Hellenistic History and Culture

HELLENISTIC CULTURE AND SOCIETY

General Editors: Anthony W. Bulloch, Erich S. Gruen, A. A. Long, and Andrew F. Stewart

Hellenistic History and Culture

EDITED AND WITH AN INTRODUCTION BY

Peter Green

UNIVERSITY OF CALIFORNIA PRESS
Berkeley   Los Angeles   London

The publisher gratefully acknowledges the contribution
provided by the General Endowment Fund of the
Associates of the University of California Press.

University of California Press
Berkeley and Los Angeles, California

University of California Press, Ltd.
London, England

Library of Congress Cataloging-in-Publication Data

Hellenistic history and culture / edited and
  with an introduction by Peter Green.
      p.   cm.—(Hellenistic culture and society: 9)
  Includes index.
  ISBN 0-520-07564-1 (cloth: alk. paper)
  ISBN 0-520-20325-9 (pbk.: alk. paper)
    1. Hellenism—Congresses.   I. Green, Peter. 1924–
  II. Symposium on Hellenistic History and Culture (1988:
  University of Texas at Austin)   III. Series.
  DF77.H5464   1993
  938—dc20   91-31398
                                                                          CIP

Printed in the United States of America
1   2   3   4   5   6   7   8   9

CONTENTS

v

ILLUSTRATIONS

PREFACE

This volume brings together in permanent form the lectures, the responses, and edited selections from the lively subsequent discussions, that made up the Symposium on Hellenistic History and Culture held at the University of Texas at Austin, 20–22 October 1988. I would like to thank, first, all speakers and respondents, not only for the quality of their contributions but also for their patience and conscientiousness throughout the slow and sometimes tediously demanding process of editing their spoken comments into a final printed text. This has been, in every sense, a collective effort.

I am also most grateful to Chris Francese, who tape-recorded the discussions following each session, and then carried out an exemplary job of editing the material thus collected before producing a final transcription. His task has made mine inestimably lighter. My final MS was transferred to disk by Leah Himmelhoch and then edited, most skilfully and accurately, by Catherine Fowler. The compilation of the index is the work of Roberta Engleman. To all these my sincere thanks.

Austin, Texas   *Peter Green*

ABBREVIATIONS

AA	*Archäologischer Anzeiger*
ABAW	*Abhandlungen der Bayerischen Akademie der Wissenschaften*
ABSA	*Annual of the British School at Athens*
Aelian *VH*	Aelianus *Varia historia*
Äg. Abhand.	*Ägyptologische Abhandlungen*
AHR	*American Historical Review*
AJA	*American Journal of Archaeology*
AJP	*American Journal of Philology*
Am. Stud. Pap.	*American Studies in Papyrology*
Anc. Soc.	*Ancient Society*
ANRW	*Aufstieg und Niedergang der römischen Weltgeschichte und Kultur Roms im Spiegel der neueren Forschung* (Berlin and New York, 1974–)
App.	Appian
Syr.	*Syrian Wars*
Praef.	*Praefatio, Roman History*
Ap. Rhod.	Apollonius Rhodius
Arch. Pap.	*Archiv für Papyrusforschung und verwandte Gebiete*
ARE	J. H. Breasted, *Ancient Records of Egypt* (Chicago, 1906)
Arist. *EN*	Aristotle *The Nicomachean Ethics*
Aristoph.	Aristophanes
Arr.	Lucius (or Aulus) Flavius Arrianus *Anabasis*
Athen *Deipn.*	Athenaeus *Deipnosophistae*
ATL	B. D. Meritt, H. T. Wade-Gery, and M. F. McGregor *The Athenian Tribute Lists*, 4 vols. (Princeton, 1939–53)
BAR	*British Archaeological Reports*
BASP	*Bulletin of the American Society of Papyrologists*
BGU	*Berliner griechische Urkunden* (Berlin, 1895–)

BIFAO	*Bulletin de l'Institut Française d'archéologie orientale*
*CAH*²	*Cambridge Ancient History,* 2d ed. (Cambridge)
CGF	G. Kaibel, ed., *Comicorum Graecorum Fragmenta* (Berlin, 1899)
Chron. d'Ég.	*Chronique d'Égypte*
Cic.	Marcus Tullius Cicero
Ac.	*Academica*
Fin.	*De finibus*
Phil.	*Philippicae*
Tusc.	*Tusculanae disputationes*
CIL	*Corpus inscriptionum latinarum* (Berlin, 1863)
CJ	*Classical Journal*
C. Ord. Ptol.	M. T. Langer, ed., *Corpus des ordonnances de Ptolémées* (Brussels, 1964)
Corp. script. hist. byz.	*Corpus scriptorum historiae byzantinae* (Bonn, 1828–97)
CP	*Classical Philology*
CQ	*Classical Quarterly*
CRAI	*Comptes rendus de l'Académie des inscriptions et belles-lettres*
Curt.	Quintus Curtius Rufus *Historiae Alexandri Magni Macedonis*
Dan.	The Book of Daniel
Diog. Laert.	Diogenes Laertius *De clarorum philosophorum vitis libri decem*
Dion. Hal.	Dionysius of Halicarnassus *Antiquitates Romanae*
D-K	H. Diels and W. Kranz, *Die Fragmente der Vorsokratiker,* 12th ed. (Dubin, 1966–67)
DS	Diodorus Siculus *The Library of History*
Epict. *Diss.*	Epictetus *Dissertationes (Discourses)*
FGrH	F. Jacoby, ed., *Die Fragmente der griechischen Historiker,* 16 vols. (Berlin and Leiden, 1923–58)
FHG	C. Müller, ed., *Fragmenta historicorum graecorum,* 4 vols. (Paris, 1841–70)
G&R	*Greece and Rome*
GGM	C. Müller, ed., *Geographici graeci minores,* 2 vols. (Paris, 1861–82)
GRBS	*Greek, Roman and Byzantine Studies*
Hdt.	Herodotus *The Histories*
Hero Alex. *Pneum.*	Hero Alexandrinus *Pneumatica*
Helck, *Lexikon*	*Lexikon der Aegyptologie,* ed. W. Helck et al., Wiesbaden, 1982
Helck, *Verwaltung*	W. Helck, *Zur Verwaltung des mittleren und neuen Reiches,* Leiden, 1958
Helck, *Wirtschaftgeschichte*	
	W. Helck, *Wirtschaftgeschichte des alten Aegypten im 3. und 2. Jahrtausend vor Chr.,* Leiden, 1975

HSCP	*Harvard Studies in Classical Philology*
HTR	*Harvard Theological Review*
*IGI*³	David Lewis, ed., *Inscriptiones graecae*, Voluminis I editio tertia fasciculus I, (Berlin and New York, 1981)
Inschr. Ilion	Peter Frisch, ed., *Die Inschriften von Ilion* (Bonn, 1975)
I. Philae	A. Bernand, ed., *Les Inscriptions grecques de Philae*, vol. 1, *L'Époque ptolémaïque* (Paris, 1969)
JARCE	*Journal of the American Research Center in Egypt*
JEA	*Journal of Egyptian Archaeology*
Jhrb. Heid. Akad.	*Jahrbuch der Heidelberger Akademie der Wissenschaften*
JHS	*Journal of Hellenic Studies*
JJP	*Journal of Juristic Papyrology*
JJS	*Journal of Jewish Studies*
Jos.	Flavius Josephus
Ant.	*Antiquitates judaicae (Jewish Antiquities)*
BJ	*Bellum judaicum (The Jewish War)*
C. Ap.	*Contra Apionem (Against Apion)*
JRS	*Journal of Roman Studies*
Just.	Justin *Epitome of Trogus Pompeius*
L-S	A. A. Long and D. N. Sedley, *The Hellenistic Philosophers*, 2 vols. (Cambridge, 1987)
I Macc., II Macc.	The First and Second Books of Maccabees
MÄS	*Münchener ägyptologische Studien*
MDAIK	*Mitteilungen des deutschen archäologischen Instituts, Abteilungen Kairo*
Meiggs-Lewis, *GHI*	R. Meiggs and D. M. Lewis, *A Selection of Greek Historical Inscriptions to the End of the Fifth Century B.C.* (Oxford, 1969)
Milet	T. Wiegand, ed., *Milet: Ergebnisse der Ausgrabungen und Untersuchungen seit 1899* (Berlin, 1914)
Münch. Beitr.	*Münchener Beiträge zur Papyrusforschung und antiken Rechtsgeschichte*
Mus. Helv.	*Museum Helveticum*
Nock, *Essays*	A. D. Nock, *Essays on Religion and the Ancient World*, 2 vols., ed. Z. Stewart (Oxford, 1972)
O. Bodl.	J. G. Tait et al., eds., *Greek Ostraca in the Bodleian Library at Oxford and Various Other Collections*, 3 vols. (London, 1930, 1955, 1964)
OGIS	W. Dittenberger, ed., *Orientis graeci inscriptiones selectae*, 2 vols. (Leipzig, 1903–5)
P. Amh.	B. P. Grenfell and A. S. Hunt, eds., *The Amherst Papyri*, 2 vols. (London, 1900–01)
P. Cair. Zen.	C. C. Edgar, ed., *Zenon Papyri: Catalogue général des antiquités égyptiennes du Musée du Caire*, 5 vols. (Cairo, 1925–40)

P. Col. Zen.	W. L. Westermann et al., eds., *Zenon Papyri: Business Papers of the Third Century B.C. Dealing with Palestine and Egypt*, 2 vols. (New York, 1934, 1940)
P. Edg.	C. C. Edgar, ed., "Selected Papers from the Archive of Zenon," *Annales du service des antiquités* 18–24 (1918–24)
P. Enteux.	O. Guerand, ed., Ἐντεύξεις: *Requêtes et plaintes addressées au Roi d'Égypte au IIIe siècle avant J.-C.* (Cairo, 1931)
P. Fuad Univ.	D. S. Crawford, ed., *Fuad I University Papyri* (Alexandria, 1949)
P. Hib.	B. P. Grenfell et al., eds., *The Hibeh Papyri*, 2 vols. (London, 1906, 1955)
P. Lille	P. Jouguet, P. Collart, J. Lesquier, and M. Xoual, eds., *Papyrus grecs* (Paris, 1929)
P. Lond. Zen.	T. C. Skeat, ed., *Greek Papyri in the British Museum*, vol. 7, *The Zenon Archive* (London, 1974)
P. Mich. Zen.	C. C. Edgar, ed., *Zenon Papyri* (Ann Arbor, 1931)
P. Par.	J. A. Latronne, B. de Presle, and E. Egger, eds., *Notices et textes des papyrus grecs du Musée du Louvre et de la Bibliothèque impériale* (Paris, 1865)
P. Rain.	J. Karabacek, ed., *Mitteilungen aus der Sammlung der Papyrus Erzherzog Rainer*, 6 vols. (Vienna, 1887–97)
P. Rev. Laws	B. P. Grenfell, ed., *Revenue Laws of Ptolemy Philadelphus*, (Oxford, 1896); reedited by J. Bingen, *Sammelbuch griechischer Urkunden aus Ägypten*, Beiheft 1 (Göttingen, 1952)
P. Tebt.	B. P. Grenfell et al., eds., *The Tebtunis Papyri*, 4 vols. (London, 1902–76)
P. Yale	J. F. Oates and A. E. Samuel, eds., *Yale Papyri in the Beinecke Rare Book and Manuscript Library* (New Haven and Toronto, 1967)
P. Zen. Pestm.	P. W. Pestman, ed., *Greek and Demotic Texts from the Zenon Archive (P. L. Bat. 20)* (Leiden, 1980)
Paus.	Pausanias Periegeta
Plat.	Plato
Apol.	*Apology*
Charm.	*Charmides*
Rep.	*Republic*
Symp.	*Symposium*
Plin. *NH*	C. Plinius Secundus *Naturalis historia*
Plut.	L. Mestrius Plutarchus of Chaeronea
Adv. Col.	*Adversus Colotem (Against Colotes)*
Alex.	*Life of Alexander*
Demetr.	*Life of Demetrius*
Eum.	*Life of Eumenes*
Isis	*De Iside et Osiride*

Marc.	*Life of Marcellus*
Mor.	*Moralia*
Pyrrh.	*Life of Pyrrhus*
St. rep.	*De Stoicorum repugnantiis (Stoic self-contradictions)*
P-M	B. Porter and B. Moss, *Topographical Bibliography of Ancient Egyptian Hieroglyphic Texts, Reliefs and Paintings*, vol. 5 (Oxford, 1937), vol. 6 (1939), vol. 7 (1952); 2d ed., vol. 2 (1972)
PMG Page	D. L. Page, ed., *Poetae melici graeci* (Oxford, 1967)
Polyb.	Polybius *The Histories*
Porphyr.	Porphyrius of Tyre *Reges Macedonum*
PSI	*Papiri greci e latini, Pubblicazioni della Società per la ricerca dei papiri greci e latini in Egitto* (Florence, 1912)
RCK	D. Dunham, *The Royal Cemeteries of Kush*, 5 vols. (Boston, 1950–63)
RE	A. F. von Pauly, G. Wissowa, W. Kroll, and K. Ziegler, eds., *Realencyclopädie der classischen Altertumswissenschaft* (Stuttgart, 1893 – Munich, 1978)
REA	*Revue des Études Anciennes*
REJ	*Revue des Études Juives*
RAL	*Rendiconti della reale Accademia dei Lincei*
RIDA	*Revue internationale des droits de l'antiquité*
Riv. Filol.	*Rivista di filologia e di istruzione classica*
RN	*Revue Numismatique*
SAOC	*Studies in Ancient Oriental Civilizations* (Chicago, 1931–)
SB	F. Preisigke et al., eds., *Sammelbuch griechischer Urkunden aus Aegypten* (Strasbourg, 1915–)
Schol. Theocr.	C. T. E. Wendel, *Scholia in Theocritum Vetera* (Leipzig, 1914)
SEG	*Supplementum epigraphicum graecum* (Leiden, 1923–)
SEHHW	M. I. Rostovtzeff, *The Social and Economic History of the Hellenistic World*, 3 vols. (Oxford, 1941); 2d ed. (1952)
SIG[3]	W. Dittenberger, ed., *Sylloge inscriptionum graecarum*, 3rd ed., 4 vols. (Leipzig, 1915–24)
SSEA Journal	*Journal of the Society for the Study of Egyptian Antiquities*
Stob.	Ioannes Stobaeus (John of Stobi)
SVF	H. von Arnim, ed., *Stoicorum veterum fragmenta*, 4 vols. (Leipzig, 1903–5, 1924)
Syncell.	Syncellus the Chronographer *Chronographia*
Tac. *Hist.*	Cornelius Tacitus *The Histories*
TAPA	*Transactions and Proceedings of the American Philological Association*
Theocr. *Id.*	Theocritus *Idylls*
Thuc.	Thucydides *History*

Tod, *GHI* 2   M. N. Tod, *A Selection of Greek Historical Inscriptions,* vol.
                    2, *From 403 to 323 B.C.* (Oxford, 1948)
UPZ   U. Wilcken, *Urkunden der Ptolemäerzeit,* vol. 1, *Papyri aus
                    Unterägypten* (Berlin and Leipzig, 1927); vol. 2, *Papyri
                    aus Oberägypten* (Berlin, 1935–57)
Val. Max.   Valerius Maximus *De factis dictisque memorabilibus*
Vell. Pat.   C. Velleius Paterculus *Historiae romanae*
W. Chr.   L. Mitteis and U. Wilcken, *Grundzüge und Chrestomathie
                    der Papyruskunde* (Leipzig, 1912)
WO   *Die Welt des Orients: Wissenschaftliche Beiträge zur Kunde
                    des Morgenlandes* (Wuppertal, 1947–)
Xen.   Xenophon
  Mem.   *Memorabilia*
  Cyr.   *Cyropaedia*
YCS   *Yale Classical Studies*
ZPE   *Zeitschrift fur Papyrologie und Epigraphik*

Introduction:
New Approaches to the Hellenistic World

Peter Green

Where there is much desire to learn, there of necessity will be much arguing, much writing, many opinions; for opinion in good men is but knowledge in the making.

MILTON, AREOPAGITICA (1664)

Historians are . . . carried along by the general cultural movements of their own times, such as Romanticism, Positivism, or Marxism. They are as much affected as anyone else by the evolution of ways of thinking about the behavior of men in society. . . . Original ways of looking at the past direct the search towards new kinds of evidence. Eventually these seams become exhausted and the venerated leaders are challenged by iconoclasts who become in time the patrons of new orthodoxies.

NORMAN HAMPSON, THE PERMANENT REVOLUTION: THE FRENCH REVOLUTION
AND ITS LEGACY, 1789–1989 (1988)

Why are we looking at the same things we looked at fifty years ago and coming up with completely different conclusions?

A. E. SAMUEL, SYMPOSIUM ON HELLENISTIC HISTORY AND CULTURE (1988), IN
DISCUSSION.

Despite all the benefits of sophisticated modern communication systems, scholarship remains an essentially lonely business. The world is large, one's area of specialization limited; kindred spirits tend to be widely scattered. Bibliographies, periodicals, and, ultimately, books ensure that our ideas are disseminated; the exchange of offprints is a crucial element in the sharing of knowledge. But the time lag between an inchoate idea in the head and the formulation of that idea into a rational theory is considerable, while the period from the written concept to its final publication can be—*experto credite*—even longer. Thus during much of one's research one lives in a private—and for a great deal of the time not unwelcome—limbo, working alone, trying out one's ideas on, at most, a few close professional friends, and often not even doing that, at least until a fairly advanced stage in one's thinking. The picture may differ somewhat for scientists; but in that cluster of ancillary specialties which

1

composes our own area of research in the classics, not least for the Hellenistic period, I think this sense of isolation, especially in the early stages
of any project, is endemic.

It also undoubtedly explains why academics who are neither job hunting themselves nor selling their own recent Ph.D.'s still flock enthusiasti-
cally, often through appalling winter weather, to meet old friends, exchange shoptalk, and even listen to papers, at APA/AIA meetings. The
impulse to attend these grisly social reunions, year after year, needs to
be an exceptionally strong one, perhaps because classics, as a discipline,
does not provide so rich an assortment of those specialist literary confer-
ences that proliferate under the aegis of institutions such as the MLA,
and that have been memorably satirized by David Lodge in his novel
Small World. When we decided to organize such a symposium at the
University of Texas, Austin, our chief aim was, precisely, to facilitate the
exchange of ideas on Hellenistic history and culture between a group of
widely scattered experts based in the United States and in Britain. We
also tried, for the sake of intellectual stimulus and profitable debate, to
bring into confrontation scholars whose conflicting opinions might be
expected to ensure not just good entertainment (though of course, as
some participants were not slow to point out, this consideration had
indeed occurred to us) but also, and more important, a thorough scrutiny
of all new theories, old dogmas, and overcomforting *idées reçues*.

Professor David Halperin, rather flatteringly, has credited me with
being a *provocateur*, a mischief maker—rather, one gathers, in the spirit
of Sherlock Holmes, of whom it was said, in *A Study in Scarlet*, that he
was quite capable of trying out the latest poison on his friends, not out
of malice, but in the disinterested pursuit of scientific knowledge. If so,
I can hardly claim to be oversuccessful at stirring up trouble, since what
emerged from this symposium was not, in the first instance, a series of
irreconcilable differences but a whole range of illuminating and unfore-
seen agreements. Debate, when it did occur, tended to be on topics already well aired in print, and, it could be argued, dependent more on
personal temperament than on hard evidence—for example, the socio-
legal status of the Macedonian monarchy: model of constitutionalism or
ad hoc power-base for warlords? or the "biographical fallacy" in literary
criticism; or that perennially baffling puzzle, Antiochus Epiphanes' motives for his root-and-branch attack on Jewish religion. No surprises
there. It was, rather, the revealing insights, the fertilizing phrases, the
unexpectedly converging or parallel lines of research from different sub-
disciplines, the sense that in this great variegated Hellenistic mosaic a
new pattern was emerging, of which we had all become part without
knowing it (rather like Molière's M. Jourdain talking prose unawares),

that gave our meeting its special, indeed unique, sense of urgency and excitement.

At the same time this phenomenon does, on reflection, give cause for a certain amount of historiographical concern: serendipitous concinnity is all very encouraging, but one begins to wonder whether our old friend the zeitgeist may not have been exerting its unseen prior influence on most of us behind the scenes. Why *are* we looking at largely the same evidence and coming up with different conclusions? Why, more or less independently, are we stressing areas (such as the frontier problem) in which our predecessors took comparatively scanty interest? We have, of course, learned to look out for *their* explicable prejudices and ad hominem motivations—but what about our own? We know, for example, that Rostovtzeff's position regarding the Russian Revolution almost certainly dictated his interpretation of the Greek economic system, emphasizing private property and a laissez-faire market. Yet is is only beginning to occur to us that his centralized, dirigist, authoritarian model of Ptolemaic administration, so ably criticized by Professor A. E. Samuel in his presentation, in fact owes a great deal to Marxist, no less than to Keynesian, theory. Ideas currently in the air tend, like viruses, to be infectious as well as invisible. It may, equally, be no accident that the current challenge to this (papyrologically based) thesis of a Ptolemaic planned economy has surfaced at a time when the patent and acknowledged bankruptcy of the Marxist system is transforming the history of Eastern Europe.

In his stimulating monograph *The Shifting Sands of History: Interpretations of Ptolemaic Egypt*, Professor Samuel reminds us that "it is desirable to consider the effects of modern experience on the treatment of that period," and he notes various major trends and events during the past century and a half that have contributed to shaping the ancient historian's preconceptions about his craft.[1] The liberalism engendered by the American, French, and Greek revolutions too soon found itself competing with a new and flourishing colonial imperialism, as the triumphant nation-states shouldered the White Man's Burden or were seduced by the dream of Manifest Destiny. Residual guilt over the nastier aspects of military conquest complicated the issue by forcing these new expansionists to advance behind the morally uplifting banner of cultural proselytization. To do this they unashamedly, and often in all likelihood unconsciously, borrowed the language and imagery of Christian missionaries bringing light to the benighted heathen, aided in this (at least as regards Alexander) by section 6 of Plutarch's early essay *De Alexandri Magni Fortuna aut Virtute* (*Mor.* 329A–D). Though Alexander was by far the most

---

[1] A. E. Samuel, *The Shifting Sands of History: Interpretations of Ptolemaic Egypt*, Publications of the Association of Ancient Historians, no. 2 (Lanham and London, 1989), ix.

notable beneficiary of this exercise in historical sanitization, he by no means stood alone.

What is our position today? Two world wars, plus such horrors as the Holocaust, Hiroshima, the Gulag Archipelago, and the murderous depredations of various committed extremists—the Khmer Rouge, the IRA, assorted Middle East bombers and hijackers—have left most Western historians with an ingrained distrust, not only of totalitarianism (whether of the Left or the Right) but of all ideological politics whatsoever; not only of the *Führerprinzip* but of the validity, let alone the attainability, of principles as such. The chief casualty, ideologically speaking, has been hope: idealism—and, a fortiori, *Idealismus*—is today not even a dirty word, but a bad joke. We live in a world of pragmatic calculation, where the dominant concern is self-interest. For many of us *ataraxia* seems a logical goal, and *lathe biosas* a desirable motto. We are obsessed by economics, Great Power competition, and the ingenious devices of applied science. It is hard for us to think of soldiers as heroes. Egalitarianism and multiculturalism have rendered *elitist* a pejorative term—while at the same time competing uneasily with a more-than-Alexandrian academicism and such knee-jerk nationalist phenomena as an obsession about flag burning.

Feminism, similarly, is undermining traditional male assumptions in a society that also contrives to be more preoccupied with sex than any civilization since that of Julio-Claudian Rome. We sneer at experts and bureaucrats while remaining helplessly dependent on them. We complain about the loss of cultural values while energetically deconstructing all the criteria on which such values ultimately rest. Our talent for paradox, in short, eclipses that of the Socratic tradition, on which Professor Long has thrown so much new light. As for religion, we manage a balancing act in this field too: largely skeptical, as academics, about the efficacy of Christianity, we nevertheless do not underrate, as historians, the continuing force in human affairs of passionate faith (after the Rushdie affair, who could?), and thus we are perhaps in a better position to understand just what the "deification" of human leaders implied. At least we have got beyond the point of treating it solely as political flim-flam, or even as cynically provided opium for the masses. (In this connection I note with surprise, in retrospect, that during discussion Euhemerus—to dynastic cults what de Gobineau was to Aryanism—only got mentioned once, by Professor Burstein, while none of us thought of bringing up the notorious ithyphallic hymn with which Athens greeted Demetrius Poliorcetes in 290.) On the one hand, intellectual loss of religious faith; on the other, snake handling, Holy Rollering, and astrology, with Islamic fundamentalists burning books and issuing death sentences in the background. The paradox continues.

The relevance of all this to Hellenistic historiography should be readily apparent. We are what we eat, and that includes the apple from the Tree of Knowledge. Scholars know this, and remind us of it at intervals. The Swiss historian Eduard Füter was well aware, as early as 1911, that the changes in European society after the Franco-Prussian War of 1870 profoundly affected the assumptions of all later Western historians, whatever their chosen field of study.[2] Croce's assumption that all history is contemporary history[3] should be viewed in the same light. But the reminders sometimes are forgotten in the excitement of pursuing new lines of thought; and thus the searching question posed by Professor Samuel (apropos the visual arts, but it has universal application), and placed at the head of this introduction as an epigraph, is one that merits careful and detailed consideration. During the symposium itself it was, understandably, sidelined in favor of new aperçus on specific aspects of Hellenistic society; but now, I think, the time has come to take stock of the revisionist findings that we shared and to evaluate them, in perspective, as the product of our own day and age.

At the same time, of course, we have to bear in mind certain important caveats. While the zeitgeist can never be ignored as an influence—least of all when we flatter ourselves we have made due allowance for it—neither is it all-dominant. To a degree that might surprise behaviorists (but not, of course, Dr. Johnson), the intellect and the will do remain free agents. What is more, as Professor Pollitt hinted in discussion, a fashion or trend, no less than new evidence, may start useful inquiry by pointing us in directions we might otherwise never have turned to; and in any case—I hope this is not whistling in the wind—commonsense precautions should save us from the worst excesses of academic behaviorism.

Let us start with the big question: Why, during the past decade or two, has the Hellenistic Age come to enjoy such extraordinary vogue as an area of study? And why—even more interestingly—have its achievements been upgraded to a point where the old buzzword "decadence" is now dismissed as a regrettable solecism, on a par with patronizing anthropological references to "the savage mind"? The remarkable, and rapid, rehabilitation of Hellenistic philosophy, so strikingly demonstrated by Professor Long and other scholars, is the most obvious instance of this trend, but by no means the only one. Alexandrian literature is attracting more and more attention in its own right, and not merely as a precursor of, and model for, the writers (less neoteric than is often

---

[2] E. Füter, *Geschichte der neueren Historiographie* (Munich and Berlin, 1911); cf. Peter Green, *Essays in Antiquity* (London, 1960), 52ff.

[3] Best analyzed by R. G. Collingwood, *The Idea of History* (Oxford, 1946), 201–4.

claimed) of late Republican and Augustan Rome. Professor Bulloch's description of Callimachus as "the most outstanding intellect of this generation, the greatest poet that the Hellenistic age produced . . . a great poet in his own right"[4] would have raised academic eyebrows not so long ago. Alexandrian science, most notably in the fields of mathematics, astronomy, and medicine, is rapidly becoming a growth industry, as the work of scholars such as White, Scarborough, Lloyd, Von Staden, and Neugebauer eloquently attests. Hellenistic art—I am thinking in particular of Professor Pollitt's magnificent new survey[5]—has undergone a similar upward revaluation. Most recently of all—and perhaps this is the most immediately notable feature of this symposium—a great deal of interest has shifted from the supposed centers of power to the periphery, creating the basis for a series of "frontier studies" that will (it seems safe to say) profoundly modify our assessment of the political, economic, and cultural history of the Hellenistic Age. To take the most dramatic example raised: simply by treating the Tiber as a frontier, by reexamining the relations between Rome and the Greek East in such terms, scholars are, at a deep and radical level, transforming our underlying preconceptions—little changed hitherto, in essence, since Droysen's day—of *Hellenismus*.

This generally bullish academic market has been brought about (as Professor Samuel hinted during discussion) by a variety of disparate factors, not all the product of the zeitgeist. The great mass of systematic groundwork carried out early in this century by pioneering giants such as Wilcken, Berve, Grenfell and Hunt, Rostovtzeff, and Dittenberger—all, significantly, in the first place papyrologists or epigraphists—depended upon an immense influx of raw material to be edited, published, and collected, and it was in consequence particularist to a degree. Its great virtue was to make generally available a large quantity of more or less fragmentary texts, both literary and nonliterary (with the occasional substantial bonanza such as the Aristotelian *Athenaion Politeia* and, more recently, Menander's *Dyskolos*). Its faults were, first, a tendency either to generalize rashly from the merely local and parochial,[6] or else, per contra, among more cautious scholars, not to see the wood for the papyrus trees; and second, the unthinking retrojection of modern assumptions—often economic[7]—into ancient sociocultural patterns where they were inapplicable.

---

[4] A. W. Bulloch, *The Cambridge History of Classical Literature*, vol. 1, *Greek Literature* (Cambridge, 1985), 549, 570.

[5] J. J. Pollitt, *Art in the Hellenistic Age* (Cambridge, 1986).

[6] Cf. Peter Green, *Alexander to Actium: The Historical Evolution of the Hellenistic Age* (Berkeley and London, 1990), xx–xxi.

[7] Cf. Samuel, *Shifting Sands*, 51ff.

The foundations, then, were being laid early, with a textual emphasis that, while avoiding the worst excesses of anachronistic bias, also failed to provide an overall view. General interest followed much more slowly. The three tumultuous centuries between Alexander's death and Octavian's victory at Actium were ignored as far as possible and denigrated, in general terms, as a sad falling-off from the classical apogee. Greek achievement was still to a remarkable extent identified with the Greek *polis*, so that Philip of Macedon's victory over a handful of leading Greek states at Chaeronea in 338 came to be seen as a watershed in Greek history, after which nothing, in a sense, mattered: Hellenistic culture was bourgeois, decadent, and materialist; Periclean idealism was dead; the *idiotai* and *apragmones* had triumphed; *ataraxia* was the goal. When this society fell victim, finally, to the Roman military machine, with its crass and philistine efficiency, the feeling was that these degenerate Greeklings had got no more than they deserved (as more than one member of the symposium observed, the anti-Roman prejudice among modern Hellenists is notable).[8] Byzantium, and a fortiori, modern Greece, despite its amazing twentieth-century literary renaissance, fared even worse: I vividly recall the comment of one eminent scholar, who declared (apparently in all seriousness) that he could have nothing to do with a society capable of making ἀπό govern the accusative case. It was this powerful climate of opinion that also felt the need to distort Alexander's pursuit of κλέος into altruistic missionary work on behalf of Greek (meaning fifth-century Athenian) culture.

The impact of World War II proved, ultimately, inimical, if not fatal, to this kind of thinking. What popular journalists labeled the Century of the Common Man (against which Evelyn Waugh fought so notable a rearguard action in *Brideshead Revisited*) had no time at all for upper-class elitists who were soft on Platonic homoeroticism and the kind of *de haut en bas* social planning (seen, now, as fascism or worse) so prominent in the *Republic* and the *Laws*. Victims of real totalitarianism were equally unenthusiastic: Sir Karl Popper produced another catchy label, that of the Closed Society. The attitude with regard to sex was ambivalent: Platonic (or Solonian) pederasty might carry objectionable elitist overtones, but the new permissive generation of classical scholars (bliss was it in that pre-AIDS dawn to be alive) lost no time in abolishing all forms of literary censorship (Aristophanes—whom Thomas Arnold had declared that no man could safely read till he was over forty—totally unexpurgated; Martial no longer in Italian; four-letter words running riot). This, in itself an excellent advance, reinforced that glaring misconception so popular

---

[8] Those familiar with the late Professor T. B. L. Webster will recall his elegant off-the-cuff diatribes on this topic.

among nonspecialists, the notion of Greek society as a kind of sexual free-for-all. But it also, more importantly for our present discussion, opened up a significant aspect of the Hellenistic zeitgeist with which many people felt they could identify: the romantic, psychologically sophisticated attitude to erotic passion, best exemplified by Medea's violent obsession with Jason as delineated so skillfully by Apollonius Rhodius in book 3 of his *Argonautica*.[9]

Further, the very existence of canons of good taste—something intimately bound up, as its critics were not slow to point out, with the elitist attitude—was, inevitably, challenged; and with the rejection of such criteria (or, at least, of the current ones) the barriers that had held scholars back from an honest appraisal of Hellenistic art and literature were at one stroke removed. An interesting, and still only partially explored, consequence of this release was that Chaeronea came to be seen less and less as a violent dividing line between the old world and the new. Features identified with the Hellenistic world, and supposedly the result of direct political oppression or the destruction of democracy, were found flourishing long before Philip's victory, in the early fourth and even the late fifth century. Aristophanes' last play, the *Plutus* (388), has more in common with the bourgeois social comedy of Menander than with a politically engaged satire such as the *Acharnians* (425). No accident, I feel, that both Professor Robertson and Professor Pollitt found themselves stressing the *continuity* of Greek art through this difficult transitional period rather than the disruptions putatively occasioned by external events; or that Professor Long should have backtracked to Socrates as the role model for systematic Hellenistic thinkers experimenting in the exercise of philosophical power.

The loosening and realignment of aesthetic standards has been a two-edged business. We all, I think, welcome the increased range of appreciation and flexibility of judgment that it brings with it; at the same time there is a price to pay, in the shape of alternative experimental systems, ranging from Marxism to deconstruction, designed to reintroduce a set of rules, a yardstick to decide what's good and what's bad (even, perhaps especially, for those who argue that "good" and "bad" have no real meaning). Post-Chomskyan grammar argues, in effect, that Humpty Dumpty was right, that words or idioms mean just what we want them to mean, that ἀπό—to return to an earlier point—can take any case it pleases and that to hold out for the genitive is mere sentimental antiquarianism. By

---

[9] It is instructive to compare the tone of modern commentators—e.g., Francis Vian, Budé ed., vol. 2 (Paris, 1980), 39ff., or R. L. Hunter, *Argonautica, Book III* (Cambridge, 1989), 27ff.—with that of an earlier scholar such as G. W. Mooney, *Argonautica* (London, 1912), 36–37.

the same token, any slang or patois, however debased, can now claim linguistic autonomy and can deflect all criticism by labeling it racist, elitist, or both. In this brave new world the charge of *corruptio optimi pessima* is a dangerous one to bring. To watch our new academic Alexandrians walking such a tightrope is the most intriguing paradox of all.

Still, advantages have accrued. The "base mechanic arts" of the Hellenistic world, long ignored (as Professor White so vividly demonstrates) by scholars with no less class-bound a sense of the banausic than their ancient counterparts, today form a flourishing field of advanced research: technology can no longer be dismissed, by ivory-tower humanists, as a business fit only for artisans. This kind of functional egalitarianism is ethnic as well as class based; hence, in recent years, the fashionable march toward multiculturalism, with its conscious downgrading of the Western, Greco-Roman tradition as such, and its assault on the ingrained concept of Hellenes versus barbarians (e.g., Isocratean panhellenism, and such subtly patronizing essays on the theme of the Noble Savage as the Pergamene sculptures of Gaulish warriors, dying with Homeric panache, but still safely defeated). This movement has produced, in addition to *parti pris* propaganda like Martin Bernal's *Black Athena—ex Africa semper aliquid noui*—the far more important, and stimulating, preoccupation with frontiers and frontier cultures offered here in the presentations by Professors Burstein and Holt. Now we have cleared our minds of the missionary cant about cultural proselytization, we can clearly see, first, that Ptolemaic or Seleucid outposts of empire were ghettos in an alien and resentful environment,[10] and second, that, in Professor Holt's words, "the aim of the Hellenistic states was less to annex these fringe areas than to exploit them with as little involvement and expense as possible" (p. 59). In other words, the removal of the need to justify imperial expansionism, by Alexander or his less romantic successors, has killed a myth and made it correspondingly easier to see what was actually going on; these Nubians and Bactrians now interest us in their own right, and not merely as the uncivilized targets for Greco-Macedonian conquistadors.

The benefits of such a change in outlook are varied and often unpredictable; once we stop taking Hellenic assumptions of superiority and justified aggression (e.g., in the matter of panhellenism) at face value, the evidence stares us in the face. It is not always welcome: S. K. Eddy's pioneering work *The King Is Dead: Studies in the Near Eastern Resistance to Hellenism, 334–31 B.C.* (1961) got a notably cool reception. At a more mundane level, Alexander scholars have begun to accept the idea (some more reluctantly than others) that their hero simply took over the gov-

---

[10] Cf. Green, *Alexander to Actium*, ch. 19, 312ff.

ernmental bureaucracy of any country he conquered, putting in an offi-
cer of his own at the top to skim off the profits, a habit continued by the
Diadochoi. As Professor Delia persuasively demonstrates, this is true
even of Egypt.[11] The pharaonic system (and indeed perhaps even some
Persian satrapal survivals, an earlier overlay) continued throughout the
Ptolemaic period, aided by a middle-level corps of Greek-speaking
Egyptian interpreters, and giving point to the seldom quoted comment
of Augustus, who may be presumed to have understood these matters,
that he was amazed at Alexander's lack of interest in organizing the
territories he had conquered.[12] No accident either, perhaps, that in a
decade of strangling bureaucracy, governmental corruption, weak leadership, and financial waste, Professor Samuel should be questioning the
effectiveness, even the very existence, of a Ptolemaic dirigist economy
centrally controlled by the king. The alternative scenario he presents,
that of an independent civil service going its own way while producing
just enough in the way of flattery and fiscal returns to keep the government happy, puts me irresistibly in mind—*si parua licet componere mag-
nis*—of the central thesis embodied in that politically acute British sitcom
"Yes, Minister." The striking resemblance suggests to me that Professor
Samuel may well have tapped a perennial vein in human nature, of the
kind that appealed to Thucydides.

   This brings me to what must be the most powerful factor, emotionally
speaking, that has contributed to the contemporary renaissance in Hellenistic studies. This is something many of us have experienced; from a
personal viewpoint I can do no better than repeat here what I wrote in
the introduction to my own survey of the period:[13]

> As my work proceeded, it acquired an unexpected and in ways alarming
> dimension. I could not help being struck, again and again, by an over-
> powering sense of *déjà vu*, far more than for any other period of ancient
> history known to me: the "distant mirror" that Barbara Tuchman held up
> from the fourteenth century A.D. for our own troubled age is remote and
> pale compared to the ornate, indeed rococo, glass in which Alexandria,
> Antioch, and Pergamon reflect contemporary fads, failings, and aspira-
> tions, from the urban malaise to religious fundamentalism, from Veblen-
> ism to *haute cuisine*, from funded scholarship and mandarin literature to a
> flourishing dropout counter-culture, from political impotence in the indi-

---

[11] Professor Burstein, too, has been working along very similar lines in a paper entitled
"Alexander in Egypt: Continuity or Change?" in *Achaemenid History: Proceedings of the Achae-
menid History Workshop*, vol. 8, edited by Heleen Sancisi-Weerdenburg and Amélie Kuhrt
(Leiden: forthcoming), an early draft of which he kindly communicated to me.

[12] Cited by Plutarch, *Mor.* 207D 8: ἐθαύμαζεν εἰ μὴ μεῖζον Ἀλέξανδρος ἔργον ἡγεῖτο
τοῦ κτήσασθαι τὴν ἡγεμονίαν τὸ διατάξαι τὴν ὑπάρχουσαν.

[13] Green, *Alexander to Actium*, xxi.

vidual to authoritarianism in government, from science perverted for military ends to illusionism for the masses, from spiritual solipsism on a private income to systematic extortion in pursuit of the plutocratic dream. Contemporary cosmological speculation seems to be taking us straight back to the Stoic world-view, while Tyche has been given a new lease of life by computer analysts, who prefer to describe it, with pseudo-Hellenistic panache, as "stochasticism."

Obviously, such parallels can be overworked, and apparent resemblances sometimes turn out, on investigation, to be meretricious. But at least they have the merit of stimulating new lines of research, even if we are tempted to wrestle with the problems of antiquity by the hope that they may, in the fullness of time, shed some light on our own.

That we will bring our own preconceptions, and those of our age, to the task, is, as Croce saw, inevitable. The breaking of old prohibitions will always produce new ideologies; we can no more resist the lure of pattern making than our predecessors could. History, and historians, like Heracleitus' river, never stand still. Each generation will, for whatever reason, reassess the past in its own terms. That is one (perhaps oversimplistic) answer to Professor Samuel's original question: revaluation of the Hellenistic era was overdue. Fifty years or less is the life of a good translation (something equally dependent on the zeitgeist);[14] no historical interpretation can hope to survive much longer, and Professor Samuel's choice of time span was entirely apt. What I have tried to suggest here is why—or part of the reason why—our various essays in revisionism took the harmonious line they did. What none of us could have foreseen individually—something that I hope emerges in the pages that follow—was the collective sense of excitement and discovery, the sparking of fresh ideas, generated by this sharing of individual explorations. It remains an occasion none of us will forget. Let us hope that in this case opinion will indeed prove to be Milton's "knowledge in the making."

[14] Cf. Peter Green, *Classical Bearings* (London and New York, 1989), chap. 16, 256ff.

The Macedonian Imprint on the Hellenistic World

N. G. L. Hammond

Monarchy is a red rag to a republican, and I suppose there are republicans among you today. Greeks too thought poorly of monarchy. Even Isocrates, who curried favor with Philip, made this clear: if a Greek wanted to become a king, he had to go to the backwoods as Philip's progenitor had done and impose himself on people of a different race (see figure 1). Aristotle, who outlived Philip and Alexander and saw the Macedonian monarchy at work, condemned monarchy as a political institution and judged it fit only for barbarians, who were incapable of organizing their own affairs and so became subservient to a king—whereas the Greeks, being both spirited and intelligent, conducted their own affairs in a sensible manner and rejected any form of subjection. Yet the hallmark of the Hellenistic world was monarchy. Almost every successful general, whether Macedonian, Greek, Bithynian, Cappadocian, or of mixed race, set himself up as a king. One exception was Sosthenes, who made his Macedonians in Macedonia take an oath of loyalty to himself not as king (as they were prepared to do) but as general.[1] Was he a republican, a forerunner of Oliver Cromwell? The answer is probably no; and his reason was surely that he was not a member of the royal house and saw no hope in 279–277 of establishing himself as king permanently. The fact is that monarchies ruled over as many parts of the Hellenistic world as remained unconquered for some three centuries (excluding Greece and most of Sicily).

What sort of monarchy was it? Most scholars have believed that Alex-

---

[1] Just. 24.5.14, in ducis nomen.

ander became the successor of Darius and therefore a king of a despotic type, and that his own successors ruled as absolute monarchs except in Macedonia itself. That is a mistaken view. Plutarch long ago observed[2] that Alexander never called himself βασιλέων βασιλέα, this being the Greek equivalent of a Persian royal title.[3] He had no desire to set himself up as the heir of Darius, for he had come to liberate not only the Greek city-states but also Lydians, Carians, Egyptians, Babylonians, and other Asian peoples from Persian rule. His propaganda—and indeed his purpose—was different. He was to be King of Asia from the moment he crossed the Hellespont, and as he cast his spear into Asian soil he cried out: "I accept Asia, spear-won, from the gods."[4] He prayed then that "those lands would welcome him not unwillingly."[5] It was to be his kingdom, and the Asians were to be his people. Accordingly he ordered his army not to pillage; he gave a military funeral to Persian commanders who fell in battle against him; he sent peasants back to cultivate their own fields; he told the Lydians to live by their own customs and to be free, put Ada in control of Caria and gained the cooperation of Carian cities, and confirmed many Phoenician and Cyprian kings in their positions. Whenever a claim was made for or by Alexander, it was as King of Asia—in the prophecy at Gordium, in his belief that the claim was confirmed by thunder and lightning, in the letter to Darius ("Come to me as Lord of all Asia" and "send to me as King of Asia"), and in his own words on the spoils dedicated to Athena at Lindos "having become Lord of Asia." Others acclaimed him as King of Asia, from the army in 331 after the battle of Gaugamela down to the envoys from Libya in 323.[6] Moreover, Alexander was demonstrably not the king of the Medes and the Persians; for their lands were subject to his satraps, and the pretender to their throne was sent for judgment and execution "to the gathering of Medes and Persians,"[7] just as other offenders, such as Musicanus,[8] were sent to their home country for similar judgment.

As King of Asia Alexander set his own standards. They were those not of Persia but of Macedonia: in short, tolerance of religions, respect for local customs, continuance of local government, and coexistence, as in the Macedonian kingdom. He believed that these standards—so alien to European imperialism—worked; for he said that he would have little difficulty in winning Arabia, because he would allow the Arabs to admin-

[2] Plut. *Demetr.* 25.3.
[3] See Meiggs-Lewis, *GHI* no. 12, pp. 20–22.
[4] DS 17.17.2.
[5] Just. 11.5.11.
[6] Arr. 7.15.4.
[7] Arr. 4.7.3.
[8] Arr. 6.17.2.

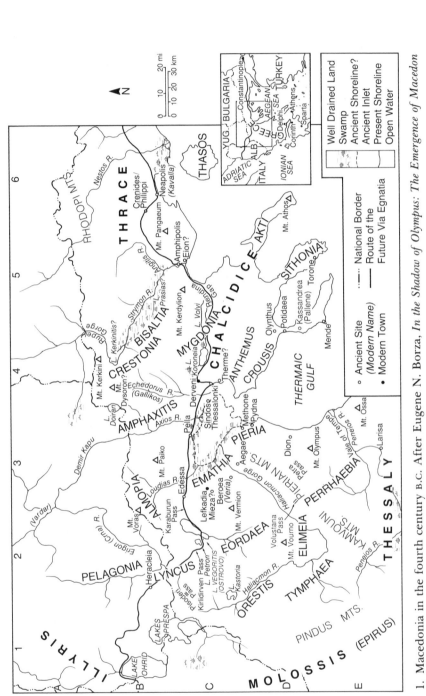

1. Macedonia in the fourth century B.C. After Eugene N. Borza, *In the Shadow of Olympus: The Emergence of Macedon* (Princeton: Princeton University Press, 1990), p. 302.

ister their state in accordance with their customs, as he had done in India.[9] At the same time he was King of the Macedonians. Even during his illness he acted in the traditional manner—banqueting with his friends, bathing in a pool such as has been found at Pella, sacrificing as custom demanded each day, issuing movement and operation orders to his officers, and discussing with them what promotions should be made to fill vacancies in command posts.

One Hellenistic ruler aimed to win Alexander's titles and Alexander's kingdoms: Antigonus set his one eye on both. In 316 he was treated as "Lord of Asia,"[10] and he was said by Seleucus to be aiming at "the entire kingship of the Macedonians,"[11] that is, to be king of Macedones wherever they were. There is a significant contrast in terminology: king of a territory and king of persons.

I turn now to the nature of the Macedonian monarchy, on which some new light has recently been shed. The monarch is described first by Herodotus and then by Thucydides as "king of Macedones."[12] "King" and "Macedones" make up the official state. The king may address the Macedones in assembly; the Macedones may honor the king.[13] They both appear in the fragmentary inscription of the treaty between Perdiccas II and Athens;[14] for he and other royals and then leading commoners are the official representatives of "Makedonon." One or other stands for both in some official documents, such as the treaty between Amyntas III and the Chalcidians,[15] and in relations with the Delphic Amphictyony, where in 346 votes were given to Philip or to "Macedones,"[16] contributions were recorded "from Macedones," and delegates were sent "from Alexander." The terms were used together until the end of the free Macedonian State. Rome proclaimed at the Isthmian Games in 190 her victory over "King Philip and Macedones"; and then at Rome and at Delphi her victory over "Macedones and King Perseus."[17] The two parts operated the State. What did the Macedones do? They elected, and, when they wished, they deposed a king (e.g., Amyntas III).[18] The Macedones decided cases of treason, the king prosecuting. The Macedones in assem-

---

[9] Arr. 7.20.1.
[10] DS 19.48.1.
[11] DS 19.56.3.
[12] Hdt. 9.44.1; Thuc. 1.57.2.
[13] E.g., Philip V in SIG^3 575 (vol. 2, p. 71).
[14] IG^3 no. 89 (pp. 105–8); cf. ATL 3:313–14 n. 61, N. G. L. Hammond and G. T. Griffith, *A History of Macedonia*, vol. 2, *550–336 B.C.* (Oxford, 1979), 134–35.
[15] SIG^3 no. 135 (pp. 177–9); cf. Tod, GHI 2 no. 111 (pp. 30–34).
[16] Paus. 10.8.2.
[17] SIG^3 652a (p. 213), CIL I xxvii (p. 48).
[18] Porphyr. frag. 1 in FHG 3:691.

bly were addressed by the king or by his guardian—for instance by
Philip to take the offensive against Bardylis, and by Alexander to win the
Kingdom of all Asia—and in each case they decided what to do, whether
meeting in Pella or on the bank of the Hydaspes.[19]

In all meetings of Macedones of which we know the Macedones met
under arms: certainly for the election of a king, for trying a case of
treason, for deciding to attack Bardylis, and for deciding to win all Asia.
The conclusion seems to be clear, that the Macedones were serving soldiers; and we may add ex-soldiers, because Olympias asked to be tried
by all Macedones and because Antigonus held an assembly of Macedones
at Tyre which consisted of the soldiers with him and men resident in the
area, that is, soldiers settled there.[20] It is equally clear that not all men
capable of bearing arms in Macedonia in the geographical sense were
"Macedones"; for that title was given only to the elite infantrymen (being
the Hypaspists and the Phalangites) and to the Companion Cavalry, the
two groups making up the "Companions." They alone were "the citizen
troops." Diodorus, following a Hellenistic historian, probably Diyllus,
described the Macedonians whom Alexander chose to send home in 324
as "the oldest of the citizens" (τῶν πολιτῶν);[21] and then, following Hieronymus, a contemporary writer, in 323 described Antipater as being
short of "citizen soldiers" (στρατιῶται πολιτικοί).[22]

Let us turn now to the Macedones serving in the Hellenistic kingdoms.
In our literary sources they are always distinguished from the Asian and
Egyptian troops, even from those "armed in the Macedonian manner"
(e.g., at Paraetacene, Gabiene, and Raphia),[23] and it is they who form
the Royal Infantry Guard. They were in a category of their own. It was
these troops who outlawed Eumenes and others in 321, and it was they
and the ex-servicemen in Syria who outlawed Cassander provisionally,
if he was unwilling to make a U-turn. They acted as an assembly and
passed decisions in the name of "the Macedones with Antigonus" in 315
(τὰ δεδογμένα τοῖς μετ᾽ Ἀντιγόνου Μακεδόσι).[24] When it was known
that Alexander IV was dead and that the Temenid line was at an end,
Antigonus and his son Demetrius were proclaimed kings in 306 by "the
army",[25] and Plutarch[26] described the proclamation as being made at the
palace of Antigonus by "the assembly" (τὸ πλῆθος being used here by

[19] Curt. 9.1.1–3.
[20] DS 19.61.1.
[21] DS 17.109.1.
[22] DS 18.12.2.
[23] Polyb. 5.82.2.
[24] DS 19.61–62.1.
[25] App. *Syr.* 54.
[26] Plut. *Demetr.* 18.1.

Hieronymus, as it was of the assembly which abandoned the last plans of Alexander; it was used also of the assembly which elected Roxane's baby to be king in 323). The proclamation of Ptolemy as king was made, according to Appian, "by his own household troops" (ὁ οἰκεῖος αὐτοῦ στρατός), also in 306.[27] Another interesting proclamation was that of Ptolemy Ceraunus after his murder of Seleucus at Lysimachea, the capital city of the dead Lysimachus, in 281. Ptolemy rode to the palace and was proclaimed king by the Royal Guard, and he then presented himself, wearing the diadem and accompanied by the Royal Guard, to the army of Seleucus, which accepted him.[28] On this occasion he was given the cognomen Ceraunus "by the army,"[29] just as Philip had been called Arrhidaeus by the infantrymen in 323.[30] Similarly Arsinoë received a diadem and was acclaimed queen of Ptolemy Ceraunus by the assembled army.[31]

The cases of proclamation which I have considered were all of leading persons. More difficult was the election of a minor or an incompetent as king and the appointing of guardians (*epitropoi*) or managers (*epimeletai*) to serve during his minority. In 323, on Alexander's death, the leading Macedonians, meeting under arms, set up four guardians for Roxane's baby-to-be, and obtained an oath of loyalty from those present and later from the Macedonian cavalrymen; they intended next to obtain the agreement of the Macedonian infantrymen. But the infantrymen bucked; they chose Arrhidaeus the half-wit. In the end Arrhidaeus and the baby-to-be were elected by the whole company in the presence of the corpse of Alexander, "so that his majesty should be witness to their decisions."[32] Very much the same process was enacted in 208 at the palace in Alexandria in Egypt, to which the two leading Macedonians summoned the Hypaspists, the household troops (ἡ θεραπεία), and the officers of the infantry and the cavalry.[33] The two leaders then announced the deaths of the king and queen, crowned their five-year-old son as king, and read out a will of the king in which they themselves were named as guardians. The ceremony was accompanied by the display of two urns which were said to contain the ashes of the deceased king and queen (we may compare the presence of Alexander's corpse at the election of Arrhidaeus and the baby-to-be in 323). Later the two leaders obtained the oath of loyalty to the king from the Macedonian soldiers

---

[27] App. *Syr.* 54.
[28] Memnon, *FGrH* 434 F8.
[29] Trogus, *Prologue* 17: cognomine Ceraunus creatus ab exercitu.
[30] Just. 13.3.1.
[31] Just. 24.3.2: ad contionem quoque vocato exercitu.
[32] Just. 13.4.4: ut maiestas eius testis decretorum esset.
[33] Polyb. 15.25.1.

(αἱ δυνάμεις), "the oath which they had been accustomed to swear at the proclamations of the kings."[34] It is clear that Polybius was referring here to the general custom of the Macedonian troops in Macedonia, as well as at the Macedonian court in Egypt.

I hope that I have now cited enough instances to support the conclusion that the pattern of the Macedonian State in Macedonia was duplicated in the so-called Hellenistic kingdoms of Lysimachus in Thrace, of Antigonus and Demetrius in Asia, of Ptolemy in Egypt, and—we may assume—of the Seleucids. Thus the state in each case consisted of the king and the Macedones who had elected him and had taken an oath of loyalty to him. He commanded them in war; they served as elite troops and were in distinction to any others in the King's Army, αἱ βασιλικαὶ δυνάμεις. We do not know how often and on what issues the king consulted the assembly of his Macedones. But we do know that when he failed to keep in close touch, as Demetrius II did in Macedonia, he was certain to fall from his position. Thus the imprint of the Macedonian State was stamped indelibly on the states which we call "the Hellenistic kingdoms."

I turn next to some consideration of the Macedones as a whole. Within what became Macedonia they went through three phases. First, when the kingdom consisted only of Macedones by birth, in the period before 358, these racial Macedones were the Μακεδόνες αὐτοί of Thucydides' analysis, whereas the people of Upper Macedonia were nominally "subject races" (ἔθνη ὑπήκοα) and in a different sense Macedones.[35] By 359 the Macedones numbered about 10,000 (comparable to the Athenian hoplite army of 490), and it was an assembly (ἐκκλησία) of this size which was persuaded by Philip to go forth and attack Bardylis' Illyrians.[36] The king could well have addressed an electorate of that size. After 358, selected men of Upper Macedonia were taken fully into the Macedonian State as soldiers—both cavalrymen and phalangites—of the King's Army; and by 336 the number of citizen soldiers—Macedones—had risen to some 30,000, domiciled over a much wider area than in 359. At short notice the king could address only those of them who were relatively close at hand, and in particular the household troops. A preliminary decision by them might be enough in itself for the king to act; alternatively, their decision might be confirmed or rejected by a larger assembly of Macedones (examples of a two-stage process include those of Alexander in Hyrcania and Demetrius in Thessaly).[37] Philip added

[34] Polyb. 15.25.11.
[35] Thuc. 2.99.
[36] DS 16.4.3.
[37] Plut. *Alex.* 47.1–4, *Demetr.* 37.

many Greeks and some persons of other races to the circle of his Friends and Companions; but only some of them were made Macedones by him. The next stage began gradually under Alexander, and increased rapidly with the troubles after his death, namely the recruitment by the king or by his generals of more men from Lower and Upper Macedonia, who on entering the King's Army were made Macedones. For example, in 334 the newlywed officers on leave were to recruit cavalrymen and infantrymen "from the territory" (ἐκ τῆς χώρας),[38]—that is, not from Antipater's troops—and in 331 recruiting officers were to enlist "suitable young men,"[39] again, not from Antipater's troops. During the Lamian War Sippas, Leonnatus, and Craterus each individually recruited more and more men from within the Macedonian kingdom. There will have been others who went from Macedonia overseas, to serve in armies in Asia and Egypt in the thirty years up to the Battle of Ipsus in 301. Thereafter the sons of Macedones established overseas were sufficient to maintain elite forces in the Hellenistic kingdoms (an early example being the sons of Alexander's Hypaspists).

I turn next to the other peoples in the Macedonian kingdom. They lived on land which had been won by the spear of the king and which was thenceforth the king's possession. The earliest known example of such possession is Anthemus, an area which Amyntas offered to Hippias, the banished tyrant of Athens. Some inscriptions, just published or about to be published, provide other examples. Julia Vokotopoulou generously showed me one such inscription before publication. In it the frontiers of several small Bottiaean cities of southeast Chalcidice are laid down by the fiat of Demetrius, c. 290, and there is mention of an earlier royal grant of land to the Ramaioi, probably by Philip II in 348. Another inscription, just published by her, contains these words: "King Alexander gave to Macedones Kalindoia and the places around Kalindoia—being the lands of Thamiscus, Camacae and Tripoea."[40] These had been four cities of the Bottiaei of northern Chalcidice (three of them being named as city-states in an earlier inscription). They had been won by the spear of Philip II in 348. Now in 335/4 Alexander gave the site of the largest (Kalindoia) and the lands of three other cities (but not the sites) to "Macedones," which I take to be the other half of the Macedonian State. The intention is clear: Kalindoia is to be a Macedonian city, a *polis Makedonon* (like Oesyme in Scymnus 656–57). The people of Kalindoia were no doubt planted elsewhere; but the people of the three cities which lost their lands

---

[38] Arr. 1.23.7.
[39] DS 17.49.1.
[40] Cf. Hammond, *Ancient Macedonia*, vol. 4 (Thessaloniki, 1986), 87ff.

but not their towns presumably stayed on as villagers associated with the new Macedonian city.

A third inscription, published in 1984,[41] shows Alexander in 335/4 both confirming arrangements made by Philip and making new ones on the same principle: he gave land to Philippi to possess (ἔχειν), and on the other hand he granted Philippi the right to cultivate certain land, and the Thracians the right to cultivate other land—each of them, it seems, paying rent to the king. Thus land won by Philip from the Thracians in 356 was Philip's and was inherited by his successor, Alexander. The king was owner of the land, τῆς χώρας.

This relationship between the king and spear-won land (γῆ δορίκτητος) and its peoples was taken overseas by Alexander. As he landed in the Troad he "accepted Asia from the gods, won by the spear"[42]—a proleptic claim, which he made good. He thus became King of Asia, the land which henceforth belonged to him and his successors. He made this clear at Priene in 334. Like Philippi, Priene was a free Greek city to the extent that it owned its land, conducted its own affairs, and did not pay annual tax to the king; but it was subject to the king's overall rule and policy. In an ordinance of 334 Alexander granted ownership of some land to citizens of Priene, and he made the non-Prienians live in villages and pay tax to the king. In this ordinance at Priene, Alexander said: "I know that the land is mine" (χώραν γινώσκω ἐμὴν εἶναι).[43] Those words later were to apply to most of Asia; for example, in 324 the Epigonoi were brought from the newly founded cities and "from the spear-won land."[44]

The Successors made the same claim. When the Temenid line came to an end, each of the generals in power "possessed the land allocated to himself as if it was a kingdom won by the spear."[45] Moreover, as with Philip and Alexander, this land was hereditable. Even if actual possession was not achieved, the claim remained. Thus Antiochus the Great claimed possession of eastern Thrace, because his ancestor Seleucus had defeated Lysimachus in war and taken his whole kingdom "won by the spear."[46]

Next, what was the relationship between the king and the native peoples on the spear-won land? Within the Macedonian kingdom Philip and Alexander left these peoples—Illyrians, Thracians, Paeonians, and

[41] C. Vatin, *Proc. 8th Epigr. Conf.* (Athens, 1984), 259–70; cf. L. Missitzis, *Ancient World* 12 (1985): 3–14, Hammond, *CQ* 38 (1988): 382–91.

[42] DS 17.17.2; Just. 11.5.10.

[43] Tod, *GHI* 2 no. 185.11 (p. 243), and Hammond, *The Macedonian State* (Oxford, 1989), 216 n. 25.

[44] Arr. 7.6.1.

[45] DS 19.105.4.

[46] Polyb. 18.51.4: δορίκτητον.

Greeks—to run their internal affairs as before, whether in a tribal system, or under a monarchy, or as a *polis*. They paid taxes to the king, and they worked the land which he chose to give or to let to them. They were no part of the Macedonian State. They had to accept that State's foreign policy, and they had to obey the king's commands. But they enjoyed great advantages: security; prosperity; freedom of language, law, and religion; no large expenditure on armaments and mercenaries; and the right of appeal to the king. A very few served in the King's Army as light cavalry and light-armed troops. The main function of these native peoples was to promote the economy of the kingdom and thus to enable it to maintain its regular army of Macedones. As need arose, the number of peoples on the land was increased by the transplantation of Illyrians, Gauls, Thracians, and Getae to work the lands of Lower Macedonia especially. We do not know of any risings by the native peoples or by the transplanted peoples.

The relationship between the king and the native peoples of Asia and Egypt was very similar. After the battle of the Granicus River Alexander told the peasants of Mysia "to return to their own property," that is, to cultivate it as theirs; and he gave the same order to the Indian peasants of the Indus delta.[47] At Sardis he granted the use of their own customs and laws to the Lydians and left them "free," that is, free to manage their own affairs in their own way, but of course to be subject to the overall kingship of Alexander and to pay taxes to him; and he continued on the same principle, which he intended to apply also in Arabia.[48] As he advanced, the proportion of Macedones to the peoples on spear-won lands decreased. He therefore began early to train elite troops from the native peoples: Lydians, Lycians, Carians, Egyptians (6,000 according to the Suda s.v. βασιλικοὶ παῖδες); and from 330 onward, mixed forces of Macedonian and Asian cavalry, parallel units of Asian troops (especially the 30,000 Epigonoi), and finally a phalanx mixed in each section.

The Macedonian policy of coexistence, cooperation, and joint military service succeeded both in the Macedonian kingdom and overseas. "Philip created one kingdom and people out of many tribes and nations."[49] Alexander created another kingdom, the Kingdom of Asia, by applying the same Macedonian principle but over a vastly greater area. Yet even at his early death there was no rising by the native peoples. The extent to which the Successors imitated Alexander cannot be exaggerated. "The kings imitated Alexander with their purple robes, their bodyguards, the inclination of their necks, and their louder voices in conversation," wrote

[47] Arr. 1.17.1, 6.17.6.
[48] Arr. 7.20.1.
[49] Just. 8.6.2.

Plutarch.[50] They imitated him in policy also. Let us take as an example
Eumenes, a Greek of Cardia, who might have organized his satrapy on
some Greek model. But he was more Macedonian than the Macedonians:
he relied on his Friends, exacted an oath of loyalty from the Macedones
in his army, gave them purple hats and cloaks, formed for himself a
Cavalry Guard of 300, and an Infantry Guard of 1,000 men chosen by
a *dogma* of his Macedones.[51] He had his own system of Pages, of whom
two squadrons of fifty each served close to him in battle (Alexander
too, according to Diodorus, had had Pages to guard him in Asia).[52] But
Eumenes owed his successes equally to the native troops whom he recruited, especially in Cappadocia.

Next, the king and the city. In the seventh and sixth centuries the
Macedones destroyed or expelled the previous inhabitants of the rich
coastal plain west of the Axius, and most Macedones then abandoned
the pastoral way of life and settled in tight communities, based on the
"companies" (παρέαι) of their pastoral life. These communities called
themselves *poleis*, cities, self-managing centers of local loyalty. Aegeae,
Alorus, Pella, Ichnae, and Heracleum were certainly *poleis* at the turn of
the sixth century, and each had its own distinctive citizenship and territory. The Macedonian State created new cities of Macedones within the
expanding kingdom, as we have seen at Kalindoia. Such a city was created
not by attracting individuals (as a new town would do today) but by
transplanting a community of Macedones; for example, the Macedones
of Balla were transplanted to Pythium, a town of Perrhaebia. Philip V
carried out just such a policy: "He uprooted the citizen men with their
women and children from the most distinguished coastal cities and
planted them in the area now called Emathia."[53] It was a two-way process,
the displaced population of Emathia being transferred elsewhere. Such
transplants of populations were used by Philip II in order to mix old
and new populations together in both Macedonia proper and Upper
Macedonia.

The Macedonian cities within the kingdom, old and new, managed
their own affairs—financial, religious, diplomatic, and military—and in
the last war against Rome the cities sent envoys to the king, offering
their own money and their own reserves of grain for the campaign.[54] In
physical terms the kingdom consisted of two parts: αἱ πόλεις καὶ ἡ χώρα,
"the cities and the countryside" (so divided by Pyrrhus and Lysimachus,

[50] Plut. *Pyrrh.* 8.1.
[51] Plut. *Eum.* 7.2, 8.6.
[52] DS 17.65.2.
[53] Polyb. 23.10.4.
[54] Livy 42.53.3.

according to Plutarch).[55] But it was, rather, the cities which formed the basis of Macedonia's military and economic strength.

Similar developments were promoted in the Kingdom of Asia by Alexander and then by his successors. The already established cities, both Greek and non-Greek, received favored treatment in terms of land and taxation. Populations were transferred (e.g., for refounding Tyre and Gaza, and for many Seleucid foundations); and expanding trade brought prosperity to these cities. They managed their own affairs, like the cities in the Macedonian kingdom, but within the overall authority of the king. New cities were founded with a modicum of Macedonians and Greeks, who were directed initially by Alexander and then were welcomed by the Successors. These cities included within their territory a large element of local indigenous people, like the villagers attached to Macedonian Kalindoia. It is important to stress that these were not Greek cities in any political sense; for the Greek city was a city-state, fiercely independent, riven by *stasis*, racially exclusive, and intolerant of royal rule. Their function, as in the Macedonian kingdom, was to produce the military and economic resources which the Hellenistic kingdoms required for survival. The history of what A. H. M. Jones called the "Greek City" of the Hellenistic and Roman periods in Asia[56] was rather the history of the Macedonian city—perhaps the greatest contribution which the Macedonian State made to human civilization.

RESPONSE: E. N. BORZA

Professor Hammond has given us a rich paper, full of intriguing suggestions about connections between the traditional Macedonian monarchy and the kingships of the Hellenistic period. He sees in the Macedonian state the antecedents for what followed in the Hellenistic era. The implications of what he has suggested are far-reaching and should be important to all of us interested in political and cultural continuity in the ancient world.

In order to acknowledge the validity of Professor Hammond's thesis, we must be prepared to accept two things: first, that his reconstruction of the institutions of the Macedonian state is valid; and second, that his interpretation of the Hellenistic legacy of these institutions is correct. I leave the Hellenistic aspect to others better qualified to comment, and shall limit myself to the first question: are Professor Hammond's views a fair representation of Macedonian institutions?

I cannot deal in detail with all of the matters raised by Professor Ham-

---

[55] Plut. *Pyrrh.* 12.1.
[56] A. H. M. Jones, *The Greek City from Alexander to Justinian* (Oxford, 1940).

mond, and offer the following in the way of commentary. First, I should like—though with a brevity that neither scholar nor subject deserves—to raise a few critical points that may, I hope, suffice to reveal the nature of what I perceive as a major problem in treating these matters. Second, I wish to address the larger context of describing the Argead dynasty of Macedon,[1] and to suggest why it is so difficult to develop analogues or parallels between what Hellenistic kings did and the activities of their Macedonian predecessors.

The heart of Professor Hammond's argument lies in his reconstruction of the relationship between the Macedonian king and his people, the Macedones, in the Argead period. His attempt here and elsewhere to define the Macedones as the Macedonians-at-arms has met with general approval. Professor Hammond correctly demonstrates that the epigraphical evidence—on this point, the best kind of evidence—from the late fifth and early fourth centuries shows that the king is βασιλεὺς Μακεδόνων. The same evidence also reveals that all treaties are made with the king personally; the only other persons mentioned are the king's descendants or living members of his immediate family, the Argeadae. This would remain true through the reign of Alexander the Great, where "King Alexander" alone marks all of the surviving treaties.

The numbers of the Macedones are still largely guesswork. Professor Hammond gives 10,000 Macedones in 358 and 30,000 in 336. This is in fact the number of infantry in the Macedonian army during Philip's campaign against the Illyrian Bardylis (DS 16.4.3) and the number at the commencement of Alexander's reign.[2] But there is nothing in the evidence cited to connect these numbers with the total citizen population beyond the unproved assumption that the whole citizen levy was enrolled in these campaigns. Perhaps the citizen rolls were actually larger, as Alexander was able to draw on extensive human resources in exchanging veterans for fresh troops during his Asian venture.[3] This could have been accomplished had large numbers of new men been made Macedones under Alexander, but Professor Hammond argues that this process began only "gradually under Alexander and increased rapidly . . . after his death." We are thus left somewhat confused not only by the

---

[1] Throughout I prefer "Argead" to Hammond's "Temenid," as I hold that the tradition of a Temenid (Argive Greek) origin for the Macedonian royal family is a story probably derived from the propaganda of Alexander I; see my "Athenians, Macedonians and the Origins of the Macedonian Royal House," *Hesperia*, suppl. 19 (1982): 7–13.

[2] For detailed discussion of the numbers in Alexander's army see N. G. L. Hammond and F. W. Walbank, *A History of Macedonia*, vol. 3, *336–167 B.C.* (Oxford, 1988), 86–87.

[3] On Alexander's manpower reserves see A. B. Bosworth, "Macedonian Manpower under Alexander the Great," *Ancient Macedonia* 4 (1986): 115–22, and "Alexander the Great and the Decline of Macedon," *JHS* 106 (1986): 1–12.

problem of numbers, but also by the definition of what a Macedonian was at any given moment.

Professor Hammond cites some new inscriptions from Chalcidice showing the disposition of king's land to Macedones and perhaps others. I wonder if such an act of settlement conferred with it citizenship (one thinks of similar circumstances during the Roman Republic), or whether these land grants may not have been a reward to veterans who already were Macedones? Griffith has maintained that the latter situation may have prevailed in Chalcidice in Philip II's time, but that so few Macedones were settled as to leave the basic Greek character of the population not much altered.[4] In the end, the award of royal land grants might account for an increase in the numbers of Macedones.

It appears that Professor Hammond is on the right track in his attempt to frame the problem as one that necessitates understanding the relationship between the troops (Professor Hammond's "citizen troops," the elite infantry and Companion Cavalry) and the king, and the Macedonians and the king, and whether these two—troops and Macedonians—are synonymous. But I am not entirely persuaded that our sources, many of which are late and imprecise, use these terms with the precision that both Professor Hammond and I would wish. In short, I am less certain about the definition and numbers than is Professor Hammond.

Moreover, I am unable to share Professor Hammond's fine distinction between Alexander as King of the Macedones and as King of Asia. The late Stewart Oost pointed out that the sources do not discriminate between kingship or lordship over Asia.[5] The title is not official in any sense, but general, at least as far as we can tell from the ancient writers, who are mainly centuries removed from these events. As Oost pointed out, it would be as if Napoleon's troops had proclaimed him "Emperor of Europe." I thus cannot accept that our sources' comments about Alexander's titles in Asia have any significance for describing his formal relationship with his own peoples.

To continue, Professor Hammond suggests that these citizen-soldiers both elected and deposed their kings. Now we have surviving the names of sixteen historical Argead kings, beginning with Amyntas I in the late sixth and early fifth century and ending with Alexander IV, son of the conqueror, who was murdered in 311/10. (Those who accept that Argaeus and Amyntas IV were kings would have eighteen names on their list.) Yet we have only a single dubious reference, in a late writer, for the

[4] In N. G. L. Hammond and G. T. Griffith, *A History of Macedonia*, vol. 2, 550–336 B.C. (Oxford, 1979), 365–79.

[5] S. I. Oost, "The Alexander Historians and Asia," in Harry J. Dell, ed., *Macedonian Studies in Honor of Charles F. Edson* (Thessaloniki, 1981), 265–82.

Macedonians deposing a king in accordance with due process.[6] Of my list of sixteen, exactly half were murdered. Of the remainder, half appear to have died of natural causes or were killed in battle, and we have no information about the others.[7] The only possible instance of a king being deposed would be that of young Amyntas IV, for whom Philip might have served as regent for a year or two; but I am among those who believe that Philip was king from the start.[8]

As for the selection process—and this is central to Professor Hammond's theme of continuity between the Argead and Hellenistic periods—we have, in fact, information about only three successions, those of Philip II, Alexander the Great, and Arrhidaeus. Insofar as limited evidence permits us to say, the procedures used in all three successions differ from one another. Some sort of assembly may have participated in the choice of Philip; at least Philip was addressing an assembly as part of the process (DS 16.3.1), but we lack evidence that Philip was *elected* by the army as the sole method of succession.[9] Further, Philip's rule was quickly challenged by Argaeus, who marched immediately to secure the support of the local population, a move forestalled by Philip (DS 16.2.6–3.3). No assembly is mentioned in the case of Alexander's succession,[10] even though he is portrayed as courting and winning support through tactful statements (DS 17.1.2; Just. 11.1.8). As for Arrhidaeus, it was an extraordinary scene in Babylon in the early summer of 323, and, while not all of the details have been accepted as historically accurate, the

---

[6] Porphyr. frag. 1 (= Syncell. 261D) in *FHG* III, p. 691, part of a garbled and largely untrustworthy account of Macedonian rulers of the early fourth century.

[7] Archelaus was killed by a lover, Amyntas II by Derdas, Pausanias (probably) by Amyntas III, Alexander II by Ptolemy, Ptolemy by Perdiccas III, Philip II by Pausanias, Philip III by Olympias, and Alexander IV by Cassander. Moreover, there were additional conspiracies against at least Amyntas III and Alexander III, and a number of potential rivals were dispatched in the struggles for succession of Archelaus, Philip II, and Alexander the Great. Death from natural causes: Alexander I, Perdiccas II, Amyntas III, and Alexander the Great.

[8] The matter of Philip's regency is not settled. The strongest argument favoring a regency is offered by Adrian Tronson, "Satyrus the Peripatetic and the Marriages of Philip II," *JHS* 104 (1984): 120–21. I am, however, inclined to accept the view of Griffith, *History of Macedonia* 2:208–9, 702–4, who is persuasive in arguing that Amyntas never ruled.

[9] DS 17.2.2. Justin (11.1.8) mentions a *contio*, the same word used by Curtius (10.7.13) to describe the crowd assembled at the time of Arrhidaeus' selection, but this is not to be taken as meaning a formal electoral assembly (*pace* Griffith, *History of Macedonia* 2:391) any more than is Hammond's *plethos* (see below, note 13).

[10] Contra Hammond, *History of Macedonia* 3:30, who cites Arr. 1.25.2 as evidence for Alexander's "election" to the throne of Macedon. Arrian says nothing of the kind in this passage, and in the brief mention of Alexander's accession in the appropriate place (1.1.1), Arrian wrote παραλαμβάνω, the same verb used by Plutarch (*Alex.* 11.1), which, among its various meanings in this context (e.g., "receive," "succeed to," etc.), does not mean "elect."

general sense of what went on is undeniable.[11] It all boils down to this: for the whole history of the Argeadae there is preserved a detailed account of only this one scene of succession, characterized by chaos, ambition, fear, and political maneuvering. If there were constitutional procedures for selecting a king, they were not in evidence. If the "army assembly" was constituted to elect a king, why did it not function in June 323? And why (if one accepts the story of the king's last words) did a small group of generals ask the dying Alexander about *his* choice of successor? Who would enforce such a decision? In the course of the confusion, Perdiccas held the ring (whatever that signified), Ptolemy proposed rule by a junta, and a throng of soldiers pushed for Arrhidaeus.

The evidence for later fourth-century successions—the only Argead successions for which we have information—permits the following conclusion: groups of persons participated in the selection of the king, as the king ruled, in some sense, with the consent of the governed (here I concur completely with Professor Hammond's underlying assumption). This is a component of kingship resting on generalship, an ancient tradition in several societies in which commanders led with the consent of their troops. Those who shared in the king's selection probably (but not always) included members of the royal family, important barons and military chiefs, parts of the army, and, perhaps, of the civilian population—although I should not like to press the last point. The extant evidence suggests that the selection was not fixed according to established, constitutional procedures, but depended upon the political and military circumstances at hand. Even an autocratic king needed the support of the army, some troops of which might be consulted or exhorted if the situation required that, as in the cases of Philip II and Arrhidaeus. But acclamation by the army, which may have been a normal, ritual part of the process, is not the same as election, a procedure marked by political agreements and compromises made on another level. There is in fact no evidence proving that the sovereign power to elect a king rested with any particular group of persons. Succession appears rather to be the result of a series of political and military decisions made by those in a position to do so, and the manner in which they conducted themselves was a response to the circumstances of the moment.[12]

Thus, while I can accept much of what Professor Hammond says about

[11] DS 17.117.3–118.2, 18.1.3–2.4; Arr. 7.26.3; Curt. 10.5.4–10.20; Just. 12.15.8.

[12] When Polybius (15.25.11) refers to troops at the Ptolemaic court swearing loyalty as they were accustomed to doing at the proclamation of kings, it is not as clear to me as to Hammond that our source is referring to some old Macedonian custom rather than to a feature of the court of the Ptolemies. The passage is evidence only of the swearing of loyalty; loyalty may be crucial to the success of a would-be monarch, but Polybius does not equate the acclamation of loyalty with the formal procedure of choosing a monarch.

the nature of the Macedonian citizenship through the age of Alexander, I am somewhat skeptical about the power of that citizen body to effect momentous decisions, such as the election and deposition of their kings. But there is also a logical inconsistency in Professor Hammond's position. Even if we accept that some kind of assembly of troops selected and deposed kings (and I do not accept this), they did so because they were Macedones, citizens of a Macedonian monarchical state. To claim the perpetuation of the process into Hellenistic times would require defining the citizen body of the Ptolemaic and Seleucid kingdoms in the same way for the same reason. Professor Hammond has not done this, and I am not certain that the analogy is possible. But I leave that matter to those well versed in matters of Hellenistic ruling and ruled classes.[13] As for Antigonid Macedonia, I suspect that things were much as they had been before the age of Philip and Alexander, although this is an impressionistic view.

There are several other points in Professor Hammond's paper that require a similar response, that is, that I do not see in one or two isolated instances, cited by late sources, a sample of evidence statistically sufficient to lay down a general rule, especially when much of that evidence concerns the reign of Alexander, whose career may be unique because of its geographical setting and multiethnic complexity. The most that can be said is that there appear to be some features of the reigns of Philip and Alexander that may have established precedents for the Hellenistic kingships that followed. But, if Kienast and Fredricksmeyer are correct,[14] Philip's kingship was tending toward an Asian absolutist model,

[13] Hammond cites several situations from the Hellenistic period suggesting that there was a functioning army assembly that made important decisions, especially regarding the appointment and deposition of rulers. But the evidence does not always support Hammond's view. For example, Hammond argues that the *plethos* mentioned by Plutarch (*Demetr.* 18.1) in his descriptions of the crowning of Antigonus and Demetrius is an assembly. But this misinterprets Plutarch. Τὸ πλῆθος is a throng of soldiers *saluting* Demetrius and Antigonus; but Antigonus is *crowned* by his friends (οἱ φίλοι), and Demetrius receives the diadem from his father. Moreover, Plutarch's account of the crowning of Antigonus and Demetrius is part of a longer passage which goes on to describe the assumption of royal status by all the first-generation Successors, and there is a complete silence on the procedures of accession used by Ptolemy, Lysimachus, Seleucus, and Cassander. There is little more here and in other evidence cited by Hammond (e.g., note 9 above) than small contingents of soldiers, normally household troops, proclaiming a new king. These are ad hoc incidents, more akin to the proclamation of Claudius as emperor by the Praetorians rather than manifestations of an institutional procedure.

[14] Dietmar Kienast, *Philipp II. von Makedonien und das Reich der Achaimeniden*, Abhandlungen der Marburger Gelehrten Gesellschaft, 1971, no. 6 (Munich, 1973), and E. A. Fredricksmeyer, "Divine Honors for Philip II," *TAPA* 109 (1979): 39–61, "On the Background of the Ruler Cult," in *Macedonian Studies*, 145–56, and "On the Final Aims of Philip II," in W. L. Adams and E. N. Borza, eds., *Philip II, Alexander the Great and the Macedonian Heritage* (Washington, 1982), 85–98.

and most of Alexander's kingship was exercised for eleven years amid almost constant campaigning thousands of miles from home. It is difficult to believe that either of these royal administrations was "normal," although I confess that the dearth of information about political and social institutions before Philip makes it as dangerous for me to claim that Philip and Alexander were unusual as it does for Professor Hammond to claim that they were part of a continuing tradition.

As for the king and the city, Professor Hammond raises the possibility that the Macedonian city in the Hellenistic and Roman world was "perhaps the greatest contribution which the Macedonian State made to human civilization." Now we cannot deny that the Macedonians were city founders and refounders from the time of Archelaus to the age of Philip and Alexander. But I cannot attach much significance to this Macedonian custom, or regard it as very different from what Greeks had traditionally been doing for centuries. There were, roughly speaking, only two kinds of inhabited communities in the Balkans for people who had settled into an agricultural or commercial pattern: towns and *poleis*. The custom of European settlement, until quite recently, has been to live in defensible towns that lay near trade routes and had access to fresh water and farmland. The Macedonians lived this way both as the result of their natural evolution and because their kings forcibly moved people into such settlements from time to time, as Professor Hammond points out. That the towns managed many of their own affairs should not surprise us, especially as the Argead monarchy seems not to have been highly bureaucratized. But it would appear that a major difference between Macedonian towns and Greek towns is that the Greeks selected their own magistrates and legislated on their own behalf in *poleis* that were politically autonomous.

As this is a major difference, I am not clear about Professor Hammond's phrase *polis Makedonon*, and what the distinction is between it and a Greek *polis*. I think a better analogy would have been between Macedonian towns and the larger towns that were part of the Athenian *polis*, excluding the town of Athens. All central Macedonian towns whose sites are known were located on prime farmland, and, as Professor Hammond has shown by his use of the new Chalcidic inscriptions recently recovered by our Greek colleagues, good farmland in Chalcidice was used to settle persons in towns. And when Philip II took Amphipolis, he may have settled some Macedonians therein, but the infrastructure that had managed this city for nearly a century continued as before.[15] That is, Amphipolis continued to maintain all of the characteristics of its former status as a *polis*, save one essential one: it was no longer politically

---

[15] Griffith, *History of Macedonia* 2:230–42.

independent. Can any of these settlements, new or old, properly be called a *polis*, when political authority resided in the monarchy?

Now Professor Hammond apparently understands this. This is the Argead model he sees establishing the pattern for the eastern cities of the Hellenistic and Roman periods, and certainly no one would wish to deny Professor Hammond's claim concerning the historical importance of those centers. But I fail to see that this is a peculiar Macedonian institution. The characteristic Macedonian institution was the monarchy itself, replanted throughout the Asian and African rim of the eastern Mediterranean as an attempt to legitimize the conquests of Alexander's successor generals, but even so hardly a unique form of government in that part of the world. Furthermore, as the general pattern of settlement in the Greek as well as Macedonian world was through towns, the development of cities in the eastern Mediterranean seems to me to be a perfectly natural, indeed, the only possible, means of social organization.

Perhaps my quarrel with Professor Hammond on this point is only one of emphasis. We agree that the cities of the East were important. He sees this as an outgrowth of a Macedonian custom; I see it as a more common and natural means of establishing settlements or of perpetuating existing urban centers. The relationship of these cities to their ruling monarchs was, as Professor Hammond points out, similar to what may have existed in old Macedon, but I do not view this as something especially characteristic of the Macedonian heritage so much as the only situation possible if one is to have cities within a far-flung monarchy.

Professor Hammond is correct when he points out that these self-governing Hellenistic cities were not city-states, since, like Macedonian cities, they were ruled by the king. Yet he calls the Macedonian cities *poleis*. I agree that the Macedonian and Hellenistic cities were alike; but I see neither as a proper city-state in the Greek sense, if by that we mean they were autonomous. Still, it may in the end be a moot point: who would be willing to argue that Mytilene or Naxos or Carystos were not *poleis* just because they were ruled by Athens in the fifth century B.C.? I think that Professor Hammond is on the right track in attempting to define the relationship between kings and cities in Macedonia, but I am unpersuaded that this is significant for an understanding of the cities of the early Hellenistic world. Self-managing cities existing within larger monarchies in the East had rarely been independent, and one wonders whether their Hellenistic status is not as much due to traditional city-monarchy relationships in the East as to the fact that Macedonian kings now ruled there.

Nevertheless, it is not certain that Professor Hammond is wrong in the end. One of the more remarkable aspects of his career is the unusual prescience or intuition he has shown about some things, most notably his identification of the modern village of Vergina as the site of ancient Aegeae. As ancient historians, we are most of us, on occasion, intuitive and impressionistic when confronted with scanty evidence. Professor Hammond's argument about the cities remains, in my view, just that—impressionistic—but I am intrigued by the implications of it, and await the recovery of more epigraphical and archaeological evidence from Macedon itself to test the hypothesis more accurately.[16]

Now, let us examine a methodological context for what Professor Hammond and others of us attempt to do when tracing the long course of Macedonian institutions.[17] At the core of his argument lies a conviction that the Macedonian monarchy operated according to a set of procedures that had been established through custom over a long time. There are two basic schools of thought about the Macedonian "constitution," if by that term we mean the customs and institutions by which a society was regulated. One school holds that the Macedonian kingdom was run according to a generally accepted set of traditions within which various groups held and exercised customary rights which the king oversaw and

[16] Pella is only now emerging from the ground. It is Hippodamian in plan, and appears similar to the grand cities of Asia Minor and the Levant in the Hellenistic period. But the dating of much of Pella is still imprecise; we have virtually no archaeological chronology for the city from its refounding by Archelaus about the year 400 B.C. down to the later fourth century. As for Aegeae, we have only scattered buildings; but perhaps further excavation based on the new magnetometer readings will reveal something of its fourth-century plan. Dion, which holds so much promise in theory, is still being dug mainly at Roman levels. The very site of Therme is in dispute, and the early history of Thessaloniki lies beneath its Roman, medieval, and modern overlay.

We know, in fact, very little about these towns. To judge by what slight evidence has been recovered through excavation, their physical appearance would seem to differ somewhat from that of their Hellenistic counterparts. To the best of my knowledge no major religious monument (and here I include the small Eucleia monument at Aegeae), such as a temple, has yet been recovered inside a Macedonian town. Pella has an agora, but it may be middle or late Hellenistic. Whether Aegeae had one or not will be known only from further excavation. The agora, so typical for Greek *poleis*, as the center of the kind of self-management that Hammond attributes to Macedonian towns, thus far is missing. There are other differences, having to do with the distribution of burial sites and small shrines, but I have no time to explore them beyond this brief reference. A trickle of inscriptions describing city procedures and officials continues to appear, but, as yet, of insufficient quantity and quality to judge the extent to which the institutions that governed these towns are indicative of self-government or royal rule.

In brief, there is not enough literary or archaeological evidence to make a strong case for the self-governing *polis*-type urban center having existed in Macedonia itself. Further, since the Hellenistic urban center in the eastern Mediterranean may, as I believe, have resulted from a natural organic evolution coupled with Greek influences in new city planning, a link between Macedonian cities and those of the Hellenistic East has yet to be established.

[17] Some of what follows reflects an argument presented in detail in my recent work, *In the Shadow of Olympus: The Emergence of Macedon* (Princeton, 1990).

guaranteed. This is what I shall call the "constitutionalist" position. The other school believes that the kingdom was centered on the autocracy of the monarch himself, who did precisely what he wanted, or—more exactly—what he could get away with.

But what is the evidence for these institutions? Unfortunately for those of us who are historians attempting to seek order (and even reason) out of the chaos of events, the Macedonians are a people who are mainly silent about themselves, and there is no Polybius for the Argead period. Nearly all our information about political and social institutions in early Macedon comes from the age of Philip and Alexander; and any attempt to retroject such evidence into earlier Macedonian history requires large assumptions about the continuity of institutions from the classical period into the later fourth century and the Hellenistic era. If the advocates of constitutionalism use this continuity as an operating methodological assumption, they should also be able to trace the continuation of these institutions into the Hellenistic period, or, if not, to posit when and why there was a break.

The constitutionalist position was laid out forcefully more than half a century ago by Friedrich Granier,[18] and much of the discussion since then has evolved in support, modification, or rejection of his views. Using evidence mainly from the Hellenistic period, Granier concluded that the Macedonian kingship evolved from a primitive chieftainship, in which the king was a first among equals, chosen by his fellow warriors. As Macedonian institutions became more formal, an organization of Macedonian men-at-arms came into existence, marking a transition to something akin to a sovereign military assembly. As the population became more settled and the Macedonians were transformed from a warrior society into a landed aristocracy, the nobility usurped popular sovereignty. In the fourth century, however, the assembly was revived to provide the monarchy with support against the nobility. The army assembly acquired some judicial functions and even selected the king or regent. All parties were aware of their rights, although in practice the king ruled as an autocrat. Nonetheless, the relationship between king and people was regulated by two constituent functions of the army assembly: the right to elect the king, and the right to sit as judge and jury.

Granier's book proved influential, and, although some details in it were found unacceptable, its basic thesis—that the Macedonians lived according to traditional customs—long remained unchallenged. Over the years it has been extended and modified by others, including André Aymard, Pierre Briant, and Professor Hammond himself; and while

---

[18] *Die makedonische Heeresversammlung: Ein Beitrag zum antiken Staatsrecht* (Munich, 1931).

some small differences exist, these are all variations on the constitutionalist theme.[19]

This constitutionalist view remains an attractive hypothesis, despite
the fact that there is no evidence from antiquity to support the kind of
political evolution that Granier described. Moreover, the fragments that
have been used to prove the existence of an assembly at any period
have been drawn from late authors far removed from the scene, or have
referred to events in the Hellenistic era. The major challenge to the
constitutionalist position has been led by Malcolm Errington, who has
received some support from Robert Lock and Edward Anson.[20] The
critics' position may be summarized thus: (a) Granier and others have
constructed a theoretical model based upon an unacceptable assumption,
namely that peoples' rights were recognized by Macedonian kings but
not realized in practice; (b) the evidence used to support the model comes
mainly from the Hellenistic period, and the assumption that there was
an institutional continuity from early Macedon to the Hellenistic period
is unproven; (c) the evidence from the reign of Alexander the Great
that shows occasional meetings of the army for some judicial or forensic
purpose describes a special situation—an exception to the rule, not the
rule itself; and (d) there is no supporting evidence from reliable contemporary writers, such as Aristotle. The sources centuries removed are for
the most part ignorant about early Macedonian institutions and anachronistic in describing institutional terms and procedures.

In my view the modern critics have struck a telling, though perhaps
not fatal, blow at the constitutionalist position, which must remain what
it has always been: a theoretical construction largely unsupported by
evidence from antiquity. Now it could be argued that it is not methodo-
logically incorrect to develop a theoretical model by extending a body of
information from a relatively well-documented period into an era lacking
sources. That is, if one could show that there was a constitutional structure in the Hellenistic period like that in the age of Philip and Alexander,
it would not be unreasonable to suspect that its origin lay back in the

[19] Aymard, "Sur l'assemblée macédonienne," *REA* 52 (1950): 115–37, and "Basileus
Makedonon," *RIDA* 4 (1950): 61–97, both reprinted in Aymard's *Études d'histoire ancienne*
(Paris, 1967); Briant, *Antigone le Borgne* (Paris, 1973); and Hammond, *History of Macedonia*
2:150–65, 383–404.

[20] Errington, "Macedonian 'Royal Style' and its Historical Significance," *JHS* 94 (1974):
20–37, "The Historiographical Origins of Macedonian 'Staatsrecht,' " *Ancient Macedonia* 3
(1983): 89–101, and "The Nature of the Macedonian State under the Monarchy," *Chiron*
8 (1978): 77–133; Lock, "The Macedonian Army Assembly in the Time of Alexander the
Great," *CP* 72 (1977): 91–107; Anson, "Macedonia's Alleged Constitutionalism," *CJ* 80
(1985): 303–16, and "The Evolution of the Macedonian Army Assembly," *Historia* 40
(1991): 230–47.

earlier period of Macedonian history for which there is no evidence. But the critics have shown that these institutions did not exist under the autocratic rule of the Antigonid dynasty of Hellenistic Macedon. Assuming that they had been in place earlier, what made them vanish? The only possible answer lies in the reigns of Philip and Alexander: the autocracy of the latter in particular was legendary, and he may well be said to have killed prior constitutional arrangements. But this is the very monarch whose reign appears to have provided us with much of our information about the rights of the Macedonians. We are thus driven to the improbable conclusion that the constitutional arrangements of the Macedonian monarchy collapsed under the absolutism of that very king whose reign provides evidence of their existence. This simply will not do. The more probable alternative is that the interaction between Alexander, his commanders, and his troops in assembly was a unique situation, resulting from the extraordinary circumstances of a Macedonian army operating far from home and lacking the normal forms of support and references.

To present such a minimalist picture of Macedonian institutions without offering an alternative may not be satisfactory. Perhaps one can offer—lacking evidence—a theoretical model. But what model? The "Homeric" model is attractive, but it, too, is fraught with problems of evidence and method that are part of the ongoing struggle to understand Dark Age Greece. Moreover, we lack information about the social and economic support enjoyed by Macedonian kings to match what we know about the relationship of Homeric chieftains with other members of their community. Besides, the Macedonian king was clearly more autocratic. There is no contemporary Greek model, certainly not the constitutionally constrained monarchy of the Spartans. Illyrian and Thracian models come to mind, but these appear to be too tribal and are, in any case, imperfectly understood. Fifth- and fourth-century Macedon may have been influenced by the Persians, but no serious analysis can be offered until there is a clearer notion of Persian-Macedonian relations in the fourth century before the age of Philip and Alexander.[21]

In sum, I hold that we do not know enough about early Macedonian institutions to describe the extent to which they were preserved in the Hellenistic period. Certainly, some aspects of the reigns of Philip and Alexander do appear to have continued at least into the early Hellenistic

---

[21] Shortly after the conclusion of the present symposium an article appeared by Alan E. Samuel, "Philip and Alexander as Kings: Macedonian Monarchy and Merovingian Parallels," *AHR* 93 (1988): 1270–86, in which a "warlord" model was offered. Samuel attempted to show that the tie that bound king and people was the winning of land; and surely there is considerable evidence—as Hammond has pointed out in his paper—of the importance to Macedonians of "spear-won land" (γῆ δορίκτητος). This may be an idea deserving greater emphasis in Hammond's arguments.

era. But I regard as unproven this attempt to show that such features were a part of traditional Macedonian monarchy—what Professor Hammond calls the "pattern" of the Macedonian state. I agree that the Macedonians had a vital impact on the history of western Asia and the eastern Mediterranean world; but that had little to do with the migration of Macedonian institutions to distant places. In fact, the true "Macedonian imprint" was due to the conquest carried out by Alexander's armies, thus removing from western Asia the political power that had for centuries blocked the penetration of Greek culture. Their conquest replaced Asian rule with Macedonian rule. To the extent that a cultural transformation followed, it was, in my view, due rather to a continuation of local traditions and the influence of pockets of Hellenism than to the establishment of anything distinctly Macedonian.

DISCUSSION

E. S. Gruen: Plutarch is surely right that Alexander shunned the title "King of Kings." I have no quarrel with the facts presented by Professor Hammond. But the interpretation I find a little more difficult. Professor Hammond's paradoxical version is that Alexander avoided the designation because it was too restrictive: "King of Asia" was meant to be a more sweeping title. Then he goes on to say that Alexander did not want to succeed Darius but wanted Darius to remain as the King of the Medes and Persians, as would his successors. I have three problems with this. First, if Alexander was willing to have Darius retain his throne, what was the symbolic significance of Alexander *sitting* on that throne? Secondly, if he expected Darius' heir to be king to the Medes and Persians, why did he send him to Macedonia to learn Greek? And third, if Darius was to be King of the Medes and Persians, would he also retain the title "King of Kings"? Which kings would he then be king of? Perhaps Alexander avoided the title "King of Kings" for a simpler reason—that is, the negative connotations that this phrase had in the Greek world, at least since the time of Xerxes and Aeschylus' *Persae.*

N. G. L. Hammond: If you look at the letter, which, I think, gives the actual sense of what Alexander wrote to Darius, he says that Darius can be king over other kings, and this must mean that Darius could retain the hereditary title "King of Medes and Persians," *basileus basileon.* It is kings within the Medic and Persian state that he is king of, not all the kings of the world. I think the point of confusion is that Persian kings could claim the title "King of Asia." But so could the kings of, say, Phrygia and Macedonia. To be King of Asia does not mean to be king of the Medes and Persians. Alexander claimed to be king of all of Asia. He thought of India as being the end of Asia. Asia to him was a geographical concept. He didn't know the limits of it, but it was a clear concept.

P. Green: Alexander is in fact equating Asia with the entire Persian domain. So in fact whether he was called King of Kings or not was a moot point.

N. G. L. Hammond: No, Asia was more than the area controlled by Darius at his death. Alexander went beyond that. Darius, for example, didn't control the Indus valley.

A. E. Samuel: I am dubious as to whether we can use the evidence for Alexander to describe Macedonian kingship as an institution. That is, although I would be inclined to say that we can describe Alexander as a king, and can talk about his kingship, in terms of patterns of behavior, overall we get the impression from the sources that Alexander became increasingly suspicious of his generals and was worried about their reaction to what he was doing. I am concerned about whether or not we can really use the evidence about Alexander on items. As an Alexander historian I know some of those stories are true, but I'm not sure which ones. And I'm not sure which stories come out of the tradition to amplify it, or which ones establish the tradition. To depend on any single piece of evidence to describe the situation which pertained at the time of Alexander seems to me to be depending on evidence that is really shifty. So I incline to a minimalist position simply because I don't have any evidence.

N. G. L. Hammond: It's obviously important to decide which of the original sources of information were used by the later writers. And that I've endeavored to do for three Alexander historians and I hope to go on to the sources of Plutarch's *Alexander* and of Arrian. That seems to me to be a vital foundation which hasn't been properly laid. It will always be controversial, but some points one can probably establish. If you accept the word of Arrian that he was following Aristobulus and Ptolemy, then you have a fairly solid basis to go on. Things which he says are *legomena* are just stories he knows are not trustworthy, and so we know it too.

S. M. Burstein: Professor Borza's minimalist position on the question of the constitution of Macedonia I accept as a statement of the evidence. But he also slipped in a redefinition that might actually be very promising. Errington, as I see it, has been fundamentally attacking a straw man. What Granier, Briant, and the others have done is to devise for Macedon something akin to Mommsen's *Staatsrecht*, a precise model with rigid rules and formulas. That is easy to knock down. It has been done convincingly. However, Errington has come perilously close to positing something unparalleled: an autocracy in which the murder of Clitus is *normal*. The king can do anything. A Merovingian warlord might get away with a murder—many murders—but not even the Merovingian system ever assumed that this was normal behavior. Professor Borza appears to be suggesting that there *was* a set of Macedonian constitutional traditions, but that we just don't know what they are. Is that correct?

E. N. Borza: I think so, yes. Leon Mooren has written on these matters recently and has taken a plausible moderate position, somewhere between Hammond and Errington, though a bit closer to the latter. The heart of the question remains: What is the relationship of the king of the Macedonians to the Macedonians? If my position is accepted—and I hope Professor Hammond will agree with what follows—the king of the Macedonians had a working relationship with his army, as did any good general in antiquity. And this relationship is not the law of the jungle. I would never claim that, even though Errington may appear to do so; in fact, I know personally that he believes that even the jungle has laws. Whatever the nature of the Macedonian "constitution," it arises from a mutual understanding of the nature of that relationship. We have the most evidence for it from the expedition of Alexander, although his reign may be an unusual situation. Even though the "rules" are difficult for us to recover, they seem—some notable exceptions aside—to have worked tolerably well.

I do not believe that the evidence supports the notion that Macedonian kings were elected and deposed through some popular procedure, although I accept, on the basis of three later-fourth-century successions for which we have evidence, that troops played some part in the process. It is a political process, but not necessarily a constitutional process following some rigid theoretical model.

N. G. L. Hammond: One comment on Greek and Macedonian cities: The Macedonians called their cities *poleis* and other Greek writers called them *poleis*. They were in that sense cities. But the Greek city was not able to coexist with local peoples peacefully. The Greek cities in Asia soon ceased to grow, for they tried to subject the native peoples to serfdom. Aristotle said: When you conquer Asiatics, reduce them to serfdom, make them subject to the Greek city-states. So the Greek *polis* was racially exclusive, not capable of extension to whole areas in the East. But the Macedonian *polis*, as we see it being created, was a mixture of Macedonians and other peoples. This is what happens in Asia. It's a Macedonian *polis*, not a Greek type.

The Hellenistic Fringe:
The Case of Meroë

S. M. Burstein

Interaction between Greek and non-Greek cultures is one of the constants of Greek history, and never was it more intense than in the Hellenistic period. Multitudes followed Theocritus' advice (*Id.* 14.57–68) and sought their fortunes in the new Macedonian kingdoms that emerged from the wreckage of Alexander's empire. Their experiences and those of the native subjects of the Macedonian kings among whom they settled have been the subject of numerous studies.[1] On the periphery of the Hellenistic kingdoms, however, were other peoples, peoples that succeeded in preserving their independence, but whose fates were intertwined with those of the Macedonian kingdoms. There also Greeks and non-Greeks and their cultures met, but as equals instead of ruler and ruled. The purpose of this study is to consider the results of one such encounter, that between Ptolemaic Egypt and the kingdom of Meroë in the central Sudan (see figure 2).

Relations between Ptolemaic Egypt and its southern neighbors occupy little space in Hellenistic histories. Much of this neglect is the result of the fragmentary character of the extant sources that is the bane of all Hellenistic studies. The ancient evidence, both Greek and Meroitic, was once extensive. Pliny the Elder (*HN* 6.183) lists six men who traveled in Meroitic territory in the Hellenistic period and wrote accounts of their experiences; they included Dalion, who explored the southern Sudan, and Simonides the Younger, who lived in Meroë for five years. Of their

---

[1] Fundamental is Claire Préaux, *Le Monde hellénistique*, 2 vols. (Paris, 1978); see esp. 2: 545–65.

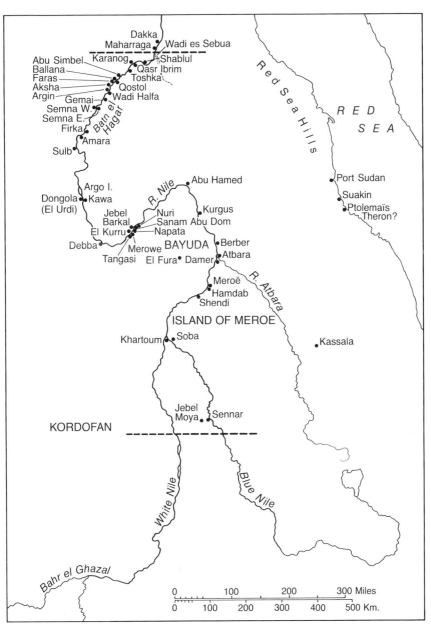

2. The Meroitic kingdom. After P. L. Shinnie, *Meroë: A Civilization of the Sudan* (London: Thames and Hudson, 1967), p. 17, fig. 2.

works and also those of Ptolemaic officials such as Pythagoras, *nauarch* under Ptolemy II,[2] only fragments remain; this is true also of works based on them, such as the pioneering *Geography* of Eratosthenes of Cyrene and the *On Affairs in Asia* and *On the Erythraean Sea* of the second-century-B.C. historian Agatharchides of Cnidos.[3] Meroitic evidence has suffered similarly severe losses. Nubian historical inscriptions in Egyptian virtually cease with the reign of Nastasen in the third quarter of the fourth century B.C.,[4] while those in the still undeciphered Meroitic language are few and, in any event, only begin in the second century B.C. Worst of all, much of the rich evidence once contained in the large royal and noble cemeteries near Meroë and in the ruins of the ancient city has been lost through looting in antiquity and the crude excavation methods employed by the first modern archaeologist to work at Meroë, Sir John Garstang, who dug in the royal city between 1909 and 1914.[5] The deficiencies of our sources, however, are not alone sufficient to account for the neglect of the history of Hellenistic Meroë. Equally important was Meroë's peripheral character, both geographically and politically.

The Meroitic kings claimed sovereignty over all Nubia, from the first cataract in the north to Sennar in the south. The reality was different. The Meroitic heartland lay in the famous Island of Meroë, the triangle of land formed by the junction of the Nile and Atbara rivers, about six hundred miles south of Egypt, and separated from it by the barren and forbidding Nile valley in lower Nubia, with its numerous rapids, the so-called cataracts.[6] With sufficient effort these obstacles could be overcome, as they were by the pharaohs of the eighteenth and nineteenth dynasties, who incorporated all of Nubia into the Egyptian empire. Faced with these same obstacles, however, most Egyptian dynasties pursued less aggressive

---

[2] F. Lasserre, "Pythagoras," *Der kleine Pauly* (Munich, 1972) 4:1269.

[3] Cf. Truesdell S. Brown, *The Greek Historians* (Lexington, 1973), 182–94, for a brief account of Agatharchides and his works. An annotated translation of *On the Erythraean Sea* is now available: Agatharchides of Cnidus, *On the Erythraean Sea*, ed. Stanley M. Burstein, Hakluyt Society Publications, 2d ser., vol. 172 (London, 1989). For a survey of the Hellenistic historiographic tradition concerning Nubia see Stanley M. Burstein, "The Nubian Campaigns of C. Petronius and George Reisner's Second Meroitic Kingdom of Napata," *Zeitschrift für ägyptische Sprache und Altertumskunde* 106 (1979): 97–101. The principal literary and epigraphical sources concerning ancient Nubia are collected and translated in László Török, *Der meroitische Staat 1*, *Meroitica* 9 (Berlin, 1986).

[4] Fragments of an inscription commemorating the visit of the early-third-century-B.C. king Sabrakamani to the temple of Amon at Kawa are extant. Török, *Staat*, no. 28.

[5] For brief surveys of archaeological activity at Meroë see P. L. Shinnie, *Meroë: A Civilization of the Sudan* (London, 1967), 24–28, and William Y. Adams, *Nubia: Corridor to Africa* (Princeton, 1977), 71–90, 295–96.

[6] Cf. Claire Préaux, "Sur les communications de l'Ethiopie avec l'Egypte hellénistique," *Chron. d'Ég.* 27 (1952): 257–81, and Claude Vandersleyen, "Des obstacles que constituent les cataractes du Nil," *BIFAO* 69 (1969): 253–66.

policies toward their southern neighbors, maintaining a strong defensive position on Egypt's southern frontier while relying on diplomatic ties with the increasingly Egyptianized elites of Meroë and its predecessors to ensure a steady supply of the various Nubian products—ivory, gold, ebony, exotic animals and their skins, and slaves—desired by Egyptians.[7] Even were our sources fuller, therefore, the history of Egypt's relations with Nubia would still be episodic in character, a history marked by long periods of relative peace punctuated by occasional military intervention —by Egypt in Nubia or, less frequently, by its Nubian clients in Egypt—whenever circumstances suggested the possibility of gaining a temporary advantage. Such was also to be the pattern of Egyptian-Nubian relations during the Hellenistic period.

The story of Greek contact with Nubia prior to the early third century B.C. is quickly told. In what became the standard Greek account of Meroë and its environs, namely the long digression on the Nile in the second book of his *On Affairs in Asia* (DS 1.37.5), Agatharchides of Cnidos claimed that prior to the reign of Ptolemy II "Aithiopia," that is, the Nile valley south of Egypt, was closed to the Greeks. *Stricto sensu* this is incorrect, but Agatharchides' exaggeration is understandable. Pre-Hellenistic contact between Greeks and the Upper Nile valley is attested, but it was sporadic and insignificant. Graffiti on the colossi of Ramses II at Abu Simbel attest to the participation of Greek mercenaries in the Nubian campaign of Psamtek II in 593 B.C.,[8] and their continued service as members of the Egyptian garrison at Aswan is confirmed by hieroglyphic evidence.[9] Thereafter, evidence for Greek penetration of the central Sudan is lacking for three centuries. Like his Egyptian and Persian predecessors, Alexander garrisoned Elephantine (Arr. *Anab.* 3.2.7), but that was only prudent in view of the attempts, documented in hieroglyphic inscriptions, by fourth-century-B.C. Meroitic rulers to exploit Egyptian weakness in order to expand their influence in lower Nubia.[10] My attempt to credit Alexander with activity in Nubia on the basis of references in Hellenistic and Roman sources to an Aithiopian expedition led by Callisthenes has, however, found few adherents;[11] and no one has attempted to rehabilitate Arrian's reference (*Anab.* 7.15.4) to an "Aithio-

[7] Good recent accounts are Inge Hofmann, *Der Sudan als ägyptische Kolonie im Altertum* (Vienna, 1979), and William Y. Adams, "The First Colonial Empire: Egypt in Nubia, 3200–1200 B.C.," *Comparative Studies in Society and History* 26 (1984): 36–71.

[8] Meiggs-Lewis, *GHI* no. 7.

[9] *ARE* 4:994; cf. Hdt. 2.30–31.

[10] Harsiotef campaigned as far as the first cataract in the mid–fourth century; cf. E. A. Wallis Budge, *Annals of Nubian Kings* (London, 1912), 130–31, line 94.

[11] Stanley M. Burstein, "Alexander, Callisthenes and the Sources of the Nile," *GRBS* 17 (1976): 135–46.

pian," that is, a Meroitic, embassy to Alexander in 324 B.C., as has been done for the Roman embassy. The implications of the Meroitic evidence are similar. Finds of Greek imports are almost unknown in pre-Hellenistic Meroitic sites; and the special treatment accorded the only one whose archaeological context is known—namely the famous Sotades Vase found in Tomb S 24 in the South Cemetery at Meroë and now in the Museum of Fine Arts, Boston—suggests that the few that did reach Meroë were valued precisely because of their rare and exotic character.[12] Only in the 270s B.C. did this situation change, with the decision by Ptolemy II to mount a full-scale military campaign in Nubia.

No account of the campaign is extant, and except for a possible allusion to a Meroitic raid on Ptolemaic positions near Aswan in a fragmentary third-century papyrus (*SB* no. 5111), no details survive concerning its course. About the campaign itself, therefore, hardly more can be said than that Agatharchides' reference to Ptolemy II recruiting five hundred cavalrymen in the Aegean suggests that preparations were on a considerable scale.[13] Fortunately, the situation is clearer with regard to the origins of the war and its implications for relations between Ptolemaic Egypt and Meroë in the third century B.C.

Fragments of a speech urging war by a now unidentifiable Ptolemaic adviser from the first book of Agatharchides' *On the Erythraean Sea* indicate that, in Thucydidean terms, the pretext for attack was the Meroitic activity in Lower Nubia alluded to above; and the results of the campaign reflected this concern. Theocritus, who celebrated the Nubian campaign as one of the significant achievements of the first decade of Ptolemy's long reign, observed (17.86–87) that Ptolemy "cut off a part of Black Aithiopia." This phrase has usually been interpreted as an allusion to the annexation of the Dodekaschoinos, that is, the roughly seventy-five-mile stretch of the Nile immediately south of the first cataract, which from this time on formed the estate of the great new temple of Isis Ptolemy II built at Philae,[14] together with the important gold mining region, east of the Nile in the Wadi Allaqi, whose horrors Agatharchides described so vividly in the fifth book of his *On the Erythraean Sea* (frags. 23–29).[15]

---

[12] The rhyton was found in situ set against the core of the tomb superstructure immediately behind the tomb chapel: *RCK* 5:383–84.

[13] *On the Erythraean Sea*, F 20 (Burstein) = *GGM* 1:119. For the connection of this fragment with Ptolemy II see Stanley M. Burstein, "The Ethiopian War of Ptolemy V: An Historical Myth?" *Beiträge zur Sudanforschung* 1 (1966): 20.

[14] Cf. Kurt Sethe, "Dodekaschoinos: Das Zwölfmeilenland an der Grenze von Ägypten und Nubien," in *Untersuchung zur Geschichte und Altertumskunde Ägypten* (Leipzig, 1905) 3: 59–92. For the temple and its history see P-M 6:206–10 and Gerhard Haeny, "A Short Architectural History of Philae," *BIFAO* 85 (1985): 207.

[15] E.g., *SEHHW* 1:383, Adams, *Nubia*, 334, and Jehan Desanges, *Recherches sur l'activité des Méditeranéens aux confins de l'Afrique* (Rome, 1978), 257–58.

Graffiti and numismatic evidence suggest, however, that this interpretation is too narrow and that to secure his hold on Dodekaschoinos Ptolemy also garrisoned the old Middle Kingdom forts at Buhen[16] and Mirgissa[17] near the second cataract, so that, at least temporarily, the whole of lower Nubia from Aswan to the modern border between Egypt and the Sudan at Wadi Halfa came under Ptolemaic control as a result of his Nubian campaign. But if preempting Meroitic ambitions in lower Nubia was the pretext for Ptolemy II's Nubian campaign, the "truest cause" for the third-century Ptolemies' continuing interest in the Sudan was something else: their desire to find a secure source of war elephants.

The military use of elephants was millennia old in Asia. The Greeks and Macedonians first encountered them in battle, however, during Alexander's campaign, at the Battle of Gaugamela in 331 B.C. and again in India in 326 B.C. Thereafter, despite their mixed record in combat, the Diadochoi assigned a high priority to the acquisition of war elephants. But in this ancient "arms race" geography placed the Ptolemies at a serious disadvantage since their Seleucid rivals controlled the land routes to India, the chief source of elephants and elephant handlers. During the reign of Ptolemy I this had not been a serious problem because of his capture of some of Alexander's original Indian elephants at the battle of Gaza in 312 B.C. But by the 270s the situation had changed, since the elephants Ptolemy II had inherited from his father were by then too old to face in battle the fresh beasts of his rival Antiochus I, and they had to be replaced. Hence the interest of Ptolemy II and his successors in Nubia, and their concern to maintain a strong presence there, with results that are clear even in our fragmentary sources.[18]

For three-quarters of a century relations between Ptolemaic Egypt and Meroë were unusually close. Elephant-hunting expeditions, sometimes

[16] For Greek graffiti at Buhen see Olivier Masson, "Nouveaux graffites grecs," *Chron. d'Ég.* 51 (1976): 310–13.
[17] Cf. Georges Le Rider, "Monnaies trouvées à Mirgissa," *RN* 6th ser. 11 (1969): 28–35, who publishes a hoard of 28 bronze coins of Ptolemy I and Ptolemy II buried c. 266/5 B.C. and a second hoard including 43 unminted flans and seventeen poorly struck bronzes with types first attested under Ptolemy II, suggesting minting activity at Mirgissa—more likely to be explained by the need to pay soldiers stationed there than as the result of forgery (as suggested by Le Rider's use of the term "imitation" to describe them). The date of the mint's activity is less clear; Le Rider favors a date not earlier than the reign of Ptolemy VI, although admitting that a date in the third century is possible.
[18] For recent surveys of Ptolemaic elephant-hunting activity in the Sudan see Jehan Desanges, "Les Chasseurs d'éléphants d'Abou-Simbel," in *92e congrès national des sociétés savants, Strasbourg et Colmar, 1967, section d'archéologie* (Paris, 1970), 31–50; H. H. Scullard, *The Elephant in the Greek and Roman World* (London, 1974) 123–45; and Inge Hofmann, *Wege und Möglichkeiten eines indischen Einflusses auf die meroitische Kultur* (Vienna, 1975), 46–111.

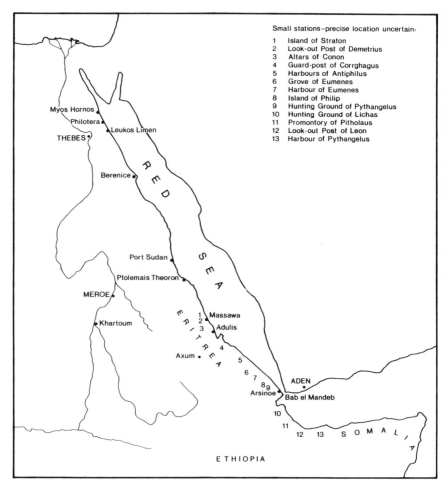

Small stations–precise location uncertain:

1   Island of Straton
2   Look-out Post of Demetrius
3   Altars of Conon
4   Guard-post of Corrghagus
5   Harbours of Antiphilus
6   Grove of Eumenes
7   Harbour of Eumenes
8   Island of Philip
9   Hunting Ground of Pythangelus
10 Hunting Ground of Lichas
11 Promontory of Pitholaus
12 Look-out Post of Leon
13 Harbour of Pythangelus

3. Ptolemaic elephant-hunting stations. From H. H. Scullard, *The Elephant in the Greek and Roman World* (London: Thames and Hudson, 1974), p. 129, fig. 13.

numbering hundreds of men,[19] repeatedly penetrated Upper Nubia, either from the north via the Nile valley or from the east via the Red Sea port of Ptolemaïs of the Hunts, while explorers traveled freely throughout Meroitic territory (see figure 3). The results are apparent in the sudden precision of Hellenistic accounts of the Sudan and in Meroitic

[19] An expedition of 231 men is mentioned in a papyrus of 224 B.C., *W. Chr.* no. 451.

4. Representations of elephants from Meroë. From P. L. Shinnie, *Meroë: A Civilization of the Sudan* (London: Thames and Hudson, 1967), figs. 27 and 48.

archaeology (see figure 4). Thus, the course of the Nile south of Egypt was accurately described and its major tributaries together with their native names were identified; the political map of northeast Africa was clarified; the Egyptianizing character of Meroitic culture was recognized; and the ways of life followed by Meroë's noncivilized neighbors were analyzed.[20] At the same time Greek luxury goods became a regular part of the funerary equipment of Meroitic kings, queens, and nobles. Aithiopia ceased to be part of the world of Greek myth and became part of the oecumene; and such it remained for the rest of antiquity.

Active Ptolemaic intervention in Nubia, however, ended in the last decade of the third century B.C., and for good reason. The poor performance of Ptolemy IV's elephants at the battle of Raphia had exposed the inadequacies of the Ptolemaic elephant corps, while the revolts of Horwennefer and Ankhwennefer in Upper Egypt forced his successor Ptolemy V to concentrate all his efforts on maintaining his hold on Egypt, a goal that was only achieved in 186 B.C. after two decades of struggle. Reoccupation of the Dodekaschoinos, which had fallen to Horwennefer and Ankhwennefer's Meroitic allies, quickly followed.[21] Thereafter, although trade with Meroë continued, the increasingly embattled second- and first-century Ptolemies limited their efforts to maintaining their control of the Dodekaschoinos, except for a brief period during the reign of Ptolemy VI when Ptolemaic power again reached the second cataract.[22] In the end, therefore, the active policy of the third-century-B.C. Ptolemies in Nubia was only an episode, with little long-term significance for Egypt. But what about its impact on Meroë?

In an important recent survey of Meroitic history the distinguished Hungarian art historian and Meroiticist László Török with some justification characterized the treatment of Meroë by Ptolemy II and his immediate successors as "intimidation."[23] Not only had Meroë suffered military defeat and loss of territory but it also had to assent to Ptolemaic claims of suzerainty. Thus, Meroë was included in the list of Nubian nomes obligated to bring offerings to Ptolemy II's new temple of Isis at Philae;[24] and, according to Callixenus (FGrH 627 F2), "Aithiopian" trib-

---

[20] A summary of the state of geographical knowledge of the Sudan in the third century B.C. is contained in Strabo 17.1.2, C 786. Cf. Burstein, "Nubian Campaigns," 997–98.

[21] For Meroitic activity in the Dodekaschoinos at this time see Adel Farid, "The Stela of Adikhalamani Found at Philae," MDAIK 34 (1976): 532–56, and Erich Winter, "Ergamenes II., seine Datierung und seine Bautätigkeit in Nubien," MDAIK 37 (1981): 509–13. The presence of Meroitic troops on the Egyptian side during the decisive battle ending the rebellion in 186 B.C. is attested in the Second Philae Decree. M. Alliot, "La Thébaïde en lutte contre les rois d'Alexandrie sous Philopator et Epiphane, 216–184," Revue belge de philologie et d'histoire 29 (1951): 435.

[22] OGIS 111.

[23] L. Török, "Meroe, North and South," in Nubian Culture Past and Present, ed. Thomas Hägg (Stockholm, 1987), 153.

[24] UPZ II 27. The claim of sovereignty is explicit in the similar inscription of Ptolemy VI, in which Ptolemy is portrayed as bringing the offerings of Nubia to Isis. Hermann Junker, Der grosse Pylon des Tempels der Isis in Phila (Vienna, 1958), 263, XXV. On these texts see Hofmann, Wege, 71–73, L. Török, "Die meroitischen Nomoi," Mitteilungen des

ute bearers took part in the great pomp Ptolemy II held at Alexandria in the mid-270s B.C.[25] Even more important, Meroë had to endure foreign penetration of its territory on a scale unparalleled since the second millennium B.C. But did this restoration of close ties with Egypt also have a significant impact on Meroitic institutions and culture? A controversial fragment of Agatharchides' *On Affairs in Asia* that is preserved by Diodorus (3.6) has suggested to scholars that it did:

> Of all their customs the most astonishing is that which obtains in connection with the death of their kings. For the priests at Meroë who spend their time in the worship of the gods and the rites which do them honour, being the greatest and most powerful order, whenever the idea comes to them, dispatch a messenger to the king with orders that he die. For the gods, they add, have revealed this to them, and it must be that the command of the immortals should in no wise be disregarded by one of mortal frame. And this order they accompany with other arguments, such as are accepted by a simple minded nature, which has been bred in a custom that is both ancient and difficult to eradicate and which knows no argument that can set in opposition to commands enforced by no compulsion. Now in former times the kings would obey the priests, having been overcome, not by arms nor by force, but because their reasoning powers had been put under a constraint by their very superstition; but during the reign of the second Ptolemy the king of the Ethiopians, Ergamenes, who had had a Greek education and had studied philosophy, was the first to have the courage to disdain the command. For assuming a spirit which became the position of a king he entered with his soldiers into the unapproachable place where stood, as it turned out, the golden shrine of the Ethiopians, put the priests to the sword, and after abolishing this custom thereafter ordered affairs after his own will. (Loeb translation by C. H. Oldfather)

Scholarly discussion of this passage with its exaggerated contrast of Hellenic sophistication and barbarian foolishness[26] has been extensive and contentious. Sir James Frazer saw in it proof that the Meroitic king was a "sacral monarch" who embodied the forces of nature and had to die when signs of failing strength appeared.[27] More recently it has been

---

archäologischen Instituts der ungarischen Akademie der Wissenschaften 8/9 (1978/79): 47–56, and L. V. Zabkar, *Apedemak Lion God of Meroë* (Warminster, 1975), 31–32.

[25] Cf. E. E. Rice, *The Grand Procession of Ptolemy Philadelphus* (Oxford, 1983), 19, 95–98. A strong case for dating the pomp to winter 275 B.C. has been made by Victoria Foertmeyer, "The Dating of the Pompe of Ptolemy II Philadelphus," *Historia* 37 (1988): 90–104.

[26] A favorite theme of Agatharchides; cf. his remarks on the Jewish Sabbath in *FGrH* 86 F20.

[27] Sir James George Frazer, *The New Golden Bough*, ed. Theodore H. Gaster (New York, 1959), 228.

dismissed as merely a doublet of Herodotus' account (2.137–39) of Saba-
kos—that is, Shabaka, the first king of the twenty-fifth dynasty—and,
like it, a typical tale of a *Kulturhero* without significant historical value.[28]
The breadth of the disagreement between these views is indicative of the
magnitude of the problems posed by this passage, not the least of which
is the reality of the custom of royal suicide itself.[29] But even a *Kulturhero*
is invoked for a reason, so it is likely that there is a kernel of truth in
Agatharchides' dramatic account, namely that a bloody confrontation
between a Greek-educated king, Ergamenes, and the priesthood of
Amon, the principal guardians of Meroë's Egyptian traditions, ended in
a major reform of the Meroitic monarchy marked by a strengthening of
the position of the king.[30] As always, the lacunae in our evidence prevent
certainty, but this interpretation is supported by four facts. First, Meroë
seems, sometime in the early third century B.C., to have replaced Napata—site of the holiest shrine in Nubia, the great temple of Amon
founded by Thutmose III in the fifteenth century B.C.—as the site of
the coronation of the kings of Meroë.[31] Second, beginning with Arakakamani, the king now generally identified with Agatharchides' Ergamenes,
the Meroitic kings and aristocracy abandoned the old royal cemetery at
el-Kurru near Napata for a new burial ground at Begarawiya just east of
Meroë. Third, Meroitic royal iconography suggests that, again beginning
with Arakakamani, the kings of Meroë adopted a new, less Egyptianizing,
style of regalia.[32] Fourth and finally, archaeological evidence indicates
that in the third century B.C. Meroitic royal patronage of several deities
apparently connected with the office of the king, but lacking identifiable
Egyptian backgrounds—namely Apedemak, Arensnuphis, and Sebiumeker—was increased.[33]

[28] Török, *Staat*, 13–15.

[29] Cf. the reservations concerning reports of similar practices in the modern Sudan in
E. E. Evans-Pritchard, "The Divine Kingship of the Shilluk of the Nilotic Sudan," in *Social
Anthropology and Other Essays* (New York, 1962), 208–9.

[30] A similar confrontation between the priesthood of Amon of Napata and the sixth-
century-B.C. Napatan king Aspelta is suggested by the so-called Excommunication Stela
(Budge, *Annals*, 113–16), as was pointed out to me by Dr. T. Kendall.

[31] This is implied by DS 3.5.1–2. The suggestion that Diodorus, or rather his source,
Agatharchides, confused Meroë with Napata (cf. Shinnie, *Meroë*, 41) is unlikely in view of
the silence concerning Napata in Hellenistic geographical sources prior to the first century
B.C. Burstein, "Nubian Campaigns," 101–2.

[32] Inge Hofmann, *Studien zum meroitischen Königtum* (Brussels, 1971), 52.

[33] On Apedemak see Zabkar, *Apedemak*. For Arensnuphis and Sebiumeker see Stefen
Wenig, "Arensnuphis und Sebiumeker: Bemerkungen zu zwei in Meroë verehrten Göt-
tern," *Zeitschrift für Ägyptische Sprache und Altertumskunde* 101 (1974): 130–50.

But did Ergamenes' reforms also include a policy of deliberate Hellenization? Meroitic studies form an interdisciplinary field, and opinions
on the extent and significance of Hellenization in third-century-B.C.
Meroë tend to divide along disciplinary lines. Egyptologists and Meroiti-
cists are inclined to minimize the implications of Ergamenes' Greek education—the product of a chance encounter with a "wandering Greek
scholar" in one notorious formulation[34]—and to limit Ptolemaic influence on Meroitic culture to that which accompanied the reestablishment
of trade with Egypt following Ptolemy II's Nubian campaign.[35] The few
classicists who have considered the problem have been more sanguine in
their conclusions. So M. I. Rostovtzeff claimed that "under Ergamenes
Meroë, the capital, and in particular its citadel with its Hellenistic palaces,
its Hellenistic bath, its Ethiopian-Hellenistic statues and decorative fres-
coes, became a little Nubian Alexandria,"[36] while L. A. Thompson maintained that Ergamenes transformed Meroë into "an approximation of a
Hellenistic kingdom,"[37] and Jehan Desanges suggested that the kings
and queens of Meroë "ont contracté des habitudes liées à la culture hel-
lénique;"[38] a miscellaneous and superficially impressive body of evidence
has been or could be cited in support of this view.[39] Besides the architectural and artistic phenomena mentioned by Rostovtzeff, it includes
imported pottery, especially amphorae but also tableware; classical
influence on Meroitic pottery; jewelry;[40] statuary either of Greek
workmanship or reflecting classical stylistic influence and themes;[41]

---

[34] Shinnie, *Meroë*, 18.

[35] E.g., Török, "Meroë," 153–54.

[36] M. Rostovtzeff, *The Social and Economic History of the Roman Empire*, 2d ed. (Oxford, 1957) 1: 302.

[37] L. A. Thompson, "Eastern Africa and the Graeco-Roman World (to A.D. 641)," in *Africa in Classical Antiquity*, ed. L. Thompson and J. Ferguson (Ibadan, 1969), 36; cf. L. A. Thompson, "The Kingdom of Kush and the Classical World," *Nigeria and the Classics* 11 (1969): 32.

[38] Jehan Desanges, "L'Hellénisme dans le royaume de Meroë," *Graeco-Arabica* 2 (1983): 277.

[39] For lists of classical imports see George A. Reisner, "The Pyramids of Meroë and the Candaces of Ethiopia," *Museum of Fine Arts Bulletin* 21, no. 124 (April 1923): 25–27; Thompson, "Kush," 33; Thompson, "Eastern Africa," 36–37; and L. Török, "Kush and the External World," *Meroitica* 10 (1989): 117–156.

[40] *RCK* 5: 175 (W. 179); Steffin Wenig, *Africa in Antiquity* (Brooklyn, 1978), no. 186 (vol. 2, p. 253).

[41] John Garstang, "Third Interim Report on the Excavations at Meroë in Ethiopia," *Annals of Archaeology and Anthropology* 5 (1913): 77–80 with pls. IX–X. Dows Dunham, "Four Kushite Colossi in the Sudan," *JEA* 33 (1947): 63–65. Adams, *Nubia*, 312–13; Wenig, *Africa*, no. 215 (vol. 2, p. 274).

auloi,[42] imported metal vessels[43] and fine glassware;[44] and Greek inscriptions and graffiti, including a column drum from Meroë inscribed with a Greek alphabet, thus suggesting that Greek was taught in the royal city.[45]

Meroitic history spans almost a millennium, but the evidence for reconstructing any particular aspect of that history, such as the nature of its relations with Greco-Roman Egypt, is, to say the least, sparse. Of the dozens of known Meroitic kings only two can be assigned approximately exact dates: Arqamani in the late third century B.C.[46] and Teqorideamani in the mid–third century A.D.;[47] and Ergamenes' coup is the only recorded event of the kingdom's internal political history. The temptation is strong, therefore, to try to form a synthetic picture of Meroitic culture by assembling miscellaneous lists of objects and culture traits with little regard for their chronology, archaeological context, or possible function in Meroitic culture. When the items cited above are viewed in the light of these three factors, however, a different picture of the extent and character of Hellenism in Hellenistic Meroë results.

Chronologically, the distribution of the items in the list is uneven. There were two peaks in contact between Meroë and Greco-Roman Egypt, namely the period between Ptolemy II's Nubian campaign in the 270s and the early second century B.C., and that between approximately the mid–first century B.C. and the early third century A.D. The overwhelming bulk of the known classical and classicizing objects date from the second of these two periods, the first being represented by only a few metal vessels of various types—goose-head wine strainers,[48] drinking cups, buckets, and basins—and fragments of wine amphorae.[49] There is a similar distinction, in the archaeological contexts in which these ob-

---

[42] Nicholas B. Bodley, "The Auloi of Meroë: A Study of the Greek-Egyptian Auloi found at Meroe, Egypt [*sic*]," *AJA* 2d ser. 50 (1946): 217–40; D. M. Dixon and K. P. Wachsmann, "A Sandstone Statue of an Auletes from Meroë," *Kush* 12 (1964): 119–25.

[43] The imported classical metal objects are surveyed and the parallel dating evidence is summarized by Inge Hofmann, *Beiträge zur meroitischen Chronologie* (Vienna, 1978), 213–30.

[44] E. Marianne Stern, "Hellenistic Glass from Kush (Modern Sudan)," *Annales du 8e congrès de l'association internationale pour l'histoire du verre, Londres-Liverpool, 1979* (Liège, 1981), 35–59.

[45] Shinnie, *Meroë*, 23. The inscription has been published in Alan R. Mallard, "BGD . . . —Magic Spell or Educational Exercise?" *Eretz-Israel* 18 (1985): 40* and pl. IV.10.

[46] Winter, *Ergamenes II.*, 509–13; Hofmann, *Beiträge*, 57–60.

[47] Hofmann, *Beiträge*, 168.

[48] Such a goose-head strainer was found in Beg. N. 7, the tomb of Arakakamani, the first Meroitic king buried at Meroë (*RCK* 4:28). For other examples see *RCK* 4:41 (Beg. S. 3, the tomb of an unidentified queen) and *RCK* 5: 78 (W. 10). The latter two are single rather than double handled.

[49] *RCK* 4: 70 (Beg. N. 8), 73 (Beg. N. 11), 77 (Beg. N. 13), 82 (Bar. 5).

jects are found, between the two regions that constituted the kingdom of Meroë: the narrow valley of the Nile in lower Nubia, and the Meroitic heartland in the steppe country of the central Sudan. In Lower Nubia they occur widely in both residential and burial sites, and classical influence is evident in the material culture of the region, most likely as a result of the profitable trade conducted by the natives with the personnel of the temples and garrisons of the Dodekaschoinos and Aswan area. By contrast in Upper Nubia classical imports are found only in two types of sites: palace complexes, and tombs identified by their architecture and the richness of their burial goods as royal or noble.[50] Finally, of the admittedly few surviving Greek imported goods found in third- and second-century-B.C. Meroitic contexts, only the wine strainers and wine amphorae represent additions to Meroë's cultural repertory, the other vessels belonging to categories of objects well attested as normal components of pre-Hellenistic Meroitic royal and noble funerary equipment.[51] Clearly, except for the possible development of a taste for Greek wine on the part of the Meroitic aristocracy, the extent of Hellenization in third- and second-century-B.C. Meroë was nugatory. This is not, however, to deny Ptolemaic influence on the culture and institutions of Hellenistic Meroë. Quite the contrary. Ptolemaic influence was considerable, but it was not Greek. One aspect of that influence, the adoption by Meroë of the use of war elephants, has even been described as Indian,[52] albeit at second hand; but in the main it was Egyptian, and for good reason.

While not themselves Egyptian, the rulers of Meroë, like the pharaohs, claimed to be sons of the sun god Re[53] and kings of Upper and Lower Egypt; conducted their government in Egyptian; celebrated their exploits in hieroglyphic inscriptions; and were buried with Egyptian rites in miniature pyramids decorated with excerpts from the Book of the Dead and other traditional funerary texts. Even the reform by Ergamenes and his successors of the Meroitic monarchy was expressed, despite their rejection of the domination of the priesthood of Amon, in forms derived ultimately from Egypt. Not surprisingly, therefore, it was the Egyptian side of Ptolemaic civilization that attracted the Meroites in the decades following Ptolemy II's Nubian campaign, particularly the form in which they encountered it at Philae, where the third- and second-century Ptolemies paraded their role as pharaoh through their patronage of an important group of temples, including ones dedicated to Isis,

---

[50] William Y. Adams, "Meroitic North and South," *Meroitica* 2 (1976): 18.

[51] E.g., cups: *RCK* 2, pl. XC AB (Nuri); basins: *RCK* 1, pl. XLI BCD (El-Kurru); buckets: *RCK* 1, pl. XLI A (El-Kurru).

[52] Hoffman, *Wege*, 144–148; cf. B. G. Haycock, "Landmarks in Cushite History," *Journal of Egyptian Archaeology* 58 (1972): 232.

[53] Bion, *FGrH* 668 F1.

the Meroitic royal god Arensnuphis, and possibly Mandulis, chief god of
the Blemmyes, Meroitic vassals who roamed the eastern deserts of Lower
Nubia.[54] As a result, in contrast to the meagerness of the evidence for
Greek influence in Hellenistic Meroë, examples of Ptolemaic Egyptian
influence are easy to find. Thus the royal titularies of the third-century
Meroitic kings echo those of the contemporary Ptolemies;[55] their regalia
included a style of crown first attested in Egypt in the Ptolemaic period,
particularly in reliefs of Ptolemy IV at Philae;[56] and at the pilgrimage
center of Musawwarrat es Sufra, south of Meroë, with the aid of Greek
architects[57] and masons[58] they built a number of important temples. Of
these temples the most revealing is the so-called Lion Temple, excavated
and partially restored by the East Germans in the 1960s. Here in an
impressive series of reliefs accompanied by texts—based on Egyptian
originals that are best attested at Philae, and inscribed in hieroglyphs
typical of the early Ptolemaic period[59]—the Meroitic king Arnekhamani,
wearing the new-style regalia with its Ptolemaic-style crown,[60] is depicted
receiving pledges of victory from the Meroitic pantheon—which, however, is headed now not by Amon but by the native war god Apedemak,
who wears a similar crown.[61] Nor was the influence of Ptolemaic Egyptian
culture in Hellenistic Meroë confined to the circle of the king. Evidence
of it has also been identified in various aspects of Meroitic public and

---

[54] Arensnuphis: P-M VI 210–11; Haeny, "Philae," 220. Mandulis: P-M 6:211; Haeny,
"Philae," 227. The existence of a temple in Ptolemaic times is not certain, although Ptolemaic patronage of the cult of Mandulis in the second century B.C. is attested by *I. Philae* 12
bis.

[55] Haycock, "Landmarks," 231; Hofmann, *Beiträge*, 53–56.

[56] László Török, *The Royal Crowns of Kush: A Study in Middle Nile Valley Regalia and
Iconography in the First Millennia B.C. and A.D.*, BAR International Series no. 338 (Oxford,
1987), 15–16, 44.

[57] The use of Greek architects is implied by the substitution of Greek for Egyptian
measures in the laying out of Meroitic public buildings. Friedrich W. Hinkel, "Ägyptische
Elle oder griechischer Modul? Metrologische Studien an historischen Bauwerken im mitt-
lern Niltal," *Das Altertum* 33 (1987): 150–62. Dr. Hinkel has informed me by letter that the
new metric system was employed in the construction of both the Lion Temple and temple
IA-300 in the Great Enclosure at Musawwarat es Sufra.

[58] The presence of Greek masons is implied by the use at Musawwarat es Sufra of letters
of the Greek alphabet as keys to aid in the assembly of architectural elements. Fritz Hintze,
"Musawwarat es Sufra: Vorbericht über die Ausgrabungen des Instituts für Ägyptologie
der Humboldt-Universität zu Berlin, 1963 bis 1966 (vierte bis sechste Kampagne)," *Wissenschaftliche Zeitschrift der Humboldt Universität zu Berlin*, Gesellschafts und sprachwis-
senschaftliche Reihe no. 17 (1968), 476 Abb. 17, 477 Abb. 18.

[59] Fritz Hintze, *Die Inschriften des Löwentempels von Musawwarat es Sufra* (Berlin, 1962),
21–22.

[60] Fritz Hintze, *Musawwarat es Sufra*, vol. 1, pt. 2, *Der Löwentempel* (Berlin, 1971), pls.
20–21.

[61] Hintze, *Löwentempel*, pls. 23c, 25, and 37.

funerary art[62] and, more importantly, cult, where the role of the god Anubis as provider of offerings for the dead becomes increasingly prominent from the late third century B.C. on.[63] Clearly, far from leading to the Hellenization of Meroë, the establishment of close relations between Ptolemaic Egypt and its southern neighbor in the decades following Ptolemy II's Nubian campaign actually facilitated the restoration of contact between Meroitic culture and its Egyptian roots, and helped make possible the Meroitic renaissance of the late Hellenistic and early Roman imperial periods.[64]

This conclusion should not be considered surprising. In Ptolemaic Egypt Hellenization was a strategy involving adoption of Greek values and a Greek way of life pursued by members of the native Egyptian elite eager to maintain or if possible improve their position and influence in a colonial society. Beyond the frontier, however, the situation was different. Protected by geography and heirs to a centuries-long civilized tradition of their own, and therefore under no similar compulsion to Hellenize, the Meroitic elite were free to select only those elements of Hellenism compatible with their traditions. In the Hellenistic period these were limited to a few imported luxuries. In the Roman period the range of imports, both material and spiritual, widened considerably, and an occasional Meroitic king, impressed perhaps by ambassadors' reports of life at Alexandria,[65] might even have a nymphaeum built at Meroë,[66] import Greek flute players, or have Greek taught at his court; but the essential pattern remained unchanged. The bulk of classical imports continued to be limited to obvious luxury goods—small portable objects of comparatively high value, such as blown glass and metal vessels—while cultural imports such as architectural forms occur only as decorative elements in buildings built in accordance with Meroë's Egyptianizing traditions.[67] Meroë's continuing economic and cultural autonomy, de-

---

[62] Robert S. Bianchi, "Ptolemaic Influences on the Arts of the Late Napatan and Early Meroitic Periods," *Meroitica* 5 (1979): 68–69.

[63] Ibid., 68; For details see Janice Yellin, "The Role and Iconography of Anubis in Meroitic Religion" (Ph.D. diss., Brandeis University, 1978).

[64] Adams, *Nubia*, 312–32. Török, "Meroë," 166–67.

[65] For the office of "Great Envoy of Rome" see L. Török, *Economic Offices and Officials in Meroitic Nubia: A Study in Territorial Administration of the Late Meroitic Kingdom* (Budapest, 1979), 104. Cf. Dio Chrysostom's reference (32.40) to "Aithiopians" in his audience at Alexandria.

[66] Garstang, "Third Interim Report," 77–81; László Török, "Geschichte Meroes: Ein Beitrag über die Quellenlage und den Forschungstand," *ANRW* II.10.1 214–17.

[67] For Alexandrian elements in Meroitic architecture see L. Török, "Traces of Alexandrian Architecture in Meroë: A Late Hellenistic Motif in Its History," *Studia Aegyptiaca* 2 (1976): 115–36, and "Zu Datierung des sogenannten römischen Kiosks in Naqa/Sudan," *AA* (1984): 145–59. On a small scale the same tendency is illustrated by the Doric column used as an offering column support found in *RCK* 5: 81 (W. 19).

spite centuries of contact with Greco-Roman Egypt, is perhaps best illustrated by two facts: first, unlike its eastern neighbor and later rival Axum, it never found it necessary to develop a coinage system; and second, the only classical god known to have received a cult in Meroitic territory is that most Egyptian of Greek deities, Sarapis.[68] Only after the fall of Meroë in the fourth century A.D. to Axumite and barbarian invasions did this situation change, first with the transformation of Meroë's northern neighbors, the Noba and Blemmyes, into *foederati*, and later, in the south, with the conversion of the various medieval successor states of Meroë to Christianity. Then a true Nubian Hellenism developed, one marked by the adoption of Greek artistic forms and the use of Greek as the official language of government and religion, but based on the Christian Hellenism of Byzantium, not the pagan Hellenism of Ptolemaic and Roman Egypt.[69] That, however, is another story.

RESPONSE: FRANK HOLT

Beyond the narrow confines of the old Balkan city-states, the enormous Hellenistic world was essentially a frontier society. Not only along the hinterlands of that world, but even in the urban heartlands of Mesopotamia and Syria, Greek colonists could exploit (at the expense of native peoples) all the opportunities of a classic frontier setting: an abundance of new resources, a low ratio of men to land, increased mobility, a mingling of many occupational and social backgrounds, and something of a safety valve for ongoing expansion and exploration. Thus the Hellenistic frontier existed at almost all points, in Memphis as well as Meroë, in Babylon as well as in Bactria, in downtown Jerusalem no less than in the deserts of Jordan. This vast frontier experience was fundamental in shaping the history and culture of the Hellenistic world, in much the same way (though many times magnified) as in the earlier colonial period associated with the Greek Archaic Age. It follows that the concept of frontier studies should be central to the study of Greek history as a whole, and to the Hellenistic Age in particular.[1]

---

[68] E. Seguenny and J. Desanges, "Sarapis dans le royaume de Kouch," *Chron. d'Ég.* 61 (1986): 324–329.

[69] Cf. Kazimierz Michalowski, "Les Contacts culturels dans le monde méditerranéen," in *Institut française d'archéologie orientale du Caire, livre du centénaire 1880–1980* (Cairo, 1980), 305–6; Tomas Hägg, "Nubien och Bysans," *Svenska Forskningsinstitutet i Istanbul Meddelanden* 9 (1984): 5–31 (English summary on p. 31). The most important corpus of Nubian Greek inscriptions published to date is that edited by Jadwiga Kuginska: *FARAS IV: Inscriptions grecques chrétiennes* (Warsaw, 1974).

[1] The argument here is not for the revival, on yet another frontier, of the famous thesis of Frederick Jackson Turner. I do believe that it was the adjustment to a new environment which stimulated the rise of a unique Hellenistic civilization, and that the frontier experi-

This, of course, has not generally been the case.[2] Greek frontier studies have failed to become a major field, quite unlike their well-developed, highly visible Roman equivalent. But while there may be no Hadrian's wall in Hellenistic history, the frontier is clearly no less important to the Greek experience than to the Roman. When speaking about Macedonia, itself a frontier society which left its strong imprint upon the Hellenistic world, Charles Edson had this to say in the first sentence of the first paper of the First International Symposium on Ancient Macedonia: "The concept of the frontier has rarely been associated with the study of Greek history."[3] It was thus twenty years ago that Professor Edson set the challenge met so admirably in Professor Burstein's paper on Meroë.

The case of Meroë reminds us that studies of the Hellenistic fringe should never be left on the fringe of Hellenistic studies. In spite of the poor state of our evidence, it is well worth asking what the furthest frontiers of the Hellenistic world were like. What, for example, brought the Greeks (and what sort of Greeks were they) to such places as Nubia, Nabataea, Characene, or Commagene? Did there develop outside the political and military frontiers of the Hellenistic kingdoms a distinctly different (and more distant) cultural frontier? Did independent states on the Hellenistic fringe find it possible to nourish themselves on the non-Greek elements of Hellenistic culture while discarding, untasted, the unfamiliar husks of Hellenism? Was there really Greek culture where there were no Greek colonists? These are important questions, but not easy ones to answer. I therefore thank Professor Burstein for making the case of Meroë both interesting and understandable. In order to test his hypothesis, I shall respond by looking elsewhere on the Hellenistic fringe for evidence of a similar frontier experience. The obvious place

---

ence (not necessarily the frontier natives) contributed at least as much to that new culture as did the heritage of the old Greek *poleis*. It is also true that some of Turner's aggressive frontier types (explorers, miners, etc.) may be found in the Hellenistic period, and that the native peoples were largely oppressed, ignored, or displaced. On closer inspection, however, much of Turner's thesis has no bearing whatever on the Hellenistic model. Most notably absent, perhaps, is the democratic stimulus which is allegedly fostered by the frontier wilderness. *That* impulse lingered weakly in Athens, perhaps, but not in the new royal cities of the east. On Turner and his influential thesis, see the works of his staunchest supporter, Roy Billington: *Frederick Jackson Turner: Historian, Scholar, Teacher* (New York, 1973), and *The Genesis of the Frontier Thesis* (San Marino, 1971).

[2] The new edition of the *CAH*, admirable in so many ways, nevertheless exhibits this shortcoming; see F. W. Walbank et al., eds., *CAH*[2] VII.1, *The Hellenistic World*, where, in a rather full index of thirty-nine pages, the word *frontier* does not find a place alongside *factories, famine, fishing, freedom*, and *fruit*. Walbank does have a "frontier" chapter in his short work *The Hellenistic World* (Cambridge, Mass., 1982), but its twelve pages are really devoted to geography and exploration.

[3] Charles Edson, "Early Macedonia," *Ancient Macedonia* 1 (1970): 17–44. The symposium was held at Thessaloniki in 1968.

to look, of course, is at the other great elephantine frontier of the Hellenistic Age; and so we turn to India.[4]

Like Nubia, northwest India and the neighboring regions of Arachosia and the Parapamisadae (see figure 5) had only marginal contact with the Greek world before the Hellenistic age.[5] The strongest western influence upon early India came not from Greece but from Persia, in much the same way that Egypt had put its stamp upon Meroitic culture long before the arrival of Ptolemaic envoys and armies. By the time the Greeks and Macedonians did arrive, both Meroë and India had become essentially independent under localized, native rule. Although Alexander did campaign in India and left there more than a dozen Greek garrisons and colonies, most of these were apparently drained away in the first bloodletting of the Diadochoi.[6] In any case, Alexander had kept a number of rajahs in power, including Porus, Taxiles, and Abisares. Within seven years of Alexander's demise, even these native rulers had been replaced by the rise of a new Indian king named Chandragupta, the founder of the Mauryan dynasty.[7]

Chandragupta's empire arose on the very fringe of the vast territories claimed by Seleucus I Nicator. In fact, Seleucus brought his army eastward to confront Chandragupta shortly after 305 B.C. While making claims of outright conquest, Seleucus conserved his energies in favor of a more useful solution: Chandragupta was acknowledged as rightful king of India, including Arachosia and the Parapamisadae, while Seleucus received as "tribute" some five hundred war elephants.[8] In about 205 B.C. Antiochus the Great again brought a Seleucid army to India, and this encounter ended in the same way as the first—with a tribute of

---

[4] While India provides an ideal model for testing Burstein's thesis on Meroë, it is certainly not the only area offering useful points of comparison. The eagerness of some of our fellow symposiasts to draw our attention westward to the Tiber frontier is perhaps the best example. Our discussions really did bear out the proposition that Hellenistic frontier studies ought to be developed further. This is only one way in which our separate thoughts were drawn together by this forum, and I take this opportunity to thank the sponsors and organizers for making this possible.

[5] See Jean W. Sedlar, *India and the Greek World: A Study in the Transmission of Culture* (Totowa, N.J., 1980).

[6] Holt, *Alexander the Great and Bactria* (Leiden, 1988), 84 n. 139, 100–102.

[7] DS 19.48; Strabo 15.2.9 C 724.

[8] Just. 15.4.21; Strabo 15.2.9 C 724; App. *Syr.* 55; Plut. *Alex.* 62.2. See H. Scharfe, "The Maurya Dynasty and the Seleucids," *Zeitschrift für vergleichende Sprachforschung* 85 (1971): 211–25, and P. H. L. Eggermont, "Indien und die hellenistischen Königreiche," in Jakob Ozols and Volker Thewalt, eds. *Aus dem Osten des Alexanderreiches* (Cologne, 1984), 74–83. The basic bibliography for these matters may be found conveniently in E. Will, *Histoire politique du monde hellénistique*, 2d ed., 2 vols. (Nancy, 1979–1982), to which should be added the exemplary treatment by Paul Bernard, *Fouilles d'Aï Khanoum* (Paris, 1985) 4:85–95.

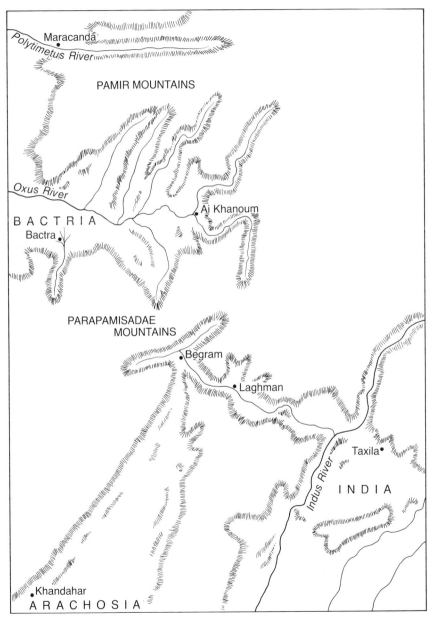

5. The Bactro-Indian frontier. Map after F. Holt.

elephants and a treaty between these states.[9] During the full century framed by these two famous attacks upon India, Seleucid contact with the East was very uneven. Some sort of marriage alliance, and the dispatch of ambassadors to the Mauryan capital, kept the first Seleucid monarchs in fairly close touch with the Mauryan dynasty.[10] By the middle of the third century B.C., however, the Seleucids began to lose control of their own eastern satrapies and soon lost direct access to India.[11] Thus, after a brief period of fairly close relations, as in the case of the early Ptolemies and Meroë, the Seleucids became preoccupied with problems elsewhere and their contacts with India were weakened. The eventual return of a Seleucid army under Antiochus III, and the renewal of the original treaty between these states, shows us the true nature of their relationship. They were independent states, neither of which could ever conquer or control the other. Theirs was never the history of the ruler and the ruled, but of the raider and the raided.

One impressive feature of the Hellenistic fringe is this remarkable similarity between the African and the Indian experience. In a number of important ways, Mauryan India was to Seleucid Asia what Meroë was to Ptolemaic Egypt. Indeed, I think it is safe to classify both Meroë and Mauryan India as Hellenistic "resource frontiers." These areas, much like Spain to the Romans or Brazil to the Portuguese, offered important commodities which could not generally be obtained from areas already under the state's control. Desirable though these materials might be, they tended to be very difficult and costly to collect, and to be located in areas not easily conquered or economically controlled. In the parallel cases of Meroë and Mauryan India, such important resources included elephants and precious metals,[12] desired by both the Ptolemies and the Seleucids, often in direct competition with each other. Professor Burstein has linked Ptolemy II's Nubian campaign to a need for new war elephants, since those of Ptolemy I were no doubt of little value by the mid 270s B.C. It is worth adding that a cuneiform tablet from Babylon records the deliv-

---

[9] Polyb. 11.39.11–12.

[10] On the Seleucid ambassadors Daimachos and Megasthenes, consult Eckart Olshausen, *Prosopographie der hellenistischen Königsgesandten* (Lovan, 1974) 1:171–74. Note also the Ptolemaic ambassador, pp. 33–34.

[11] Polyb. 11.39; Just. 41.4.

[12] On the siginificance of elephants see the standard work by H. H. Scullard, *The Elephant in the Greek and Roman World* (Ithaca, N.Y., 1974), esp. chap. 4. On mining and mineral deposits see John Healy, *Mining and Metallurgy in the Greek and Roman World* (London, 1978), esp. chap. 3. The mineral wealth of ancient India has been categorically denied by W. W. Tarn, *The Greeks in Bactria and India*, 3d ed. (Chicago, 1985), 103–9, but the ancient evidence seems convincing even if occasionally embellished with stories of gold-digging ants and gryphons: Herodotus 3.94, 102–5; Aelian *VH* 4.27; Curt. 8.5.3, 8.9.19; Strabo 15.1.30 C 700, 44 C 706, 69 C 718; DS 2.36.2.

ery of twenty elephants (via Bactria) to Antiochus I at the same time that Ptolemy II suddenly found his own needs critical.[13] Thus, the Seleucids and Ptolemies raided their respective resource frontiers whenever the opportunity or need arose. Such incursions were rarely significant military events involving genuine conquest; but since they did achieve the goal of resupplying the state with wealth, elephants, and exotica, these products were easily paraded as the spoils of war back in Alexandria or Antioch.

If I am right about the nature of Meroë and India as Hellenistic resource frontiers, what does this suggest about patterns of *cultural* interaction? First, it becomes clear that the Ptolemies and Seleucids were interested, literally, in fringe benefits, and in little else. They were fascinated by certain products, rather than by the peoples or places associated with them. In this regard, there was no "moving frontier" tied to "manifest destiny," no attempt to "convert the savages," no "Greek man's burden" in either India or Africa.

The aim of the Hellenistic states was less to annex these fringe areas than to exploit them with as little involvement and expense as possible. This particular approach did not encourage exchanges of population or of cultural traits; it did not engender serious concern for permanent or peaceful contacts. The occasional presence of Greek envoys and explorers in Nubia or India might suggest an interest in mutual understanding, but in fact they were more likely to be royal agents scouting these regions' resources. Once such resources were identified, it was easier to leave most of the actual mining or hunting to native effort and expertise. Thus, except in very small numbers, the Greeks were not motivated to move deeper into Africa or India in either a spiritual or a physical sense.

I suspect that this ambivalent attitude was largely reciprocated, and that the native rulers of these resource frontiers were less interested in Greek culture than in keeping the Greeks themselves away. From the point of view of Meroë or the Mauryans, of course, the Hellenistic states were themselves resource frontiers. Either by attack or by agreement, non-Greek rulers could acquire Greek luxury goods without necessarily involving themselves in a cultural metamorphosis. Professor Burstein has shown this quite well in the case of Meroë. For India, too, the debate over cultural influences divides itself along nationalistic and disciplinary lines. Western scholars, most of them classicists, put too much emphasis upon a thin scattering of classical references and Greek artifacts. This evidence is unevenly distributed in time and place, and subject to self-serving interpretation. Thus the discovery of Greek objects (e.g., the

---

[13] Fragment no. 92689 in the British Museum; see Sidney Smith, *Babylonian Historical Texts* (London, 1924), 150–59.

"Begram Treasure") in India is considered "proof" of the long-term dominance of Greek *culture*, while the discovery of Indian artifacts in the Hellenistic world (e.g., at Ai Khanoum) is considered "proof" of Greek *military* dominance. Classicists insist upon having it both ways at once— "heads we win, tails they lose," no matter what is found where or when.

On the other hand, some Indologists insist upon the total failure of the Greeks to penetrate the society and culture of the subcontinent. In one famous formulation of this thesis, which betrays itself by its own close borrowing from the classical world, the Greeks "came, they saw, but India conquered."[14] The truth is that each culture felt assured of its own superiority, and succeeded in remaining independent and aloof for a century or so. But beyond that point, in India as well as Africa, cultural interaction became quite pronounced. The Indologist must accept the fact that Greek culture eventually influenced the East, but the classicist must also accept the fact that Greek culture had little impact until long after Alexander.

Seleucid Asia, therefore, was not much affected by the vigorous culture of independent India. Although Asoka (c. 269–37 B.C.), the grandson of Chandragupta, claimed to have sent Buddhist missionaries to the kings of Hellenistic Asia, Egypt, Epirus, Cyrene, and Macedonia, there is no notice of their arrival in or effect upon the courts of these kings.[15] By the same token, the impact of Greek culture upon Mauryan India also seems negligible. Bindusura (c. 297–69 B.C.), the son of Chandragupta, is said to have taken an interest in acquiring certain exotic items, namely figs, wine, and a sophist. Antiochus II supplied the wine and figs, but not the philosopher.[16] Thus the third century saw little real interchange between East and West: Bindusura became no more Greek than Antiochus became Buddhist, and it would appear that it was easier for Ergamenes to find a sophist in Nubia than for Bindusura to beg one for India.

This does not mean, of course, that there were no Greeks in the Mauryan realm. Besides ambassadors and adventurers, the fringe areas of the

---

[14] A. K. Narain, *The Indo-Greeks* (Oxford, 1957), 11, later repeated in "Alexander and India," *G&R* 12 (1965): 165.

[15] Asoka's Rock Edict 13 mentions the missionaries to Antiochus II, Ptolemy III, Magas of Cyrene, Antigonus Gonatas, and Alexander (of Epirus?); for bibliography consult F. R. Allchin and K. R. Norman, "Guide to the Asokan Inscriptions," *South Asian Studies* 1 (1985): 43–50. If there was any impulse to influence the culture of a foreign state, the evidence suggests that it came from India rather than Greece, and that it was the Greeks who refused the offer. On this theme, see the thoughtful little essay by Arnaldo Momigliano, "The Fault of the Greeks," reprinted in his *Essays in Ancient and Modern Historiography* (Middletown, Conn., 1977), 9–23.

[16] Athen. *Deipn.* 14.652–53. See also 1.18e, where the exchange of exotica between the rulers of resource frontiers is complete: Chandragupta had sent Indian aphrodisiacs to Seleucus I.

Mauryan empire (particularly Arachosia and the Parapamisadae) still contained a few Greek colonies dating back to Alexander and Seleucus Nicator. This explains why Asoka set up Greek translations of his edicts at Khandahar[17] (see figure 6). The presence of these Greek colonists is proven not only by Asoka's Greek inscriptions, but by an earlier ex-voto set up there by the son of a certain Aristonax.[18] What this means, of course, is that some of the Greeks there were willing to accept Asoka's rule, though we are not sure that they embraced Asoka's religion. In fact, it would appear that the Greeks represented no more than an old colonial enclave at Khandahar, one largely impervious to Indian culture as late as the mid–third century B.C. Nor was Greek influence by any means growing. Elsewhere in Mauryan India, Asoka had no occasion to express himself in Greek. We may conclude that where there were Greek colonists on the Hellenistic fringe, there was Greek culture, but that the cultural frontier of Hellenism rarely reached beyond them in any lasting or meaningful way.

During the Mauryan period, the Greek language made no inroads into India, and only maintained itself among the colonists at Khandahar. This makes the case of Aramaic all the more important and interesting. The administrative language of the old Persian Empire was used in six of Asoka's edicts, including two examples from Khandahar and others from Taxila and the region of Laghman.[19] Even in the Greek kingdom of Bactria, Aramaic continued in use at least until the final collapse of Ai Khanoum in the latter half of the second century B.C.[20] Thus, long after the Persians had lost control of the East, and in spite of the Greek intervention under Alexander and his successors, the Persian imprint upon

[17] For references, see Allchin and Norman, "Asokan Inscriptions." It was probably from among these settlers that Asoka drew the linguistic talent necessary to render his *dharma* into Greek, both for local consumption and for his missionary activities in the West (see above, note 15). It is less clear whether Greek philosophers had become a regular part of the Mauryan court since the time of Bindusura's unsuccessful attempt to obtain one through Antiochus II, as implied by E. Will, *"Poleis* hellénistiques," *Classical Views* 32 (1988): 340 n. 28.

[18] The inscription has been published by P. M. Fraser, "The Son of Aristonax at Khandahar," *Afghan Studies* 2 (1979): 9–21; see also A. N. Oikonomides, "The Temenos of Alexander the Great at Alexandrian Arachosia," *ZPE* 56 (1984): 145–47. The reading of the inscription is contested; Fraser reaches the conclusion that the area was still under Seleucid control. For a judicious commentary, see Bernard, *Fouilles.*

[19] Consult the maps and text of Allchin and Norman, "Asokan Inscriptions."

[20] The evidence for Aramaic (and its derivatives) may be found conveniently in F. R. Allchin and N. Hammond, eds., *The Archaeology of Afghanistan* (London, 1978), 192–201; also consult W. Ball, *Archaeological Gazeteer of Afghanistan* (Paris, 1982) 2:366–67. For the additional evidence of coinage, see in particular R. Audouin and P. Bernard, "Trésor de monnaies indiennes et indo-grecques d'Ai Khanoum (Afghanistan)," *RN* 16 (1974): 6–41, esp. 28–30.

6. Greek and Aramaic translation of an edict by Asoka. Khandahar, mid–third century B.C. Photo: Délégation Archéologique Française.

the culture of this region could not be erased. Indeed, it enjoyed a re-markable resurgence in the form of Kharoshthi, a script derived from Aramaic and used by Asoka to write the Indian Prakrit language. In architecture no less than linguistics, the influence of Persia appears ever stronger during the Mauryan period. The excavated "audience hall" at Patna, the rock-hewn monuments of Bihar, and the widespread use of bell-shaped column capitals (see figure 7) all attest to Persian rather than Greek inspiration during the first century of the Hellenistic Age.[21] This

[21] The material evidence is surveyed and illustrated in M. Taddei, *Archaeologia mundi: India* (Geneva, 1970), 48–76.

7. Persian-style bell-shaped column capitals. Karli, western India. Photo: Archaeological Survey of India.

may well be a rare example of what Professor Burstein has discovered in Nubia, where Hellenistic contacts merely reinvigorated the Egyptian roots of Meroitic culture.

Beyond the third century B.C., when the Mauryan empire collapsed and India was invaded by the Greeks of Bactria, the cultural interaction of Greeks and non-Greeks was greatly intensified. Thereafter, we may trace a long and active period of cultural exchange in India, eventually giving rise to Indo-Greek states and Gandharan art. Yet, as in Meroë, this was a much later development extending well beyond the Hellenistic Age. For the first century or so following the death of Alexander the Great, as Professor Burstein has shown so well, the Hellenistic fringe was a much more complicated arena where the confrontations of Greek and non-Greek cultures produced little in the way of "brotherhood" and cultural borrowing.

DISCUSSION

D. Delia: The relief from the Lion Temple of Musawwarat that Professor Burstein showed, depicting an elephant and captives, is very reminiscent of the entryway of the Ramesside temple of Abu Simbel, with the Asiatic captives on one side and the Nubian captives on the other.

S. M. Burstein: The similarity is not surprising. The layout of Meroitic art is fundamentally Egyptian. One does often have the feeling, however, that Egyptian forms are used to express ideas that are not Egyptian, and this is particularly true in the Roman period. But the artistic idiom always remains fundamentally Egyptian.

K. D. White: Just a very general question: if there is anything to be gained at all from any kind of comparative study of the interpenetration of cultures and fringe benefits and so on, is it possible that Africa can produce *aliquid novi* here as well?

S. M. Burstein: The answer is certainly yes, especially with regard to late ancient sites. Particularly likely to produce interesting new information are sites such as Adulis in the territory of Axum, Meroë's eastern neighbor, in modern Ethiopia.

T. Watkins (U. T. student):   Both in Meroë and in Bactria there was a period without much interaction and then a period of greater interaction between Greek and non-Greek peoples. Why is this?

S. M. Burstein: The answer depends on the nature of the interaction. As far as military and political interaction is concerned, the determining factor must be the monumental logistical problems posed by the upper Nile valley, problems so severe that in the Middle Ages the Islamic rulers of Egypt abandoned the attempt to spread Islam by military means. In antiquity the requisite effort was made no more than sporadically, and then only under pressing necessity, as in the case of the third-century Ptolemies. Evaluation of the extent and character of cultural interaction is a more difficult problem, one that is complicated by two factors. First, to be honest, there is the Hellenist's prejudice against Rome. The vast bulk of the evidence I have seen for the spread of Hellenistic cultural phenomena beyond the frontiers of the Greco-Roman world dates from the Roman imperial period. This is without doubt true for the two areas I am most familiar with, namely Nubia and Dacia. Candidly, I suspect that the Hellenistic kingdoms, with their comparatively small Greek and Macedonian populations, are much overrated as political and certainly as cultural powers. The second factor is the relative strength of the various cultures in the multiethnic Hellenistic kingdoms. This is particularly important in the case of Egypt since Ptolemaic Egyptian culture was rich and vibrant, and the Ptolemies presented themselves to the Meroites as pharaohs. By contrast, Roman Egyptian culture was a culture in decline, and for good reason. Unlike the Ptolemies, the Romans did not patronize the Egyptian temples as their predecessors did; nor did the Roman officials the Meroites encountered present themselves in pharaonic guise. Thus, unlike the situation under the Ptolemies, in the Roman period the Meroitic state interacted directly with the dominant culture in Egypt, with results visible in the evidence for the greater incorporation of Hellenistic cultural elements mentioned at the end of the paper.

F. Holt: Whenever we are dealing with the interaction of two still vigorous cultures, as in the case of the Seleucids and the Mauryans, there is something of a cultural stalemate. What breaks that down is the weakening of one power and its invasion by the other. In the third century B.C. this is exemplified by the fact that in the easternmost city of the Seleucid realm (Ai Khanoum) there is a strong cultural statement: the Delphic maxims, proclaiming Greekness in an inscription set beside a gymnasium, theater, and so forth. Beyond this frontier is a cultural boundary drawn by the Hindu Kush mountains. And on the other side of that boundary, at the same time, we find Asoka putting up the Indian rival of the Delphic maxims, a set of inscriptions proclaiming the *dharma* of Buddhist India. Thus in the third century there is a cultural standoff taking place on either side of the Hindu Kush. In the second century B.C. that situation changes. The Greeks cross the Hindu Kush and conquer northwest India. Then you get this strong cultural interaction, then you finally get Greek kings issuing coins that are Greek on the obverse and

Indian on the reverse. Eventually, you even get a Greek king who professes Asoka's *dharma*. This exemplifies the process. And it is a long process, I should emphasize. Tarn and others tended to shorten it into one great spasm of brotherly interaction, and I don't think it happened that way. We should remember the famous example of this process involving Greece and Rome before and after the Macedonian wars.

E. S. Gruen: I have a frontier question that is not geographical but chronological, that is, one that concerns the frontier between the Hellenistic and Roman periods. What do you make of Gallus' invasion of Ethiopia? What did the Romans want there? Certainly they weren't interested in exporting Greek culture to Meroë, and I don't think they were interested in the resource frontier—they didn't want the elephants. What do you make of this?

S. M. Burstein: I'm inclined to agree with Colin Wells's view that the Romans never saw a frontier they didn't try to cross, and this was, I think, particularly true in the twenties B.C. Certainly, Gallus implies in his Philae inscription that when he met Meroitic envoys he bullied them into what the Latin text of the inscription clearly implies was recognition of Roman supremacy. As far as Gallus, and presumably Augustus, was concerned, Meroë had become Roman territory. The Meroites, of course, didn't see it that way; and when they struck back later in the decade, they made a symbolic statement: they took statues of Augustus back to Meroë, where the head of one was found buried under the threshold of a Meroitic building whose decoration included a painting of a Roman prisoner being humiliated. The striking thing about Augustus, however, is that he knew it paid to cut his losses when the costs of maintaining a distant and unprofitable conquest were too great. Hence his retreat from Nubia at the end of the decade. In a sense, his treatment of Nubia foreshadows his reaction to Varus' disaster in Germany. Interestingly, both cases are treated similarly in the *Res Gestae*, Petronius' expedition and the conquest of Germany being mentioned but not the later retreats. In a nutshell, though, I think that in the twenties Augustus was prepared to expand as far as possible until he discovered how far "far" really was.

What Is "Hellenistic" about Hellenistic Art?

Martin Robertson

A very long time ago I published an article which I called "The Place of Vase-painting in Greek Art,"[1] and when I sent a copy to Sir John Beazley I inscribed it "Fools rush in where angels fear to tread." I fear that a lecture with the title I've given this one needs some similar cover. When Peter Green invited me to take part in this symposium and discuss some aspect of Hellenistic art, I was delighted but in a difficulty. It is a field which I find of the very greatest interest, but one in which I have never done detailed research of my own, and I could think of no special theme to offer. So I went for the wide general question, which is indeed a very interesting one, and looks fine as a title with its question mark at the end; but in a lecture with such a title the audience may reasonably expect to be offered something in the way of an answer or answers, and this is where the trouble starts. In her account of life in a labor camp Irina Ratushinskaya writes: "Tanya is reading the journal *Literary Questions* and I poke fun by asking whether there is, anywhere in the world, a journal called *Literary Answers*? And, if there are no answers, what is the use of questions?" However, I don't think I quite accept that (nor, perhaps does Irina Ratushinskaya; after all, she was joking). A question can be interesting even when no answer comes up; even when, in the nature of the case, it is unlikely that any answer tentatively put forward would be likely to meet with general acceptance. Certainly today I have no answers, but perhaps talking round the question, in the lecture and in discussion, will not be a total waste of time.

[1] *ABSA* 46 (1951): 151–59.

To begin with, what have people said on this question before? Indeed, what have I said on it myself? I might as well start from that; and since in my *History*[2] I was not primarily aiming to break new ground, what I said there will contain a good deal of *communis opinio*. Looking at that again, I see that I seem to put a great deal of emphasis on the idea that the change from classical to Hellenistic art was not, like the change from archaic to classical, something which came about within the art, something inaugurated by the artists themselves because of discontent with established idioms and conventions, but almost entirely a reflection of changes external to art itself: change in the structure of the known world and the way it ran, Greek cities now being ruled in the main by kings who also ruled countries and cities inhabited by non-Greeks (and even those cities which maintained independence were inevitably changed by this changed ambience). Of course I make no claim to originality in this view. It is widely held; but I am now not quite so sure of its overriding truth, and I find myself more than a little worried by the way I applied, or rather, if the truth be told, failed to apply this premise to the actual art as we have it. Do the qualities, whatever we may perceive them to be, which distinguish Hellenistic from classical art really reflect in any definable way the enormous change from the classical to the Hellenistic world?

To take first one obvious problem. One would expect the inclusion of oriental peoples, with their own long and sophisticated traditions of art, in kingdoms ruled and partly populated by Greeks (for the purposes of this lecture I count Macedonians as Greek) to lead to some interaction of Greek and oriental in the art of the time. But where does one find this? Well, there is one obvious and obviously significant monument which does show something of the fusion one expects, the Mausoleum of Halicarnassus; but that is, awkwardly, a pre-Hellenistic building. Attempts to show that any part of this extraordinary architectural-sculptural complex are of Hellenistic date[3] seem to me, beyond a doubt, altogether mistaken. In any case the non-Greek features are the basic design of the building, with its stepped pyramids and high podium, and the way the sculptures are disposed in relation to the architecture; and these elements are unquestionably original. I regret to observe that in my book

---

[2] M. Robertson, *A History of Greek Art* (Cambridge, 1975).

[3] R. Carpenter, *Greek Sculpture* (Chicago, 1960), 214–16; C. M. Havelock, "Round Sculpture from the Mausoleum at Halikarnassos," in *Studies Presented to George M. A. Hanfmann* (1971), 56–64, rebutted by B. Ashmole, "Solvitur Disputando," in *Festschrift für Frank Brommer* (Mainz/Rhein, 1977), 1–20; see also G. B. Waywell, *The Free-standing Sculptures of the Mausoleum at Halicarnassus in the British Museum* (London, 1978), 252 n. 215. After studying Waywell's catalogue I find it impossible not to suppose that the whole complex and its adornment were completed in a single operation over a relatively short period.

I skate round this awkwardness in two ways. First, I put my sketch of the historical background to Hellenistic art at the beginning, not of the chapter called "Hellenistic Art," but of the one before, slyly entitled "The Second Change: Classical to Hellenistic," in which I include the Mausoleum; and secondly, I write in that chapter: "The Hellenistic situation was in certain circumstances partly anticipated before the transitional phase in the age of Philip and Alexander."[4] This sentence is in itself, I think, a fairly obvious truth. What I failed to stress is the fact—I think it is a fact, and surely a rather odd one—that when one gets to the Hellenistic Age proper one finds very little indeed in the way of original creations like the Mausoleum in a mixed Greek-Oriental idiom.

Pollitt, in his great book *Art in the Hellenistic Age*,[5] is not concerned with the Mausoleum, since it lies outside his period. He does, however, cite a related monument, which to my shame I did not mention: the Hellenistic (perhaps third-century) tomb at Belevi. He refers to its fusion of Greek and oriental elements, which he sees as carrying on a tradition initiated in the funeral car of Alexander, of which we have an elaborate description and which is another and still more deplorable omission from my book. Even these, however, seem to me to bring us back to the same problem. The oriental elements in the tomb at Belevi are all already present in the Mausoleum (the stepped pyramid) or in still earlier Lycian tombs (the rock-cut chamber), so that it could be seen as part of a local tradition in western Asia Minor rather than as reflecting the innovations of Hellenistic rulers; while Alexander's catafalque stands, like the Mausoleum, on the verge of the Hellenistic Age and seems to promise new departures—which it is oddly difficult to find realized in actual fact.

There is one monument, which both Pollitt and I discuss rather marginally (and indeed it is marginal to the Hellenistic world, geographically, historically, and stylistically): the extraordinary tomb on the mountaintop of Nemrud Dagh[6] in eastern Anatolia, overlooking the upper Euphrates, set up for himself by Antiochus I of Commagene, who reigned through the middle decades of the first century B.C. and claimed descent from both Greek and Persian rulers. Pollitt very perceptively writes of this (p. 275): "The Hellenistic ruler cult involved a fusion of Greek thought with oriental religious beliefs, and the hybrid colossi of Nemrud Dagh may be the truest, if not the most sophisticated, embodiment of it." One might add that it is not only the seated colossi which illustrate this

---

[4] Robertson, *History*, 447.

[5] J. J. Pollitt, *Art in the Hellenistic Age* (Cambridge, 1986). Belevi tomb: appendix 5, 289–90. Alexander's catafalque: 19–20.

[6] Nemrud Dagh: H. Bossert, *Altanatolien* (Berlin, 1942), figs. 1017–19; E. Akurgal, *Ancient Civilisations and Ruins of Turkey* (Istanbul, 1969), pls. 109–12; Pollitt, *Art*, 274–75, fig. 294; Robertson, *History*, 565.

8. Antiochus and Heracles. Relief at Nemrud Dagh, mid–first century B.C. Photograph from a cast in the Ashmolean Museum, Oxford.

fusion of Greek and oriental idiom in the style, but also the very odd reliefs, which show Antiochus shaking hands with his gods, Herakles (figure 8) and others; and indeed the whole layout of the huge mountain-top tumulus, with its sculptures and inscriptions. Here in any case we really do have a Hellenistic mixture of Greek and oriental in art; but it remains strange that we've had to fare so far and so long to find it.

Pollitt wonders if the Belevi tomb might be taken as suggesting that Seleucid buildings sometimes showed such a mixture. For reasons given earlier I feel doubt in this case, but the idea receives support from the remains of a Greek city uncovered on the extreme eastern verge of the Hellenistic world: Ai Khanum, on the Oxus in Afghanistan. Ancient Bactria, in which Ai Khanum lay, was a province of the originally huge kingdom of Seleucid Syria, but through much of the third and second centuries B.C. it was ruled by a series of independent Macedonian kings. A determination to keep its character essentially Hellenic is evidenced by the inscriptions, one of them a touching document: the sayings of the Greek sages, set up by a citizen who records that he copied them at Delphi. The theater too and the gymnasium, visible signs of the strictly

9. Antimachus of Bactria. Silver tetradrachm, first quarter of second century B.C. British Museum, London. Photo: Hirmer Verlag.

Hellenic cultural institutions of drama and athletics, are purely Greek in design. A big palace, on the other hand, and a quarter of smaller houses seem rather of Persian derivation in plan, yet here too the detail is often Greek: Corinthian columns and pebble mosaics.[7] It is interesting that the wonderful coin-portraits of the Bactrian dynasts are purely Greek in style[8] (see figure 9).

The most striking failure of Eastern and Greek traditions to mingle in the art of the Hellenistic world is found in Egypt, where the Ptolemies, in Pollitt's words, "were Hellenistic kings in Alexandria and the most recent dynasty of Pharaohs elsewhere in Egypt."[9] The two cultures remained virtually independent, and the arts followed their own traditions with only the most trivial and superficial borrowings on either side. There is a possible exception in the matter of personal portraiture. It is certainly in the Hellenistic Age that this branch of Greek art reaches its apogee, though no less certainly its beginnings are much earlier (there will be

[7] P. Bernard, *Fouilles d'Ai Khanoum*, Vol. 1 1973; (Paris, *CRAI* (1975): 175ff.; *CRAI* (1976): 291–92; *Bulletin de l'école française d'extrême-Orient* 63 (1976): 16ff.

[8] See, e.g., Charles Seltman, *Greek Coins* (London, 1933), 55.

[9] Pollitt, *Art*, 250.

more to say about this). It is also true that a striking realism is found in some Egyptian carved portraits which date from a time long before Greek art came into existence. Further, there are highly "veristic" portrait-heads in hard stones carved by Egyptian sculptors in Ptolemaic times, and some have held that these influenced Roman portraiture of the late Republic.[10] If continuity could be traced between these early and late Egyptian likenesses, one might think that the tradition had had an influence, through Alexandria, on Hellenistic developments. Alternatively, the late Egyptian artists might have been influenced by their Greek neighbors. In any case, some interaction seems possible, but of a strictly limited kind.

I have in the past argued for the importance of an Eastern connection of a different nature in the case of some early (pre-Hellenistic) examples of realistic portraiture in Greek art: the so-called Mausolus from the mid–fourth century, and certain satrap portraits from the same area in the first half of the century, going back to the coin-heads of Pharnabazus and Tissaphernes from the beginning of the fourth and the later fifth century respectively.[11] In these, I suggested, the realism might reflect the sense of relative freedom which a Greek artist might feel when working for a foreign patron in a milieu outside his own. Pollitt has argued against this,[12] on the grounds of evidence for such realism in Athens in the fourth century: for example, Silanion's Plato, and the notorious particularity recorded of the portrait-statues by Demetrios of Alopeke. The Plato I view a little differently, seeing in it less an interest in the rendering of the sitter's individual features than a skillful adaptation of the traditional satyr-model used for portraits of Socrates, Plato's master, whose persona he used in his writings throughout most of his life.[13] It's true, though, that the copy I chose to illustrate suits this interpretation better than the one Pollitt has! As to Demetrios, I have never questioned his importance, or sought to make the oriental connection the sole source of the idea of realistic portraiture in Greek art. I think our difference here is more one of emphasis than absolute. Happily Pollitt is the respondent to this paper, and will be able to tell us if I am misrepresenting him on this question or elsewhere. He ought of course to be the person giving the lecture. He has worked the Hellenistic field far more deeply and widely than I; but at least he is here to correct my errors, and, I hope, perhaps to offer some better answers to the question in my title than I can provide.

[10] See G. M. A. Richter, "The Origin of Verism in Roman Portraits," *JRS* 45 (1955) 39–46 (against the idea but citing its proponents).
[11] M. Robertson, *A Shorter History of Greek Art* (Cambridge, 1981), 183ff., figs. 249, 250.
[12] Pollitt, *Art*, 64.
[13] Ibid., 64, fig. 59; Robertson, *History*, 508–10, pl. 157d.

Before leaving this question of Greek portraiture and the East, however, I should say that the suggestion I once made, that the realism of the Ostia Themistocles might perhaps be due in part to its original having possibly been made while the sitter was the Great King's satrap in Magnesia,[14] now seems to me a quite irresponsible extension of the original idea. I do, however, still tend to believe that the Ostia head is a true copy of a contemporary portrait; and the likelihood that such realism was possible then has been strongly reinforced by the discovery of the marvellous bronze head in the wreck off Porticello.[15] Only the most desperate special pleading can make this other than a fifth-century Greek original, and its formidable realism is equally undeniable, though it is possible that it is not a portrait. I find myself much tempted by Professor Ridgway's theory that it does not, as commonly thought, represent a philosopher but rather the good centaur, Chiron.[16] We have diverged some way here from the Hellenistic Age, but not, I hope, unjustifiably. Realistic portraiture is a central Hellenistic interest, and its evolution cannot but be of interest to our inquiry.

Absorption of or modification by oriental influence, then, is a trivial and marginal element in Hellenistic art; and, at least in Egypt, this seems to reflect the general situation, Alexandria being a political and cultural enclave in a virtually unchanged country. How far the social and political isolation of non-Greek from Greek, so marked there, applied also in Seleucid Syria is something which I find I simply do not know.

In religion the position, even in Egypt, seems not so clear-cut; but though Sarapis is apparently of Egyptian origin there is no trace of anything unhellenic in his images. Isis was both more deeply central to Egyptian religion and destined to become more influential in the classical world; but if her cult did affect the tradition of art in the West it was really only under the Roman empire. Greek religion, of course, had taken a great deal from oriental cults long before the Hellenistic Age: Adonis, for instance, and, right at the start, Hesiod's *Theogony*, at a time when Greek art too was overwhelmingly indebted to the East. That remote, formative period, however, does not offer much of an analogy with the Hellenistic situation.

Religion, however, is one area where perhaps we really can see a change of attitude in the Hellenistic Age that does directly affect art. When, in the early second century, Eumenes II built a library at Perga-

[14] Robertson, *History*, 188, pl. 62d.
[15] National Museum, Reggio di Calabria; G. M. A. Richter, *The Portraits of the Greeks*, abridged and revised by R. R. R. Smith (Oxford, 1984), 65, fig. 29.
[16] B. S. Ridgway, "The Bronzes from the Porticello Wreck," in *Archaische und klassische griechische Plastik*, ed. H. Kyrieleis (Mainz, 1986) 2:59–69, pls. 100–101.

mon, and placed in it a reduced and modified marble version (figure 10) of Pheidias' chryselephantine Athena in the Parthenon, he surely did not put the statue there simply as an adornment.[17] Athena was the goddess of wisdom as well as arms, the library was attached to her sanctuary, and the image in the library was the goddess its patron, not simply a work of art to embellish a public building. Nevertheless, it does seem to illustrate an approach, to art no less than to religion, very different from that of Pericles and Pheidias and the other citizens of fifth-century Athens for whom the original statue was made. On the religious side, the placing of a major image of a deity in a building designed for a strictly secular purpose is hardly conceivable in archaic or classical Greece. One might even say that there were no purely secular buildings of monumental character before the Hellenistic Age. There were *bouleuteria* and such, connected with the city government; but the interweaving of religion with civic life was so inextricable that these buildings must be seen as having a strong religious side. This is no less certainly true of theater and stadium. The stoa may perhaps be counted an exception, though very many individual stoas were either placed in sanctuaries or had some direct religious or civic association. A Hellenistic library might be attached to a sanctuary and placed under a deity's protection, but the purpose for which it existed had no religious element. It was, in a new sense, a truly secular building.

On the artistic side, the thing that most sharply distinguishes the Athena in the Pergamene library from her model in the Parthenon is the very fact that she is a copy. This is not, as Pollitt has stressed, a true copy, designed to reproduce the details of the original as closely as possible, as copies made under the Roman empire surely for the most part were. She is an adaptation, a re-creation in the spirit of her own time; but still, this statue is deliberately and carefully modeled on another statue created nearly three hundred years before, a practice which surely can be called truly Hellenistic.

Eumenes' Athena is an example of one kind of statue with a religious affiliation which could hardly have been made before the Hellenistic period: the adaptation of a classical cult-figure (originally designed to be approached down the long darkness of a temple-cella) to a totally different setting and purpose. Another example typifies a quite new type of deity, whose image owes nothing to the tradition of the temple-cella: the Tyche (Fortune) made for the city of Antioch at the beginning of the Hellenistic Age (in the first few years of the third century) and constantly

[17] See M. Robertson, "Greek Art and Religion," in *Greek Religion and Society*, ed. P. E. Easterling and J. V. Muir (Cambridge, 1985), 155–90, fig. 33.

10. Athena. Marble statue from Pergamon, second century B.C., freely copied from fifth-century original. Antikensammlung, Staatliche Museen zu Berlin. By permission.

imitated in other cities over the following centuries.[18] This colossal bronze group, of which we can form some idea from descriptions and small versions (see figure 11), was set in the open air and was cunningly designed to present changing and effective views from many angles. Statues of course had been placed in the open air in Greek sanctuaries from the beginning of Greek sculpture, among them colossi, and among those some of bronze—Pheidias' Athena Promachos, for instance, on the Acropolis, and long before that the archaic Apollo at Amyclae. Certainly, however, none of these departed from the traditional principle of design which expected a statue to be looked at mainly from an area in front. In the fourth century Lysippos made several bronze colossi, especially a Herakles and a still larger Zeus at Tarentum; and these, from what we know of other works of the master, are likely to have shown some concern with breaking frontality, with insisting on the third dimension. Lysippos, more than any other sculptor, seems to look forward to the Hellenistic spirit. Eutychides, creator of the Tyche of Antioch, was his pupil, as was Chares of Lindos who, in the Colossus of Rhodes, created a bronze figure even larger than Lysippos' Tarentine Zeus, and representing Helios, one of the old gods. Eutychides, on the other hand, used the new three-dimensionality to invent a new type of image for a new goddess.

"New goddess" is not quite true. Tyche (Fortune) had been occasionally personified earlier (like almost every other abstraction in Greek thought), and even given at least one statue;[19] but, as Pollitt has emphasized, she takes on an entirely new importance in this period. An obsession with Fortune is the first of five attitudes or states of mind which he sees as particularly characteristic of the Hellenistic Age[20]—a most valuable line of approach. Besides, Eutychides' goddess is not just Fortune in the abstract. With her mural crown and the river-god swimming out from under her feet, she is firmly characterized as the fortune of a city, of a particular city: Antioch on the Orontes. Any city founded in archaic or classical times was put under the protection of one of the old deities. It is surely very interesting that so early as this the experience of the wars between Alexander's successors led Seleucus and his son Antiochus to put their new capital city under the protection of her own Chance; and Seleucus was to learn how fickle a personal Fortune can be.

Since so much in the Hellenistic world depended directly or indirectly on the favor or caprice of kings and on their changing fortunes, and

---

[18] Pollitt, *Art*, 2–3, fig. 1; Robertson, *History*, 471–72 pl. 150a, b; Robertson, "Greek Art," 189–90, fig. 44.

[19] See Robertson, *History*, 383–85 (where the assertion that the head of the Apollo from the Temple of Zeus at Olympia is carved from a separate and finer piece of marble is false).

[20] Pollitt, *Art*, 1–4 (the other four: 4–16).

11. Tyche of Antioch. Small marble statue of Roman imperial date, copied from original of very early third century B.C. Vatican Museum, Rome.

12. Ptolemy II and Arsinoë II. Gold octadrachm of Ptolemy II (285–246 B.C.).
British Museum, London. Hirmer Fotoarchiv.

since royal portraits are in the vanguard of developing realism, one might
expect that another change in religious practice—the according of divine
status to monarchs, after their death or in their lifetime—would have
had some visible effect on art; and in one point I think it does. I do not
count as an effect on art the giving of divine symbols, like Poseidon's bull
horns for Demetrius Poliorcetes, or even the transference to his portrait
of a pose associated with Poseidon.[21] These are not changes of artistic
character, and in any case they go back to Amon's ram horns for Alexander and the thunderbolt Apelles gave him. Quite different is the enormous eye given to some rulers on their coins, early and most strikingly
to Ptolemaic royal couples (see figure 12), later to some Seleucids, and
which perhaps appears first in some posthumous portraits of Alexander,

[21] See ibid., 31–33, figs. 20–22; Robertson, *History*, 516.

notably on the Alexander mosaic.[22] This, surely intended to stress the sitter's superhuman, divine character, runs directly counter to the prevailing trend towards realism. It is not a natural development within the art, but something imposed on the artist—if not by direct command then by the changed atmosphere in the world. Parenthetically, arising from the observation made just now about the inextricability from religion of civic life and government in the city-states, I have sometimes wondered if this may not help to account for the readiness with which Greek citizens acknowledged divinity in Macedonian kings. To those who had always been accustomed to think of city government as bound up with the gods, it was perhaps a comfort, when government was wrested away by an unnaturally powerful mortal, to consider him a god himself. Certainly Hellenistic monarchs shared with the Olympians not only total and irresponsible power, but with it utter unreliability in the handing out of favors or destruction.

Realistic portraiture is, of course, one of the most important manifestations of art in Hellenistic times and can be taken as one of the things which distinguish Hellenistic art from classical: individualism is another of Pollitt's typically Hellenistic states of mind. The trend, as we've noticed, existed before, but now it is far more widespread, and the aim of making a portrait look like a particular individual is far more general and more marked. Sometimes this aim is extended, in quite a new departure, from the face to the body; early in the period, for instance, the Demosthenes, and later the Chrysippos counting on his fingers[23] (see figure 13). It is true that there are still limitations on its application which do not apply in Roman portraiture. Portraits in Hellenistic as in classical Greece are still always and only of people who have made themselves a name, public figures; or rather, there are exceptions to this rule, but all late and under direct Roman influence, as in Italianized Delos.[24] I myself feel (but this is not I think universally accepted) that even the most personal of Hellenistic portraits keep something of the public as well as the individual character: the ruler, the poet, the philosopher. This is not to say that I suppose we can tell from any Greek portrait the field in which the sitter made his public name. The cautionary tale of the early classical Pindar which so many of us for so long accepted as a possible Pausanias[25] has, I do not doubt, unrecognized parallels in the Hellenistic Age. I

[22] Detail of Alexander's head from the mosaic: J. Boardman, J. Dörig, W. Fuchs, and M. Hirmer, *Die griechische Kunst* (Munich, 1966), pl. xliv. Ptolemaic pair: Pollitt, *Art*, 272 fig. 293a. Seleucid pair; ibid., fig. 293d.

[23] Robertson, *History*, pl. 161b (Demosthenes), d (Chrysippos); Pollitt, *Art*, 61, fig. 55 (Demosthenes), 69 fig. 66 (Chrysippos).

[24] Pollitt, *Art*, 73–75, figs. 73, 75–77; Robertson, *History*, 598, pl. 190d.

[25] Smith in Richter, *Portraits*, 176–80, figs. 139, 140, and frontispiece.

13. Portrait of Chrysippos. Composite cast from marbles of Roman imperial date, copied from original of later third century B.C. Louvre, Paris (marble head, British Museum, London). Photographie Giraudon.

do think, though, that every Hellenistic portrait has, together with its individuality, a public character of the kind that, in Roman art, distinguishes imperial and court portraits from the wonderful series of common men and women which has no parallel in Greece.

Nevertheless, with all these caveats, it remains evident that portraiture in the Hellenistic Age is something distinctively of its time; but I am not sure how far this really helps to answer the question we set out by asking. It is easy to point to many things in Hellenistic art which were not there in classical: the new approach to the third dimension which we've thought about already; the liking for the grotesque and unideal in the minor arts and even in the major (the Barberini Faun is the supreme example, but there are plenty more); the use of a dramatic setting for a big statue like the Victory of Samothrace (a theatrical mentality is another of Pollitt's Hellenistic states of mind); the exploration of the possibilities in reclining or fallen figures (the sleeping Ariadne, the sleeping Hermaphrodite, the Dying Gaul, the dying and the dead from the smaller Pergamene dedication); and so on.[26] Even in the straightforward single standing figure it is easy to make the same point. The "Hellenistic Ruler" in the Terme (figure 14) may not be a ruler and his date may slide up and down the centuries, but he is surely quintessentially Hellenistic.[27] Compare him to another man with a spear, the classical *doryphoros* (figure 15). Everything is different: the brutal realism of the features, the exaggerated heaviness of the muscular body, the wonderful spiral of the composition. But all this, like everything else I have been listing, is only to say—what of course we knew already—that Hellenistic art is a clearly distinct phase of Greek art. It is of course itself divisible into phases, wisely defined by Pollitt according to the historical circumstances: the age of the Diadochoi, the age of the Hellenistic kingdoms, the Greco-Roman phase;[28] only it is very difficult to fit the works of art into these phases at all tidily because different styles overlap, run parallel, recur—a variety in itself typically Hellenistic.

However, that is by the way. What I am now trying to say is that when we ask "What is 'Hellenistic' about Hellenistic art?" we do not simply mean "What distinguishes Hellenistic art from classical?" There is much in the art of the fourth century which is not found in that of the fifth:

[26] Barberini Faun: Pollitt, *Art*, 134, 137, fig. 146; Robertson, *History*, 534–35, pl. 169d. Victory of Samothrace: Pollitt, 113–16, fig. 117; Robertson, 535, pl. 137a. Ariadne: Robertson, 535, pl. 169c. Sleeping Hermaphrodite: Pollitt, 149, fig. 160; Robertson, 551–52, pl. 176b. Dying Gaul: Pollitt, 85–92, figs. 85, 87; Robertson, 531, 533, pls. 167c, 168b. Dying and dead from small dedication: Pollitt, 90–94, figs. 89, 91–94; Robertson 530, pls. 168a, 170c.

[27] Pollitt, *Art*, 72–74; Robertson, *History*, 519–20, pls. 163c, 164a.

[28] Pollitt, *Art*, 17.

14. Bronze portrait-statue, variously dated from earlier third to earlier first century B.C. National Museum of the Terme, Rome.

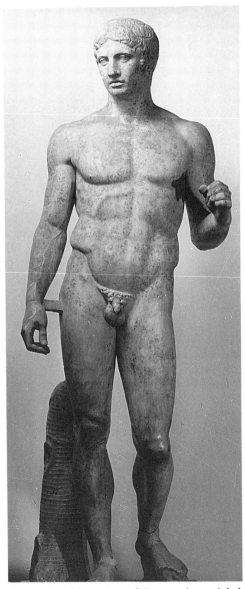

15. Youth with a lance. Marble statue of Roman imperial date, copied from fifth-century bronze *doryphoros* by Polykleitos. Museo Nazionale, Naples. Photo: Deutsches Archäologisches Institut, Rome. Reprinted by permission.

the exploration of the female nude in sculpture, for instance, or the advances in chiaroscuro in painting. It is a distinct phase; but one would hardly frame the question "What is 'fourth-century' about fourth-century art?" When we ask what is Hellenistic about Hellenistic art we surely mean, What is there about this phase of Greek art that would not have been there if the tremendous change which came over the Greek world in the last third or so of the fourth century had not taken place? If someone had knifed Philip sooner and Macedon had not got imperialist ambitions but had gone on it its old way and allowed the Greek cities to go on in theirs, Greek art would certainly have developed in many ways just as it actually did. In what way could it *not* have done so? The Hellenistic Ruler, exemplary Hellenistic figure though he be, can be traced back in a smooth sequence to classical sources. Portraiture we have already considered in this sense; the exaggerated musculature is exaggerated on the basic pattern laid down by Polykleitos; and the spiral composition, whatever the actual date of the statue, derives directly from the innovations of the pupils of Lysippos at the beginning of the third century—innovations already hinted at in the work of Lysippos himself, whose own style developed out of the Polykleitan tradition. I see nothing in this statue which needed a change in the world to bring it about.

In what we have already looked at there was one noticeable feature which seemed to stem directly from that change: the exaggerated eye in some royal portraits. Perhaps if we look harder at some of the other things we shall find that they too have something of the same character; for it can hardly be, I think, that the position is the exact opposite of that which I put forward in my *History* and quoted at the beginning of this paper: that the change from classical to Hellenistic in art was hardly at all a change taking place within the art but almost wholly a reflection of outside changes. Let us try again.

Hoping for light from a different direction I opened the new Hellenistic anthology by Neil Hopkinson,[29] and as epigraph to the introduction I found a verse in which a poet lamented the passing of the good old days when the Muses' meadow was unpolluted and it was possible for a poet to find something to write about; now everything's been said, he complained, the arts have reached their limit, and there's nowhere a man can drive his newly yoked chariot. Oh yes, I thought, that speaks very well for the visual arts too in Hellenistic times. Then I read the first sentence in the introduction, and learned (what you will be shocked that I didn't know, but I am too old for shame) that "these are the gloomy words of Choerilus of Samos, an epic poet writing in the late fifth century B.C." I remembered something I once wrote to the effect that up to

[29] Neil Hopkinson, ed., *A Hellenistic Anthology* (Cambridge, 1988).

the classical moment of the Parthenon, of Pheidias, of Polykleitos, the development of Greek art is essentially unified, a single stream; but that after that it begins to break up, different groups of artists developing different styles, so that the columnar Procne from the Acropolis can be contemporary with, and as much a child of her own time as, a wind-blown figure like the Nike of Paeonius[30] or the new goddess in the Getty. Are we really making a mistake, I wondered again, in trying to draw a sharp line in art at the beginning of the Hellenistic Age? The fifty years after Chaeronea saw a total change in the character of the Greek world, but are we really right to look for a corresponding change in Greek art? Art has its own tempo, and should we perhaps do better to make the change from classical to the next phase in Greek art come not at the end of the fourth but at the end of the fifth century? Well, surely, in a word, No; but I still think it is worth asking such questions every now and then, if only to remind ourselves how artificial and distorting our division of art into periods is. We can only study art through the imposition of such a framework, but art when it's happening isn't really like that. Conquest or revolution has a violent and immediate effect on everyday living (though often a lot even of that probably goes on with surprisingly little change), but its effect on art is much less calculable.

Of course particular manifestations of art may be directly and drastically affected. For a classical Athenian, art could include a carved tombstone; for a Hellenistic Athenian, after Demetrius of Phaleron, it couldn't; but that is not what we're talking about. Art develops continuously and changes in complex and subtle ways, sometimes gradual, sometimes sudden. Even the assertion I made just now, that up to the classical moment of Pheidias and Polykleitos Greek art developed in a unified way, is itself a gross simplification. For the archaic period it is more nearly true, and the change from archaic to classical can be made to look like a sharp break by fixing it at the moment of the abandonment of the frontal posture for statues early in the fifth century. But the seeds of change had been there all along, and in certain aspects the change was largely achieved during the second half of the sixth century; while the two sculptors of the Siphnian treasury friezes—one serenely archaic, the other struggling towards the classical—give the lie to the notion of a single development. In the early classical phase all kinds of casting around after possible styles can be seen. We have noticed experiments with realistic facial types, perhaps actual portraiture; and the wonderful new marble

[30] Robertson, *History*, 286–87, 345–46, pl. 940 (Procne); 287–88, 350, pl. 94d (Nike of Paeonius).

charioteer from Motya[31] shows that a severe-style head can be combined with a clinging drapery style derived from that of late archaic *korai* as well as with the columnar drapery more typical of the time, giving us, before the classical moment, exactly the contrast we noted after it in the Procne and Paeonius' Nike.

Even at the heart of the classical, on the Parthenon itself, the centaur heads of the south metopes are not what one thinks of as classical types; and consider the knotty anatomy of the Poseidon from the west pediment. Suppose that an Attalos or a Eumenes had anticipated Morosini with more success, taking this figure out of the gable and removing it to Pergamon. If the torso had been dug up there, how should we date it? Based on a classical model, no doubt, but perhaps carved around the time of the Great Altar? And yet of course the altar frieze, for all its Parthenonian echoes, is as profoundly Hellenistic as the Parthenon pediments are classical. There is real continuity, but there are also real breaks: between the high classical and its aftermath in the late fifth and fourth centuries, and between fourth-century classical and Hellenistic. What we should like to be able to see is a relation between this second break and the catastrophic historical background.

Much of what happened in art in the Hellenistic period is development inherent in the art itself: the overwrought muscles of the Parthenon Poseidon exaggerated in torsos of the altar frieze; the drama of the Scopasian heads from Tegea exaggerated in some giants' heads.[32] One cannot of course say that these developments would inevitably have happened whatever the historical circumstances, but I think one can say that for them simply to take place did not need the special conditions of the Hellenistic world. There is, however, one development on the altar frieze which strikes me as being of a different kind, the thing which does most to justify the transference from another historical epoch of the word *baroque*. This is the way in which, where the returns of the frieze meet the steps, there is no framing molding, and the huge giants move out of their art-world into ours, pressing hand or knee on the same steps up which the worshipper climbs[33] (see figure 16). In post-Parthenon Athens the balustrade of the little temple of Athena Nike has in the same way a

---

[31] Motya, Museo Whitaker; V. Tusa, "Il giovane di Mozia," in *Archaische und klassische griechische Plastik* 2:1–11, pls. 82–85. Both date and identification are disputed; but it seems to me likely that the garb marks the figure as a charioteer, and certain that it cannot have been carved much after the decade 470–60.

[32] Parthenon Poseidon: F. Brommer, *Die Skulpturen der Parthenon-Giebel* (Mainz, 1963), pls. 103–6. Scopasian head from Tegea: e.g., Robertson, *History*, pl. 145. Pergamene altar slabs with comparable torsos and faces: e.g., ibid., pl. 170d; Pollitt, *Art*, 98 figs. 99–100.

[33] Meeting of carved frieze with steps just visible: Pollitt, *Art*, 95 fig. 97; with steps well seen: E. Simon, *Hesiod und Pergamon* (Mainz, 1975), pl. 1.

16. Slabs of colossal marble relief from podium of Altar of Zeus at Pergamon. Earlier second century B.C. Antikensammlung, Staatliche Museen zu Berlin. By permission.

return which runs beside the steps (see figure 17). The last of the under-life-size Victories moves parallel to a visitor reaching the top step, and she too takes a step up; but the tread on which her foot rests is carved in relief within the frame and is on a smaller scale than the steps in the world outside.[34] To thus relate a figure within the representation so directly to the world without was surely a bold innovation in its time; but the frame is kept, the two worlds remain distinct. What the designer of the altar podium has done represents a far profounder break with tradition.

Does this get us any further, though? Can we relate it to anything in the thought or conditions of its special time? Or can this too be classed as a purely artistic phenomenon, the desire of an artist to break the old mold, open new ways? That of course it is, but is it that alone? Let us look back for a moment at the change from archaic to classical. The seeds of the classical were surely there in Greek art throughout its archaic phase, and the changes that mark the difference between the two periods are strictly artistic ones, developing within the arts quite naturally; but one cannot assume that the seeds would have ripened, the drastic

[34] B. Carpenter, *The Sculpture of the Nike Temple Parapet* (Harvard, 1929), pl. 1 (photo of slab), fig. 15 (drawing showing relation to steps).

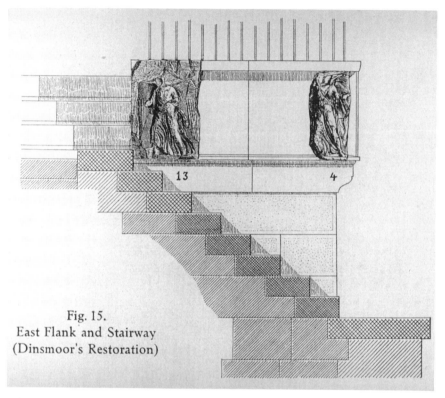

Fig. 15.
East Flank and Stairway
(Dinsmoor's Restoration)

17. Reconstruction of steps and return of carved marble parapet of Temple of
Nike on Athenian Acropolis. Late fifth century B.C. From Rhys Carpenter, *The
Sculpture of the Nike Temple Parapet* (Cambridge: Harvard University Press, 1929),
p. 84, fig. 15. Reprinted by permission.

changes actually have been made, if historical circumstances had developed differently. Certainly one could not assert that the classical revolution was a *result* of the liberation of spirit released by the repulse of the
Persian invasion, but I believe that there is nevertheless a real relation
between the two things. The art of Achaemenid Persia, technically admirable, decorative, formally beautiful, and to my mind dreadfully dull,
seems to me to offer an idea of what Greek art might have become if
some late archaic artists had not found their way to the decisive break;
and I find it easy to think that that is exactly what would have happened
if Greece had become a province of the Persian empire. I see the act of
those artists in freeing themselves from the age-old conventions as an
expression of the same spirit which brought about the realization of

Athenian democracy, flowered in literature and philosophy, and willed a successful resistance to Persia.

The problem is so elusive and difficult just because there is no break with the past, in the actual art, at all comparable to the abandonment of archaic conventions; and of course the liberation from the Persian threat was the exact opposite of what befell the Greek cities at the beginning of the Hellenistic Age. Nevertheless, I think one may be able to see that imaginative leap, by which an artist in the second century broke the frame between art and the world, as linked to another kind of liberation of thought which could hardly have come about if the Greek world had not been so violently changed in the way it was. The Olympians in earlier Greek thought inhabit their own world and visit ours unpredictably and for the most part dangerously. Their images dwell in their temples and are approached with due formality and caution. This pattern continues unbroken in formal religion, but from the late fifth century on through the fourth another strand of religious thought becomes more and more important beside it. There is the cult of Asklepios and the healing heroes, in whose shrines you can sleep, and hope that the god or *daimon* will visit you in person and heal you. The literary tradition about this is reinforced by the number and character of the marble votive reliefs dedicated in gratitude or hope. An equally great wealth of very similar reliefs attests the equal importance of the cults of Pan, the nymphs, and the rivers: gods and *daimones* who inhabit the countryside with you. These, then, at the popular level; and parallel with these, among intellectuals, widespread skepticism about the gods. Such developments belong to the later fifth and fourth centuries, and were a natural process in the world of the city-states, with popular religion naturally echoed in the art of the votive reliefs. In the changed world of the Hellenistic kingdoms, and directly influenced by the change, philosophic skepticism becomes much more cogent and much more popular. Gods are present for all to see in the mortal kings, while the traditional gods become much more dubious entities, and, even if they exist, of much less significance than the universally recognized and overriding power of Fortune, who can and does topple those divine kings, and might even at the same time, after all, shift lucky you, if not from log cabin to White House, at least from rags to riches. All this takes away much of the awe, and with the awe the fear, attaching to traditional gods and traditional stories. Such a shifting approach to religion would not in itself lead an artist to break down the barriers between the living world he inhabits and the divine one he is representing; but when his exploration of new ways in art led him in that direction it *allowed* him to do so, where an earlier artist might have felt (indeed the designer of the Nike balustrade perhaps did feel) a taboo:

representations of the gods, like the gods themselves, were better kept in their own place.

Can we extrapolate from the specific case, and perhaps suggest that this new attitude, which really is a consequence of the world change, does color artists' approach to their art over a wider range than I have been allowing? Lysippos' pupils would surely have devised the all-round, spiraling composition for statues whatever the circumstances, and whoever the patrons for whom they worked; but the Tyche of Antioch, sitting in the open above the river, is not only a programmatic creation of her time at an artistic level but profoundly a figure of the new age in a much wider sense, and a profoundly influential one. So, too, it is perhaps unlikely that a city-state would ever have provided occasion for the adaptation, like Eumenes' Athena, of an earlier statue, conceived in a religious context, to a secular one. Similarly, the portraits of the first Hellenistic kings, on their coins and in other forms, are certainly part of a development of realistic portraiture in Greek art which reaches back into the classical age and would surely under any circumstances have gone on; but it is also important that they came into being as a direct result of new needs in the new Hellenistic situation, and became themselves a determining element in the growing popularity of the genre.

This is a ridiculous mouse of a conclusion; but perhaps during the labor things may have been touched on which may lead others to contribute more valuable insights; or perhaps, more probably, things I have failed to notice may lead to that desirable result. At any rate, this seems to be as far as I can get.

RESPONSE: J. J. POLLITT

It would be appropriate to the taste and style of the Hellenistic Age if Martin Robertson and I were to confront and challenge one another with radically different views of Hellenistic art. Unfortunately, I find myself in substantial agreement with almost everything he has said, and even our minor differences of opinion—such as our differing view of the role of oriental art in the development of naturalistic portraiture—are really only matters of emphasis.

I think, however, that I can stage a confrontation of another sort that may turn out to be equally interesting. In correspondence and conversation with Professor Robertson it has become clear that this symposium has provoked both of us to take a fresh look at Hellenistic art and to reassess our earlier evaluations of its basic character. In a sense, this meeting seems to have forced us to have a confrontation not with one another but with ourselves. In his great history of the whole of Greek art[1] and in my recent book on Hellenistic art[2] both of us tended to dwell on how the innovative features of Hellenistic art could be explained as responses to new social and political conditions of the period—the wider geographical horizon in which Greek art flourished, the advent of Hellenistic kingship, the growth of large urban centers with mixed populations, and so on. It is quite natural, when you are writing books of that sort, to look for what seems new and distinctive in the period with which you are dealing. Now that we have stepped back from that task, however, both of us seem to have found that in trying to define what was new we tended to deemphasize the continuity between Hellenistic art and earlier Greek art, a continuity that we would now agree was, in fact, very strong.

In my own book on Hellenistic art I emphasize five new attitudes in the Hellenistic Age that played a role in shaping its art. A new instability in systems of government, in the settlement of populations, and in the expectations of individuals for a settled life, led, I argue, to an *obsession with fortune* that is reflected in such things as the popularity of images of Tyche, in the appeal of images of Alexander for their seemingly talismanic power, and in the fascination with dramatic reversals of fortune (as, for example, in the painting that was the source of the Alexander mosaic). I also point to a *theatrical mentality* that grew out of the conviction that life in the Hellenistic period had somehow become a play written by fortune in which one must play one's part. The popularity of images from the theater in the decorative arts; the fondness for dramatic portraits that conveyed trials of the spirit (e.g., the Lysippan portraits of Alexander); the love of dramatic narrative crises (the Granikos monument, the Alexander sarcophagus); dramatic settings both for buildings (the Pergamene acropolis, the temple of Athena at Lindos) and for sculptural groups (the "lesser Attalid group" in Athens, the Nike of Samothrace); and, on a purely stylistic level, the prevalence of the "Hellenistic baroque" style, can all be seen as emanations of this new mentality.

As others have long argued, the social instability of the Hellenistic Age and the decline of small, tightly knit communities contributed to the development of still another distinctive mind-set of the Hellenistic period, *individualism*. The interest in distinct personalities in portraiture; the concern for individual states of consciousness such as fear, pain, drunkenness (see figure 18), or erotic excitement; and the exploration of personal religious emotion in the images of Sarapis and in mysterious architectural spaces like the Arsinoeion and Hieron at Samothrace, all reflect this new concern for personal, rather than communal,

---

[1] Martin Robertson, *A History of Greek Art* (Cambridge, 1975), 445–590.
[2] J. J. Pollitt, *Art in the Hellenistic Age* (Cambridge, 1986).

18. Drunken old woman. Roman marble copy of third- or second-century-B.C. original. Glyptothek, Munich. Photo Chr. Koppermann.

19. Nilotic mosaic from Palestrina, circa 80 B.C. Museo Prenestino-Barberiniano, Palestrina.

experiences and values. The corollary, as Tarn put it,[3] of individualism was a *cosmopolitan outlook*, a sympathetic curiosity about the entire inhabited world that lay beyond one's own social and ethnic traditions. Thus foreigners, derelicts, and exotic fauna and flora are all treated with interest, and usually with sympathy, in Hellenistic art (see figure 19).

Finally, there was the *scholarly mentality* that grew out of royally subsidized intellectual centers like the Library and Museum of Alexandria, which brought a didactic, learned quality to Hellenistic art that is expressed in such things as complicated allegories—for example, the stele of Archelaos (figure 20)—and in the learned, evocative pleasure that was derived from reviving and playing with earlier artistic styles, archaism and neoclassicism (see figures 21 and 22).

[3] W. W. Tarn, *Hellenistic Civilization*, 3d ed. (London, 1952), 2.

20. Marble votic relief by Archelaos of Priene, circa 150 B.C. British Museum, London. Photo British Museum, courtesy of Trustees.

21. Neo-Attic Maenad relief. Marble, circa 100 B.C. Uffizi Gallery, Florence. Photo Alinari.

22. Terme Boxer. Bronze, second or early first century B.C. National Museum of the Terme, Rome. Photo Alinari.

It is not my intention, like some beleaguered bureaucrat in a Marxist state whose policies have failed, to recant the line of thought that I have just sketched—I still think that it has basic validity—but I would like for a moment to look at Hellenistic art from another point of view. As Martin Robertson has emphasized in his paper, after one does one's best to identify what is really original about Hellenistic art, one keeps coming back to the unavoidable observation that most of the major developments of Hellenistic art grew quite explicably, if not entirely predictably, out of earlier Greek art. Until quite late in the period, when Hellenistic artists faced the challenge of satisfying the needs and taste of Roman patrons, there are no changes that one would be inclined to call revolutionary. Precedents for most of the major developments of Hellenistic art can be found in the art of the fourth century B.C. or even earlier. For example, a realistic trend in portraiture is anticipated in a number of portraits that belong to the fourth century. I would cite, in particular, those of Xenophon and Plato (figure 23)—although on the latter, let it be noted, Martin Robertson disagrees.

Dramatic confrontations, and their accompanying pathos, can be found in the pedimental sculptures from Epidauros and Tegea, as well as in other sculptures, and literary sources suggest that they were explored in the paintings of Euphranor, Nikias, and Aristeides. The increasingly widespread use of personifications, including related groupings of personifications (e.g., *Demokratia* and *Demos* in the presence of Theseus in Euphranor's paintings in the Stoa Basileios in Athens) anticipate the didactic allegories of Hellenistic art. Personal religious emotions are anticipated in fourth-century images of Asklepios and perhaps in the unorthodox, mysterious interior of the temple of Apollo at Bassae. A retrospective view of style seems already to be present, on a limited scale, in the fifth century B.C. in the mannerism of the Pan Painter and the archaism of the sculptor Alkamenes. The "boy strangling a goose" type and other well-known Hellenistic images of children, while admittedly treated more playfully and lovingly than images of children had been in the classical period, represent the continuation of an earlier tradition of votive images of children. Even those images that are often thought to constitute social realism in Hellenistic art—old fishermen (figure 24), peasant women (figure 25), dwarfs, and the like—were anticipated in brief flashes in Greek vase painting (I think of the foreign-looking gentleman and his dog on the cup that is the name-vase of the Hegesiboulos Painter in New York [figure 26]) and apparently, judging by the literary evidence, in the art of the sculptor Demetrios of Alopeke.

In short, there are good reasons for concluding that what is "Hellenistic" about Hellenistic art is a matter of new emphasis rather than radical

23. Portrait of Plato. Roman marble copy of fourth-century-B.C. original. Fitzwilliam Museum, Cambridge. By permission.

24. Old fisherman. Roman marble and alabaster copy of original of ? 200–150 B.C. Louvre, Paris. Photographie Giraudon.

25. Old market woman. Marble, late second or early first century B.C. Metropolitan Museum, New York. All rights reserved, The Metropolitan Museum of Art, Rogers Fund, 1909.

26. Red-figured kylix attributed to the Hegesiboulos Painter. The Metropolitan Museum of Art, Rogers Fund, 1907.

departure. There is a new look to many things, but continuity with the past is equally striking.

The one period in which this general observation seems not to be entirely true occurred, as I said earlier, in the late Hellenistic period when the resources of Hellenistic art were being put at the disposal of Roman patrons. In the Greco-Roman phase of Hellenistic art there were a few developments that seem to have had no clear Greek precedent and must be viewed as altogether new. A change that was clearly unprece-dented, as Martin Robertson has observed, was the extension of the por-trait sculptor's art to represent ordinary people who could claim no pub-lic distinction. We are, of course, familiar with such portraits in Roman art, where not only prominent public officials but also people of relatively low status—freedmen, for example—commissioned portraits. In the Greek world, on the other hand, portraits had always been reserved for people who were credited with some great achievement, such as military heroes, leaders in government, victorious athletes, or renowned philoso-phers, poets, and orators. In Greek portraiture, the "average person" was simply not of much interest. When viewed against this background, that remarkable series of realistic portraits found on Delos, dating from the late second and early first centuries B.C. and representing what seem to be Italian, Greek, and eastern Mediterranean businessmen (see figure

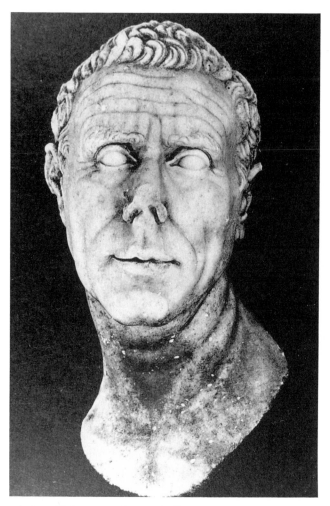

27a. Portrait from Delos, second or early first century B.C. Delos Museum. *Exploration Archéologie de Délos*, vol. xiii, pls. xxi, xxiii.

27 a, b), appears quite remarkable and clearly constitutes something new. Such evidence as there is indicates that the artists who made them were Hellenistic Greeks; but they flourished in an international culture which was something other than traditionally Greek, and this culture challenged them to create an unprecedented genre.

The atmospheric style of landscape painting that we find in the *Odyssey* landscapes (see figure 28) may be another example of an unprecedented development in Hellenistic art, although in this case, given the paucity of surviving Greek paintings, it could be argued that the Greek antecedents simply have not survived.

27b. Portrait from Delos, second or early first century B.C. Delos Museum.

A final thought. This symposium has provoked a number of interesting reflections on the role of frontiers in the Hellenistic world. The chief fountain of inspiration for the artists of the Hellenistic period was undeniably old Greece, but to the extent that they were affected by frontiers, I think it can be asserted that the most influential one was not the Sudan or the Hindu Kush; it was the Tiber.

DISCUSSION

A. E. Samuel: Why are we looking at the same things we looked at fifty years ago and coming up with completely different conclusions? For

28. Odyssey landscape: attack of the Laestrygonians. Vatican Museum, Rome. Photo Alinari.

example, the strictly Egyptian portraits of the Hellenistic period, which Egyptologists used to admit were influenced by Greek trends, are now being seen by Egyptologists as emerging directly from Egyptian traditions and precedents. Another example is the Anubis stele, which used to be considered a demonstration of the fusion of Greek and Egyptian art, having the Anubis head on the relief coupled with Greek architectural elements, but is now used as a demonstration of the separation of the two traditions. Why is this?

J. J. Pollitt: It's a deep philosophical question. (Laughter.) Why do literary classicists now undertake structuralist analyses of Virgil, and so on, whereas it didn't occur to previous generations to do such things? We continually reexamine the past in the light of ideas, theories, and problems that currently happen to interest us. I suppose that new attitudes toward works of art and literature have something to do with changing social and cultural conditions, as they did in the Hellenistic period. There seem to be inevitable changes in the things that succeeding generations find interesting and in the biases that they bring to historical studies. I doubt that this question is really answerable in a rigorous way. In some cases, as new data become available, we are virtually forced to reframe old questions and to look at monuments in a new way. This is the case with Macedonian art, for example, now that we know so much more about Macedonian painted tombs.

S. M. Burstein: One thing I have always found strikingly original about Hellenistic art is the sudden fascination with what one can only call the ugly. I am thinking of the wonderful series of statues such as the drunken old peasant woman or the crippled man going to the market. Is this in fact truly original, and in what conceivable context could these objects have functioned, aside from being experiments by the artist?

J. J. Pollitt: I myself believe that most of these old peasant women, fishermen, and so on, were votive sculptures dedicated in sanctuaries. We do have one literary reference, in Herodas, to votive sculptures of this sort in the Asklepieion at Cos. I think that the drunken old woman, the one in Munich (figure 18)—who is not really a peasant, incidentally; she wears fairly elaborate, expensive clothing—may have something to do with the Alexandrian festival called the *lagynophoria* in which aristo-crats dressed up like peasants, sat on beds of straw with their bottles, and pretended to have a rustic picnic. But that's only a guess. In any case, I do think that these statues had a serious context of some sort, probably a religious one. There are a number of difficult questions about these sculptures. For example, were they unique to the Hellenistic period?

M. Robertson: There are no precedents in monumental art, but there are some ugly people on fifth-century vases, certainly, as well as among terracottas.

J. J. Pollitt: It does seem as if a tradition that we can identify earlier in vase painting and in statuettes has suddenly been applied to monumental sculpture.

N. Yalouris (former Director, Greek Archaeological Service):   I liked Dr. Pollitt's point about the lack of revolutionary changes in Hellenistic art, that what we find here is, rather, a special emphasis on what happened in the past. This is confirmed by another fact. If we look at the literary activity of this period, all the intellectuals, poets, and philosophers devote most of their time and interest to the past, and to previous creations;

what they want is to document, explain, and preserve them. Original activity in new forms of poetry is very unusual.

J. J. Pollitt: It does seem to have been a very self-conscious period, a period in which artists had a sophisticated awareness of what had gone on before. Hellenistic artists were surrounded by a wide array of earlier monuments, and these reverberated in their minds, I think, when they did their own work. The temptation to imitate or recreate earlier styles must always have been there, and when their patrons developed a nostalgic taste for the art of the past, the artists were ready and willing to gratify it.

E. S. Gruen: What I find particularly interesting about Professor Pollitt's formulation is that he identifies originality with the involvement of the Romans! Could he elaborate a little on what characteristics exactly he sees as original in this late, Greco-Roman phase of the Hellenistic period (150–50 B.C.)? Is it simply the fact of portraiture of private individuals rather than public figures, and if it is more, to what degree is Roman patronage directly responsible for it?

J. J. Pollitt: When I spoke about new developments under the influence of Roman patronage, I didn't mean, of course, that there was no originality in Hellenistic art prior to the Greco-Roman phase. I think that the development of realistic and dramatic representations of personalities in Hellenistic portrait sculpture, for example, is one of the most original developments in the entire period. What I meant in reference to the Greco-Roman phase was that there were new genres that were completely unprecedented and were not, like most developments in the Hellenistic period, predictable extensions of preceding traditions in Greek art. Portraits of average people, as opposed to prominent public figures, were not the greatest creations of Hellenistic art, but they were something that simply had not existed before.

I also think that the full-blown stylistic historicism of neo-Attic art is another example of innovation stimulated by Roman patronage. Traces of archaistic and classicistic mannerisms do, of course, turn up earlier in Greek art, but neo-Attic statues and reliefs have a special atmosphere about them. Romans in the first century B.C., like Cicero when he had his "college year abroad" in Athens, saw classical Greek culture as something comfortably remote, essentially finished, and all the more impressive precisely because it could be viewed from a distance. They were impressed by it in the same way that we, in our impressionable student days, were impressed by college surveys in the humanities. Getting some Greek culture meant a lot to people like Cicero before they went to law school,

so to speak, and entered into the rough and tumble of Roman political
life. There was a Romantic nostalgia about the whole experience. This
feeling pervades neo-Attic reliefs. Old forms were reinterpreted in a
poetic, learned, and somewhat distant way. This effect seems to have
appealed to Roman patrons more than it did to Greeks. At first, neo-
Attic reliefs and similar sculptures were made in workshops in Athens
and shipped to Italy to be used in villas like Cicero's. Later on, many of
the sculptors migrated to Rome to be nearer to their patrons.

N. G. L. Hammond: Could I raise the question of an early example of
portraiture? The gold Alexander dedicated by Alexander I from spoils
won against the Persians, was, presumably, a recognizable portrait of
Alexander himself, made in his lifetime. A second example is the Alexander on the tetradrachm of Alexander I riding a horse with a dog under-
neath, which looks to me very much like a portrait of the king.

J. J. Pollitt: Yes, I think that there were portraits, at least from the time
of the Persian Wars, that represented the actual appearance of people,
at least to an extent. A representation of an individual doesn't have to be
intensely realistic to qualify as a portrait. The question of what constitutes
realism in a portrait is a highly subjective one. We tend to judge a portrait's realism by the number of naturalistic, idiosyncratic details that a
portraitist is prepared to, or permitted to, incorporate into an image.
But the fact that a particular work contains relatively few details of this
sort does not mean that it is not a portrait. Classical Greek portraits
seem more realistic when compared to Egyptian pharaonic portraits,
and Hellenistic portraits seem more realistic when compared to those of
classical Greece. The effects of each type were different, but they all
functioned as portraits.

K. D. White: Where if anywhere does the great series of sacroidyllic
paintings fit in, and where does the temple of Fortuna Primigenia at
Palestrina fit into this later landscape, as it were, which you have been
describing so eloquently?

J. J. Pollitt: As far as I can remember, all the sacroidyllic landscapes
belong to the later first century B.C. or later; so, while they may have
had Hellenistic precedents, what survives belongs to the early Roman
Empire. Decoration on the Fortuna temple complex went on for a long
time, and the date of the Nilotic mosaic has been debated, but it probably
belongs to the time of Sulla, as the literary evidence suggests. A Greek
painter called Demetrios the *topographos* is said to have migrated from
Egypt to Italy, where he served as host to Ptolemy VI while the latter was

in exile in Rome. Presumably he brought some sort of topographical painting with him, and this genre may be reflected in the Praeneste mosaic. The interchange of ideas between the Hellenistic world and Rome seems to be explicitly documented in this case, and once again we seem to be dealing with a form of art that was Hellenistic in origin but had an appeal for Roman patrons. Nilotic paintings, as you know, were popular in the Roman world and extend well beyond the Hellenistic period.

J. H. Kroll (University of Texas at Austin): The growth of museums and collections is very well documented in the Republican period, as the letters of Cicero show. And the major "museums" in Roman Imperial times were the great collections of Greek art in Rome, sometimes taken as spoils, and sometimes just the collections of connoisseurs. But is this an exclusively Roman phenomenon? Isn't Pergamon the best documented early location for the collection of sculpture and even copies of sculpture as museum pieces—as opposed to one of the traditional functions of art? I believe there are inscriptions from Pergamon which actually mention earlier statuary. Is that correct?

J. J. Pollitt: Yes, there are several inscriptions on bases at Pergamon that give the names of classical sculptors, most notably Myron, Praxiteles, and Kresilas. These seem to be labels rather than signatures. We can assume, I think, that one of the Attalid kings either collected some works by these sculptors, or had copies made, and exhibited his collection at Pergamon. We also know from literary evidence that Attalos II collected paintings. According to Pliny, he bought a painting of Dionysos by Aristeides from the spoils of Corinth, only to have it confiscated by Mummius.

M. Robertson: And Ptolemy III collected classical art, especially Sicyonian paintings.

J. H. Kroll: So this makes the Hellenistic kings the predecessors of the Romans, at least in the sense that the Romans were picking up on something that was well under way—at least this concern for the function of art, sculpture as something for a garden or a museum, rather than as a dedication or to honor someone. Couldn't you say, when trying to determine something specifically Hellenistic in the cultural sense about art, that there was a gradual shift from a world in which art was basically utilitarian (the archaic tradition) to a world which allowed more art for art's sake—or at least the addition of such a role for major works of art?

J. J. Pollitt: There were undoubtedly some things that were made for collectors and for the Roman art market. Much of neo-Attic art may fall into this category. I still think, however, that traditional functions—votive offerings, public commemorations, architectural decoration—can be ascribed to most works of Hellenistic art.

M. Robertson: The Pergamene and Ptolemaic collectors seem to have gone for old masters and not for contemporary work.

J. J. Pollitt: And the things that formed these collections by and large were not made for the collections; they were simply expropriated.

J. H. Kroll: Well, what about the seated boxer (figure 22), which you may see as a victory statue, but certainly isn't a victory statue in the traditional sense? Couldn't that be a museum piece?

J. J. Pollitt: We just don't have a context for it. I suppose it could have been made expressly for the art market, but I rather doubt it. I have no problem with seeing the boxer as a votive statue, originally set up in a sanctuary in some Greek city and later brought to Rome as booty.

J. H. Kroll: When do you have the first museums for sculpture built?

J. J. Pollitt: Well, clearly they existed in the first century B. C., when Pasiteles and Arkesilaos and the sons of Polykles were working for Roman patrons and selling works to collectors. We even hear, incidentally, of collectors paying extra money to get the original clay or plaster model of a particular work, so that no other copies could be made. They were intent on having the original masterpiece, not just one version among many. This mentality seems to arise at the very end of the Hellenistic period, in the last stages of the Greco-Roman phase.

At first, when most Greek art was coming to Rome in the form of booty, sculptures were exhibited in temples and in porticoes within the precincts of temples, like the Porticus Metelli. Later, when private collections were formed through the Roman art market, they were still sometimes placed in public buildings. The collection of Asinius Pollio, for example, one of the most avid Roman collectors, seems to have been housed in the library that he built into the Atrium Libertatis when he reconstructed it. Statues were also set up in baths and basilicas, although it's difficult to say whether or not such sculptures constituted "collections." It's also reasonable to assume that some private collections were exhibited in the *atria* and porticoes of houses and villas. As far as I know, the ancient world didn't have any "pure" museums, that is, buildings that were used exclusively for the display of works of art. Ancient art galleries seem always to have had other functions as well, either public or domestic.

Unfortunately, we don't have a very clear idea of how ancient sculptures were exhibited in these ancient equivalents of museums; so it's difficult to say whether they were adequate by our standards or not.

People in a Landscape:
Theokritos

Peter Levi

I must apologize for having the pretension to give this paper, which I know raises questions too naive to be answered.[1] My excuse is that I never cease to wonder about Theokritos. Virgil is already a brilliant and a thrilling poet in the *Eclogues*, but I think he got a lot wrong about Theokritos' bucolic world (figure 29)—almost everything, in fact, except the poetry, which he reproduced perfectly.[2] I have spent thirty years trying to master the lessons that Virgil learnt from Theokritos in his youngest poems. Four or five years ago when I was writing a history of Greek literature I reread most of what there is to read in Greek, and in all that long spell of reading, after Homer and Aeschylus I liked Theokritos best; he was freshest, and I was most surprised by him.[3] He came neck and neck with Plato, who took up a whole long summer. Indeed he owes something to Plato—those endless summer evenings, the dialogues

[1] Most of the modern references are in David Halperin's *Before Pastoral: Theocritus and the Ancient Tradition of Bucolic Poetry* (New Haven, 1983).
[2] Tityros, whose name comes from Philetas—cf. G. Bonfante, "Tityros e Satyros," *RAL* 39 (1984): 197—might mean a ram, the leader of the flock; but Virgil noticed in Theokritos the possibilities of the name for making a self-echoing noise like that of the opening of Theokritos' first idyll. It was, precisely, the sound of a pipe or a flute. "Tityre tu," he began, and then, in case we missed it, "Tu Tityre."
[3] Robert Wells has recently produced the best, the most telling translation of Theocritus we have had since the sixteenth century: *Theocritus, The Idylls* (London, 1988). All my verse quotations are from Wells's version. He lightened my task and made it a pleasure. I would, at the same time, like to draw attention to the impressive, and little-known, translation of Idyll 11 ("The Cyclops"), by Elizabeth Barrett Browning, *Poetical Works* (New York, Boston, 1897) 576–78.

29. Pastoral scene probably representing Theokritos. Silver dish, late Hellenistic period. The Hermitage, St. Petersburg. From *The History of the Hellenic People* (Ekdotike Athenon, 1974), vol. 5, p. 397.

of the idle in beautiful places—but I would sooner take part in an idyll of Theokritos than a dialogue of Plato, if only because of the sensuous concentration and apparent ease of the poetry, and its self-echoing noise. As Philetas claims in *Daphnis and Chloe*,[4] the echoes in the woods sing Amaryllis-yllis-yllis for ever. That trick has been reinvented many times; what persists is what du Bartas called "Écho, voix forestière, Écho fille de l'air" (*Paradis terrestre, La Seconde Semaine, Premier jour*).

---

[4] Longus 2.7: ἐπῄνουν τὴν Ἠχὼ τὸ Ἀμαρυλλίδος ὄνομα μετ' ἐμὲ καλοῦσαν.

> La gentile Alouette avec son tyre-lire
> Tire l'yre à l'iré, et tiri-lyrant vire
> Vers la voûte du Ciel, puis son vol vers ce lieu
> Vire, et desire dire, adieu Dieu, adieu Dieu.

I would like, initially, to notice a short lyric by the modern Russian poet Mandelshtam, which perhaps says more about Theokritos' technique as a poet and imitates him better than I can hope to do:

> Orioles in the deep wood: vowel length
> is the one measure of all tonal verse:
> and on one day a year pure duration
> pours out and nature's metre is Homer's.

> Like a caesura that long day dawns:
> from early morning longueur's lazy weed:
> oxen at pasture, golden indolence
> won't let you drain the whole note from the reed.

> (Trans. P. Levi)

The question I have set myself is, what kind of a world are these herdsmen living in, and what are their social relations, as presupposed by the bucolic idylls? The idylls are deliberately varied, and they offer us an entire gallery of more or less unhappy country lovers, as seen by urban or courtly eyes, not by one another, like the sheepshearing in *The Winter's Tale* observed by the king. Theokritos in his χάριτες for Hieron (*Id.* 16.36ff.) makes an apology for pastoral poetry. He remembers the cattle of the Scopadae, the shepherds, and the horses. Cycnus earns a mention because he was turned into the water bird of his name on the river Sybaris: the scholiast says he was white from birth, διὸ καὶ θῆλυν αὐτὸν εἶπεν ὁ Θεόκριτος.[5] Then he goes on to the Cyclops, and the pigs and cows in the *Odyssey*, and Laertes tilling the ground. The final praise of Hieron is a prayer for the peace of Sicily and the flourishing of the earth:

> May the old inhabitants repossess their cities,
> Build on ruins and restore what has been spoiled.
> May the fields be worked and bring forth crops once more
> While bleating flocks, too many to count, grow fat
> On the grassy plains. May the passer-by at nightfall
> Quicken his steps as the cattle are driven home.
> Let fallows be ploughed for sowing while the cicada,
> The shepherd's sentinel, high among branches, rasps
> The midday silence. Let the armoury be shrouded.
> Let poetry carry Hiero's fame through the world.

> (16.88–98)

---

[5] Schol. Theocr. 16.49 Wendel.

That is as close as the king can come to entering the idyllic world of the poems. Even the cicada is more memorable: how that tiny detail—typical of Theokritos—brings the rest to life!

The people want an old prosperity restored, an old natural order reinstated.[6] Apropos, the cattle are driven in at night but the sheep seem to be everywhere. This raises the important question of transhumance. We have been warned recently in the *Journal of Hellenic Studies*[7] not to believe too easily that ancient cattle were transhumant. In the earlier classical period I speculate that they were. Otherwise Kerambos (punished for disobeying the rules of transhumance) would not have become a stag beetle;[8] nor could the two herdsmen have met on Kithairon, thus making the story of Oedipus impossible. Louis Robert has pointed out[9] that grazing rights could be a *causa belli*; an inscription that guarantees mutual grazing rights between two cities foresees damages and infringements even so.

We know that owners were charged by the night for their cattle's grazing on temple lands at the Isthmus, and I assume that those cattle were crossing the Isthmus, as the sheep and goats from Dolianá in Arcadia did annually in living memory.[10] We know of an ancient boundary that cut off Aráchova from its grazing,[11] but that was because the grazing belonged to the Delphians: they were richer and their cattle grazed further. I do not understand how the enormous numbers of cattle sacrificed in Athens in the course of a year could graze normally inside the plain of Attica. So I assume that herdsmen wandered. In a period closer to Theokritos, we have a sad inscription from islanders seeking relief against wandering herds guarded by toughs, who grazed their flocks where they chose.[12] In the Roman period, Cicero's friend Atticus is supposed to have controlled much of the grazing of Epirus.[13] One man can physically handle only so many animals of course, but the growth of capitalism in the ancient world meant that one man could be the owner of many flocks—and of many shepherds, if they were slaves.

Very few herdsmen are named in inscriptions. Two of the few excep-

---

[6] Cf. P. Levi, *The Lamentation for the Dead* (London, 1984), 1–5.

[7] Halstead, "Tradition and Ancient Rural Economy in Mediterranean Europe: Plus Ça Change?" *JHS* 107 (1987): 79–81.

[8] Ovid *Met.* 7.353.

[9] L. Robert, "Les Chèvres d'Héracleia," *Hellenica* 7 (1949): 161–70.

[10] Personal knowledge: conversation with old villagers; confirmed by Mr. Roger Howell.

[11] Cf. Robin Osborne, *Classical Landscape with Figures: The Ancient Greek City and Its Countryside* (London, 1987), 51.

[12] L. Robert, "Épitaphe d'un berger à Thasos," *Hellenica* 7 (1949): 152; cf. "Chèvres," 161 for third-century-B.C. Herakleia, south of Naxos and west of Amorgos.

[13] Cornelius Nepos, *Life of Atticus* 25.14.3.

tions are Μάνης χρηστὸς τοῖς δεσπόταις ἤμην, surely a slave; and, in the cave at Vari: "Skyron's goatherd (dedicates) this altar to the Nymphs"—probably another slave since he has no personal name.[14] It would be interesting to know—not that they seem to care—whether the herdsmen in Theokritos are slaves or free. In the Roman period, it seems to have been conventional to reward herdsmen, or more particularly shepherds, by letting them raise a few beasts of their own among the flock. John Aubrey noticed the same custom in his own day in Wiltshire. "In our western parts (I know not what is done in the north), the sheep-masters give no wages to their shepherds, but they have the keeping of so many sheep, *pro rata*; so that the shepherd's lambs do never miscarry." "He has the keeping of so many sheep with his Master's flock. Plautus hints at this in his Asinaria, (a.3 s.1, l.36). 'The herdsman, too, who, like a mother, pastures strangers' sheep, has some of his own too, who are his chiefest hope.' "[15] When shepherds offer sacrifice at Mykale, all they can offer according to the inscribed record is a little cheese or a kid or a lamb.[16] This custom, which seems to go back at least to Theokritos, explains some otherwise perplexing moments in the *Idylls*.

It makes a lot of difference whether the herdsmen are free or not; on the whole I think they are not. It matters just as much whether or not they are travelers; that is a problem we must discuss in detail. They certainly seem to know one another quite well, and the social distinction of "cowmen top, shepherds second, and goatherds lowest,"[17] which a scholiast gives and the idylls on the whole confirm, is not sufficiently sharp to make them uneasy. Their typical songs, the βουκολικὰ, consist of a brief series of two or three lines each on a wide variety of themes, with a refrain, often strung together and quite subtly matched, almost like the matching series of haiku of the Japanese poet Basho.[18] The relationships of persons are conventional, but they are very much sharper than the languorous, scarcely differentiated landscapes, haunted by country gods and shepherds, that we find depicted in the visual arts[19]—those twisted trees and wordless conversations that tend to

---

[14] Robert, "Chèvres"; "Épitaphe."

[15] *Worlds of John Aubrey* (Folio Society 1988) 237, 181.

[16] Robert, "Épitaphe," 154.

[17] Schol. Theocr. 1.86b Wendel.

[18] See, e.g., Matsuo Basho, *The Four Seasons: Japanese Haiku* (Mount Vernon, N.Y., 1958), and *A Haiku Journey: Basho and Selected Haiku* (Tokyo, 1974).

[19] On these, cf. in general Claude Rolley, *Greek Bronzes* (London, 1986) 214–16, and in detail, Achille Adriani, *Documenti e ricerche d'arte alessandrina* (Rome, 1959), particularly the chapter entitled "Divagazioni intorno ad una coppa paesistica del museo di Alessandria." Cf. also J. Charbonneaux, R. Martin, and F. Villard, *Hellenistic Art, 330–50* B.C. (London, 1973), 164ff., with figs. 169, 176, 178, 180.

swamp our reading of the idylls. From the first idyll onwards, relationships are crisp: more is implied than is said.

Thyrsis in Idyll 1 is a shepherd, who invites a goatherd, in the name of the nymphs who own the spot, to sit and pipe, while Thyrsis looks after the goats. The goatherd refuses to pipe at noon but begs Thyrsis to sing the cowman's song, *The Passion of Daphnis*, which Thyrsis composed. All this is pure diplomacy: Thyrsis has induced the goatherd to offer him a solid bribe, three milkings of a good nanny goat, and an elaborate wooden cup as queer, on a lesser scale, as the shield of Achilles.[20] I take the description of the cup to be the goatherd's equivalent of a song. There are two strange references to travel. First, the goatherd bought his cup, for a goat and a fine cheese, from the Kalydna ferryman. Kalydna seems to be a little island north of Kos; so people, perhaps herdsmen and their flocks, move about among the islands. Or was the cup carved in Kalydna and sold in Kos? Then why to a goatherd? Is the point that a wooden cup would be terribly old-fashioned and a goatherd would treasure it? I think the goatherd traveled with the ferryman. Second, who is this Chromis the Libyan against whom Thyrsis sang in a contest? A Greek-speaking shepherd, but "Chromis" may mean he was black. The contest was local: they know one another. Is Chromis a local man, or a mildly exotic member of the floating population of the Near East? There were flourishing Greek settlements in Libya, and in Idyll 3 we have a yellow Libyan billy goat (4–5). This internationalism is apparently deliberate. Thyrsis himself is from Sicilian Etna.

The song about Daphnis seems to be set in Sicily. Daphnis is the cowman par excellence, who died of love, mourned by the wild beasts and by his own cattle, by herdsmen of all kinds, and by Priapos. The same thrilling detail as usual brings the scene to life: Daphnis grazed and watered his cattle on Mount Etna, but the nymphs of eastern Sicily failed to protect him from Aphrodites' vengeance. When he dies, nature is reversed:

---

[20] Theocr. *Id.* 1.1–63. The best discussion of this strange cup and the contradictions it embodies is that by David Halperin, *Before Pastoral*, 161ff. Was it meant as a contemporary work or an antique? In the time-scale of the poem, of course, it is new, freshly made and still fragrant from the chisel (28). The aged fisherman on a jutting rock, with his white hair and his fresh, supple strength, could be a late-fifth-century fisherman, perhaps a satyr or a papposilenos. The ivy need be no later. The woman with two bearded suitors certainly need not. But the vineyard, the foxes, and the little boy with the cricket cage on the stone wall are puzzling at any period. The landscape cup in Adriani, *Documenti*, or even the Portland Vase and its like, are much less specific, and the fineness of detail seems impossible on a cup; it suggests a trompe l'oeil painter, maybe an Alexandrian.

Let the prickly juniper bloom with soft narcissus,
Let pine be weighed with pears. Let the stag hunt the hounds,
Let the nightingale attend to the screech-owl's cries.

                                                        (132–36)

It may not help much, but my own suspicion is that Daphnis invented
the bucolic song; that he is, in fact, Boutes, the human lover of Aphrodite
of Eryx at the far end of Sicily, who, the Athenians maintained, was the
founder of the Boutiadae, a clan active and privileged on the acropolis
of Athens. Apollonios of Rhodes explained how Boutes ended up at
Eryx, having swum ashore there from the Argo.[21] I take this elaborate
bit of mythological cunning to date from the fifth century, and I assume
that Apollonios, an Alexandrian by birth, simply found it useful, just
as Kallimachos found Hekale useful. But Theokritos was a Syracusan,
Thyrsis was from Aitna, and apparently so was Daphnis. If we are right
to set this idyll in Kos, because of the ferryman of Kalydna, then the
goatherd comes from there.

After many years of suspicious resistance, I am bound to admit here
that I accept most of Gow's footnote about the Kalydnian ferryman.[22] I
think the reference in Homer (*Il.* 2.677) to the Kalydnian islands as the
islands, most notably Kalymnos, around Kos must be decisive in such a
poet as Theokritos; and we know he wrote about Kos in the great seventh
idyll, where the country people were surely masks for real poets. It does
remain possible that the cup for which the goatherd paid in cheeses is so
elaborate that it must have come from Kos or even Alexandria, and that
the poet's fancy of how such a wonderful cup might get into the hands
of a goatherd involved him in the invention of a vague Kalydnian sailor.
That is a possible reading, and then the setting is Sicily; but the goatherd
still has dealings with a sailor, and I prefer the other view. As for Kos,
it was the home of Philetas, and Tityros and Daphnis were both his
characters.[23]

Notice that the settings of the idylls are intensely and sensuously realized, but as vignettes, never complete landscapes, and with only hints as
to what country we are in. I like Wilamowitz's observation[24] that Aigilian
figs at the end of the first idyll are related to the Aigelioi of Kos and not
to the Attic deme of Aigilon (or its hero Aigilos), which is an unrecorded
village remembered for its figs only by Philemon in his treatise on Attic

---

[21] Ap. Rhod. 4.910ff., cf. Paus. 1.26.5; see *RE* 3 (1899) cols. 1081–82, s.v. "Butes (4)"
(Wernicke); P. Levi, *History of Greek Literature* (New York, 1985), 422.

[22] A. S. F. Gow, *Theocritus*, 2d ed. (Cambridge, 1952) 2:14–15.

[23] Cf. E. L. Bowie, "Theocritus' Seventh *Idyll*, Philetas and Longus," *CQ* n.s. 35 (1985):
67–91.

[24] *Ap.* Gow, *Theocritus* 2:31; cf. Paton and Hicks, *Inscriptions of Cos* nos. 393, 394, cited
ibid.

names, quoted by Athenaios.[25] Philemon may be thinking of this poem.[26] Gow takes the view that geographical names in bucolic poetry are not to be taken seriously.[27] My impression is that they are hints at the real world of the poem's characters. At any rate we should pursue them as if they are, and I believe they will turn out to make sense.

Let me offer, at least as a kind of extended footnote, a formal rebuttal of Gow's view that geographical names are used by Theokritos with cheerful insouciance and are often contradictory.[28] I have already dealt with the first idyll. But to say that "Thyrsis is Sicilian (65) and the Libyan (24) also suggests the west" is to sweep the problem under the carpet. Thyrsis and the Libyan met at some international competition, a shepherds' Olympics. In the second idyll, to say that "Lipara (133) conflicts" with all the evidence for Kos is ridiculous: the fire of Lipara is an enormous volcano, which is bound to be proverbial at least as far away as Kos. In Idyll 3 Gow is simply guessing, and so am I. In 4 and 5 his attempts to pick holes in the geography pile conjecture on conjecture: the rivers of Sybaris, Haleis, and Himera are admittedly surprising and raise a mild doubt; but even if Theokritos had invented them, which I do not suppose, only in Sybaris (which no longer existed) would he have given his own names to a landscape. But I think he knew Kroton and Sybaris. In the tenth idyll we have the old problem about Sicily and Kos. But the choice of Sicily depends here (4) upon the plant *kaktos*, which was known to Nikander and Philetas, who had no Sicilian connection, and on the song of a lark (50), which we know from the seventh idyll to have been at home in Kos, and which anyway was Demeter's bird. (Philetas, incidentally, wrote a poem about Demeter.) The other indications in the tenth idyll, such as they are, point to Kos.[29] Theokritos' world is the real world.

One might go further. The goatherd's description of his cup forms a fine matching contrast with the song Thyrsis sings, but in an Alexandrian mode of another kind; it is not bucolic song. The goatherd's language is in general queerer, quirkier, and spiky with detail. Apart from the first exquisite exchange of compliments—and even this he is not well able to sustain—the goatherd is scarcely capable of true bucolic song. Of that

---

[25] Philemon *ap.* Athen. *Deipn.* 14.652e.

[26] W. Seelbach, *Die Epigramme des Mnasalkes von Sikyon und des Theodoridas von Syrakus* (Wiesbaden, 1964), identifies the place as Aigaleon in northern Greece; but he has not noticed Theokritos, and Gow has not noticed Mnasalkes.

[27] Gow, *Theocritus* 1:xx, and notes *ad loc.*

[28] Ibid.

[29] Rivers of Sybaris, Haleis, and Himera: Theocr. *Id.* 5.123–24. Larks on Cos: *Id.* 7.23, 141. The lark as Demeter's bird: A. Lezzi-Hafter, "Demeter mit dem Vogelszepter," in *Studien zur Mythologie und Vasenmalerei*, ed. E. Böhr and W. Martini (Mainz, 1986), 87–89. Philetas' poem on Demeter: J. U. Powell, *Collectanea Alexandrina* (Oxford, 1925), 90–91.

Thyrsis gives a perfect and fully developed example. Thyrsis is a master-singer of international fame: the passion of Daphnis is his set piece, it is not impromptu, and the goatherd worships it. What a herdsman might produce on his own we learn from other idylls: specifically, from 3 and from Komatas and Lakon in 5. It seems to be just a few antiphonal, competitive verses sung impromptu, suspiciously like certain epigrams which we have only from a slightly later generation, from Mnasalkes of Sikyon for example.[30] Idyll 3 consists of the rustic, solitary *komos* to Amaryllis: a string of fragmentary love songs. Their eloquence is not bucolic, but rather belongs to the traditional nature of love songs. The singer is unnamed; Tityros, however, is looking after the goats:

> Lucky the bee as it flits through the curtain drawn
> Across your cave, dark ivy and maidenhair fern.
> O pity my restless heart! Look how I pine!
>
> Now I know Love as he is, an angry god
> Suckled by a lioness, reared in a wild wood,
> A smouldering fire that burns to the very bone.
>
> The lips may be loving though the heart is unstirred.
> Then let yourself be kissed by a clumsy goatherd,
> Girl with bright eyes, dark brow and heart of stone.
>
> (12–20)

Who *is* Amaryllis? Philetas surely invented her.[31] Does she live alone in a cave? Is she a nymph? No, common sense assumes that she lives there in the summer, keeping a few animals. He might give her a white nanny goat with kids. His own goats are on the hill, but she lives less ambitiously by the shore. He might turn away and give the goats to Mermnon's ἐριθακίς, a girl servant in diminutive form, who wants them. This landscape is quite densely populated. Olp(h)is sits on the cliff watching for tunny fish, and normal island life is going on. Can Olp(h)is be a character from Sophron's mime about tunny fishing?[32] The Tityros of Idyll 7 is a shepherd, probably native to Kos, in the song sung by Lycidas; yet he reminds us of Thyrsis, because Lycidas says that Tityros (72–73) will sing how Daphnis loved Xenea, and the hill grieved for him, and the oak trees on the banks of Himera sang his dirge. The river Himera brings Daphnis further west and closer to Boutes; but Tityros, as Lycidas imagines him, is in Kos: his song comes fresh off the mountain. Between Kos and Sicily, herdsmen's songs are apparently common property—not,

---

[30] For these epigrams by Mnasalkes see A. S. F. Gow and D. L. Page, eds., *Hellenistic Epigrams* (Cambridge, 1965), 140–44.

[31] See Bowie, "Seventh *Idyll*," 80–81.

[32] Sophron, Θυννοθήρας, *CGF* no. 162.

after all, an unlikely phenomenon. The explanation may well be that, as Bowie argues,[33] Lycidas and Tityros both come from Philetas.

The fourth idyll reveals a new world: it is a frank and salty conversation between two herdsmen. Aigon (also a herdsman) has gone off to Olympia as an athlete, taking twenty sheep. This is southern Italy, and he will have to stay in Greece at least a month in the hot season. His companion is the famous athlete Milon of Kroton (fl. mid–sixth century B.C.), so this idyll takes place in the remote past. Milon was once defeated in a test of strength by a cowman,[34] and the Alexandrians were interested in that legend;[35] so we are in either the sixth century or a vague and dateless golden age. Yet scholars identify Glauke (31) as a contemporary musician; if she is, she seems a deliberate intrusion. In this poem, "Amaryllis" is recently dead. Is she the same Amaryllis or another? Is she nothing more than a girl's name from a song? Or is this a deliberate attempt to create a web of relationships, between scarcely named characters, covering the whole Greek rural world of the Mediterranean? I suspect this Amaryllis of having one foot in the grave and the other in the sixth century B.C. Maybe Philetas buried her. Kroton had a disturbed, unhappy history: it is a queer place to choose for a golden age. I agree with Gow that the poem itself is early Theokritos;[36] it contains no great song. Battos is grazing Aigon's herd, but the father of Aigon oversees the milking; the herd are in bad condition, missing their master. Battos might steal milk if he could. The calves stray into somebody's olive grove, and Battos gets a thorn in the foot, which Korydon pulls out. This is certainly a timeless world.

> Tell me Korydon, is the old man still screwing
> That little girl he fancied, the dark-eyed one?
>
> The same as ever. It was only yesterday
> Down by the byre that I caught him on the job.
>
> You'll never rest old boy, till you beat the Satyrs
> And thin-shanked Pans at their own horny game.
>
> (58–63)

In the fifth idyll, we have the same capricious network of relationships, but in this idyll alone the goatherd and the shepherd are definitely slaves. A subversive question: in this poverty-stricken, sufficient world, where there are so many refinements of status, does slavery really seem to matter very much? It would matter to me; but does it matter to them, or

---

[33] Bowie, "Seventh *Idyll*," 68ff.
[34] Aelian *VH* 12.22.
[35] Alexander Aetol. frag. 11, *ap.* Powell, *Collectanea*, 128.
[36] Gow, *Theocritus* 1:xviii ff., 2:76.

does Theokritos think it does? He does, I think, make slavery an ironic background for ridiculous pretensions; but in these two last idylls I am not clear about how unhappy the herdsmen are. Komatas may well (in my view) be the heroic herdsman of Thourioi who was famous for his resurrection from a chest of honey.[37] Lakon (racial names for slaves are extremely common) knows Korydon from Idyll 4, and Sybaris is close to Kroton; indeed their rivalry was famous, so I imagine Idylls 4 and 5 are linked. Sybaris was famous for its luxuriousness and its obliteration. The tall stories about Aigon are surely very old.

Also, these two idylls both deal with pungently low life. It must be deliberate that they are both set long ago and far away, and yet that these conversations and songs could happen anywhere. The sense of a dreamlike confusion of time is as essential to Theokritos as the sharpness of the thorn in the foot and the lazy sweetness of the Italian grazing grounds. Even the small thefts in Idyll 5—the stolen milk, the goatskin, and the pipe—are in some way innocent; while the bets between the two slaves, a fattened lamb against a billy goat, are wholly innocuous. The erotic undertones are merely rustic and propose quite an innocent picture of life. Lakon used to be buggered by Komatas, but now he has fantasies of his own about the boy Kratidas, while Komatas has discovered girls. Lakon's girl is less credible, being introduced at the last moment, and he boasts about her only when he is sore: she is ἁ παῖς, only a figure in a competitive couplet (126–27) to answer a couplet by Komatas. The same may be said of Alkippe and Eumedes at the end of the contest (132–35). Morson, the woodman cutting heather nearby, judges that Komatas wins (138–40), and in the final few couplets of the contest Komatas without doubt has the upper hand—psychologically at least, and, I believe, even as a poet: "Moon clover and goatwort have my goats for pasture; on mastic they walk, they couch on arbutus." Lakon's reply is pretty but less thrilling: "Balm have my sheep to browse, and like roses in plenty flowers the cistus." Even in Robert Wells's beautiful version, Komatas is the more sharply sensuous of the two:

> *Komatas:* Vetch and clover are my goats' favourite browse,
> They walk on mastich and sleep among arbutus.
>
> *Lakon:* Where my sheep graze, rock-roses open around them.
> They feed on the starry balsam's favourite blossom.

The old unregenerate bugger goes his way rudely rejoicing; the old lover has beaten his beloved, the old singer his pupil; and the goatherd,

---

[37] Colin Macleod, *Collected Essays* (Oxford, 1983), 168–69, suggests that being buried alive is a metaphor (cf. Ovid *Ibis* 16 and La Penna *ad loc.*), the point being that Lycidas will be renewed as a poet. Cf. Gow, *Theocritus* 2:152, on Theocr. *Id.* 7.78.

because of the hardness and pungency of his song, has beaten the shepherd. It need scarcely be said that competitions like these are real. Antiphonal song on impromptu subjects, involving a conflict of wit and, to some degree, of poetry, has been recorded as late as the 1960s by A. L. Lloyd.[38] I have even heard it myself, as a conversation in the fields, and as a mocking comment on the slowness of our expedition, sung in Persian in the remote mountains of central Asia. That is the source of bucolic song, which Gow found so enigmatic. Living folksong enters into the heart of it.

Idyll 6 is another challenge and response, but the songs are longer: fourteen verses against twenty-one. Damoitas and Daphnis are both cowherds, both apparently Sicilians; they exchange gifts of a flute and a pipe, and the physical difference between them is very slight: "The face of one was blurred with down, the other had a beard coming." They grazed their herds together and together they sang; they kissed each other at the end, and one fluted and the other piped "while their calves frisked over the soft turf." These two are in stark contrast to the couples of Idylls 4 and 5. Galatea and Polyphemos are the theme: Daphnis sets it but Damoitas completes it. In Daphnis' song Galatea is a nymph taunting Polyphemos, whom Damoitas makes pathetic: she calls him "goatherd, clumsy lover." The love of Polyphemos and Galatea, unhappy as usual, is framed by the happy herdsmen, and they in turn are framed against the sad human poets, Theokritos and Aratos. Daphnis of course is an ancient, not a contemporary, character.

Only the famous seventh idyll is certainly meant to be contemporary. An inscription has even turned up on the island of Kos that seems to localize it, or rather to confirm its localization, not far from the spring of which Gow reproduces a photograph.[39] The characters in this idyll only seem to represent real poets, and the descriptions are the lushest and most inviting in all the works of Theokritos. The competing songs are based on a genuine bucolic tradition, no more remotely than those of Daphnis and Damoitas; but a certain unreality or surface shimmer divides this idyll from those I want to discuss more fully. It reads to us as a puzzle, and any hints it offers about real rustic life must be treated with caution.

All the same, Lycidas, the Kydonian[40] goatherd who looks the part, is of some interest, and so is the sensory sharpness of his conversation (7.11ff.):

---

[38] A. L. Lloyd, *Folk Music of Bulgaria* (London, 1964); *Folksong in England* (New York, 1967).

[39] Gow, *Theocritus*, vol. 2, pl. VIII B.

[40] Bowie, "Seventh *Idyll*," 90–91, identifies Kydonia as an island off Lesbos. But see Gow, *Theocritus* 2:135, on *Id.* 7.12.

A coarse-haired, shaggy goatskin, the colour of rust,
Smelling of milky rennet, hung from his shoulders.
Beneath lay a threadbare smock, done up with twine
About the waist, and he carried an olivewood crook
In his right hand.

(15–19)

All these conversations are in the hot season and mostly at midday. The contrast of heat and coolness, smooth and shaggy, movement and stillness, are essential to the poetry: "Now even the lizard lies asleep in its cranny, / And the tomb-haunting larks have gone to ground." The larks, I suppose, are ground-nesting birds among the shade of roadside tombs. Παίζει τάφοις, Babrius says (72.20). I find it impossible to believe in a crested lark called "tomb-crested" except as a joke in Aristophanes. In a recent *Festschrift*, Dr. Lezzi-Hafter offered a suggestion that would throw light on this idyll: that the bird on top of Demeter's sceptre is a lark.[41] I find the suggestion so attractive that I am bound to adopt it until and unless it should be disproved; though I notice also that the Athenians were led by a lark to Korone, where they worshipped Apollo Korydos.[42] I take the bird flying up behind Demeter's throne in the fifth-century Boeotian plate reproduced by Gow[43] to be a lark. The memorable festival at the end of the poem (128–57) is one that normal herdsmen never get to attend: it is the innermost sanctuary of Theokritean verse.

It is with some reluctance that I abandon the seventh idyll, because this is the last poem genuinely by Theokritos to touch on herdsmen and their songs. His fishermen share the same poverty, but the bucolic singing that makes him so famous is confined to four or five poems, unless you count Boukaïos the reaper in Idyll 10. Idylls 8 and 9, though probably not genuine, do cast a little further light on the pastoral world, in spite of their inferior verses. In the eighth idyll Menalkas does not dare to bet a lamb against a calf, because he works for his father—"stern my father is, and stern my mother, and at nightfall they count over all the flock" (15–16). A goatherd has a barking dog, just as Polyphemos had in Idyll 6 (10–11), and Menalkas has one called Lampouros (65). The destiny of most milk is as usual cheese making. Fresh milk, of course, would not keep, and we know from a fragment of Nikander[44] that on Samos and Doulichion βουγάϊος meant a milk drinker. People live in caves. Both these phony idylls are about Daphnis and Menalkas; at the end of the

[41] For "tomb-crested" larks see Gow, *Theocritus* 2:138, cf. 1:57; Aristoph. *Birds* 471–75; Lezzi-Hafter, "Demeter," 87–89.
[42] Paus. 4.34.8; cf. D'Arcy W. Thompson, *A Glossary of Greek Birds* (Oxford, 1936), 136–38.
[43] Gow, *Theocritus*, 2: pl. VIII B.
[44] Nicander frag. 131 Schneider.

first, Daphnis, ἄκραβος ἐών, *florens aetate*, marries the nymph Naïs, and in the second Menalkas addresses Αἴτνα, μᾶτερ ἐμᾶ... (15). The poet gives Menalkas a seashell from the rocks of Ikaria, near Kos, a conch that fed five people. Finally, Idyll 27 is not by Theokritos, and what light it casts is confusing. Daphnis, son of Lycidas, seduces a girl called Akrotime, daughter of Menalkas. He is a cowherd and she is (what I wish I knew more about) a shepherdess:

> Χἠ μὲν ἀνεγρομένη πάλιν ἔστιχε μᾶλα νομεύειν
> ὄμμασιν αἰδομένοις, κραδίη δέ οἱ ἔνδον ἰάνθη.

> She rose and went again to herd the sheep,   (69–70)
> Shamed in her eyes, but her heart within was glad.

The reapers in Idyll 10 are a gruff, perhaps elderly workman called Milon, given to coarse rustic proverbs, and a lovestruck young man, Boukaïos, whose name suggests a cowman and his song: in the *Iliad* Hector uses it as an insult to Ajax, as Antinoös does to Iros in the *Odyssey*.[45] Homer says βουγάϊος, not βουκάϊος, and the two citations confirm one another, but the difference of spelling is nothing. It is typical of the freakish pedantry of the Alexandrians to use a Homeric word in a corrected form. Bougaïos or Boukaïos has fallen for the girl from Hippokion's farm, the daughter of Polybotas, who must be a farm slave if not a wage laborer. She plays the flute for the reapers, and Milon's advice about her is "Take what you want and pay for it." Boukaïos sings a song about love:

> Bombyca, they call you a gipsy, sunburnt, thin.
> I call you slender child with the honey skin.

> (26–27)

The word "gipsy" stands here for the Greek *Syra*, a Syrian, which is a slave name and maybe a joke. Milon mockingly admires this song, which is indeed admirable and pathetic at the same time:

> Bombyca, knuckle-bone feet and voice like a flower—
> I am lost for words to show how lovely you are.

> (36–37)

Milon replies with what he calls the song of Lityerses; Lityerses was a form of John Barleycorn, and his only function here is to indicate a reaping song, which turns out to be a string of loosely related couplets, whereas Boukaïos's impromptu love song was more artistic, probably

---

[45] Hom. *Il.* 13.823; *Od.* 18.79.

because love songs were like that.[46] Like the *Works and Days* of Hesiod, Milon's song begins formally, but it soon tails off into proverbs and satiric verses. The encounter remains undecided.

Boukaïos would like a pair of Amyclaean sandals (35)[47]; at present we must think of him as barefooted, like Battos in the fourth idyll. The cattle graze, the world of these poems is unshod. Sex and poverty are the only troubles, but dreams overcome both, and song consoles for both. Sex in fact is sex without consequences. Priapos has presided over everything that happened since Idyll 1. Desire comes easily and in many forms; and so perhaps does the fulfillment of desire. "There is in empty kisses sweet delight" (*Id.* 27.4). Sometimes the world of Theokritos is like Plato's, as shameless and yet as virtuous; the opening of the seventh idyll recalls Plato's *Republic* in its carefully detailed setting and the meeting of friends. But Theokritos is not a philosopher, or at least his philosophy is in reserve, unspoken. His technique is a little Chekhovian; he likes resonance and echoes and counterechoes, and he hints at far more than he precisely reveals. (With Aischines and Thyonichos, for example, in Idyll 14, we discover only gradually where we are, after the poem has hooked us.) His great urban set pieces, Idylls 15 and 2, the *Festival of Adonis* and the *Pharmakeutria*, only gradually reveal themselves. The same is certainly true of his brief bucolic idylls. We read the characters, surmise a world (or an age of the world), and overhear an enchanted singing; and that is all. I assume it was meant to be all. We may well wish that some ancient professor, a lesser Aristotle or a Xenophon, had written us a treatise on the subject matter of Theokritos, but no one was interested enough to bring it to life except Theokritos himself. All we have really is the poetry; the learned *scholia* hardly amount to much.

The intrusion of love poetry of various kinds into the herdsmen's world calls for tactful observation, because when we are presented with poetry of a unique nature we are not always able to see what is being mixed with what. Mnasalkes of Sikyon makes it clear, in his seventh epigram,[48] that love is not a proper theme for herdsmen. His epigram is addressed to a syrinx, a pair of Pan-pipes, that he finds in a shrine of Aphrodite. The point is that he *does* find it there, and I assume that he may be thinking of Theokritos:

---

[46] The flute song included in Powell, *Collectanea*, 199, is not a bad analogy to the form of composition.

[47] References to Amyclaean sandals collected by Gow, *Theocritus* 2:202; cf. Suda s.v. Ἀμύκλαι. Elsewhere in Theocritus (*Id.* 12.13) *Amyklai* stands for Sparta, in a passage that seems to derive from a glossary of homosexual dialect words.

[48] Gow and Page, *Hellenistic Epigrams*.

Syrinx what are you doing here with the Foamborn?
Why did you stray here from a shepherd's lips?
Here are no cliffs or glens, but only loves
And longing. The wild Muse lives on the mountain.

I do not think it is too pedantic to suggest this poem is about wordless music, the kind of piping heard by lost travelers in the Alps, echoing from the rocks, according to Lucretius, and taken to be Pan (4.577–89). Pan plays a small part in Theokritos: he is a name to swear by, and Daphnis, dying, hails Pan as his master because of his piping. But Daphnis is dying of love, and as Mnasalkes says, wild music lives on the mountain. "O Pan, are you ranging the long hills of Lycaeus / Or the heights of Maenalus?" Daphnis asks (1.123–24), and bids him

Come, master, and take this pipe of mine, sweet-smelling,
Fastened with wax, the lip-piece delicately bound.
Love drags me into the darkness where no songs sound.

(1.128–30)

But the truth seems to be that the love theme was essential to bucolic song, if only because it was essential to the death story of Daphnis. This argument is, of course, based on a myth, and a late version of a myth; but love also occurs in the stray impromptu stanzas sung in competition, or simply strung together in the fields. Men and animals come together in the shade at fresh water in the heat of the day and of the year. Why is there no piping, though there may be singing, when Pan sleeps at midday? Because it is not only Pan who sleeps, and because the use of the pipes is to lead animals out in the morning and home in the evening. The Greeks used pipes as we use sheepdogs. In the heat of the day animals may stray, as Theokritos has them stray whenever the herdsman's eye has been off them, but normally they lie stinking in the shade of trees, like their human guardians. I have heard the *klarino* played at midday high up on Mount Pelion, but that was by an itinerant musician on his way to a festival. Other times, other customs.

The first idyll is an aberrant masterpiece: its mourning music, its theme of a love-death, and its refrain to the Muses, are adapted from various sources to a work of high art, just as the second idyll is adapted from magical language that we could never recognize by knowing only the second idyll. The love songs of the Amaryllis idyll (3) suggest a wider variety of loosely related themes, but although the situation is realistic and rustic enough, the poetry here sounds far more sophisticated than the real impromptu serenade would. The classical references to Hippomenes and Melampous and Adonis and Endymion are enchanting, but not truly rustic. They are part of international grand mythology;

they are in fact literary. (One would not expect, for example, to find them all together in a shepherd's speech in Aristophanes.) The fourth idyll is full of hints about real herdsmen, but not exactly herdsmen's song. The description of the grazing grounds which is gradually built up has an amazing casual-sounding grace; the sound is genuine but the trick is literary. The sound is the recognizable sound of Greek poetry, in its most refined form, sounding as clear through the dialect as William Barnes does in English (a kind of Tennyson by other means), and making cunning use of the most peculiar and knobbly words to produce that fresh and sighing effect only a poet as good as Theokritos can produce: a sound worth all the generations of effort that lie behind it. Our truest, or nearest to true, example of bucolic song is in Idyll 5, the contest between Lakon and Komatas, two slaves, one of them just touched with obscure mythological grandeur. I think that Virgil understood how this poetry worked, and learnt to reproduce it gleefully. That of course is another story.

> May I set
> The winnowing fan in another year's heaped grain
> While the laughing Goddess clutches her poppies and sheaves.
>
> (7.155–57)

RESPONSE: DAVID M. HALPERIN

For Pratt C. Remmel, Jr.

When I was writing my love poems, which sprouted out from me
on all sides, and I was dying of depression,
nomadic, abandoned, gnawing on the alphabet,
they said to me: "What a great man you are, Theocritus!"
I am not Theocritus: I took life,
and I faced her and kissed her,
and then went through the tunnels of the mines
to see how other men live.
And when I came out, my hands stained with garbage and sadness,
I held my hands up and showed them to the generals,
and said: "I am not a part of this crime."
They started to cough, showed disgust, left off saying hello,
gave up calling me Theocritus, and ended by insulting me
and assigning the entire police force to arrest me
because I didn't continue to be occupied exclusively with metaphysical
   subjects.

But I had brought joy over to my side.
From then on I started getting up to read the letters
the sea birds bring from so far away,
letters that arrive moist, messages I translate
phrase by phrase, slowly and confidently: I am punctilious
as an engineer in this strange duty.
All at once I go to the window. It is a square
of pure light, there is a clear horizon
of grasses and crags, and I go on working here
among the things I love: waves, rocks, wasps,
with an oceanic and drunken happiness.
But no one likes our being happy, and they cast you
in a genial role: "Now don't exaggerate, don't worry,"
and they wanted to lock me in a cricket cage, where there would be tears,
and I would drown, and they could deliver elegies over my grave.

This is not a personal confession, but Robert Bly's translation of "Carta a Miguel Otero Silva, en Caracas" (Letter to Miguel Otero Silva, in Caracas), a lengthy lyric poem composed in 1948 by Pablo Neruda.[1] I have chosen this poem because it articulates a notion of Theocritus that Professor Peter Levi and I can join in repudiating. Theocritus the elegist, the weepy love poet, the metaphysician, caged with crickets behind the bars of his own artistry and self-absorption (cf. *Id.* 1.45–54)—that is not the poet whom Professor Levi and I admire: Neruda's Theocritus, I think it is fair to say, is not our Theocritus. We do not suppose, to be sure, that Theocritus could easily pass Neruda's test of social engagement. Theocritus is not a revolutionary, a social reformer, or even a militant social critic. But he is not wholly immersed in the world of his own sentiments. I doubt that anyone could come away from hearing Professor Levi's paper without a just appreciation of Theocritus' skill as a social observer, his keen interest in the details of "how other men live," and his sympathetic engagement with the world around him.

    I begin by emphasizing the extent of my agreement with Professor Levi, because I shall have scant occasion to do so again. I hope none of my sweetly reasonable fellow discussants will take offense if I say that to agree with the speaker is a kind of professional betrayal in a scholarly commentator. Even worse, it is alien to the spirit of bucolic exchange, as Professor Levi has described it.

    Despite this shameful inability of mine to rise to the bucolic occasion, I can declare that my outlook on Theocritus really does differ from that

---

[1] Robert Bly, ed., *Neruda and Vallejo: Selected Poems*, trans. Robert Bly, John Knoepfle, and James Wright (Boston, 1971), 118–27; cf. Robert Bly's introduction, "Refusing to Be Theocritus," 3–15.

of Professor Levi; in what follows, I shall try to magnify our disagreement in the interests of scholarly controversy. In fact, I cannot help but suspect that Professor Peter Green, when he invited me to comment on Professor Levi's paper, must have been indulging his own well-known bent as a *provocateur*, a mischief maker. To engineer an exchange between Professor Levi and myself on the subject of Theocritus was surely to construct an exercise calculated to drive each of us deeper into his own established identity, putting on public display Professor Levi's marvelous and highly personal intuitions about ancient authors, his splendid eye for the significant detail, his incomparable knowledge of the Mediterranean and its inhabitants, and his dazzling hit-and-run tactics as a literary critic, all the while exposing more plainly to view my own hopelessly academic relation to the subject, my tedious concern with literary categories and schemes, and my cautious, perennially dreary interpretative style. I must now give up the struggle against Professor Green's typecasting and submit myself to the inevitable: against necessity, as Simonides said, even the gods do not fight.[2]

Professor Levi's Theocritus is a poet of nature, a Hellenistic Mandelshtam, tuning his verse to the rhythm and cadence of the seasons, capturing in language the sonorities of the classical landscape. My Theocritus is, characteristically enough, "the first academic poet," as his most recent American translator, Daryl Hine, has called him[3]—or perhaps I should say, the first *great* academic poet: a writer whose artful language, lavished on uncouth subjects, creates an effect of deliberate incongruity which is designed to forestall any reader's attempt to wallow complacently in Theocritus' sensuous images.[4] Rather than dilate further upon *my* Theocritus, however, I wish to examine more closely that alien creature, Professor Levi's Theocritus, in order to determine what it is about him, exactly, that seems so unfamiliar to me.

Professor Levi's Theocritus is at once a romantic and a realist, whose poetry combines "sensuous concentration" with keen observation of social realities. The *Idylls* invite us to while away "endless summer evenings . . . in beautiful places" even as they present to us a window on the life of rural Greece in the Hellenistic period. These two tendencies in Professor Levi's Theocritus—the evocative and the documentary—are not in principle contradictory ones, but I often find them difficult to harmonize in

---

[2] Simonides, frag. 37.29–30 = *PMG* Page, no. 542 (p. 282).

[3] Daryl Hine, trans., *Theocritus: Idylls and Epigrams, with an Epilogue "To Theocritus"* (New York, 1982), ix. I have reviewed Hine's translation in *The Yale Review* 74 (1984–85): 587–96.

[4] See David M. Halperin, *Before Pastoral: Theocritus and the Ancient Tradition of Bucolic Poetry* (New Haven and London, 1983), esp. 219–37.

Professor Levi's handling of them. I can never tell in advance which details in Theocritus Professor Levi will take to be simple reflections of contemporary reality and which he will derive from the inherited traditions of Greek poetry, history, and myth; nor have I fathomed the logic that governs his choices in specific instances. And yet it makes some difference to our reading of Idyll 1, for example, whether we consider the fictive "internationalism" of Theocritus' pastoral world (to which Professor Levi rightly calls our attention) purely facetious, a pretty fantasy of performing herdsmen who manage to acquire within the confines of their little society an international prestige, or whether there really was "a shepherd's Olympics," as Professor Levi calls it, a periodic pan-Hellenic festival for talented rustics. The latter possibility, I think, would have struck a sophisticated Alexandrian audience as hardly less comical than the annual convention of village idiots in Woody Allen's Russian idyll, *Love and Death*, which is perhaps closer in spirit to Theocritus on this point than is Professor Levi's reconstruction. In any case, what I have difficulty understanding about Professor Levi's interpretation is why he believes in Chromis the Libyan in Idyll 1 (even though Virgil treats Chromis as a standard pastoral persona in Eclogue 6) but in neither Olpis the fisherman nor Amaryllis in Idyll 3, preferring to relegate them to a lost mime of Sophron's and to a lost work of Philetas', respectively. (Philetas seems to have become, since E. L. Bowie's recent essay,[5] an all-purpose dumping ground, a popular interpretative resort for scholars who wish to dispose of anything in Theocritus for which they have little explanatory use.) Professor Levi's Theocritus, it seems, can be counted on to be a reliable witness to the Hellenistic world whenever documentation is needed, and to be a sensuous and allusive scene painter when it is not.

   Similarly, Professor Levi concedes that Theocritus is quite vague about the chronological settings of the idylls: "The sense of a dreamlike confusion of time is as essential to Theokritos as the sharpness of the thorn in the foot and the lazy sweetness of the Italian grazing grounds," he remarks, apropos of Idyll 4, concluding, "This is certainly a timeless world." But when we come to geography, Professor Levi delivers a different verdict: "Theokritos' world is the real world," he says, and he opposes A. S. F. Gow's view that Theocritus' use of geographical names is arbitrary and inconsistent. Far from being casual in his treatment of geographical detail, Professor Levi's Theocritus sets many of the bucolic Idylls in some quite specific locale—though it is difficult, evidently, to say exactly where. Professor Levi places Idyll 1 on Cos, but not very confidently; he admits that a Sicilian location for the poem is possible.

---

[5] E. L. Bowie, "Theocritus' Seventh *Idyll*, Philetas and Longus," *CQ* n.s. 35 (1985): 67–91.

Although I agree that in this case Cos is the likelier setting, I find it significant that Professor Levi, an established authority on Pausanias and an expert on the geography of the Mediterranean, is still unable to determine the poem's dramatic setting to his complete satisfaction. Theocritus can surely have had few readers so well informed as Professor Levi; if even he cannot definitively establish the setting of Idyll 1, who can? I am forced to conclude that Theocritus attaches a different sort of value to the place-names he sprinkles throughout his poems, that he chooses them for their literary associations, or their euphony, or their arcane preciosity: the Kalydnian ferryman is surely meant to demonstrate the skill with which Theocritus could lift a relevant detail from the Homeric catalogue—at least as much as he is meant to situate the first idyll on Cos. The epithet "Kalydnian" would indeed seem, though not decisively,[6] to place Idyll 1 on Cos; but that is not the point.

Professor Levi's positivism becomes more intrusive when he moves from geography to social forms. Speaking of Idyll 10, for example, he notes that Boukaïos' love song is "more artistic [than Milon's reaping song], probably because love songs were like that." Similarly, in the course of discussing the ivy cup in Idyll 1, Professor Levi enumerates a number of possible surviving artistic models and wonders whether Theocritus intended the cup to represent a contemporary work or an antique. I believe that Professor Levi has been taken in by Theocritus' ability to produce what critics nowadays call "an effect of the real": the ivy cup is modeled, surely, not on any of the artifacts Professor Levi mentions, but on the Shield of Achilles in the *Iliad* and on the Shield of Heracles in a poem which Theocritus' contemporaries, such as Apollonius, ascribed to the authorship of Hesiod.[7] Theocritus secures the epic descent of his ivy cup by reweaving in his own hexameters the verbal texture of those earlier poems. The vineyard scene on the goatherd's cup, which apparently frustrates Professor Levi's search for a model among the plastic arts, is actually an amalgam of the Homeric and the pseudo-Hesiodic sources, as he is well aware. I therefore stand by my previous interpretation of the cup as a complex literary symbol designed to advertise to the learned reader Theocritus' characteristic *modus operandi*—namely his elaboration, in a humble material, of insignificant but poignant and hitherto neglected details from the great archaic epics.[8]

Professor Levi's positivism crops up again when he treats the exchange

---

[6] A. S. F. Gow, *Theocritus*, 2d ed. (Cambridge, 1952) 1:xx, 2:14–15.

[7] See Rudolf Pfeiffer, *History of Classical Scholarship*, vol. 1, *From the Beginnings to the End of the Hellenistic Age* (Oxford, 1968), 144, for Apollonius' theory about the authorship of this poem.

[8] Halperin, *Before Pastoral*, 167–81.

of insults between the two herdsmen in Idyll 5. Taking those herdsmen at their word, Professor Levi assumes that, as he puts it, "Lakon used to be buggered by Komatas." That inference is particularly puzzling to me, because Professor Levi clearly understands the convention governing the exchange of abuse between herdsmen—"antiphonal song on impromptu subjects involving a conflict of wit and to some degree of poetry" is how he describes it—and he can claim to have heard it himself. I, of course, cannot make the same claim, sticking close to my desk as I do while Professor Levi is off exploring the wilds of Afghanistan, but—like the good academic I am—I can claim at least to have *read* about these rustic contests, specifically in the oral histories from Sicily collected by Gavin Maxwell in the 1950s and published by him in a marvelous book entitled *The Ten Pains of Death*. In chapter 3 of that book, Maxwell interviews a shepherd boy who describes the song-form known as *botta e riposta*, alternating couplets of challenge and reply, thrust and counterthrust, which are sung by adjacent herdsmen at night. These herdsmen can hear but not see, let alone bugger, one another: they are too far separated, pasturing their animals in different locations. Maxwell's informant, speaking of the sexual abuse that is an integral part of these exchanges, explains, "We don't take offense at what we sing to each other—if we did we wouldn't sing them, or else we'd go and beat each other up."[9] Here, then, is another point at which Professor Levi's documentary approach to Theocritus' realism leads him astray.

When T. S. Eliot writes, "Under the brown fog of a winter dawn, / A crowd flowed over London Bridge, so many, / I had not thought death had undone so many" (*The Waste Land*, 61–63), he is not simply describing London but is alluding, as he helpfully informs us in his Notes, to Dante. We should not draw firm conclusions from his verses about the size of the crowd that traveled across London Bridge during the winter of 1921, although I do not doubt that it was indeed sizable. My Theocritus is closer to Eliot than is Professor Levi's Theocritus; I like him that way. But if the real Theocritus could hear us wrangling over him, in our lamentably unbucolic fashion, I shouldn't be surprised if he remarked, in the words Neruda used to fend off the ambiguous compliments of his own overenthusiastic interpreters, "Yo no soy Teócrito" (I am not Theocritus).

DISCUSSION

K. Galinsky (University of Texas at Austin): Professor Halperin said there is the "effect of the real," what Gow called verisimilitude, in Theo-

---

[9] Gavin Maxwell, *The Ten Pains of Death* (New York, 1960), 50.

critus' poetry. The real question, I think, is to what point can you push the positivism of geographic and other realities, and at what point do you start with this sort of fuzzy evocational interpretation? What are the boundaries here?

P. Levi: I think it's Gow who's vague about geography, not Theocritus, and certainly not his audience, all of whom knew infinitely more about the Mediterranean than any of us ever can, because, for one thing, we don't live there. But I think that while Theocritus is a poet of very precise sense impressions—the thorn in the foot isn't a bad example—and also very precise about things, quite precise about relationships, the whole of his poetry adds up with all his positivism to a slightly cloudy general picture, as Virgil's does too, I suppose. I don't know if you'll agree with me about Virgil—the world of Virgil's *Eclogues* is one that one can't understand and isn't perhaps meant to understand as a world. And yet line by line it's all so precise.

D. M. Halperin: I agree that that kind of precision of detail is one of the characteristics of Theocritus' poetry, and I'm not trying to deprive would-be historians of a historical source in Theocritus. If we had further information about these details we would be justified in saying that Theocritus used them precisely. But it's hard to judge that in the absence of corroborating evidence, and I would never be happy simply to take Theocritus' word at face value. The inescapable question for the interpreter is: What is the literary valence, the function and meaning, of supposed *realia* in Theocritus' poems themselves? The answer will determine how one reads Theocritus; it never would have occurred to me to read him for documentary information.

S. Burstein: Clearly, the geography of Theocritus' poems should not be pressed too closely. I was, however, particularly intrigued by the suggestion that the antiphonal singing competitions, which the textbooks single out as an example of the artificiality of pastoral poetry, may actually be anchored in the reality of rural life. Would it, therefore, be correct to say that Theocritus gained his effects by exploiting his audience's experience of two different realities: the literary tradition of which they could recognize echoes in his poetry, and the world around them?

D. M. Halperin: I think so. I wouldn't want to suggest that Theocritus composed in some other universe, that his poetry falls to earth like a meteor. We can be pretty confident about the historical reality of antiphonal song in the pastures of ancient Greece, but only because we know about it from other sources. But to me, as I read Theocritus, the reality it makes available to us is the reality of the history of reading in the Hellenistic world, especially in the early Hellenistic world. *That* Theocritus conveys extremely vividly, the sense of a new light that's being shone on all sorts of details of the previous literary tradition, and even on its textual variants.

A. E. Samuel: I'm intrigued by the assumption that the ancient Greeks knew the Mediterranean world thoroughly, much more than we do. I teach in Toronto, which is two and a half hours from Dallas and an hour from my birthplace in New York, and this week I've been asked twice whether I have to teach in French; and this is an environment where people are quite alert to what's going on in the world.

P. Levi: I assume that Theocritus was read, firstly, by a circle of poets and literary people, based upon that curious museum in Alexandria, and that there must also have been some learned men in the court. And those people knew the way from Cos to Sicily as well as the back of their hands.

J. Scarborough: I have a question on the realities of plants, flowers, agriculture: Are we or are we not dealing with particular places that grow particular flowers? We discuss altitude, climate, and islands that have flowers which other islands do not. To me the mastic is real. It's not symbolic.

P. Levi: Well, the mastic, I agree, is real. But I'm worried about that cactus that is supposed to tie the poem down somewhere where it may not be meant to be tied down. Although we know there are different kinds of plants in different kinds of places, we don't know what there could have been on one or another Mediterranean island, unless we're told that something grows only in one place. I'm sure that Theocritus meant to be accurate about such things, but I don't myself possess the knowledge by which I could test his accuracy. He knew illustrated manuscripts, and they must have annotated where things were to be found.

D. M. Halperin: I would agree that the plants are real. But I also think that some plants are more real than others. I think that the ivy winding around the top of the ivy cup in Idyll 1 goes back to Homer and tragedy, and to wooden vessels said either to be used by rustics or made of ivy. I think Theocritus is elaborating various notions having to do with cups in the previous literary tradition.

J. Scarborough: The audience would know Homer very well all the way from childhood. But they also would know the plants. I think we can assume that the botany would be ordinary stuff. If he got it wrong people would say, Hey, you got it wrong.

D. M. Halperin: Well, what do you make of the passages in tragedy where people are given bowls made of ivy wood? It seems hard to imagine how a large bowl could be made of ivy wood.

J. Scarborough: It could be made of more than one piece.

P. Levi: I want it to be more like my wife's grandfather's old Irish black-thorn stick, which I possess; it's a great cudgel, and it still has the ivy that was around the branch twining around the stick. So that if somebody carved, say, a cup out of oak, it is conceivable that he was proud to have left the ivy around the outside of the cup he was carving. That's my hypothesis. As for Euripides, he is as foolish about the ivy bowl as he is about geography.

S. M. Burstein: Our two speakers have presented two dramatically different assessments of the reality of the supposed rural background of Theocritus' pastoral poems. I would like to know how each of them views Idyll 15. Certainly, Theocritus would seem to have tried to create the illusion of a specific location in space and time for that poem.

D. M. Halperin: My initial response is that there was some fascination on the part of propertied Alexandrians with the lives of "little people" of all sorts, not just herdsmen and other country folk. Think of all those portraits of slaves and low-life characters on mosaics and terracottas, for example.

P. Levi: Since in the poem some of the women are said to be Syracusan by blood, they can't be in that sense of the word low-life. And if you want something to illustrate this, there are, or used to be, a lot of funeral monuments in the museum in Alexandria—personally I've never seen them anywhere else—with the most hideous bourgeoises with their hair all round them all painted in vivid color, all made of terracotta. That's the analogy, rather than those very beautiful Negro heads that you get.

D. M. Halperin: Both the low life of Idylls 2 and 15 and the country life of the pastoral idylls create very much the same effect poetically for Theocritus. They provide for him a world distant from that of his own society, one in which strong emotions can be represented directly. This ironic or comic distance makes possible, paradoxically, a portrayal of passion free from irony.

K. Galinsky: Professor Levi, you said that Virgil got everything wrong about Theocritus except his poetry. Knowing ancient *imitatio*, I think that's not a bad record. But what is it exactly that you feel he got wrong? Is it the geography, or the insects, or what?

P. Levi: I don't feel that he knew or cared about what degree of reality might underlie Theocritus. In fact *we* don't know. David Halperin and I learned only the other day that the rennet that is used in Theocritus, which a man stinks of from cheese making in Idyll 7, is seal rennet. I suppose this must explain why the seals are said to stink so badly in the *Odyssey*. After all, why does he think seals smell that bad? Presumably because they're associated with rennet and cheese making. That's the kind of point Virgil didn't understand. I don't think he would know that rennet meant seal rennet.

K. Galinsky: So? (Laughter.) I'm being facetious, but this gets us back to the basic question, the level of reality in Theocritus. So if Virgil didn't pick that up, if he didn't know about the seals, what else did he miss?

P. Levi: To exaggerate the contrast I would say that Virgil's *Eclogues* read like a Mozartian opera, where Theocritus reads more like some drama of the age of Shakespeare.

K. D. White: A clarification about Idyll 15: Is Professor Halperin really telling us that there's a lack of reality in this poem? Are we not on the streets of Alexandria at all, but rather in some imaginary place? What is your picture of Idyll 15?

D. M. Halperin: I think we would know better exactly where we were in Idyll 15 if we could check Theocritus' poem against more reliable historical sources. In the meantime, we can only speculate—not very securely. At any rate, what is interesting about Theocritus is not the points of correspondence between the real world and the poetry—I concede to you that there may well be many such correspondences (although we may never discover what they are)—but something else. I can't imagine why anyone would read Theocritus for such correspondences unless he or she had some extraliterary motive for doing so, such as being a historian of the Hellenistic period.

P. Green: I think Idyll 2 is the perfect meeting ground for these two approaches. I'm interested in magic. We have in this poem formulas known from the Greek magical papyri—all genuine. And yet at the same time the magic becomes a metaphor and a symbol. It is the magic of literature, the magic of love. In the same way Ovid, for example, picks up this metaphor later in great detail. You have there, it seems to me, a congruence between the kind of social observation that Professor Levi posits, which in fact is very close and very accurate, and the kind of literary craftsmanship that Professor Halperin is after. Theocritus seems to blend them there.

D. M. Halperin: Yes, but to draw a neat distinction between accurate social observation, on the one hand, and literary extrapolation or exploitation, on the other, is to run the risk of distilling spurious, preliterary "facts" from the poetry of Theocritus. Even a good historian may be misled by such a practice. To conclude, for example, from the similarity of magical formulas in Idyll 2 and in the Greek magical papyri that Theocritus' representation of magic in Idyll 2 is "basically" accurate, however idiosyncratic his *poetic* treatment of the scene may be, would not only be incautious—it would be to miss part of what Theocritus was up to, *and* it would be to mischaracterize the general practice of ancient magic. For, according to a paper on the magical papyri by Jack Winkler, in his new book *Constraints of Desire*, the vast majority of erotic magical spells surviving in the Greek magical papyri are designed to be used by men against women, not by women against men. The picture we get in Theocritus and Virgil, then, seems to be quite untypical with respect to one very material point, and it would be unwise to lump the represented magic in their poetry in the category of "reality" pure and simple, on the basis of lexical correspondences with the papyri, without allowing for the possibility that our poets may have injected a good deal of imagination even into their portrayal of "facts," of social and erotic practices.

P. Green: Winkler's point is of course largely true—though there are gender-neutral or gender-alternative spells—and of considerable social significance. But it doesn't really affect the point I was making, which was to do rather with the techniques and *materia magica* employed (where there *is* great similarity between the papyri and our literary sources) rather than with the operators, whether male or female.

P. Levi: Suppose that most women were illiterate. Then women's magic would be carried on woman to woman and would be traditional, whereas men's magic would be scribbled down in a mannish and pedantic way.

Hellenistic Ethics and Philosophical Power

A. A. Long

The legacy of the Hellenistic philosophers is unique in one respect. Since the sixteenth and seventeenth centuries, the English language has appropriated the words *stoic(al)*, *skeptic(al)*, *epicure(an)*, and *cynic(al)* as ways of describing character, attitudes, and behavior. These terms have lost some of their Greco-Roman connotations, but they continue to preserve a significant link with their origins. If we call someone today a stoic or an epicurean, we are making a comment on an ethical outlook; we are calling attention to highly general characteristics which imply certain basic attitudes to life and exclude others. The terms presuppose consistency on the part of the person they are applied to. We don't expect someone who is stoical on Monday to be cynical or epicurean on Tuesday. As terms denoting persistent dispositions, these words are similar to *introverted/extroverted, intense/laid-back*, and so forth.

The three greatest Greek philosophers, Socrates (portrayed in figure 30), Plato, and Aristotle, have left no such legacy. We speak of Platonic love and Socratic irony, but we have not turned *Socratic* and *Platonic* into terms denoting an ethical type. Professional philosophers might call one of their number an "Aristotelian," but it would not be clear, without explanation, what this meant. The peculiarity of the Hellenistic philosophers in this respect appears to be quite general. It is not informative to describe a nonphilosopher as a Cartesian or a Kantian or a Hegelian. To understand the special significance of Hellenistic ethics, we should try to probe this peculiarity. Here I want to approach it as a question concerning the intellectual history of Hellenistic philosophy in its formative years. A comprehensive answer would have to include subsequent devel-

30. Socrates. British Museum, London. From G. M. A. Richter, *Portraits of the Greeks* (London: Phaidon Press, 1965), vol. III, fig. 561.

opments of the Hellenistic schools, their reception at Rome, and their entry into the Renaissance. My focus will be restricted to asking what it was about the ethical projects of the innovative Hellenistic philosophers that prepared the way for this curious legacy. Why did their philosophy, and in particular their ethics, lend itself to description as a *hairesis*, a "choice" or "policy" or "persuasion"?[1] What can we learn about ethics

---

[1] For an exhaustive study of the history and application of the term *hairesis*, cf. J. Glucker, *Antiochus and the Late Academy* (Göttingen, 1978), 159–92.

and its history, and about the cultural politics of Hellenistic Athens, by reflecting on the mutual exclusivity and determinacy of early Stoicism, Epicureanism, and Pyrrhonian Skepticism—I mean the notion that an ethical praxis requires commitment to a view of life so sharply defined that it identifies you as an adherent of just one school? What can we learn about the same matters by drawing attention to paradigms, concepts, and approaches that exhibit striking similarities between the different schools?

It is commonly said that Hellenistic philosophy derived much of its special character from social and political crisis.[2] Individuals, unsettled by turbulent change, are thought to have found the traditional institutions and values of the *polis* an inadequate context for defining their lives. It is not clear, however, that this is either true or explanatory. The primary impediments to happiness, according to Epicurus, are fear of divine control of the world and fear of death (e.g., *Kyriai Doxai* 11–12). Conditions of life at Hellenistic Athens seem no more appropriate to that diagnosis than those of the age of Pericles. Many Hellenistic philosophers, it is true, propose ways of life that discount or eliminate or reorient conventional objects of fear and desire. But that, so far from being new, had been the dominant thrust of philosophical ethics since Socrates. We are inclined to overlook this point because the huge presence of Aristotle intervenes between Socrates and early Hellenistic philosophy.

Aristotle's work in ethics and politics is an extraordinary analytical achievement, but in an important respect it is untypical. Its great strength lies in Aristotle's clarification and ordering of formal concepts—such as virtue, choice, pleasure—and in his balanced accommodation of a range of heterogeneous values. In much of its detailed content, however, it is highly conservative; and that is a central feature of Aristotle's methodology. He is concerned to give proper consideration to values and practices that were highly prized in Greek culture. He does not question the foundations of "gentlemanly" conduct, as prescribed by tradition, and he does not challenge basic political institutions or the status of women and slaves. He never suggests that it could be reasonable to establish one's life on a unitary conception of the good, or to look to the nature of things in general as a foundation for ultimate values. His ethical outlook is pluralist, in the sense that it acknowledges competing claims on a person's attention. But it does not treat the question, "What should I do?" as one which could invite a set of radically discrepant answers by enlightened people.

In this respect, Aristotle's ethical outlook is strikingly different from

---

[2] See, for instance, E. Bevan, *Stoics and Sceptics* (Oxford, 1913), 32. I have questioned the usefulness of such claims in *Hellenistic Philosophy*, 2d ed. (Berkeley and Los Angeles, 1986), 2–4.

that of Socrates and Plato. That point can stand, I trust, without detailed justification. But we also need to distinguish Socrates from Plato, in order to focus our inquiry into the special character of Hellenistic ethics. Plato was Socrates' profoundest interpreter and transmitter; but it is Socrates, rather than Plato, who most clearly anticipates the tenor of Hellenistic ethics. It was Socrates who gave currency to the notion of a "wise man," whose life is an extraordinary challenge to conventional views on human needs and priorities and yet a paradigm of excellence and happiness. Socrates founded no school, and he was too idiosyncratic and complex to be fully appropriated by any of his immediate followers. But the challenge of Socrates persisted, transmitted to the Hellenistic world through different intermediaries—Antisthenes and Diogenes (the Cynic Socrates), Aristippus (the Cyrenaic and hedonist Socrates), the Socrates of Plato and Xenophon, and eventually, in the Academy, the skeptical Socrates.[3]

What is Socratic about Hellenistic ethics? Not, or not necessarily, a doctrinal inheritance—central though that is in the case of Stoicism—but a particular view of what ethics should be about: the questioning of convention, the removal of fears and desires that lack any rational foundation, a radical ordering of priorities around the notion of the soul's health—or, to borrow a fine expression from Foucault, cultivating "a technology of the self."[4]

I will explain this notion in more detail shortly, but a more general point needs to be made first. The new Hellenistic schools seem, at our distance in time, extraordinarily one-sided in their ethical orientations. The Stoics insist that pleasurable and painful sensations make no difference to genuine happiness. The Epicureans claim that virtue, though a necessary instrument of happiness, must be subordinate to pleasure, which is the sole thing that is good in itself. The Pyrrhonists center happiness exclusively in skepticism. Ordinary intuitions lead one to think that the most satisfactory life should be based on a balanced range of goods and attitudes—an Aristotelian specification—rather than such one-sided options.

But if we are genuinely searching for a plan of life that will secure long-term happiness and excellence, it seems unduly limited to presume that an ethical philosopher should be thoroughly accommodating to ordinary intuitions, since some of these are presumably problematic in various ways. That was certainly not the Socratic impulse. Suppose, instead, that a philosopher finds such confusion and inconsistency and source of

[3] I have explored a number of aspects of this large topic in "Socrates in Hellenistic Philosophy," *CQ* n.s. 38 (1988): 150–71.
[4] Cf. *Technologies of the Self: A Seminar with Michel Foucault*, ed. L. H. Martin, H. Gutman, and H. Hutton (University of Massachussetts Press, 1988), 16–49.

disquiet in many current ideas about the good life that he sees his task as one of reconstituting the self on new foundations. The test of an ethical project of this kind will not be its descriptive and analytical effectiveness in handling the whole range of cultural data, but how well it works as an "art of life." Perhaps ethics is unavoidably one-sided, and we just have to decide whether the Epicurean or the Stoic way is the one for us. It is certainly striking that the innovative Hellenistic philosophers did not plump for some comfortable middle ground, and we should infer from this that their mutual exclusiveness was part of their appeal.

In addition, we need to think of ethics in the early Hellenistic period as a hot subject. The boldness of the various options recalls the earliest days of Greek philosophy when each thinker patented his own cosmological thesis. At that time the exciting thought had dawned that new truths about nature were waiting to be discovered. Hellenistic philosophers show a similar confidence in their ethical inquiries. Their project is to make individual happiness an accessible objective, something whose foundations can be fully ascertained and shown to depend on two conditions—correct understanding of the world and excellence of character. One ethical option helped to generate another through interschool controversy and contact. Early Stoicism derived much of its impetus from opposition to Epicureanism, and the schools in general propagated specific versions of their own "wise men." Some options, like early Pyrrhonism, faded out, or were assimilated into another philosophy, as happened with the absorption of the Cyrenaics into Epicureanism. But at the period with which I am concerned, the early years of the third century, the range and variety of the options reached its maximum. Even a totally forgotten figure can show the significance of this cultural phenomenon. The Cyrenaic Hegesias adopted as his version of the *telos*, "living without bodily or mental pain" (Diog. Laert. 2.95). He drew an inference concerning the efficacy of death in removing us from bad things as distinct from good ones, and so many of his audience committed suicide that Ptolemy Philadelphus prohibited him from lecturing (Cic. *Tusc.* 1.83).

Comic poets mocked the philosophers' failure to agree on specifications of "the good" (cf. Philemon, frag. 71 Kock), but there is remarkable consensus among the philosophers about the type of character that their ethics seeks to produce. Epicurus is said to have recommended Pyrrho's character but his own doctrines (Diog. Laert. 9.64). I propose that we see this character type as a new kind of hero, a living embodiment of philosophical power, a figure whose appeal to the Hellenistic world consisted in self-mastery.

The Socratic Legacy of Self-mastery
Our religious and ethical traditions have so familiarized us with the notion of self-control that it seems hard to imagine a society which had such

a notion in only a tenuous form. Yet I believe this was the case with Greece prior to Socrates. It goes without saying, of course, that Greeks from Homer to Aeschylus could express and practice self-restraint, refrain from acting on first impulse, deliberately undergo extraordinary privations, and develop paradigms of single-minded endurance, such as Odysseus and Heracles. I acknowledge that they had terms such as *sophrosyne* and *aidos*, which it might sometimes be proper to translate by "self-control." But self-control, as I am using that expression, is something different. What I have in mind is a pre-Freudian notion of a self that is completely transparent to reflection, and over which its owner claims such complete authority that he finds himself in total charge of where his life is going and indulges his emotions and appetites only to the extent that he himself determines.

A self with this degree of authoritativeness, transparency, and concentration is largely alien, I think, to Greek experience and conceptualization before Socrates.[5] Authority was always diffuse and divisive in traditional Greek culture, whether we refer to religion, politics, or individual scales of value; and I need hardly illustrate the rarity of self-control in my sense from the situations and persons of classical Greek history and literature. The development of the Greek term that eventually captures it best, *enkrateia*, is remarkably suggestive. This word does not occur before Plato and Xenophon. The corresponding adjective is found earlier, but solely in reference to physical or political power over something, and not as an attribute of a person's character. Callicles in the *Gorgias* (491d 9) says he does not understand Socrates when he talks of "ruling oneself." Socrates, almost certainly with irony, says he means nothing complicated but, as the many say, *sophrona* and *enkrate heautou*, "ruling the pleasures and passions within himself."[6]

In this passage it is the unfamiliar expression, *enkrate heautou*, which

---

[5] Support for this claim can be drawn from the careful work of Helen North in her book *Sophrosyne, Self-knowledge and Self-restraint in Greek Literature* (Ithaca, N. Y., 1966). North (69) finds mastery of passion the "new emphasis in Euripides' interpretation of" *sophrosyne*; and she also writes (70): "Certain Sophists appear to have been among the first to develop systematically the concept of *sophrosyne* as the control of man's lower impulses and appetites." This seems to me to be correct provided that we include Socrates among "certain Sophists."

[6] I go a step further than T. Irwin who, in a note on *Gorgias* 491d 4 in his translation for the Clarendon Plato series (Oxford, 1979), says that "though Socrates suggests that the many recognize the possibility of self-control, it is actually quite hard to find evidence of this view in pre-Platonic Greek." Irwin's best example is Antiphon, D-K 87 B58 (also cited by Dodds in his commentary on the *Gorgias*), where *sophrosyne* is characterized as follows: ὅστις τοῦ θυμοῦ ταῖς παραχρῆμα ἡδοναῖς ἐμφράσσει αὐτὸς ἑαυτὸν κρατεῖν τε καὶ νικᾶν ἠδυνήθη αὐτὸς ἑαυτόν. For all we know, Antiphon here may reflect the influence of Socrates' oral discourse.

is used to gloss the hackneyed term *sophrona*, so that the latter can denote a disposition of the self in terms of ruler (reason) and ruled (pleasures and passions).[7] It was the life and philosophy of Socrates, I suggest, that primarily prompted this use of *enkrates* and gave a purchase for the new noun *enkrateia*. As characterised by Xenophon, Socrates was "the most *enkrates* of all men over sex and bodily appetite, most hardy (*karteros*) in relation to winter and summer and all exertions, and so trained for needing moderate amounts that he was easily satisfied when he had only little" (*Mem.* 1.2.1).[8] I will return to this focus on frugality. Further evidence for the novelty of the concept of self-control is the rarity of Plato's use of *enkrates* without the addition of the reflexive pronoun. In other words, he feels the need to spell out the "self" that is controlled (e.g., *Rep.* 3.390b). An exception to this, but a highly revealing one, is his description of "the man within,"—that is, the soul's rational part—as *enkrates-tatos* (*Rep.* 9.589b 1). In context, however, it is clear that this refers to the sovereignty of reason over spirit and appetite, the two lower parts of the soul. By the time of Aristotle and the early Hellenistic philosophers the psychological and ethical sense of *enkrates* and *enkrateia* is so well established that the reflexive pronoun can be elided. The words on their own connote self-mastery. What began as an artificial use of language has been naturalized by familiarity with its reference—a new view of persons as quasi-political entities. The concepts of authority, power, ruler and subject, stable government and insurrection have become ways of analyzing the self.

   The fertility of these notions in Plato's philosophy is so well known that we tend to think of them as his special outlook. Plato, however, is part of a creative process that began with Socrates and, as I will show, continued to develop in early Hellenistic philosophy. The seminal contribution of Socrates is evident not only from his decisive influence on Plato and Xenophon, but also from dominant characteristics of the other Socratic schools. Self-mastery is the keynote of the philosophies of Antisthenes, Diogenes, and even the hedonist Aristippus, whose most famous

---

[7] Note the very similar passage, *Rep.* 4.430e, also an elucidation of *sophrosyne*. Here, in support of analyzing *sophrosyne* as κόσμος τις and ἡδονῶν τινων καὶ ἐπιθυμιῶν ἐγκράτεια (cf. also *Symp.* 196c), Socrates invokes the expression κρείττω αὑτοῦ as one that is in popular use, and then pokes fun at it. The fun involves the difficulty of supposing that one and the same person can be both master and subject of himself. Plato surely makes so much of this point precisely because self-mastery was not a notion whose implications for the structure of the self were familiar in everyday discourse.

[8] North, *Sophrosyne*, 118ff., notes the importance of *enkrateia* for Xenophon's portrait of Socrates. At *Mem.* 1.5.4 Socrates proposes that it should be regarded as the foundation of *arete*.

dictum was that he "had" Lais but was not "had by" her.[9] It is less obtru-
sive in Aristotle, for reasons already mentioned. (And he has a technical
distinction between *enkrateia* and *sophrosyne* which seems pecular to himself, *Arist. EN* 7.1151b 32). Aristotle finds existing political systems and
conventional values sufficiently authoritative to provide the main param-
eters of an educated moral sensibility. His evenhandedness is one of the
reasons why his ethics has worn so well, but it is not the kind of thing to
excite the radical young.

That excitement, it is obvious, was what Socrates generated in Alcibiades and his other companions. Socrates could join in a symposium and
be sober as a judge when everyone else was falling around. He could
sleep with his arms around Alcibiades, and display no signs of sexual
arousal. He could be tried on a capital charge, and exhibit himself as the
most authoritative of all citizens. He appeared wise and claimed to be
ignorant. In life and in philosophical conversation, he was a paradox,
authoritatively subversive, a private citizen with a public mission, a man
who went his own way.

To understand the popular impact of Hellenistic ethics, it is essential
to see the leading figures as interpreters and embodiments of the Socratic
paradigm. They will provide their audience, as Socrates had done, with
reasons for cultivating a life that is admirable by many of the criteria of
conventional morality; but convention, for convention's sake, will play
no more part in their reasoning than it did in that of Socrates. The ethical
outlook the leading Hellenistic philosophers offer is radically unconven-
tional in many of the attitudes it prescribes, and this radicalism is to be
seen as a consequence of the technologies of the self that are central to
their project. Hellenistic ethics transfers to the self traditional notions of
leadership and political control. But, as I shall argue, we should not see
this transference as merely an internalization of external authority, a
metaphorical withdrawal from the external world and its power relations. The consequence of internal power over oneself is conceived as
the foundation of supreme authority *tout court*. Thus an Epicurean is

---

[9] For the testimonia on this, cf. G. Giannantoni, *Socraticorum reliquiae* (Naples, 1983),
vol. 1, no. IV A 96. I am not suggesting that Aristippus had a use for the term *enkrateia* in
its Socratic sense of mastering pleasures and passions. Xenophon's Socrates (*Mem.*
2.1.1–34) tries to persuade Aristippus that he needs to cultivate *enkrateia* by arguing that
the life of a ruler is superior to that of a subject. Aristippus nimbly sidesteps the argument
by insisting that there is a third option, a life neither of rule nor of slavery, but of "freedom,"
which is the best route to happiness. It is in virtue of this notion and his claim to be able
"always to make the best of circumstances" (Diog. Laert. 2.66) that we may credit Aristippus
with an interest in autonomy or self-mastery.

promised divinity—"you will live like a god among men"—and the Stoic sage is the *only* king.[10]

Philosophical Leaders and Society

Hellenistic society is an age of kings, political and philosophical, temporal and spiritual. In this it differs from the era of Socrates. For our reflections on self-mastery and philosophical power in this later time, the institution and experience of monarchy are important, as they were perceived to be in the relationship between many kings and philosophers: Diogenes and Alexander, Pyrrho and Alexander, Zeno and Antigonus Gonatas, Sphaerus and Ptolemy Euergetes, Arcesilaus and Eumenes of Pergamon.

The daily lives of Hellenistic philosophers and their pupils are known to us only in crude outline. What do stand out in bold relief are some of the salient ways in which they captured the general attention of their world. I will focus first on Zeno (portrayed in figure 31).

It was precisely for *enkrateia* that Zeno became proverbial at Athens: the saying was "more *enkrates* than the philosopher Zeno" (Diog. Laert. 7.27), meaning, of course, that he was the paradigm of self-mastery or empowerment.[11] Frugality, contentment with poverty, rejection of overtures from Antigonus Gonatas, and detachment in social behavior are just about all that the biographical tradition offers by way of justification for this renown.[12] We know nothing about any tests of fortitude that he passed with flying colors. Yet the tradition, some of it drawn from contemporary or near-contemporary writers, is unanimous on his exemplary self-control and independence. The epigrammatist Antipater of Sidon wrote an epitaph of Zeno which reads: "Here lies Zeno, dear to Citium, who reached Olympus, not by piling Pelion on Ossa nor performing the labors of Heracles. The path he found to the stars consisted in *sophrosyne* alone" (Diog. Laert. 7.29). In another epigram, by Zenodotus (Diog. Laert. 7.30), Zeno is represented as someone with a civilizing mission to Greece, the founder of self-sufficiency (*autarkeia*), who gave up

---

[10] Epicurus makes this statement in his *Letter to Menoeceus* (Diog. Laert. 10.135). For the Stoics' claim, cf. *SVF* 3:332.

[11] Zeno's successor Cleanthes called the state of the soul which is displayed in the cardinal virtues "strength and power" (ἰσχὺς καὶ κράτος), Plut. *St. rep.* 1034D (*SVF* 1:563), and in the same context listed as the first such virtue *enkrateia* (the field of which is "steadfastness"), followed by courage, justice, and *sophrosyne*. For a similarly prominent placing of *enkrateia*, cf. Chrysippus in *SVF* 3:297.

[12] In characterizing Zeno as καρτερικώτατος and λιτότατος, Diogenes Laertius (7.26) uses two terms that became ubiquitous among historians for praising virtuous political leaders or peoples uncorrupted by luxury: cf. DS 10.12.11, 37.3.2, 37.5.1; Dion. Hal. 6.96.2, etc.

31. Zeno. Museo Nazionale, Naples. From G. M. A. Richter, *Portraits of the Greeks* (London: Phaidon Press, 1965), vol. III, fig. 1089.

wealth, discovered a "manly doctrine," and toiled at establishing a school that would be "mother of fearless liberty." "He teaches poverty and gets disciples" was the comedian Philemon's comment on what he calls Zeno's "newfangled philosophy" (Diog. Laert. 7.27). All three passages draw attention to Zeno's power, a power that consists in the advocacy and practice of a life indifferent to all conventional forms of dependence.

I turn next to the Skeptic Pyrrho. In his case we have the eulogistic testimony of his chief disciple, Timon. Timon invites his readers to see Pyrrho as a paradigm of equipoise, set apart from "the famed and un-famed alike, unstable bands of people, weighed down on this side and on that with passions, opinions and futile legislation" (L-S 2B).[13] Pyrrho travels light. He acts "so easily and calmly" and is so detached from the other voices that Timon likens him to the sun in his role as man's leader and luminary (L-S 2D). Apart from Timon, the biographical tradition stresses Pyrrho's self-conscious cultivation of a mind-set that would make him as near as possible impervious to circumstances (cf. L-S 1A–C). He is said to have talked to himself as a way of practicing to be virtuous; and a string of anecdotes is recorded concerning his ability to withstand pain and danger.

Similar stories about other contemporary philosophers abound in the tradition. Zeno's cult of poverty has precedents in the actions of the Cynic Crates, who gave up all his wealth (Diog. Laert. 6.87), and Stilpo of Megara (see below). A related phenomenon is conversion—the contrast between a lifestyle before and after association with a philosopher. We are asked to believe that Polemo, who became head of the Academy, was converted by Xenocrates from a dissolute way of life to a "stubborn" consistency of character, so that he "did not even turn pale when a mad dog bit him in the thigh" (Diog. Laert. 4.17). Apocryphal though many biographical anecdotes must be, in the case of the Hellenistic philoso-phers they largely derive from Antigonus of Carystus who was close enough in date to his subject matter to have appeared ridiculous if the general tenor of his biographies was fabrication. We have to believe, I think, that many philosophers led lives that seemed largely consistent with their theories, and that they did strike their audiences as men who had liberated themselves to a remarkable degree from conventional sources of anxiety.

From Epicurus (portrayed in figure 32) there is the moving first-per-son testimony of his death-bed letter to Idomeneus (L-S 24D):

---

[13] References of the form "L-S 2B" are to A. A. Long and D. N. Sedley [L-S = Long-Sedley], *The Hellenistic Philosophers* (Cambridge, 1987), where numerical headings (as here "Tranquillity and Virtue" under the general rubric of "Early Pyrrhonism") are subdivided alphabetically.

32. Epicurus. Capitoline Museum, Rome. From G. M. A. Richter, *Portraits of the Greeks* (London: Phaidon Press, 1965), vol. III, fig. 1153.

I wrote this [note the past tense] to you on that blessed day of my life which was also the last. Strangury and dysentery had set in, with all the extreme intensity of which they are capable. But the joy in my soul at the memory of our past discussions was enough to counterbalance all this. I ask you, as befits your lifelong companionship with me and with philosophy: take care of the children of Metrodorus.

Hellenistic philosophy, it seems, was something that could deliver the happiness that it promised.

I have suggested that we look to the notion of self-mastery as a crucial element in its success. For Socrates this notion was predicated on a reconstruction of priorities as between the claims of reason and moral integrity—the health of the soul—and the demands of the body and material possessions. The Hellenistic philosophers inherit the same interest in reorientation, but in their case self-mastery and its rationale also involve a reconstitution of the sociopolitical world, something which Socrates left alone. I don't mean that Zeno or Epicurus or Pyrrho were participants in the political process, but that their noninvolvement in it should be construed as an active stance of leadership or power-politics corresponding to the worldview of their own philosophies. Pyrrho, we are to take it, does not inhabit a world of determinate truth and ethical values, and so the way he cares for himself and presumably for others is decisively shaped by his doctrine of the indeterminacy of nature. Epicurus offers his garden as the symbol of an alternative society in which the world is conceived as something constructed by friends for the pursuit of his philosophy, liberated from fear of death and the divine. Zeno lives in the public eye, but in a manner which displays his indifference to the conventional marks of success and his profound satisfaction with what others would call asceticism. His followers, apparently, unlike those of Socrates, adopt the lifestyle of their mentor.

Modern anthropologists have accustomed us to think of selves and their interests and needs as social constructs. It seems clear that the Hellenistic philosophers had a strong inkling of this notion. Their common emphasis on austerity and frugality is not simply a recommendation to prune one's diet and give up unnecessary luxuries, but an invitation to enter an alternative world and acquire a new self. One is what one eats, just as one is what one thinks. And, one may add, one is what one desires, what one enjoys, what one takes pleasure in, and what gives one pain. The happy and virtuous self that the Hellenistic philosophers seek to define is at its most distant from ordinary attitudes and satisfactions in the area of needs and motivations.

Once again, we find much common ground between the philosophical options. A Pyrrhonian wise man, according to Timon, "will not decline or choose" (L-S 2J) and Timon describes desire, *epithymia*, as "the first of all bad things" (L-S 2I). Pyrrho's alternative world is one in which self-mastery is achieved by discovering that there is no reason for saying "I want." In Stoicism, *epithymia* is the mark of a person who mistakenly supposes that conventional goods are what he needs in order to be happy; *lype*, "mental distress," denotes the unjustified passion consequent on believing, again mistakenly, that you have been deprived of some component of your happiness.[14] Ordinary psychology, where these terms are at home as descriptions of normal phenomena, is inverted, for the purpose of a reconstructed self which will view the world with eyes undiverted by passion. The Epicurean technology of the self retains a nonpejorative use for *epithymia* and *lype*. An Epicurean wise man has desires and feels mental pain, but his desires are restricted to those which are "natural and necessary" for his happiness. His character and attitude to past and future are so constituted that he always achieves a preponderance of pleasure over pain.[15] No less than the Stoic he is happy on the rack (L-S 22Q)—a thesis already known to Aristotle, who calls it absurd (*EN* 7.1153b 19). Underlying all three of these different philosophical selves is the notion that many common desirables and deficiencies are mere convention with no basis in human nature or an enlightened understanding of the world.

Several remarks are required if we are to evaluate these ethical strategies in their historical situation. First, they are not advanced as take-it-or-leave-it maxims but as principles grounded in three carefully reasoned but quite discrepant views of "nature"—nonteleological and nontheocentric in the case of the Epicureans, teleological and theocentric in the case of the Stoics, and radically indeterminate in the case of the Pyrrhonists. Their rationale is explicitly not Aristotelian *endoxa*, a balanced assessment of conventional wisdom about the good life, but a constitution of the good life according to the Epicurean, Zenonian, or Pyrrhonian view of the nature of things.

Second, they trade heavily on the notion of a perfectly "wise" man. Every school, by this date, has its *sophos*, its paradigm of someone perfected in its own philosophy. Yet the Stoics, as was widely cited against them, withheld that title from any of their scholarchs, and in general the *sophos* was taken to be an abstract idealization. Christianity has familiarized us with the notion of unachievable imitation of a perfect model, but *imitatio Christi* must fall short for theological reasons that did not trouble Greek philosophers. Chrysippus characterized the Stoic sage as the equal of Zeus in virtue (L-S 61J), and, as already mentioned, Epicurus advocated a praxis that would make someone live like a god among men. It

---

[14] See L-S 65A–B.
[15] See L-S 21B–C, F, I, T.

was not piety that distanced the *sophos* as a practical ideal, but, as Pyrrho is nicely reported to have said, the difficulty of divesting oneself of being human (L-S 1C).[16]

There is a deep paradox here, which brings me to a third point. Paradox was a fundamental part of Greek philosophy from its beginnings. Here again, Aristotle stands out by his difference. In taking over the term "paradox," we have lost its connection with *doxa*, and so we tend to think of philosophical paradoxes as either mere puzzles or perversity. But a paradox is literally a thought that is incongruous with commonplace beliefs. Hence Parmenides' deduction of a world of truth totally at variance with mortal "opinions" is most literally a paradox. Greek philosophers trade on paradox because the dialectical tradition, via its Eleatic origins, trained them to think in terms of a dichotomy between conventional opinion and unascertained truth. On this way of looking at things, the world is, so to speak, up for grabs. Our beliefs should be grounded, based on reasons, and mere convention is not a sufficient reason for belief. The fruitfulness of this standpoint for the development of Greek speculative thought is self-evident. Interpreters of Greek ethics, in spite of the so-called Socratic and Stoic paradoxes, have yet, I think, to take its measure. Plato's *Republic* is a gigantic paradox in the Greek sense that I have explained. The ethical writings of Aristotle are not.

I suggest that we are intended to view the ethical strategies of the innovative Hellenistic philosophers as paradoxical, in the sense that they are designed to shock and intrigue and undermine complacency. We have yet to see what aspects of traditional thought their ethical *logos* leaves intact, but salvation of tradition is clearly less their concern than following the argument wherever it takes them.

The fourth point I want to make about the general tenor of Hellenistic ethics brings me back to the notion of power and Hellenistic monarchy. On the whole, as I have already suggested, it is correct to see Hellenistic ethics as a development of Socratic tendencies, rather than a direct response to supposedly new problems and situations. It does seem probable, however, that the concentration of power in the hands of Hellenistic monarchs and generals, together with the vicissitudes these figures experienced, helped to give currency to the notion of a related yet strikingly different paradigm—a self that is authoritative and utterly consistent in all circumstances, and whose power consists in an inversion of monarchical appurtenances, minimal possessions, minimal material needs, hierarchical subordination of conventional interests to a controlling rational

---

[16] Cf. Chrysippus, L-S 66A: "For this reason, then, owing to the extreme magnitude and beauty [of justice], we seem to be talking fiction and not on the level of man and human nature."

outlook, and adaptability. Thus we may place Stilpo of Megara's response to Demetrius, son of Antigonus, when he wished to restore Stilpo's plundered property: "I have lost nothing that belonged to me, since no one has removed my education, and I still have my reason and understanding" (Diog. Laert. 2.115).[17]

The response is theatrical, and a fifth point is in order here. By the time of Roman Stoicism, the term *prosopon*, "role," had become a way of designating a person's character and the "performance" expected of him. Epictetus makes it clear that a character in this sense is something that is partly determined by circumstances—one's role as a son, a citizen, and so forth—but still more importantly, by one's choices and understanding of "who one is" (cf. Epict. *Diss.* 1.2, 2.10). Epictetus had a clear forerunner in Panaetius' celebrated theory of each person's four *personae*, known to us through Cicero's report in *De officiis* 1.107–17, but there can be little doubt that the theatrical image goes back to the early days of the Stoa. Zeno's independent-minded follower Aristo described the wise man as "like the good actor who, whether he puts on the mask of Thersites or Agamemnon, plays either part in the proper way" (L-S 58G); and Antigonus Gonatas is said to have lamented the "staging" (*theatron*) of which he had been deprived by Zeno's death (Diog. Laert. 7.15). Epicurus made love of theater an attribute of his wise man (L-S 25H). Philosophers then as now were frequently mocked as mere "performers," and the fact that the profession could be abused by cultivation of its trappings does not imply that its serious practitioners avoided theatricality. The subject deserves detailed scrutiny, but here I focus on just one aspect.

Zeno and other Hellenistic philosophers were theatrical in the sense that they intended their lives to be seen as highly self-conscious choices of a determinate role. Living the part was, of course, demanded by consistency with their doctrines, especially doctrines specifying strenuous routes to happiness. But, leaving aside the competitive features of publicly conducted dialectic and the exhibitionism proper to any effective lecturer, theatricality made the point that a way of life could be quite deliberately chosen and cultivated—that it need not be an old suit of clothes which had to be worn because nothing else was available. The notion of self-mastery, which I have emphasized so strongly, presupposes just such a self-conscious choice of a life, an understanding of who one is, as Epictetus remarked.

---

[17] One may compare Alexander the Great's supposed contacts with the Cynic Diogenes, and the probably fictional exchange of letters between Antigonus Gonatas and Zeno (Diog. Laert. 7.7–9).

Connections with Popular Morality

Although the Hellenistic philosophers share a common view on the link between happiness, excellence, and self-mastery, and agree on much that these require in the sphere of practical reason and desire, they remain, as I began by saying, quite distinct. A choice between Stoicism or Epicureanism involves fundamental decisions about one's whole orientation—one's theology, cosmology, and daily practice. The power that these philosophies promise is not a simple recipe for personal autonomy but two divergent ways of understanding where one is positioned in the world.

This systematic and comprehensive outlook distinguishes Stoicism and Epicureanism from the ephemeral philosophies of life that sprang up around the same time. It also, of course, distinguishes them from popular morality. But we can perhaps learn something about the philosophical options in ethics by noticing attitudes they share, or fail to share, with sentiments voiced in the comedies of Menander.

Contrary to what is sometimes said, Menander's theater seems to me to show little respect for philosophy. It is high-grade soap opera where conventional people get into and out of messes generated by stereotypical attitudes to wealth, inheritance, sex, and the like. Knemon in *Dyskolos* is a rare case of someone who has chosen and stuck to an eccentric lifestyle through misanthropy that has a philosophical resonance. Remarking on his mistake at treating himself as "self-sufficient" (*autarkes*, 713–14)—a sure dig at contemporary philosophy—he adds, wryly, that if everyone had lived like him there would be no more lawcourts, prisons, or wars. We are reminded of Zeno's austere *Republic* (cf. Diog. Laert. 7.32–33).

More typical is the slave Daos' comment on Chairestratos' depression in *Aspis* 336ff.: "Practically all ailments stem from anguish (*lype*); and I know you have a peevish and melancholic nature. The next thing will be getting a doctor here—a philosophical one who says the trouble is pleuritis or phrenitis." But though Menander follows the general run of Greek comedy in mocking philosophy, he also provides a rich stock of the moralizing platitudes that people did, presumably, exchange in daily life. The sample I will draw from consists of *gnomai* isolated from their dramatic context. Even so, they show that popular morality was in touch with certain key sentiments of one or other Hellenistic philosophy.

First, some examples that dwell on the authority of reason.[18] "Reason is the sole manager of mortals' life" (438). "Reason conquers present misfortune" (515). "Every virtue is commanded by holy reason" (69). "Let reason be the leader of every office (*arche*)" (68). "Conquer passion

---

[18] My citations from Menander, unless a play is specified, are taken from Jaekel's Teubner edition of the *Sententiae*.

by reasoning well" (528). All Greek philosophers would endorse these viewpoints, but one is particularly reminded of the Stoics who chose the military term *hegemonikon*, "commanding faculty," for the mind.

Next, a representative selection of sentences that focus upon pleasure or pain (*lype*). "No mortal's life is free from pain" (65). "No evil is worse for men than pain" (563). "To live free from pain is the pleasantest life" (749), a statement which could come straight out of Epicurus, as could the following also: "Flee pleasure that brings later damage" (806) and "How much pain we suffer on account of pleasures" (863). "Never make yourself a slave to pleasure" (512) and "The prudent man is not caught by pleasure" (777) endorse the standard philosophical line on the disparity between self-mastery and self-indulgence.

Other lines recommend the value of education, the superiority of virtue to wealth, the incomparable worth of the soul, and so on.[19] Yet antiphilosophical sentiments are hardly less common, for example: "Human affairs are chance, not good planning" (*Aspis* 411), "No one lives the life that he chooses" (105), "Some people do well who think badly" (236), "There is no one who does not reproach fortune" (611), "The wise man does not seem to be well adapted in all respects" (599), "No man will succeed in being completely happy" (596). In general then, it seems, there are interesting echoes of philosophical ethics in Menander, approving and disapproving. Superficial and undeveloped though they are, they show that philosophers such as Zeno and Epicurus could have counted on some support, and some interesting opposition, for their systematic views in the untutored opinions of their audience.

Collectively too they show the uncertainty and confusion of popular ethics in the Hellenistic world and thus its distance from philosophy. Aristotle had made a similar point in his own lectures on ethics, noting the discrepancy between the opinions of the "many" and the "wise" on what happiness is, and adding: "[of the many] the same person keeps changing his mind, since in sickness he thinks it is health, in poverty wealth" (*EN* 1.1095a 20–25). This reactive, circumstantial view of happiness is rejected by all Greek philosophers but by none more strongly than the Hellenistic pioneers who have concerned us in this paper. They are disposed not simply to minimize external fortune's control over a person's state of mind, but to specify a consistent attitude that can ensure happiness against internal threats to its stability; for example, the attitudes described as Epicurean "untroubledness" or Stoic "good flow of life." Neither attitude will satisfy someone who identifies happiness with everything that is prized in popular morality. But such a person, an Epicurean or a Stoic will say, has failed to see that you cannot simultane-

---

[19] Cf. Jaekel 2, 50, 124, 384, 436, 565, 684, 843.

ously be a hedonist and someone who regards the perfection of reason
and obedience to moral norms as the sole human good. The mutual
exclusivity of these ethical theories is an inevitable consequence of each
system's attachment to its own internal consistency and allocation of fundamental priorities. Stoics think that their ethics would be totally undermined if pleasure or health or anything other than the virtues were
deemed "good" and a necessary constituent of happiness (*SVF* 3:37). The
Epicurean Diogenes of Oenoanda "affirms now and always, with a great
shout, that for all Greeks and foreigners pleasure is the *telos* . . . and the
virtues but the means to the end" (L-S 21P).

Such insistence upon doctrinal integrity, as I began by saying, is essential to the conception of the Hellenistic schools as distinct "sects" or *haire-
seis*. This nomenclature advertises their *practical* significance, as a striking
example will show. Dionysius of Heraclea, originally a follower of Zeno,
got the name "Turncoat" because in later life he suffered from pain so
severely that he was unable to sustain the doctrine that pain is quite
indifferent for happiness (Diog. Laert. 7.166) and abandoned the Stoa
for the Cyrenaics (or possibly the Epicureans). Dionysius' apostasy marks
him out as a failed Stoic, but also as someone who takes consistency so
seriously that he expects his own experience to be adequately validated
by the school of his allegiance.

On one understanding, values and the quality of a life are not things
that we choose, but predetermined social and psychological contexts in
which we locate ourselves as best we may: I am in pain, therefore I am
unhappy; I have won a lottery, therefore I am happy; you have injured
me, therefore I will injure you. An example to illustrate the point: Daüs
in Menander's *Aspis* (1–18) had expected his master to return from war
"famous" and "hale," with prospects of a great future—an elegant lifestyle, a title, a fine marriage for his sister. But Cleostratus has been
"snatched away" *paralogos*, "unreasonably," cheating Daüs' expectations.

The big idea of Hellenistic ethics is the unreasonableness of assuming
that a socially predetermined, un-thought-out context could ever be a
basis for long-term happiness and excellence. For that, it suggests, you
have to make a choice between systematic attitudes—Stoicism or Epicureanism let's say—each one of which constitutes a whole culture to itself.
Try to imagine a single affiliation incorporating your political party, your
religion, your form of therapy, your cosmology, your psychology, your
fundamental values—an affiliation which unified all that's involved in
being, say, a Christian, Jungian, Marxist, utilitarian believer in the big
bang. Then, I think, you have a loose analogy to one of the leading
Hellenistic schools in their most challenging phase, and a reason for
thinking of them as experiments in philosophical power.

RESPONSE: PAUL WOODRUFF

Hellenistic philosophy, as Professor Long points out, called on its adherents to make a choice of more than a school. A *hairesis* brings with it a systematic attitude toward everything—toward the cosmos, society, and the details of your life, right down to, and including, your attitude toward such details as this morning's breakfast. Not surprisingly, therefore, the names of these Hellenistic choices—stoical, cynical, and so on—came down to us as names for attitudes toward life that are not in any technical sense philosophical.

I want to look further into what is distinctive about Hellenistic philosophy along the lines that Professor Long has suggested.

Defining the period. In the first place, I think it wise to distinguish Hellenistic philosophy from the philosophy of the Greco-Roman period. From Cicero onward we find philosophy frequently in the hands of amateurs, whose approach to philosophy is colored by the circumstances of their active lives: Cicero the orator, Seneca the courtier, Marcus Aurelius the emperor, and last but not least, Sextus the doctor. At the same time, these thinkers' active lives were colored by their philosophy. This mutual coloring of active and philosophical lives is more characteristic of the Greco-Roman than of the Hellenistic period.

Our modern use of such words as *stoical* and *cynical*, I suspect, owes more to Roman than to Hellenistic usage. The debasement of these words began, so far as I can tell, in Roman times. The blurring of the lines that divided the schools—the movement toward the mashed-potato eclecticism of Antiochus of Ascalon—freed these words from their hard-edged technical meanings. Even as early as the first century of our era, the word *stoic* was so debased that it was used for the resistance of the aristocrats to the principate in Rome, although it is hard to see what Zeno or Chrysippus would have found to approve in Helvidius Priscus' vain and tradition-bound opposition to Vespasian.

The commonplace, which Professor Long rightly criticizes, that Hellenistic philosophy derived its special character from the crises of its times, owes its currency to the fact that much of what we know of Hellenistic philosophy comes from texts written by amateurs of the Greco-Roman period. The truth, I think, is as Professor Long says: that Hellenistic philosophy took its character more from its origins than from its times. And the chief origin is, of course, Socrates.

Still, some truth must be granted to the commonplace. Ethics as developed by Socrates, Plato, and Aristotle was in the service of political theory; Hellenistic ethics was not. Aristotle's ethics was explicitly a footnote to his politics. We moderns apply a Hellenistic structure to the organization of the fields of philosophy, and so we tend to ignore this in our teaching. But Aristotle, in subordinating ethics to politics as a field, was squarely within the Socratic tradition. The virtue that concerned Socrates was primarily the virtue political leaders ought to have. Plato, of, course, considered virtue to be a delicate plant that can be nurtured only on ideal political soil. In the classical tradition from Socrates to Aristotle, ethics states the goals of politics, and politics states the conditions under which the good life described in ethics is possible.

All of this is changed in the Hellenistic period. With the decline of the *polis* and the rise of monarchies comes the emergence of ethics as an independent field in philosophy, as one of the three great legs of the tripod. This is how we still teach it today. The mythical lawgiver, moral hero of the classical period, whose goal was the moral betterment of his people, has given way to the monarch whose role is more that of the mythical gods: to be a being of a higher order altogether, indifferent to ethical considerations.

The new political climate of the period forced Hellenistic ethics to be detached from politics, and this meant two things. First, the theories of Hellenistic ethics were more abstract than those of their classical predecessors. Teachers of Hellenistic ethics did not much care whether their goals were practical in view of the conditions under which people lived. Concrete social and political issues did not interest them. In particular, they did not ask whether better politics would make the good life easier to live. Second, Hellenistic ethics put enormously increased emphasis on individual choice as opposed to public policy; hence the importance of *hairesis*.

There is, then, some truth to the idea that the philosophy of this period reflected its history. But much of the character of classical ethics survived the changes that brought in the Hellenistic period. We shall see that the continuity of Hellenistic ethics with the classical tradition is more striking than the changes that parallel the decline of the *polis*. We need to ask from what sources Hellenistic ethics derived its special character. Professor Long is right that the influence of Socrates is crucial, but other sources also are important.

Socrates. Here the picture is rather complicated. All of the Hellenistic schools are plainly Socratic; one of the main issues they fought over was who among them was the true heir of Socrates. Professor Long is right about the kind of importance Socrates had for the Hellenistics: it was Socrates' life, not his teachings or his arguments, that meant the most. Socrates' life was, for most of the Hellenistic schools, a model of the life to which a philosopher should aspire. Professor Long makes the wonderfully provocative suggestion that the very conception of self-mastery, or *enkrateia*, was due to the need of Socrates' successors to conceptualize what was special about Socrates' way of life. Around this concept cluster the main ideas of Hellenistic ethics. Also, as Professor Long suggests, it explains why the various ideals of the schools are deeply ingrained dispositions, and not just academic theories, and why the ideals of those schools persist (albeit in somewhat debased form) in conceptual structures expressed in modern European languages: there was a specific sort of settled self-mastery that each school taught. Socrates' life stood as an icon for each of these.

It is not that Socrates' teachings did not matter; plainly they did, in an historical sense. The minor Socratic schools, for example, were precisely the ancestors of the great Hellenistic schools, and transmitted Socratic doctrines to them. The point is this: once formed, the Hellenistic schools venerated Socrates as an icon but were not much interested either in historical questions about what he believed or in interpretive questions about the sources for Socrates. It was not until Roman times that we see clear evidence that quarrels among the schools were carried into quarrels about the meanings of Plato's texts. Indeed, I think it is important to keep in mind that, although Hellenistic thinkers owned books of Plato, and read them, they did not, so far as I can tell, appeal to such works in any way while developing their views. The serious study of Platonic texts, along with the idea that philosophy is to be developed by the study of Platonic texts, seems to have been new in the Roman period. A remarkable feature of Hellenistic philosophy is its lack of interest in the history of thought. Philosophers generally do try to move forward by looking back and correcting their ancestors. Plato, for example, worked by writing against Heracleitus and Protagoras; Aristotle, against Plato and the pre-Socratics. What is unusual about the Hellenistic philosophers is that they worked by writing mainly against each other. That is why, I think, they showed little interest in the actual teachings of Socrates on ethical matters.

The same is true of the Socratic method as reproduced in Plato. Although members of the Academy notoriously laid claim to the method,[1] they did not practice it except in a very loose sense. Socrates used his method to refute people; whether Arcesilaus used his method in the same way is a matter of dispute. The out-and-out refutation of an opponent is, of course, inconsistent with the stated goals of the Academy, and with Arcesilaus' disclaimer of all knowledge. Socrates, through refuting others and ultimately, I would say, through refuting himself, proved that

---

[1] Cic. *Ac.* 16, 46; *Fin.* 11.1.2; in a different vein, Sextus Empiricus *Outlines of Pyrrhonism* 1.234. Opponents of the Academy resented its members' claim to Platonist ancestry (Plut. *Adv. Col.* 1121f–22a).

no one—not even Socrates—knew anything (*Apol.* 22d 1). But Arcesilaus stopped short of that, and disclaimed knowing even that he did not know.[2] Arcesilaus' skepticism was more radical than Socrates', and the method appropriate to it is different on a number of technical points. I have argued elsewhere that Socratic methods were revived in the Roman period and put to skeptical use during the first phase of the Pyrrhonist revival.[3] This conclusion is highly controversial, but the negative point ought to be accepted by all: Hellenistic argument did not show much direct influence of Plato's texts.

Other sources. Socrates gave to Hellenistic ethics its flavor and its ideal of a life in control of itself, as Professor Long says. But from what source did Hellenistic ethics derive the qualities that distinguish it from the classical tradition?

Certainly not from the alleged turbulence of Hellenistic life. All life is turbulent. Hellenistic philosophy turned away from the conditions of life in any case; its schools were all remarkably academic, far removed from the concerns of real life. The main influences on the later development of each Hellenistic school came from other schools of the same period.

In their origins, however, the Hellenistic schools owe much to Aristotle, who served as a hinge between classical and later philosophy. Professor Long is quite right that the content of Aristotle's ethics is out of line with earlier and later developments alike. But Aristotle's systematic approach to philosophy as a whole, certain aspects of his method, and even certain technical distinctions which he made, all divagated from Plato in significant ways, and so provided a new background for the development of Hellenistic ethics.[4] The stream of influence from Socrates to the Hellenistic schools was not entirely pure; new elements did flow in from Aristotle.

The stream of the Socratic tradition was mingled with other waters as well, some of these quite exotic. A striking case in point ties in with the interest of this symposium in the fringes of Hellenistic civilization. The founder of skepticism, Pyrrho, took as his ideal *ataraxia* ("undisturbedness" or "detachment"), a goal which was much admired by Epicu-

---

[2] Cic. *Ac.* 1.45.

[3] See my "Aporetic Pyrrhonism," *Oxford Studies in Ancient Philosophy* 6 (1988): 139–68.

[4] For an influential discussion of the Aristotelian background to Epicurean philosophy, see David J. Furley, *Two Studies in the Greek Atomists* (Princeton, 1967). On the extent to which Stoicism followed Aristotle, see Brad Inwood, *Ethics and Human Action in Early Stoicism* (Oxford, 1985), chap. 1. For the Aristotelian background to Academic skepticism, see J. Glucker, *Antiochus and the Late Academy* (Göttingen, 1978), 34 n. 79. Some part of the skeptical method of the Academy may be due to Aristotle (Cic. *Tusc.* 2.3.9; but see 5.4.10).

rus and which became the ethical goal in different ways of several Hellenistic schools. Where did this ideal come from?

First, it is important to see that *ataraxia* and related concepts are not quite the same as self-mastery. If, when Socrates saw what was inside Charmides' clothes, on that famous occasion (*Charm.* 155d), he was excited but fought down his excitement by sheer power of will and forced himself back to philosophy—that would be a clear case of self-mastery. But if Socrates felt no excitement at all, and was quite unmoved by the sight of Charmides' beauty, that is a kind of temperance that requires no self-mastery and is much closer in spirit to the ideal of *ataraxia*. Was Socrates really excited, or was he joking about how the future tyrant's good looks could be turned to tyrannical uses? It is hard to say; the point is that these are two different ideals, and that the Hellenistic ethicists were interested more in developing a character that did not need to be mastered than in learning to master one's own character. Pyrrho's ideal was to be like the pigs in the foundering ship, who went right on eating without a pause (Diog. Laert. 9.68). That is not self-mastery. Rather, it is the goal of living in accordance with an idealized nature.

Ataraxia is of course known to us mainly as an Epicurean ideal; but, as Sedley has pointed out, Epicurus may well have learned this ideal from Pyrrho, whom he admired.[5] And where did Pyrrho get the idea? Pyrrho learned this, we are told, from certain naked philosophers he met in India. Although Western scholars are reluctant to believe that their ancestors could have been influenced by the Orient, the tradition on this point is fairly convincing.[6]

The special character of Hellenistic ethics. What is most distinctive about Hellenistic ethics, I want to suggest, is not its Socratic character, and indeed has nothing to do with its origins. It is the amazingly academic character of each of the schools after their foundation and before the Roman period. Hellenistic ethics, like the rest of Hellenistic philosophy, was mainly self-generating. It grew out of a prolonged and highly technical debate among the schools. This is not to deny that its practitioners lived in accordance with their beliefs. But, as professional philosophers, many of them were concerned with fine points that could not have made

---

[5] Diogenes Laertius testifies to the impression Pyrrho made on Epicurus (9.64). For the hypothesis that Epicurus learned of *ataraxia* from Pyrrho, see David Sedley, "Epicurus and His Professional Rivals," in J. Bollack and A. Laks, eds., *Études sur l'épicurisme antique*, Cahiers de philologie no. 1 (Paris, 1976), 136–37.

[6] The evidence is due to Ascanias of Abdera, cited by Diogenes Laertius (9.61). The tradition is taken seriously by Everard Flintoff, "Pyrrho and India," *Phronesis* 25 (1980): 88–108; he is followed by Sedley, "The Motivation of Greek Skepticism," in Myles Burnyeat, ed., *The Skeptical Tradition* (Berkeley, 1983), 15.

a difference in ordinary life. Stoics, especially, were accused of this sort of concern by the Academy. The Socratic ideal, as Professor Long points out, had become an abstract ideal. It was still the goal for living, but it was not a goal any of us could expect to win in human life, and it was therefore one that required considerable effort—not without mental gymnastics—to articulate.

In Long's wonderfully evocative phrase, the Hellenistic schools were "experiments in philosophical power." He has shown how these experiments derive from a Socratic model, and how they resonate with models of power in Hellenistic monarchies. I would add only that these experiments depended on sustained, analytical thought, carried out through vigorous debates spanning two centuries, and that this debate is one of the most distinctive features of the period.

DISCUSSION

A. E. Samuel: I wonder if Professor Long would respond to what Professor Woodruff said about *ataraxia* as opposed to *enkrateia*?

A. A. Long: Professor Woodruff was quite right to bring up the Indian connection. I'm much less skeptical than I used to be about this. The real problem is that it's very hard to date Indian documents which seem to contain something like the skeptical tropes. But they may have been around at that time. To come to your point directly: I think the precise notion of untroubledness does not have Socratic parallels. Nonetheless the passage I quoted from Xenophon about Socrates being most *enkrates* is suggestive. It's almost there. Perhaps what Pyrrho's experience showed was just the possibility of living in an even more exotically strange way than the life of Socrates had suggested. And I think the Greek historians of the later Hellenistic period are fascinated by the exotic—I remember Diodorus talking about the untroubled Fisheaters, the *ichthyophagoi*. We can get quite a lot of mileage out of the Socratic impulse, but we perhaps need something else also.

S. M. Burstein: In one important way Epicurus differs from most of his rivals. He was political in a way they were not and could not be, since he was an Athenian citizen whereas philosophers such as Zeno were metics. Thus, unlike them, his decision not to participate in Athenian public life represented a deliberate and perhaps even subversive choice on his part, a choice which, as his letters reveal, he recommended to others. Could this conscious rejection of the citizen's role by Epicurus be part of the reason for the almost universal condemnation of him and his philosophy in antiquity?

A. A. Long: Well, as for Zeno, he had a very long life. And I take it that, as is often the case with radical thinkers, he became more respectable with age. Zeno's *Republic*, probably his earliest work, was very subversive, abolishing marriage and temples and currency. As to Epicurus, he took part in city life, he took part in festivals. So what is he not taking part in? He is not taking part in the competitive element—he's not standing for office. I think you're right that he's clearly making a political statement of some kind. Of course his way of life is parasitical upon there being some form of society which will provide the basic wherewithal. It's interesting that Marxists have always been very attracted to Epicurus. We've got a new fragment that says that when the Epicurean ideal world is constituted, *then* there will be no need for city walls, but for now we still need them.

P. Green: I think there is a basic distinction between Epicureanism and the other Hellenistic philosophies in that Epicureanism first of all set itself up very much as a way of life, as something more like a commune or a religion. We also find a disinclination to change the development of thought. This is the nearest you get to a body of dogma. Also—something that the antics of the televangelists keep reminding me of—how extremely well-heeled Epicurus was from the contributions of the faithful. It's all very different from the kind of thing that both Professor Long and Professor Woodruff were positing as a general principle—something I would absolutely agree on—that is, an intellectually developing and rigorously thought-out doctrine. This is the one that's quite different.

A. A. Long: I will grant you that Epicureanism has a sense of almost monastic development. You start as a novice and gradually advance toward more developed teaching. But the notion that it's indoctrination, if that is what you were getting at, is not correct, I think. All three of these philosophies we've been talking about are involved in a radical reconstruction of the world. But clearly what Epicurus spent most of his time doing was some pretty advanced philosophy. It won't do to think of Epicurus as the leader of some popular sect, like Jim Jones. The thirty-seven books of *On Nature* were very tough going indeed. In that little extract from the letter I read you he says that the real essence of happiness is doing philosophy.

P. Green: What I meant was that there was far less change allowed in the evolution of Epicurean thinking after Epicurus' death.

A. A. Long: This is often said, but it's not quite clear that we know it for sure. Philodemus, for example, recounts four different Epicurean lecture courses he's heard, and there are some quite substantial differences there. And there are quite a lot of things in Lucretius we have no knowledge of directly from Epicurus. For example, the swerve of the atom. I think you're right in general: Epicureanism is the most introverted of the philosophical movements, but perhaps for philosophical reasons.

A. E. Samuel: Firstly, do you think, as Professor Woodruff suggested, that the schools were trying to establish untroubledness, or do you insist that they were trying to establish self-mastery—which are, again as he suggested, quite different goals? Secondly, where do you fit the Cynics in?

A. A. Long: Professor Woodruff was pointing out that in the case of Socrates you want to distinguish between the character in which you succeed in mastering certain impulses on the one hand, and *sophrosyne*, in which you are so wonderfully well-adjusted that you just don't have these impulses. When I use the term *self-mastery*, perhaps I am shifting between these slightly; but then I think that's in the very nature of the case, because a Stoic, for example, would say that the state you want to be in is one in which reason rules. Reason can be ruling in the wise man even though he's gone beyond having any of the sort of lubricious impulses that are successfully mastered by self-control in its conventional meaning. Unless reason is ruling, then something else will take control. The notion of self-mastery as I am using it simply implies that the self is in principle capable of being ruled either by reason or by irrational impulses. Whether you have a unified view of the soul as the Stoics had or a tripartite view as Plato had, in both cases I think you can correctly talk about self-mastery.

A. E. Samuel: It seemed to me from what you were saying that the goal of the schools was to achieve control of the self, and this implied that there would be, or might be, a struggle in doing that. Whereas Professor Woodruff was suggesting that the schools were aiming at creating a pattern of living in which one was untroubled.

A. A. Long: That's the *telos*, that's the final stage, *ataraxia*. The steps on the way to that are going to be extremely rigorous. Now, to come to your other question, the Cynics are a very important seed from which Stoicism develops, yet Stoicism develops so successfully while the Cynic remains such a way-out figure—and here I want to disagree with something that Professor Woodruff said; I don't think it's correct to say that the Stoics are not interested in philosophical history. I think they are very inter-

ested in it. They're wanting as far as they can to appropriate the philosophical tradition, and I think they did actually study certain of Plato's
dialogues. It wouldn't be very *good* philosophical history by our criteria.
But I don't think the Stoics would ever want to say, "We discovered all
this."

P. Woodruff: I didn't mean to say that they did. But I do think the Stoics
did not *use* the history of philosophy in the way that Plato and Aristotle
did.

P. Levi: There is in bucolic poetry quite a lot of the cult of *ataraxia*.
Virgil says, *deus nobis haec otia fecit*. I take it that *otium* must mean something like *ataraxia*. Is it then a criticism of philosophy that Theocritus,
although he has people unhappy in love, constantly insinuates that you
can be perfectly happy if you only happen to be living in a nice place in
the country without much ambition, like the girl translated from Pro-
pertius by Ezra Pound as "happy selling poor loves for cheap apples"?
That's roughly the ideal of that kind of poetry. Is this a criticism of
philosophy or is it an attempt to approach it?

A. A. Long: I don't think they're talking about the same thing. Too
much *otium* might be a very bad recipe for *ataraxia*. *Otium* simply meant
having time on your hands, not being preoccupied with duties; but *ataraxia* is an internal state.

D. M. Halperin: I was struck by how much of what you described as
being distinctive of the Hellenistic schools can be paralleled in earlier
periods of Greek culture. Especially the theme of self-mastery, and the
theatricality of the moral act in classical Athens. In earlier periods, at any
rate, the choices that people make don't dramatize a particular lifestyle
or a philosophical outlook peculiar to the people who make such choices;
they don't seem to express one particular *hairesis*, that is, but a way of
fitting into the society. In the *Odyssey*, for example, everyone is watching
Telemachus to see by his actions if he fits in. But what they're looking to
see is not what particular kind of person he will be, but whether he will
become the same sort of man that his father is. Later on in the classical
period people are always watching the young to see how they will behave
and whether they will be worse or better than their fathers, and the
young men know that they're being watched. During the Sicilian debate
Nicias says to the young men, Don't be ashamed to vote for peace or
think that people will call you a coward if they see you voting for peace.
It's clear that people, especially the young men, are watching over their
shoulders to see who's looking at them. But no one thinks that the result

of being watched or judged is to have oneself thrust into one particular category. It's just a question of better or worse, of whether you're a good sort of person or not, not what kind of person—what individual type—you are. Now, what changes, according to you, in the Hellenistic period? And is the change that occurs a change only within philosophy, or within society at large?

A. A. Long: Before Socrates, all you were saying is absolutely right. And it's the life of Socrates—and above all Plato's reflections on it, plus those of the other Socratic followers, who suddenly got hold of the notion that you could actually make experiments and think out a well-organized life—which is totally discrepant in many ways from the way in which society normally operates. The obvious example is the challenge to Socrates in book 2 of the *Republic* to prove that a just person will be happy even if the world gives him all the opprobrium that it would normally attach to injustice. It's this kind of philosophical experimentation. So we agree on that.

D. M. Halperin: What I'm wondering is, do you really believe that it was all due to Socrates, who just started a fad, and that people started living differently because of Socrates? Did Socrates invent the self as we know it?

A. A. Long: I am not defending the old-fashioned view that the Hellenistic world suddenly got a great taste for philosophy. I take it that this is one case in which the frontier of the Tiber makes a difference. Philosophy by the Roman period has become very diffuse and popularized. But in the fourth century it is still something practiced by a very small number of people. I would defend the notion that the life of Socrates is sufficient to produce these changes, because the evidence is there.

A. Mourelatos (University of Texas at Austin):   I am struck by the career of the theater image. It's a fascinating idea that somehow it could be used precisely to convey this choice that the individual makes, when that very same image had been used by Plato to convey the exact opposite. I'm thinking of the *Republic*, where the last thing you want is *mimesis*, people picking up *prosopa*, because this is what turns them to heteronomy and inauthenticity, not to be true to your real self, but just to be doing the kind of playing that the sophists do.

A. A. Long: Plato doesn't say that we don't need role models. It's just that the ones that society has adopted are inadequate.

P. Woodruff: Very clearly he says that we should imitate Forms such as Justice and the Good.

A. Mourelatos: But I'm thinking specifically of the great worry that if you emphasize the theater image, you're moving in the direction of the sophists, you're moving into the cult of appearances. This point was not discussed, and somehow the theater image popped up without any mention of the obverse side of it.

A. A. Long: I see your point. But, from a reader's perspective, Plato's dramatic dialogues are, precisely, a staging of Socrates' philosophical life.

S. Shapiro (U. T. student):   I think that the Hellenistic philosophies as Professor Long has described them are in some ways more like religions than philosophies, especially in the importance of the personal life of the leaders like Pyrrho, and the importance of conversion and a dramatic change in lifestyle. This reminds me of early Christianity.

A. A. Long: I agree. According to Chrysippus, the final stage that you should study in philosophy is theology. He had a pun on this: he said theology is the *telos* and the *teletai*. Now "religion" is a very difficult word to analyze. What it means in a Greek context and what it means in our time are so different. Greek religion was so fluid; in a sense you could almost choose your religion. You could choose your gods. Hesiod gives a long passage about Hecate, who was never a major deity in the public sphere. But for Hesiod she is. I think that point was made well in an earlier discussion about the notion of the divine person. What religion is going to involve in your sense is perhaps spirituality.

S. Shapiro: Also a whole way of life based on a worldview completely involving the entire self.

E. Gruen: The taking on of a persona may correspond to a *hairesis*. But the analogy is a troublesome one. If you can put on the mask you can also remove it. Therefore it lacks innate authenticity, and casts doubt on genuine self-mastery. Will such *tranquillitas* in the end really be authentic?

A. A. Long: The Stoic is not saying that we should all be stage players. He is trying to say that it is possible for you to decide the role you wish to play in the world. And that's going to carry with it certain implications. One of them is that you can't play two roles at the same time. You can't be both Agamemnon and Thersites. The notion that you can just take the mask off is going to be countered by all sorts of other defenses. After all, this is not just a role for an hour, it's a role for life.

The Ptolemies and the Ideology of Kingship

A. E. Samuel

It is now almost exactly a century since Grenfell and Hunt presented us with the *Revenue Laws Papyrus*, a text which prompted the modern emphasis on the nature of Ptolemaic monarchy as intricately bureaucratic and centrally organized. Over the years, that monarchy and its administrative structure have been variously conceived, with assessments ranging from almost unalloyed approval of a government seen as innovative and progressive,[1] to the most recent condemnation by the late Eric Turner of an oppressive rule which squeezed Egypt so severely as to bankrupt it for the future.[2] I am not going to be so banal as to suggest that the truth lies somewhere in between. It doesn't—not, at least, as I see it—but is, rather, to be found outside the whole structure which the papyri have created for us as an edifice of administration and monarchic ideology.

Almost all the evidence we have for the administration and the conceptualization of monarchy in Egypt after Alexander the Great begins with the reign of the second Ptolemy,[3] and it is to this king that we attribute

---

[1] As M. Rostovtzeff, *SEHHW*, throughout his detailed treatment of Philadelphus' reign, and especially 1:271–74, 407–11, 415. A recent summary of the structure of Ptolemaic administration within Egypt may be found in R. S. Bagnall, *The Administration of the Ptolemaic Possessions Outside Egypt* (Leiden, 1976), 3–10.

[2] *CAH²* VII.1, 134–59.

[3] The bulk of the literature is enormous, and begins with general studies of Macedonian kingship and the monarchy after Alexander. In my view, the overview of monarchy in the eastern Mediterranean elaborated by Claire Préaux in *Le Monde hellénistique* (Paris, 1978) 181–294, is still by far the fullest and most useful review of the evidence. In English, see F. W. Walbank's discussion in *CAH²* VII.1, 64–100, the bibliographies there, and Leon Mooren, "The Nature of the Hellenistic Monarchy," in *Egypt and the Hellenistic World*, eds.

much of the conceptualizing of the administrative organization of Egypt for Greek and Macedonian exploitation. Ptolemy II Philadelphus has the credit for great progressive government in the appraisals of some historians, while by others he is blamed for exhausting the Egyptian economy. In the early part of his reign he continued the active Aegean policy of his father, but two major naval defeats, along with a very different international situation, limited his potential for following the patterns of military success achieved by his father and Alexander the Great. We see Philadelphus' great accomplishment to have been the creation of a wide-ranging Greek-speaking bureaucracy in Egypt, an extensive series of regulations for controlling the economic life of the country, and an accommodation of Egyptian religious and legal practice which allowed the natives to carry on their lives for the most part in the manner to which they were accustomed, while at the same time the Macedonians and Greeks in Egypt could establish themselves in as intimate a relationship as the Egyptians to the land and its gods.

To those familiar with the papyrus texts of Egypt, a number of documents come immediately to mind to exemplify royal regulations. The *Revenue Laws Papyrus* of 259 B.C. (see figure 33), though fragmentary, has many columns extant dealing with tax farming, orchards, and vineyards, as well as elaborate rules which demonstrate to us the detailed control over the growing, pressing, and selling of oil. Other texts give us similar but perhaps more specialized manuals. *P. Hib.* 198 (c. 240 B.C.), for example, with regulations issued at various times during the reign of Philadelphus and the beginning of that of his successor, deals with a number of subjects, mainly cleruchic matters, the problem of security along water routes, and judicial issues.[4] Within texts like these come quotations of royal regulations—orders or *prostagmata*, inserts or inclusions in administrative compendia the purposes of which are not always clear. As the documents in the collection of royal ordinances compiled

---

E. Van't Dack, P. Van Dessel, and W. Van Gucht (Louvain, 1983), 205–40, which returns to earlier views of the Macedonian monarchy as the basis for later structures. L. Koenen has recently reviewed the evidence for Egyptian influence over monarchical ideology, in "Ägyptische Königsideologie am Ptolemäerhof," in *Egypt and the Hellenistic World*, 143–90, in such matters as accepting the notion of "love" as a "pillar" of ideology, and arguing that Egyptian nomenclature lies behind royal names; but it is noteworthy that any such Egyptian conceptualization is always translated and rendered in Greek, and Koenen admits that the attraction of Egyptian royal ideology in the choice of cult names could only be conceived as occuring "in einer sublimeren Weise" (169).

[4] It may have been compiled for the use of the strategus, as R. S. Bagnall suggests, "Some Notes on *P. Hib.* 198," *BASP* 6 (1969): 73–118, a discussion which makes clear the nature of the text as a compendium.

33. Revenue Laws of Ptolemy Philadelphus (259 B.C.), col. 56, lines 7–13. Bodleian Library, London. From E. G. Turner, *Greek Manuscripts of the Ancient World*, 2d ed., edited by P. J. Parsons, University of London Institute of Classical Studies Bulletin Supplement 46 (London, 1987), p. 128, pl. 76.

by Marie-Thérèse Lenger illustrate,[5] the extant papyri collect related *prostagmata* issued at different times over what can be a rather long period, and they may be intermixed with other regulatory or explanatory material.

The formal structure of the individual decrees also helps to demonstrate the manner in which the king (or his officials) framed his commands. The orders generally begin in Philadelphus' time with the minimal "King commanding," although the slightly longer "King Ptolemy commanding" is also known. They deal with specific issues, sometimes in direct response to a query or request made of the king. Occasionally there is a circular notice, as in the case of a document included in the *Revenue Laws Papyrus*, addressed to the "*strategoi* and the hipparchs and the hegemons and the nomarchs and the toparchs and the *oikonomoi* and the *antigrapheis* and the royal scribes and the libyarchs and the chiefs of police." These are all officials, but of quite a variety of competence, and the general address of the text gives some insight into the attempt of royal authority to reach simultaneously many branches of the administration. But even so, the text referred to is not general, but rather a specific regulation, of which copies were being disseminated.

For the most part, the texts in which we have preserved these royal commands seem to take their origin from the desire of individuals to have compendia of documents, rather than from a wish on the part of the administration to regularize information or procedure. For example, column 38 of the *Revenue Laws Papyrus* states that it was "corrected" in the bureau of Apollonius the *dioecetes*—the finance minister, as he is generally regarded. Whether it was the copied text which was so corrected, or whether this papyrus itself was the corrected text, we have the sense that some person, either a private party wanting to know the rules, or, perhaps more likely, a bureaucrat lower in rank, was assembling regulations and referring to higher authority to get them right.

Generally, the complexity and divisions of the bureaucracy have been explained as motivated, at least in part, by a desire to reduce the possibility of cheating by providing for checks on one another by the various officials. The existence and interaction of these many officials, at the levels of administration in Alexandria, at the levels of nome, toparchy, and village, can also be observed not only in the texts which deal with official duties and regulations but also in individual documents arising out of business dealings and official activities which we are fortunate enough to possess for the latter part of the third century. A series of small archives like those in the Petrie collection and those pertaining to

[5] *Corpus des ordonnances des Ptolémées*, Académie Royale de Belgique, Classe des Lettres, Mémoires 57, pt. 1 (Brussels, 1964).

the finds from Hibeh on the east bank of the Nile give us insight into the personal and official business of a quite wide range of Hellenes active in Egypt at this time, including some of the public works carried on by Cleon, an architect and engineer whose performance came to the (adverse) attention of the king. The great archive of papyri relating to the activities of Zenon, the agent of Philadelphus' *dioecetes* Apollonius, provides a wealth of data about the activities of Greeks in Egypt at the end of Philadelphus' reign and into the next.

Zenon himself is an almost perfect exemplar of what I believe to be characteristic of administrative activity in the period—a kind of blending of official supervision of royal interests and entrepreneurial private activity which occurred whenever it was possible. Zenon himself was, of course, not an official at all; but his position as manager of the gift-estate of 10,000 arouras which Apollonius held in the Fayum meant that he was a vital cog in the private domain of an important person in Alexandria. As such, he had access to power; and such access meant that, in the realities of power, he could intervene in the activities of official appointees in the administration. There are many texts which show appeals to Zenon for help.[6] Similarly, Zenon might find himself carrying out tasks which, narrowly defined, would be official; but in fact he was involved because his boss, Apollonius, needed something done, and having Zenon do it was the easiest procedure. A text of 254 B.C., *P. Lond. Zen.* 1973, nicely illustrates the point:

> Apollonios to Zenon greeting. As soon as you read this letter, send off to Ptolemaïs [the town] the chariots and the other carriage animals (?) and the baggage mules for the ambassadors from Pairisades [the king of Cimmerian Bosporus] and the delegates from Argos [the city in Greece] whom the King has sent to see the sights of the Arsinoite Nome. (trans. Skeat)[7]

Time and time again our texts show us that the line between official and private activity was fuzzy, that official authority might be used to achieve private ends, that private resources would be enlisted for the accomplishment of official tasks. This blend of official and private is particularly notable in the special case of Ptolemaic tax farming. It seems clear from this and many other aspects of administration in Egypt in the third century B.C. that there was no clear idea of a distinction between

---

[6] E. g., *P. Col. Zen.* 9 and 11, the latter a letter of three Kaunians asking Zenon to use his influence with Apollonius; possibly *P. Lond. Zen.* 2039, a petition to the king, was meant to be handled by Zenon, as the editor argues. See on this the comments of Edgar in the introduction to *P. Mich. Zen.*, pp. 38–40. The existence of *enteuxeis* (e.g., *P. Col. Zen.* 83) in general in the archive shows how Zenon was somehow intruded into the judicial process.

[7] Cf. also, e.g., *P. Col. Zen.* 71, which mentions "the stones which you sent to Apollonius, he brought to the king, and they pleased him a great deal" (11.15–19).

public and private,[8] a distinction which is so important in our own attitudes toward government activity. Actions which if taken by officials today would produce shouts of "Corruption!" across parliamentary aisles, were normal in the bureaucracy of Ptolemaic Egypt; further, the idea on which such complaints are based—that of a conflict of interest on the part of officials—was either unknown or wholly inconsequential to that administration. The distinction is perhaps entirely modern, imposed, in some measure at least, by a "translation mentality," along the lines of that observable in the differentiation of land categories—whereby we translate one type of land holding we find designated in the papyri, *ge idioktetos*, as "private" land, and distinguish that land from other, differently named categories such as royal, temple, and cleruchic, which we see as "public" land. The distinction evaporates if we consider *ge idioktetos* to mean something like "land held personally," whereupon that land becomes parallel to other types of holdings, rather than contrasted with them.[9]

From the beginning of the analysis of the administrative texts found in the papyri, interpretation has been influenced by the notion of this division between state and private activity. For a long time, Rostovtzeff's search for a form of capitalism affected the conceptual debate in which figures like Max Weber and Karl Polanyi differed from the great classical historian on the fundamental nature of the economy. For the most part, Rostovtzeff prevailed, and accounts of the Ptolemaic economy and administration have presented matters as centrally controlled, growth oriented, inventive, entrepreneurial, and progressive. I have elsewhere challenged the idea that growth was an object,[10] and the supposed benefits of Philadelphus' activity are denied in Eric Turner's contribution to the second edition of the *Cambridge Ancient History*, volume 7, part 1, where we find not only a reinterpretation of the hitherto admired centralized authority as much more ad hoc but also an argument for conceiving the bureaucracy as schematized along agricultural lines to serve one set of needs, with other officials organized on a financial basis to serve the concurrent money economy. Turner ultimately saw the situation in mid-third-century Egypt as one in which the crown, needing funding for

---

[8] Remarked by Dorothy Crawford, "The Good Official of Ptolemaic Egypt," in *Das Ptolemäische Ägypten, Akten des internationalen Symposions 27–29 1976 September in Berlin*, ed. Herwig Maehler and Volker Michael Strocka, (Mainz am Rhein, 1978), 201.

[9] Which helps to explain why even quite early, as in *P. Lond. Zen.* 2016, 241 B.C., we see cleruchic land quite formally bequeathed. I deal with this matter somewhat more extensively in *The Shifting Sands of History*, Publications of the Association of Ancient Historians no. 2 (Lanham and London, 1989).

[10] *From Athens to Alexandria: Hellenism and Social Goals in Ptolemaic Egypt*, Studia Hellenistica no. 26 (Lovanii, 1983).

its wars, drained the economy so severely as to push the country into internal troubles evinced as early as the reign of Euergetes.

Turner's view, like those of all his predecessors, is based on the assumption that what we find in our texts reflects a directed and in significant measure planned system, one which we can evaluate in terms of both intent and achievement. But if we accept the possibility that no one in Egypt at that period had a clear idea of "state" versus "private" interest—and that even so admired an organizer as Philadelphus was still fumbling his way toward running a large territory with Greeks who had no more idea than he had about the manner in which a king should and could relate to a bureaucracy—then we may see even more dramatic differences between earlier views and a new emerging one.[11]

To Greeks who saw the relationship between the individual and the state as organic, with the individual a functioning part of the whole (rather than a distinct segment with interests potentially opposing the whole), the traditional idea that the individual's prosperity oscillated with that of the whole made perfect sense, and a clear demarcation between "public" and "private" was inappropriate. Accordingly, public administration was exiguous in most Greek city-states, and the system of fulfilling the city's needs by liturgies suited the prevailing ideology of government. It is this model which was carried to Egypt in the years of Ptolemy I, and it was with this, I suggest, that Ptolemy II also worked. To us, it is clearly inappropriate for the operation of an economy like that of Egypt. This was gradually perceived in the course of the third century B.C., as first Ptolemy I and then his successor found themselves forced to devise practicable methods of achieving their main aim, which was in essence, while Hellenizing the existing bureaucracy, to continue collecting rent and tax revenues over a very extensive tract of land, from a large number of people whose language they did not understand[12] and who functioned in a different social and economic system from that to which the Greeks were accustomed.[13]

No doubt, what could be taken over from the past was simply continued, an assumption so reasonable that it has been accepted by many without argument, but which really needs to be fleshed out by specifics

---

[11] For Rostovtzeff's view of the ("alien" to Greeks) concept of the Ptolemaic state as the private property of the kings, and the view that the Greek economic system called for "private property recognized and protected by the state as the basis of society, and the free play of economic forces and economic initiative, with which the state very seldom interfered," see *SEHHW* 1: 269–73.

[12] See, for remarks along these lines, ibid., 2: 1080.

[13] An important cultural gap emphasized by J. Bingen, *Le Papyrus Revenue Law: Tradition grecque et adaptation hellénistique*, Rheinisch-Westfälische Akademie der Wissenschaften, Vorträge G 231 (Opladen, 1978), 9–11.

in order to provide any real guide to the manner in which Soter and Philadelphus set to work to exploit the land.[14] The question is part of the whole problem of putative continuation, which cut across the board and which affects our understanding of most social structures in Ptolemaic Egypt—religious, artistic, technological, and legal, as well as administrative. The problem is inevitably made more complex, and the interpretations of the evidence more subtle, by the fact that continuation and innovation in any given area were in practice by no means uniform for both Greek and Egyptian society. That the Egyptians went their own way in many areas, while the Greeks followed Hellenic patterns, is well known; the separate Egyptian and Greek cults of Isis are one example of the phenomenon. In the area of monarchy, what can be seen as continuation of ideology for Egyptians can be quite irrelevant to the Hellenic situation; in administration, the fact that demotic terms cannot always be exactly or reliably related to Greek makes for serious problems in identifying continuation of practice.

To whatever extent Ptolemy I adopted or adapted the structure of the bureaucracy he found when he arrived in Egypt, there is no doubt that by the time of his son's reign the king was saddled with an administrative system of great size and complexity. I suggest that this administration, which to us seems so "rational" precisely because of its complexity, in fact became so complex as a direct consequence of its irrationality: the new was built up piecemeal, and the old changed only as circumstances required, inconsistent modifications often taking place as various methods proved imperfect or failed. Our tendency to see the growth of the bureaucracy as answering some master plan may lead us to misunderstand, seriously, the purposes of even some of the most important actions which we know the early Ptolemies took; we should really consider standing some of our assumptions on their heads. For example: The cleruch system may have been devised, not to provide a means of compensating soldiers, but rather for the purpose of putting as many Greek-speaking people on the land as possible, in order to facilitate the collection of rents and taxes. This would help to explain why in Egypt we find the settlers scattered rather than settled in cities; the crown may have needed them out there.[15]

If this view of the genesis of the administrative structure has validity,

---

[14] An exception is Thomas's argument that the offices of *dioecetes* and nomarch were not Ptolemaic innovations: "Aspects of the Ptolemaic Civil Service: The Dioiketes and the Nomarch," in *Ptolemäische Ägypten*, 187–194.

[15] In particular, if we accept R. S. Bagnall's persuasive argument that the cleruchs hark back to an influx of soldiers at the time of Ptolemy I ("The Origins of Ptolemaic Cleruchs," *BASP* 21 [1984]: 7–20), we might have expected the initial settlement to follow the urban patterns familiar to Greeks.

it is also true that the system didn't work. The evidence of unrest in Egypt during the reign of Ptolemy III Euergetes, native revolts in the reigns of the fourth and fifth Ptolemies, and a long period of internal disruption and division lasting for most of the second century, all show that the apparent stability of mid-third-century Egypt did not last. The reason for the troubles is less clear, however. It may well be that, as Turner argued, the strain imposed on the economy by the extortion of Ptolemy II's regime led to resistance on the part of the peasantry, and that the economic deterioration of the countryside caused by Philadelphus was as important a factor in the developing instability of government as were political events like the costs of the Syrian war which lasted from the accession of Euergetes to 240, and the succession to the throne of three minors in a row—Ptolemy IV Philopator, Ptolemy V Epiphanes, and Ptolemy VI Philometor.

The political problems were, at least cumulatively, a serious burden, and the decades of trouble, lasting almost all through the second century, clearly had an effect on the administrative structure. Although Euergetes' attack on Syria in the early 240s was treated as a great success by the synod of priests who issued the Canopus Decree, congratulating the king on his victory and issuing thanks for his benefactions (such as the recapture of the statues of the Egyptian gods), Euergetes in fact had to end the war in order to deal with domestic troubles. The victory in 217 of Philopator against Seleucid forces at Raphia may have made the eastern region of the country secure; but there was a price to pay in the rising self-confidence of Egyptian armed troops, who were first used, successfully, on that occasion. In any case, for two decades after 206 B.C., native dynasts ruled in the area around Thebes, and despite brief successes at the turn of the century, the authority of Alexandria was not firmly reasserted until 186 B.C. Even that did not put Alexandria in solid control of Egypt, for there were other native usurpers in central and upper Egypt in 164 and then again thirty years later. At the same time, quarrels within the ruling family produced civil war and periods in which there were separate and antagonistic centers of government. The conflict between Ptolemy VIII and Cleopatra II reached such a pitch of bitterness as to induce the king to murder and dismember a son whom the two had produced. Even after the reign of Ptolemy VIII ended with the king's death in June 116 (his reconciled rival Cleopatra II died a few months later), a new reign, and a new set of dynastic quarrels, began with the establishment on the throne of Cleopatra III, the second wife of Ptolemy VIII, jointly with her son by Euergetes, Ptolemy IX Soter II.

So long a period of feuding in the royal family inevitably brought disruption, some of it well documented. Ptolemy VIII Euergetes II at one point expelled large numbers of his Greek-speaking opponents from

Alexandria, a sweep which significantly diminished the intellectual population, and was responsible for both the deterioration of that city's cultural life and the spread of culture more broadly to other points in the Mediterranean. We also have a copy of the precautionary will which Euergetes II made in 154 before going to Rome: he left the Romans his kingdom if he died without heirs, a notice which was intended to warn his brother that there would be no gain if he, Euergetes, were to be killed. The will was published prominently; our copy is an inscription erected at Cyrene.[16]

We also have documents at a lower level of activity, papyri from Egypt which not only trace the recognition of various rulers in different parts of the country but also include complaints, letters, and petitions reporting turmoil and unrest. From the end of the reign of Euergetes II comes the publication of the amnesty decree recorded in *P. Tebt.* 5, issued in 118 in the name of Euergetes II and his two queens, the earlier dissident Cleopatra II and Cleopatra III. The provisions for a reordering of economic and administrative affairs not only illustrate the difficulties besetting the peasantry and population of the countryside, but also accord with the evolution of the administration which earlier documents show. After the mid–third century, the point at which we have our clearest evidence for the workings of the bureaucracy, changes inevitably took place. The large number of petitions extant from the end of the reign of Euergetes I and the beginning of Philopator's, with their demonstration of judicial procedure carried out in the office of the *strategos*, graphically demonstrate one way in which that nominally military official's brief expanded into the area of civil administration. The same kind of slurring over what are to us clearly separated administrative categories can be found later in the second century at lower levels, as officials like village scribes, who early do not seem to have had administrative or judicial authority, exercise powers which seem simply to have accrued to them. When I first looked at this problem years ago, I saw the phenomenon of the growth of power of a village scribe as a shift in structure, on the assumption that the bureaucracy implied a rational and planned division of roles; now, the evidence rather suggests to me that blurring of roles and exercise of power by officials on an ad hoc basis was always characteristic of Ptolemaic structure.

The trend of my argument is to suggest that the bureaucracy may have developed in a way very different from that envisioned heretofore. Rather than being a system developed entirely from the top, on rational principles for planned purposes, it my have evolved in answer, not only to a desire to achieve specific objectives on the part of the king or other

---

[16] *SEG* 9, 7.

senior officials, but also to wishes on the part of Greeks in Egypt to find administrative posts and get themselves some benefit from their official positions.[17] In all probability, the complex bureaucracy which we see in mid-third-century Egypt resulted from just this pressure. I think it quite likely that by 250 B.C. a very large proportion of the noncleruchic Greek-speaking individuals of Egypt had found their way into one administrative billet or another,[18] and that the bureaucracy developed its own momentum. The administrative checks and controls which our papyri attest in all likelihood reflect, not a careful plan established in Alexandria, but rather a desperate attempt on the part of the crown to get some control over a structure which, at the lowest village levels, was practically autonomous. Just as we now realize that the *diagraphe tou sporou* was not a directive from on high in Alexandria setting out the areas to be sown in various crops on the basis of rational planning but was rather, in the first instance, drawn up in the villages as a forecast of the coming crop,[19] so we should understand the entire bureaucracy to reflect, not a rational plan, but rather the aggregate of the day-to-day activity of officials at various levels. Once Ptolemaic adventurism overseas came to an end in the first half of the third century, the ambitions of the king's men had to turn to the exploitation of Egypt, and this was most easily achieved through the administration.

These Hellenes carried out their task in Egypt with no sense of the structure of an administrative state, and without much notion of distinguishing between "private" and "public" roles. They did what they had to do; they responded to demands from superiors when they could not do otherwise, and they seized any opportunity to take advantage of the weaknesses of those below them in the administration or subject to them

---

[17] That administrative posts were desirable is demonstrated by the fact that people were willing to pay to get them, as in the payments and required cultivation agreed to by Menches in return for reappointment as *komogrammateus* of Kerkeosiris in 119 B.C. (*P. Tebt.* 9 and 10. Cf. Crawford, "Good Official," 201).

[18] In a study of mine for which I had a different focus ("The Greek Element in the Ptolemaic Bureaucracy," in *Acts of the Twelfth International Congress of Papyrology,* Am. Stud. Pap. no. 7 [Toronto, 1970], 450) I found that of the identifiable Greek-speaking individuals of Hibeh, whether or not with Greek names, a significant proportion could be seen to have official billets. The figures: Greek names, minimum individuals identified, 17.4% with official titles; maximum individuals (assuming nonidentity of the same names) 9.5% with official titles; non-Greek names, minimum number of individuals, 13.5% officials; maximum individuals, 9.0% officials. In larger and more important administrative centers, the proportions would obviously increase significantly.

[19] See *P. Yale* 36 and accompanying discussion. The conclusion now seems confirmed by the demotic "Karnak Ostracon," published by E. Bresciani, "La spedizione di Tolomeo II in Siria in un ostrakon demotico inedito da Karnak," in *Ptolemäische Ägypten,* 31–37, which calls for a survey of the agricultural situation.

in the population. It was easiest to keep the officials above them happy with the steady flow of goods and revenues by putting the pressure on the producers, while they could take advantage of the myriad opportunities which might emerge out of day-to-day activity, by making loans, by buying and selling where profit could be turned, and, of course, by any illegal diversions of the royal revenues. Upper levels of the administration responded in various ways to theft of the king's goods and to the petitions and complaints which filtered up through the system. Royal directives against abuses betrayed an optimistic lack of of understanding of what was developing.[20] A document like *P. Tebt.* 703, of the time of Euergetes I, illustrates the manner in which an official, generally thought to be the *dioecetes* in Alexandria, tried to guide, or control, a local *oikonomos*, not only listing some of the duties of the junior but urging him to correct abuses by officials and abuses of the past, so that all would realize that misbehavior and wrongdoing were ended; the inducement of higher positions was dangled before the *oikonomos*, and there was an implied threat that only by following these orders would he be safe.

I doubt that the overall position of the administration changed much after the middle of the third century. The general pattern I have outlined—the use of administrative positions for gain, the ignoring of any line between activity affecting the well-being of the individual official and the benefit of the crown—remained characteristic of the system.[21] The autonomy of officials at lower levels increased with time,[22] as the number of Greek speakers in Egypt grew as a result of natural increase, and more and more of them crowded and confused the system. That development may have borne the greatest responsibility for the deterioration in the economic life of Egypt attributed by so many scholars to the second century.

While the bureaucracy went its own way in minor corruption and in countless little transactions for the benefit of officials, the enormous potential wealth of Egypt assured the crown of a continued flow of revenue. Kings and officials in Alexandria—child kings and adults, their guardians and advisers—had an adequate supply of crops, and the revenues from them, throughout the Hellenistic period: Egypt remained an

---

[20] The difference between military and civil administration is illustrated by a story told about Harry Truman. When asked what he thought his successor, General Eisenhower, would find most difficult about the presidency, Truman responded, "When he gives an order, and nothing happens."

[21] For a survey of the overall problem, see Claire Préaux, *L'Économie royale des Lagides* (Brussels, 1939), 514–33.

[22] Ibid., 523–24.

enormously productive domain down to the reign of Cleopatra VII.[23] If there were occurrences which might curtail the flow to Alexandria, the bureaucracy simply increased pressure on the population—much easier to do than arguing with senior officials. The woes of the peasantry were caused less by a rapacious monarchy than by a steadily growing army of bureaucrats lining their pockets and then covering themselves against any complaints from superiors by draining the producers to meet expectations, even in difficult times.

Thus we need to see the bureaucracy of Egypt as receiving its impetus only in part from the monarchy, and in any case not developed as a rational structure for the execution of policy but growing partly of its own momentum and partly from royal attempts to control it. In such a context the monarchy is not quite the whole government, but rather an institution making up only part of the structure, albeit nominally and conceptually at its head. The administrative structure and bureaucracy were complex and highly articulated, but they were not completely answerable to the monarchy. Officials could and did function independently of Alexandria, and seem to have been relatively indifferent to the contests for power between various members of the dynasty. The royal court existed alongside the bureaucracy and was more powerful than the bureaucrats insofar as it disposed of military and police personnel; but though that power enabled the kings to control the country by force and to draw a steady flow of resources from it, it did not allow them to operate and supervise the administrative structure closely. Just as the Latin expression for Alexandria, *Alexandria ad Aegyptum*, expressed a geographic concept of the relationship between the great city and the land of the Nile, so the geographic concept serves to describe the nature of the Macedonian administration: by Egypt, yet not of it.

If this argument—that the bureaucracy did not develop primarily from the plans and objectives of Philadelphus or others who followed him—be sustained, then our current understanding of the ideology of the dynasty must change. We can no longer understand Philadelphus' kingship as worked out in terms of his establishment of administrative control over the land,[24] and we must be open to giving greater weight to

---

[23] Or at least to the reign of Auletes; see T.R.S. Broughton, *AJP* 106 (1985): 115–16, citing Athen. *Deipn.* 5.206 c–d, which asserts that Auletes dissipated the "treasure of the Ptolemies."

[24] There is no doubt about the reclamation work in the Fayum, summarized by Rostovtzeff, *SEHHW* 1:360–362, and illustrated by *P. Lille* 1, (which L. Criscuolo argues did not relate specifically to Apollonius' *dorea* at Philadelphia: "I Mariaruri nell' Egitto tolemaico," *Aegyptus* 57 [1977]: 109–22). Criscuolo's discussion is concerned to show that the title "ten-thousand aroura holder" relates not to a grant holder but to a manager of a district of that size in the reclamation project of the Fayum. W. Clarysse, "Egyptian Estate-holders in the Ptolemaic Period," in *State and Temple Economy in the Ancient Near East: Proceedings of the*

other items of evidence than we have done up to now. An important item is the conceptualization in Theocritus' seventeenth idyll. In this eulogy to Philadelphus, patterned on the Homeric hymns, Theocritus praises Ptolemy, in Homeric language, for virtues which are themselves Homeric—the fighting prowess, the munificence, the wealth, the genesis from divinity, with which we associate Homer's kings. There is certainly no reflection of any characteristics which would suggest that Ptolemy II was different in quality from those kings. There is praise of Philadelphus' great father, Ptolemy, associated not only with divinity through his descent from Heracles but also, by proximity, to Alexander. Himself a god, the great conqueror and his relation to Ptolemy are presented in terms reminiscent of descriptions of Zeus seated on Olympus. Throughout the poem there are, in fact allusions to Zeus. "We begin with Zeus," Theocritus opens his paean of praise; he also ends with the Olympian, a traditional way of closing such a poem.

In an idyll which follows many of the patterns of early Greek poetry, Ptolemy II is praised in terms applicable to kings far back in Greek tradition, at a time before the emergence of the city-states of old Greece, and long before the conquests of Alexander and the wars of the Successors. The ideology of monarchy is the same as that on which Alexander patterned his kingship: divine descent, warrior prowess, reverence toward the gods, and generosity toward men from his great wealth. These are characteristics stressed by the Alexander tradition in its account of the world conqueror's accomplishments, and Theocritus applies them to Ptolemy. While we cannot, of course, assert, on the basis of a single work, that this concept of Ptolemy II as monarch exhausts the attributes of kingship as envisioned by him and his contemporaries, it is certainly clear that the qualities listed by Theocritus would have been prominent among those regarded as flattering to the king, and it is most likely that there were no "royal" characteristics of greater import to the concept of kingship.

There is every likelihood that the attributes of kingship emphasized by Theocritus were those understood as kingly by the first Ptolemy. In any case, by the middle of the third century, Theocritus' Philadelphus was available as a god, at least for ordinary purposes like the swearing of the royal oath. A text like *P. Hib.* 38 of Philadelphus' thirty-fourth year, dealing with the sinking of a Nile ship, ends with the following text: "I swear by King Ptolemy and Arsinoë Philadelphus, brother and sister gods, and the savior gods their parents that what statements have been

International Conference Organized by the Katholieke Universiteit Leuven from the 10th to the 14th of April 1978, Orientalia Lovanensia Analecta no. 6, ed. E. Lipinski (Leuven, 1979) 2: 737–93, points out a number of reasons which put *P. Lille* 1 in the vicinity of Philadelphia.

written above are true."[25] This is a different formulation from the struc-
turing of the dynastic cult with a priest of the *Theoi Adelphoi*, which *P.
Hib.* 199 shows to have taken place at least two decades earlier. Much has
been written on the subject of the Ptolemaic dynastic cult, but, while our
technical knowledge—dates, expansion, priesthoods, and the like—has
advanced with the publication of more and more documents, we have
not progressed much in our understanding of how the dynastic cult fitted
into either religion or the ideology of monarchy.[26] I think it is fair to say
that there is still no agreement on how the cult might have been valuable
to the *politique* of the monarchy, or whether it had any real religious
role for the Greeks in Egypt. While the use of the royal oath shows the
adaptation of the Greeks in Egypt to the idea of the divinity of the kings
in a formal sense, it does not show their resort to the cult for purposes
like those for which they might turn to the cults of, let us say, Isis, Sarapis,
or Asclepius.

It is also clear that the dynastic cult of the Ptolemies never spread
throughout the Mediterranean world in the way that we find the worship
of Isis and Sarapis did; and this may well indicate a difference in the
attitude toward it. In any case, as Dunand points out, the Ptolemies were
not directly involved in the propagation of these cults, and their establishment for the most part was a matter of individual initiative.[27] The dynastic cult was largely a phenomenon restricted to Egypt itself, and that has

---

[25] That these oaths are intended to be taken seriously is indicated by the lack of formula
in the earliest period. Cf., for example, *P. Lond. Zen.* 2045, swearing to Zenon "by your
tyche and the *daimon* of the king." The elaboration of the oath is illustrated by *P. Fuad Univ.*
3–4.

[26] Probably because it has not been as much studied or discussed as we would expect:
two and a half pages (96–98) in *CAH*[2] VII.l, three (255–57) in Préaux's *Monde hellénistique*,
describing the establishment of the dynastic cult as a cult of Alexander, then the development of the cult of the living sovereigns under Philadelphus and the modifications under
subsequent kings. There are studies which try to place the cult in its context in time and
place in terms of development and cults of other monarchies: L. Cerfaux and J. Tondriau,
Le Culte des souverains dans la civilization gréco-romain (Tournai, 1957), 193–208; F. Taeger,
Charisma: Studien zur Geschichte des antiken Herrscherkultes (Stuttgart, 1957), 287–309 n. for
Egypt. Taeger (297) sees the religious aspect of the cult as "questionable," and this is a
judgment often made, although P. M. Fraser, *Ptolemaic Alexandria* (Oxford, 1972) 1:225,
refuses to dismiss it "as a fiction designed purely to give prestige to holders of paper
priesthoods." This latter is the view of J. Ijsewijn, *De sacerdotibus sacerdotiisque Alexandri
Magni et Lagidarum eponymis* (Brussels, 1961), the only full-dress review of the priests to
that date; insofar as Ijsewijn carries through his discussion of specific priests, it shows the
priesthoods to have been held by members of the court circle.

[27] F. Dunand, "Cultes égyptiens hors d'Égypte: Nouvelles voies d'approche et d'inter-
prétation," in *Egypt and the Hellenistic World* (Leuven, 1983), 80–81; Dunand provides a
valuable survey of recent scholarship on the spread of the Egyptian cults, while at the same
time suggesting approaches to their interpretation.

been taken to meant that it existed only where it was supported directly by the crown. On the other hand, cults of individual sovereigns, kings and queens, dedications and temples, combine to show members of the dynasty treated as divinities, either individually or in assimilation to other deities in Egypt. Similarly, the evidence of sculpture, like the many small stone heads of Philadelphus[28] which were attached to bodies of cheaper materials like wood, are inexplicable unless they were used as cult figures by private persons.[29] Thus, despite all the uncertainties in the material, there is no doubt that the idea of the Ptolemaic monarchy definitely included a notion of the divinity of the king, a notion which extended to the Greeks and Macedonians and was established in the ideology as early as the middle of the reign of Philadelphus.

Military leadership had certainly also been an important aspect of monarchy for the Macedonians. Moderns have tended to downgrade this aspect of kingship for the Ptolemies, seeing Soter's policy as a cautious dependence on Egypt which he never risked in pursuit of other objectives, and Philadelphus' behavior as that of an unwarlike personality who abandoned even restricted objectives when they became difficult or expensive to achieve. Yet a connected account of his military activities, often neglected in favor of describing his administration, reveals them to have been by no means negligible. Although all modern scholars recognize that by the mid 250s Philadelphus' position in the Aegean was much inferior to that which he had taken over from his father, his lack of success in military affairs does not necessarily indicate a distaste for them, and a realistic assessment of his use of warfare hardly justifies the common judgment that he was unmilitary and pacific in character. He was involved in war almost incessantly for a large part of the first three decades after he came to the throne,[30] and we can even find traces in the

---

[28] There are many examples, such as the Dresden head, inventory 2600/A28, or Alexandria inventories 22.185 and 19.122.

[29] This is the conclusion of Helmut Kyrielis, *Bildnisse der Ptolemäer*, Archäologische Forschungen no. 2 (Berlin, 1975), 145–48. While Kyrielis may exaggerate the centralizing quality of Philadelphus' reign, and assumes more direction of developments than the king was in fact able to achieve, it is interesting that he sees (158–64) a significant difference in the practice of royal representation in Egypt from that characteristic of the other kingdoms of the period.

[30] It is certainly clear that he used the conflict in the Seleucid dynasty in about 280/79 to make acquisitions in the Aegean area, although details are difficult to discern. In the first years of his reign he regained Samos, which had belonged to Lysimachus as late as 282 (cf. *OGIS* 13 = *SIG*³ 688, and *SIG*³ 390); and he took over Miletus, where in 280/79 Antiochus I was stephanophor, while in 279/8 a gift of Philadelphus is recorded (*Milet*, vol. 1, part 3, p. 123). Between 274 and 271, it seems, he fought a war with Antiochus I, the First Syrian War. For most of the next decade, Ptolemaic forces were involved in the Aegean in support of Athens and Sparta in the Chremonidean War; then, about 260, they plunged into the Second Syrian War, which lasted perhaps to about 253 and brought

papyri of the mustering of his forces. The now-famous Karnak ostrakon found in 1969/70 refers in the year 28 (258) to the king's victory over the philo-Persian king, and alludes to Philadelphus' military activities in either the first or second Syrian wars.[31] Citing this text and others long known, Eric Turner has reconstructed Egyptian history in the second quarter of the third century as a period of intense and expensive warfare, which meant that by the 250s the crown was squeezing everything available out of the economy.[32] Whether or not one agrees with his assessment of the extent to which the administration was being centrally run, Turner's claim of military strain and expense better reflects the evidence of international activities by Philadelphus than does the traditional picture of the pacific and genial king. Finally, the evidence of Appian and Callixenus, which tends to be ignored or discounted, for the huge military resources of Philadelphus is in fact not contradicted by any other testimony; and even if the numbers given are exaggerated, as moderns subjectively decide, the forces were still very great indeed.[33]

I have, so far, delineated two areas of activity in which we can see actions that affect the image of the monarchy: the establishment of a cult based on a king who is a god, and the heavy involvement of the king and his resources in military adventure. There were, of course, other characteristics of kingly behavior which Philadelphus exemplified. An important feature of Alexander's kingship had been the image of culture and philohellenism the conqueror presented, and in that Philadelphus managed to outstrip his predecessor. There is no need here to show, even in the broadest outline, the manner in which Philadelphus built on

---

various results and troubles, including revolts by "Ptolemy the Son," which unhinged his control over some of the cities in western Anatolia. We can trace some of the events, like the shift of Ephesus to Ptolemy in about 262, and its return to Seleucid control in about 258; and we are told of important naval battles, Cos and Andros, which Philadelphus' forces lost. These, however, involve serious dating problems, which make for difficulty in tracing the history of Ptolemaic fortunes in the Aegean.

[31] Bresciani, "La spedizione di Tolomeo II," 31–37. The king is either Antiochus I or Antiochus II, depending on how one chooses to date the allusion in the document.

[32] *CAH*² VII. 1, 135–59.

[33] Appian, *Praef.* 10, claims a land army of 200,000 infantry, 40,000 cavalry, 300 elephants, 2,000 armed chariots and an arms store for 300,000 additional troops; plus a naval force of 2,000 punts and small craft, 1,500 triremes of various classes and equipment for double that number, and 800 thalamegas. Callixenus, reported in Athen. *Deipn.* 203a, states that in the grand procession of Philadelphus, held c. 275, the military parade included 57,600 infantry and 23,200 cavalry, all properly uniformed and armed. Both authors claim documentary sources for their figures: Appian, the so-called *basilikai anagraphai*; and Callixenus, the *graphai penterides*, cited as available for further details of the grand procession in Athen. *Deipn.* 197d. Athenaeus, in a passage between that dealing with the procession and that dealing with the great "40" of Philopator, *Deipn.* 203d, gives some specific details for Philadelphus' navy, a text that may go back to Callixenus.

the accomplishment of his father in making Alexandria a great center of culture in the Mediterranean. It is enough to point out that his use of patronage, together with the projects and facilities of the Library and Museum, made his court renowned as a paradigm of cultural munificence and ensured that when, a century later, a Jew in Egypt was drafting his "Letter of Aristeas" to explain the manner in which the Hebrew scriptures came to be translated into Greek, it would be Philadelphus of whom he would think when it came to giving credit for the accomplishment. The attraction to Alexandria, on a permanent or transient basis, of figures like Theocritus, Callimachus, and Archimedes assured the king of a truly royal reputation for the future, not only through Theocritus' hymn, in which the poet recorded his greatness for posterity, but in his association with the writing and accomplishments of most of the great scientists and literary figures of the age. More generally, the wealth and generosity which Theocritus claims for Philadelphus[34] are both exemplified by the almost incredible expense and display associated with the great procession,[35] as well as by Appian's report that the king had 740,000 talents in his treasury and was noted for his revenues, his extraordinary spending, and the extent of his building programs.[36]

Another notable aspect of Ptolemaic kingship was the evolution of the traditional group of royal Companions we remember from the accounts of Alexander. Ptolemy, like the other Successors, had a circle of advisers, courtiers, and agents known as Friends—Greeks, Alexandrians, and Macedonians on whom he could rely and whom he used for military, administrative, and diplomatic purposes. Quite a number of these are attested for the reign of Ptolemy I, in literary and epigraphical sources, and many of them received honors from the Greek cities associated with Ptolemy.[37] Philadelphus too had his *Philoi*, and there are such attested, although in

---

[34] *Id.* 17.95–111.

[35] Now extensively treated in a commentary by E. E. Rice, *The Grand Procession of Ptolemy Philadelphus* (Oxford, 1983), arguing effectively (124–25, 138–50) for the credibility of the text here and in the description of the enormous tent of Philadelphus in Athen. *Deipn.* 196a–97c, and the spectacular ships of Philopator in *Deipn.* 203e–6c.

[36] App. *Praef.* 10. Athenaeus refers to his great wealth in *Deipn.* 203c.

[37] Not only for Ptolemy but also for the other early rulers, G. Herman's analysis of the honorary decrees indicates that "the impression conveyed is that the ties between the honorands and the rulers were informal, casual and uninstitutionalized." "The 'Friends' of the Early Hellenistic Rulers: Servants or Officials?" *Talanta* 12–13 (1980–1981): 107. Herman argues cogently that the vagueness of the references in the early period reflects a negative attitude toward court officials on the part of citizens of Greek cities, who accordingly omit these references from decrees intended to honor such men; as attitudes toward the holding of titles changes, so these titles appear in Greek inscriptions with greater frequency. The negative attitude may also reflect Greek civic unfamiliarity with bureaucracy itself, seeing official titles as reflecting servile status rather than office.

dwindling numbers, in the reign of Euergetes and then in even lesser numbers later on under successive members of the dynasty. Comparatively few references to the Friends or their activities exist in the papyri; the Friends were clearly functionaries in Alexandria and at the level of the immediate circle of the king and court. In addition to Friends, there also seem to have been men with the titles of Bodyguard and Chief Bodyguard, but the attestation of these is much scantier and they seem to have been fewer; in any case such offices seem to have lapsed soon after the end of the third century.

A very different pattern of titling emerged in Egypt in the second century, as Mooren's study shows.[38] While the practice of appointing individuals at the court to the position of Friend continued, a second system of titling, an honorific one, grew up, whereby higher officials in the administration were given honorary court titles, graded in rank according to the administrative offices they held. These titles and their holders—unlike the Friends, who appear primarily in inscriptions and literary texts—turn up for the most part in the papyri pertaining to the administration of Egypt, and with the greater amount of evidence there, can be traced more clearly in our documentary record. We can see, for example, that from about 197/6 on there were six ranks in the honorary titulature and that later in the century, in the reign of Ptolemy VIII, two more were added. This honorific hierarchy, as Mooren has pointed out, is a characteristic feature in the development of administrative structures, whereas the circle of Friends, who actually serve the king in the court, is "spontaneous," with an explanation which "is sociological."[39] Furthermore, when we are considering the nature of the monarchy, patterns like that evinced by the functioning of a circle of Friends or Companions, whose relationship with the king is bilateral, direct, personal, and nonhereditary, show a very different sense of the relationship between the king and his *pragmata* than do patterns such as those inherent in stratified honorific appointments. Mooren's examination of the two patterns and his demonstration of the shift in the early second century offer an important confirmation of what we have been finding in connection with the conceptualization of the monarchy and its relationship to administration and government. For the third century, and the earlier the more so, the crown seems to have relied on, and governed extensively through, the traditional Macedonian group surrounding the

---

[38] L. Mooren, *The Aulic Titulature in Ptolemaic Egypt: Introduction and Prosopography*, Verhandelingen koninklijke Academie Wetenschappen, Letteren en schone Kunsten van Belvie, Lett. 37 no. 78 (Brussels, 1975).

[39] Ibid., p. 2.

king.[40] Only in the second century, and, significantly, during the rule of a minor king, does there emerge a strong association of bureaucrats with the monarchy, through the establishment of a system of honorary titulature which asserts court rank for administrators.[41]

The shift suggests a significant change in the government of Egypt, and a development of the ideology of monarchy as well. It seems to me that so long as Soter, Philadelphus, and Euergetes were able, they used their Friends, members of the court circle, as much as they could in the carrying out of official tasks, and that they continued to do so even while the administration was growing larger and more difficult to control.[42] The story of the trio of Philadelphus, Apollonius, and Zenon is one of the king dealing with all sorts of issues and arranging all sorts of matters through his "Friend" Apollonius,[43] who in turn uses his agent Zenon for royal as well as personal duties. What the Zenon archive shows, I suggest, is not the success or failure of the new administrative structure in either improving or exploiting Egypt—depending on one's view—but rather the continuing effectiveness in mid-third-century Egypt of direct administration by the court.

Direct administration might work, but the bureaucracy was growing of its own impetus. By the end of the third century, with the domination of Philopator by his high officials, and then with the accession of the minor Epiphanes, the stage was set for a great change. I have no doubt that the shift in administration and the royalization of the bureaucracy had to do with the domination of affairs by Sosibios and Agathocles, and then the events involving and following their regency in Alexandria. These two—particularly Agathocles, together with his sister Agathocleia, mistress of Philopator—have a bad press in our ancient sources, and this ancient disrespect has been carried on by many moderns; but in fact the preservation of the Ptolemaic monarchy against Antiochus II owes much

[40] As Herman remarks, " 'Friends,' " 116, the early period seems to show a lack of "administrative differentiation or specialization" among these high-ranking officials, a general phenomenon to which the Ptolemaic court conforms.

[41] This view of motivation expresses somewhat differently the conclusions reached by L. Mooren in *La Hiérarchie du court ptolémaïque*, Studia Hellenistica no. 23 (Louvain, 1977), 50–61, which also sees that in essence the hierarchy of titulature has its value in differentiations of rank within the bureaucracy.

[42] P. M. Fraser, *Ptolemaic Alexandria* (Oxford, 1972) 1:101–5 draws the distinction between the court circle (used for administering the empire), and the internal administration of Egypt (that of the "state" as a "dual administration"), which became blended in the second century.

[43] We do not know Apollonius' rank, but we do know that the king had direct resort to him.

to them.[44] The will of Ptolemy IV (allegedly forged) made them *epitropoi* for the minor child Ptolemy V; soon after the death of Philopator and the accession of the new king were announced in 204, Sosibios died (perhaps by the end of 203), and not much later Agathocles and his sister were killed in a rising led by one Tlepolemos, who then assumed the regency. In all this period, a native revolt was disturbing Egypt, and Antiochus continued to press against Egypt from the east, and it was an Aetolian refugee to Alexandria named Scopas to whom the military was entrusted. Scopas was well known as a general, and he was effective for a while against Antiochus, briefly regaining much of Palestine. But in 200, at Panium, Antiochus decisively defeated him, and forced him to surrender and vacate Palestine the next year. We later hear of him, after the Roman defeat of Philip V and the negotiations for a peace between Antiochus and Ptolemy V, failing in revolt, his life ended by self-administered poison (197). The engineer of Scopas' destruction and the peace with Antiochus was another Aetolian, Aristomenes, who had taken over as regent from Tlepolemos; and Aristomenes himself ended his life by poison within a few years.

I tell of this period in such detail to shed light on the ineffectiveness of the king at that time. Egypt was governed by court officials who faced the need to gather funds, troops, and support in order to repel external invasion, put down domestic insurrection—they didn't easily do that—and even maintain the king against a revolt like that of Scopas. For a king, with a reliable group of Friends and with the authority of divinity, this would have been a difficult enough task. Without the mystique of kingship it was even harder, and it is easy to see how nonroyal administrators (and then guardians of a minor king) like Sosibios, Agathocles, and Tlepolemos depended even more than the third-century kings on the bureaucracy. It was only the bureaucracy, which had functioned alongside the court, that could provide them with the resources and the support they needed; and it is, therefore, very soon that the bureaucrats begin to get their rewards in the shape of court-related titles and prestige. At the same time, the ministers in Alexandria were eager to conciliate those native elements who still had importance and at the same time offered potential support—that is, the temple aristocracy, whose favor could be curried with money and gifts. Again, by no accident, it is precisely at this time, the beginning of the second century, that we have the promulgation of the Rosetta decree. Similar to the Canopus decree of about forty years earlier in its praise of the king, but striking

---

[44] The factions and relationships among the highest personages in the court in this period are detailed by Leon Mooren, "The Ptolemaic Court System," *Chron. d'Ég.* 60 (1985): 214–22.

in its differences of style and language, the Rosetta stone shows how the initiative in this mode of honoring the king had passed from the Greek-speaking court to the Egyptian priests themselves.

The *philanthropa* which emerge from the court at the end of the second century B.C. have traditionally been explained as efforts to stabilize the countryside and the administration after a long period of dynastic conflict between Euergetes II, his brother, and his sister. There had been open warfare in the land between the forces of the kings and queens a number of times during this period, but our documents reflect practically none of this.[45] That there was military strife appears clearly from a papyrus like the letter of Esthladas to his parents, telling of the dispatch of forces against rebels in Alexandria in 130.[46] In fact, however, we trace events much more through the dating formulas in papyri of the period, which, by naming one or another of the rival claimants, reveal in a more pacific way who was recognized as ruler in a given place, and when. It is, in fact, this pacific characteristic of the texts that I want to stress. In the period of most intense dynastic warfare, 132–130, the bureaucrats made an effort to date their documents as best they could by whichever monarch they thought to be in power—but what counted was the form of the documents, rather than loyalty to any individual ruler. Texts written at Thebes try to indicate the situation with parallel dating by rival sovereigns, such as "year 40 which is year 2,"[47] or dating by one only—Euergetes II or Cleopatra II. A text like *BGU* 993 is indicative: a division of inheritance dated by Euergetes II and Cleopatra III, using the normal dating formula by king and queen and the priests and priestesses of the dynastic cult, refers to those priests casually as "being in the camp of the king." The documents show that the scribes were quite aware of the dynastic strife, but that they carried on with business as usual despite the turmoil which in Thebes, whence many of these texts originate, was quite close.

[45] It would be gratuitous to cite a vast list of normal documents like *P. Par* 65 (146 B.C.) and *P. Ahm.* 35 (132 B.C.) to illustrate the continuing regular work of the bureaucracy in troubled times, but it is worth pointing out the steady flow of tax receipts on ostraca at Thebes before, during, and after the period of greatest turmoil, 132–130 B.C. (e.g., *O. Bodl.* 168–88, *WO* 341–52), and to cite the petitions (and other documents) of the third quarter of the century among the Tebtunis papyri which attest the bureaucracy working in its usual way, with the writers suffering the same kinds of troubles and expecting officials to deal with their problems as did petitioners before Egypt had experienced such severe dynastic trouble.

[46] *W. Chr.* 10. There are only a few documents which reflect the unrest in the period, and they are often cited. Others include *P. Tebt.* 61 (b); the land survey of 118–117 B.C., which mentions land that had been allowed to become dry during the *amixia* (of unspecified date); *P. Tebt.* 72.45, referring to land up to the thirty-ninth year (132/1 B.C.) before the *amixia*.

[47] For a discussion and references, see my *Ptolemaic Chronology* (Munich, 1962), 146–47.

We know that turmoil continued in Egypt for some time after the reconciliation between Euergetes II and his sister,[48] but eventually there emerged the document which all historians cite as denoting both the troubles of the period and the attempt at a settlement, *P. Tebt.* 5 of 118. The joint decree of the king, his sister, and his wife, which provides for an amnesty for all crimes but murder and sacrilege, also remits debts for various taxes and charges, confirms many privileges of priests and temples, forbids a number of malpractices by officials, ratifies the separate procedure through Greek or native courts, and provides many benefactions I need not enumerate here. While the turmoil in the land doubtless led to failures on the part of tax collectors to enforce regulations; caused the destruction of some of the houses and temples, the rebuilding of which is allowed by the decree; and offered greater scope to officials to maintain the oppressions forbidden by the text, the bureaucracy of Egypt still functioned, for the most part, as it always had done throughout the period. Some of the debts might well represent collections diverted to rebel forces, while remissions revealed the intention to avoid dispute about payment as much as a desire to exhibit generosity to the populace.

The *philanthropa* represented by many provisions of the decree show an aspect of the conception of appropriate kingly behavior which was, although inherent in earlier texts, not nearly so prominent or developed. The *enteuxeis*, or petitions, of which we have a good number from the end of the third century, form one category of texts which show the concept of the king as the direct source of benefit and justice to the populace. There is no doubt that the petitions themselves were processed by the bureaucracy (indeed they acknowledge that explicitly); but the terminology of the appeals makes the king the source of the *euergasia* which the petitioner requests. In the same way, the *philanthropa* present the notion of the king as the kindly protector of his people, generous, merciful, beneficent. This idea inheres in the direct relationship exemplified by the petitions of the end of the third century, and forms part of the ideology of kingship which is taken to have been developed by philosophers and propagandists of the second century; and it is in the course of that century that we see these concepts reflected in official texts.[49]

---

[48] As usual, most texts show the bureaucracy functioning normally, but there are the occasional documents which refer to the strife: *W. Chr.* 11 indicates the existence of armed conflict between the towns of Crocodilopolis and Hermonthis in Upper Egypt in 123, while *PSI* 171 refers to *amixia* in the area of Ptolemais in 122–121.

[49] M.-T. Lenger, "La Notion de 'bienfait' (philanthropon) royal et des ordonnances des rois lagides," *Studi in onore di Vincenzo Arangio-Ruiz nel xlv anno del suo insegnamento*, M. Lauria et al. eds., vol. 1 (Naples, 1951), points out (485–86) that with one exception (*P. Enteux.* 81 of 221 B.C.) the royal grants of *philanthropa* are all later than the third century

Despite the settlement at the end of the reign of Euergetes II, dynastic conflict continued, and the strength of the kings dwindled further. Certainly after Soter II there was no Ptolemy whose behavior as a king might be seen to emulate many of the abstract concepts of kingship; and there is nothing at all about the kingship of these later monarchs that might offer ideals for others to follow. It is probably true that the kings from Philopator on had little respect among Greeks; certainly Polybius' derogations suggest that he, writing in the mid–second century, had concluded that the Ptolemies had become voluptuaries and had failed as rulers. Yet certain basic qualities of kingship which had been developed under the earlier members of the dynasty continued to characterize the manner in which the Ptolemies presented themselves. The dynastic cult established for the divine king continued to the very end of the dynasty in good enough health to be taken over by the Ptolemies' Roman successors; there continued to exist the traditional court, with Friends around the king, and with royal encouragement to Alexandria as a cultural center. After the third century, of course, there was not much possibility of the kings demonstrating military proficiency—apart, perhaps, from civil war—as Roman tutelage of the Ptolemies from Philometor on meant that not even in defense could a king make a showing against foreigners. And, as we can clearly see from the papyri of the last century of Ptolemaic rule in Egypt, Cleopatra VII was no more a part of the administrative structure or in control of the bureaucracy than were her predecessors of two centuries earlier. The development of the tradition represented by the *philanthropa* continued, and the later Ptolemies clearly represented themselves as concerned for the welfare of the people, issuing decrees that dealt with benefits to temples and priests, asylum grants, tax exemption. The practice of recording temple grants in epigraphic form ensures that we have a significant number of such *philanthropa*, but a text of Auletes' reign, granting to cleruchs both privileges and absolution from

---

B.C.; she also notes, however (487–88), the general phenomenon of *philanthropa* issued by the kings outside Egypt in the third century B.C., as well as the use of the term for benefits requested or received from Ptolemaic officials and important personages. The theoretical or philosophical demand for *philanthropia* on the part of kings is as late as Aristeas, *Letter*, 208 (cf. W. Schubart, "Das hellenistische Königsideal nach Inschriften und Papyri," *Arch. Pap.* 12 [1937]: 10; for bibliography and connections of "Aristeas" with second-century-B.C. Jewish thought, see D. Mendels, " 'On Kingship' in the 'Temple Scroll' and the Ideological *Vorlage* of the Seven Banquets in the 'Letter of Aristeas to Philocrates,' " *Aegyptus* 59 [1979]: 127–36); but the appearance of the term with a strong sense of "human benevolence," or the use of the plural as "benefits" associated with the royal *philanthropa* as early as the third century B.C. (e.g., *Inschr. Ilion* 33 = *OGIS* 221, c. 274 B.C.; *SIG*³ 548, Delphi) as well as the general sense of "favors" (e.g., *P. Col. Zen.* 9), shows how well the concept was established in usage before the second century B.C. For detailed references, see Lenger, "Notion de 'bienfait,' " 487–88 nn. 30–34.

crimes,[50] shows us that the kind of administrative amnesty illustrated by the Tebtunis text of the latter part of the reign of Euergetes II continued on into the next century. And the image of the monarchs providing for protection against exaction of excessive payments by officials, monarchs "greatly hating the wicked and adjudging a common and universal vengeance,"[51] recurs in the so-called last decree of the Ptolemies, an order of Cleopatra VII dating to 41 B.C.

I have tried to indicate here that the ideology of Ptolemaic kingship was most emphatically not one of administration or governorship. We look back at Ptolemaic Egypt, particularly in the third century, as an exemplar of highly controlled and organized administrative structure, but kingship as the Ptolemies exemplified it—as they were seen by others and portrayed in their own official documents—did not relate to the effectiveness of administration or the positioning of the monarch at the top of the hierarchy. Much of what had made up monarchy, what it meant to be a king in the time of Alexander and the Successors, continued to be stressed under the Ptolemies; some aspects were more emphasized and expanded as conditions permitted, others dwindled in prominence as the situation dictated. More and more the divine aspect of the monarch was promoted; so long as the king had the power, warfare and military action remained an important aspect of royal behavior. The king maintained a court—brilliant when possible—and a coterie of Friends and advisers, whom he used as his agents of preference for the operation of an orderly stratified administrative structure. We see the king exhibiting concern for the welfare and fair treatment of weak and complaining taxpayers, commanding the bureaucrats to avoid oppression and excessive exactions, acting as the protector of the people against the administration rather than as the overseer of the government. The monarchy existed alongside the bureaucracy, in a sense, rather than being part of it; and the king could always be seen as a figure qualitatively, not just quantitatively, different from other members of the administration. In the ideology of Ptolemaic monarchy, the king was not the supreme power of government, nor did he represent the state, he was, rather, a unique figure looking after the land and its people and ruling by qualities of character rather than position.

RESPONSE: DIANA DELIA

Alan Samuel has sensibly argued that the ideology of Ptolemaic kingship is connected with the way in which Egypt was administered. He has

---

[50] *BGU* 1185, 60 B.C. = *C. Ord. Ptol.* 71.
[51] *C. Ord. Ptol.* 76.22–23.

challenged the traditional claim that the Ptolemies absolutely dominated a tightly knit, rationally organized state. His conclusion that they did not is significant—not only for our understanding of the administration of Ptolemaic Egypt per se but because it inspires reappraisal of basic presuppositions about the interrelationship of monarchy and bureaucracy in practice and in theory.

At a symposium on Hellenistic history and culture, the Hellenocentric thrust of Professor Samuel's paper is, of course, appropriate. As a social historian of Greek and Roman Egypt, I nevertheless feel some concern. It is clear that the Ptolemies retained the traditional administrative nome divisions of Egypt and that the office of nomarch continued, although by the second half of the third century B.C. nomarchs would relinquish military and many other powers to the newly imposed nome officials known as *strategoi*.[1] Ptolemaic papyri attest to state monopolization of the cultivation and manufacture of papyrus, oil, and textiles, state control of the production of salt, and close supervision of quarries and mines. Other documents indicate that the cultivation of grain was controlled by means of state distribution of seed, in return for which farmers were required to pay a portion of their harvests. These subjects have been addressed in the prolific economic studies of M. I. Rostovtzeff and Claire Préaux as well as by other scholars.[2] *P. Rev. Laws*, dating to 259 B.C., further demonstrates that money taxes were levied on other manufactured goods and agricultural products as well.[3] *P. Tebt.* 703, dating to the late third century B.C., discloses the minute attention paid to all potential sources of revenue, including enumeration of livestock and the inspection of sown fields and weaving houses to assess productivity and to guard against peculation. Nevertheless, the intense interest of the Egyptian state in revenue matters did not spring full-grown out of the head of Ptolemy II Philadelphus in the manner of Athena, but instead ought to

---

[1] J. D. Thomas, "Aspects of the Ptolemaic Civil Service: The Dioiketes and the Nomarchs," in H. Maehler and V. M. Strocka, eds., *Das Ptolemäische Ägypten* (Mainz, 1978), 194: see also H. Bengtson, *Die Strategie in der hellenistichen Zeit*, 2d ed., vol. 3 (Munich, 1967).

[2] *SEHHW* 1:275–313; C. Préaux, *L'Économie royale des Lagides* (Brussels, 1939), 61–435; C. Préaux, "L'Économie lagide, 1933–1958," in *Proceedings of the Ninth International Congress of Papyrologists* (Oslo, 1958), 200–32. See also W. W. Tarn, "Ptolemy II," *JEA* 14 (1928): 257–58; N. Lewis, *L'Industrie du papyrus dans l'Égypte greco-romain* (Paris, 1934); S. Calderini, "Ricerche sull'industria e il commercio dei tessuti in Egitto," *Aegyptus* 26 (1946): 13–83; F. Dunand, "L'Artisanat du textile dans l'Égypte lagide," *Ktema* 4 (1979): 47–69; M. Schnebel, *Die Landwirtschaft im hellenistischen Ägypten*, Münch. Beitr. no. 7 (Munich, 1925), 94–185; N. Hohlwein, "Le Blé d'Égypte," *Études de Papyrologie* 4 (1934): 22–120; C. Bradford Welles, "On the Collection of Revenues in Grain in Ptolemaic Egypt," *Festschrift F. Oertel* (Bonn, 1964), 6–16; Z. M. Pakman, *The Taxes in Grain in Ptolemaic Egypt*, Am. Stud. Pap. no. 4 (New Haven and Toronto, 1968).

[3] *P. Rev. Laws*.

be understood as a continuation of pharaonic practice.[4] For example, the Palermo stone indicates that a biennial census of cattle took place as early as the Old Kingdom.[5] Middle and New Kingdom documents attest to an elaborate system of taxes and show that land was resurveyed after the annual Nile inundation to determine the liability of Egyptian peasants to pay a portion of their harvest to Pharaoh, as they later would to Ptolemy.[6] Moreover, royal officials regularly supervised expeditions to Egyptian quarries and mines.[7] The elaborate instructions imparted to royal viziers, especially Rekhmire, suggest that they carried out the functions which the Ptolemies would later apportion among their *dioecetes*, nome *strategoi*, and *chrematistai*.[8] Hence, as the Ptolemies indeed retained or adapted pharaonic administrative institutions,[9] it follows that their ideology of kingship to some extent also derives from pharaonic prototypes.

In response to Rostovtzeff's grand view that the Ptolemaic administration was more refined, more logical, more comprehensive, more, shall we say, quintessentially "Hellenic" than its pharaonic antecedents,[10] Professor Samuel now posits the claim that the Ptolemaic bureaucracy was not rationally ordered, that it was not planned, and that it developed on an ad hoc and piecemeal basis as specific needs arose and former methods, proving to be inadequate, were abandoned. He raised a similar suggestion some twenty years ago in connection with his seminal study of the nomarch's bureau in the third century B.C.[11]

The lack of distinction that existed between public and private activity has also been duly emphasized by Professor Samuel. To be sure, the

---

[4] C. Bradford Welles, "The Ptolemaic Administration in Egypt," *JJP* 3 (1949): 28–37, 47.

[5] *ARE*, Breasted, vol. 1, secs. 76–167; see also Helch, *Lexikon* 4:652–54.

[6] H. Goedicke, *Die königliche Dokumente aus dem Alten Reich* (Weisbaden, 1967), 56, 72; Helck, *Wirtschaftsgeschichte* 141–55; Helck, *Verwaltung* 138–45. See also P. C. Smither, "A Tax Assessor's Journal of the Middle Kingdom," *JEA* 27 (1941): 74–6.

[7] Helck, *Wirtschaftsgeschichte*, 182–94; Helck, *Lexikon* 2:55–68.

[8] Helck, *Verwaltung*, 2 n. 1 and 17–50; T. G. H. James, *Pharaoh's People* (Chicago, 1984), 51–72; W. C. Hayes, "Egypt: Internal Affairs from Tuthmosis I to the Death of Amenophis III," *CAH*[3] II.1, 354–57. For the instructions to Rekhmire, see Breasted, *ARE*, vol. 2, secs. 663–761. See also Thomas, "Aspects," 191–92, for a parallel to the *dioecetes* during the Persian period.

[9] See, for example, Préaux, *Économie*, 570, and J. H. Johnson, "Ptolemaic Bureaucracy from an Egyptian Point of View," in M. Gibson and R. Biggs, eds., *The Organization of Power: Aspects of Bureaucracy in the Ancient Near East*, = *SAOC* no. 46 (Chicago, 1987), 141–49.

[10] *SEHHW* 2:1079.

[11] "The Internal Organization of the Nomarch's Bureau in the Third Century B.C.," in *Essays in Honor of C. Bradford Welles*, Am. Stud. Pap. no. 1 (New Haven and Toronto, 1966), 213–29; see also E. Turner, "Ptolemaic Egypt," *CAH*[2] VII.1, 148–49.

Zenon archives demonstrate Apollonius' use of official authority to attain private ends and the deployment of his private resources to accomplish official tasks.[12] Nevertheless, as Dorothy Crawford has pointed out, since Ptolemaic officials appear to have received no regular salaries, this lack of distinction between public and private spheres of interest promoted corruption, as administrators abused their official positions in order to line their own pockets.[13] Reiterated exhortations to royal officials to be fair and just suggest that, although quite the contrary state of affairs frequently prevailed in fact, excessive exploitation was nonetheless condemned in principle as abusive.[14] As Hermann Bengtson aptly observed, every administration is only as good as the men who comprise it.[15]

What is most exciting is the way in which Professor Samuel links these two bold theories, arguing that administrative activity, far from being the coherent result of royal planning, was rather the aggregate of activities of exploitative officials, and that what has traditionally been touted as a system of administrative checks and balances actually represents "a desperate attempt on the part of the crown to get some control over a structure which, on the lowest village levels, was practically autonomous." Hence the king, according to this theory, existed alongside the administrative bureaucracy, intervening only to check abuses or to curb the rapacity of his administrators. At the same time, however, I wish to point out that a symbiotic relationship continued between the two, since the king depended on his administrators to collect the revenue that he used for military and personal ends, and the administrators ultimately owed their appointments to the king; these selfish considerations, on occasion, surely reconciled the tension and conflict between royal and administrative objectives. Moreover, at least one pharaonic precedent for the discordant state of affairs that Professor Samuel has described comes to mind: the New Kingdom edict of Horemheb, which outlines the measures that this king intended to pursue to check the flagrant corruption of fiscal and other administrators similarly abusing their positions for personal gain.[16]

In keeping with Professor Samuel's premise that the ideology of Ptolemaic kingship was intimately connected with the way in which Egypt

---

[12] The Zenon archive is divided among several private collections, most notably *P. Cair. Zen.* I–V, *P. Col. Zen.* III, *P. Edg., P. Lond. Zen.* VII, *P. Mich. Zen.* I, and *P. Zen. Pestm.*

[13] "The Good Official of Ptolemaic Egypt," in *Ptolemäische Ägypten,* 201; see also Préaux, *Économie,* 514–33.

[14] See, for example, *UPZ* I 113 (156ᵃ).

[15] "Die ptolemäische Staatsverwaltung im Rahmen der hellenistischen Administration," *Mus. Helv.* 10 (1953): 176.

[16] On this large stele, which was displayed against the ninth pylon of the Karnak complex, see Breasted, *ARE,* vol. 3, secs. 45–59; R. Hari, *Horemheb et la reine Moutnedjmet, ou la fin d'une dynastie* (Geneva, 1964), 302–18; and C. Aldred, "Egypt: The Amarna Period and

was administered, let us turn to some of the aspects of royal ideology mentioned by him.[17] The first of these is that, from the reign of Ptolemy II Philadelphus on, the king was worshipped as a god. This claim, while on the surface appearing to be "minimalist," initially troubled me in view of the proverbial skepticism harbored by certain Greek intellectuals concerning the divinity of any living monarch. One need only recall Demosthenes' scathing response to the motion to deify Alexander at Athens: "Let him be a son of Zeus and Poseidon also, if he wishes"[18] or the Cynic Diogenes' provocative rejoinder, "Then make *me* Sarapis!"[19] Even if these anecdotes are totally apocryphal, they nonetheless reveal a certain resistance among Greek intellectuals to the substitution of *theos* for *basileus*.[20] As C. Bradford Welles succinctly observed, "no Greek, ancient or modern, ever thought that anyone was really superior to himself."[21]

Nevertheless, in 279/8 B.C., the first *Ptolemaia* was celebrated at Alexandria to honor Ptolemy II Philadelphus' deified parents, the "Savior Gods," Θεοὶ Σωτῆρες, Ptolemy I Soter and Berenike I.[22] The seventeenth idyll of Theocritus similarly alludes to the institution of the cult of the defunct Soter at Alexandria by 270 B.C.[23] Claire Préaux's suggestion that the dynastic cult of the Ptolemies at Alexandria developed out of an original hero cult in honor of Alexander as founder of the city appears to be sound, and it implies that subsequent Ptolemies were incorporated therein by virtue of royal succession.[24] Nevertheless, as early as

---

the End of the Eighteenth Dynasty," *CAH*[3] II. 275–77. Note as well A. B. Lloyd, "The Late Period, 664–323 B.C.," in B. G. Trigger et al., *Ancient Egypt: A Social History* (Cambridge, 1983), 336.

[17] Note the earlier discussion by C. Préaux: "L'image du roi de l'époque hellénistique," in F. Bossier et al., eds., *Images of Man in Ancient and Medieval Thought: Studia G. Verbeke* (Leuven, 1976), 53–75.

[18] Hypereides, *in Demosth.* 31 (p. 19 Blass); Aelian *VH* 5.12; cf. Athen. *Deipn.* 6.251b and Val. Max. 7.2.13.

[19] Diog. Laert. 6.63. See also C. Habicht, *Gottmenschentum und griechische Städte*, 2d ed. (Munich, 1970), 28–36 and passim.

[20] See also J. R. Hamilton's interpretation of Arrian *Anab.* 7.14.6: "The Origins of the Ruler Cult," *Prudentia* 16 (1984): 11–12, *contra* J. P. V. D. Balsdon, "The Divinity of Alexander," *Historia* 1 (1950): 385.

[21] *JJP* 3 (1949): 38.

[22] Kallixeinos in Athen. *Deipn.* 5.203a = *FGrH* III 627. See also E. E. Rice, *The Grand Procession of Ptolemy Philadelphus* (Oxford, 1983).

[23] 17.16–17. Cf. Philo *Leg. ad Gaium* 138.

[24] C. Préaux, *Le Monde hellénistique* (Paris, 1978) 1:225–57, followed by P. M. Fraser, *Ptolemaic Alexandria* (Oxford, 1972) 1:215–20, and Turner, "Ptolemaic Egypt," 168. See also W. Otto, *Priester und Tempel im hellenistischen Ägypten* (Leipzig, 1905) 1:175–85; Habicht, *Gottmenschentum*, 109–23; and F. W. Walbank, "Monarchies and Monarchic Ideals," *CAH*[2] VII.1, 97. On hero cults, see L. R. Farnell, *Greek Hero Cults and Ideas of Immortality* (Oxford, 1921); and A. D. Nock, "The Cult of Heroes," *HTR* 37 (1944): 141–74, reprinted in Nock, *Essays* 2:575–602.

272/1 B.C., Ptolemy II Philadelphus and Arsinoë II (figure 34) assumed the appellation Θεοί 'Αδελφοί ("Brother and Sister Gods") and received a cult that was associated with the cult of Alexander.[25] How then can we explain the "great leap," as Turner dubs it, from the cult of deceased ancestors to the veneration of living men? I would suggest that the two may be reconciled as distinct manifestations of divinity. The former was an extension of the hero cult instituted on behalf of Alexander; the latter was reverence generated by the manifestation of royal power.

In contrast with the Judaeo-Christian perspective of omnipotent, omniscient, and omnipresent divinity, the term *theos* possessed an extended range of meanings for an ancient Greek. It might denote an Olympian deity, a demigod, a hero, or a Hellenistic sovereign; it also was associated with miracle workers, the so-called divine men. Divinity was not construed as an absolute, but instead was an unstructured abstract signifying varying levels and nuances of power.[26] Hence it was in recognition of power, of achievements capable of exciting the popular imagination (to paraphrase Arthur Darby Nock),[27] that the earliest Greek ruler cult was established in 404 B.C. Even if the Ptolemaic dynastic cult originated as a form of royal propaganda, its continued success attests to popular belief.[28] As Simon Price, and now Professor Long, have both observed, it is futile to ask whether Greeks actually believed in the divinity of rulers; the only palpable evidence of their mental state is participation in cult or ritual.[29]

Although one might well be tempted to interpret the metaphorical description of Ptolemy II Philadelphus as θεὸς ἄλλος "another god," by Callimachus in his Delian Hymn,[30] as hyperbole (representing either an expression of official propaganda or else a public manifestation of

[25] *P. Hib.* 199.11–17 (272/1[B.C.]); L. Cerfaux and J. Tondriau, *Un Concurrent de Christianisme: Le Culte des souverains dans la civilisation gréco-romaine,* Bibl. Theol. 3d ser., vol. 5 (Tournai, 1957), 262ff. See also Fraser, *Ptolemaic Alexandria* 1:216, and Turner, "Ptolemaic Egypt," 168.

[26] H. Goedicke, "God" *SSEA Journal* 16 (1986): 57–58; S. R. F. Price, "Gods and Emperors: The Greek Language of the Roman Imperial Cult," *JHS* 104 (1984): 80; and S. R. F. Price, *Rituals and Power: The Roman Imperial Cult in Asia Minor* (Cambridge, 1984), 29–30, 247. Cf. Farnell, *Greek Hero Cults,* 370, on the conscious distinction drawn by Greeks between heroes and gods. See also E. Bickermann, "Consecratio," in *Le Culte des souverains dans l'empire romain,* Entretiens sur l'antiquité classique no. 19 (Vandoeuvres-Genève, 1972), 7–8.

[27] "ΣΥΝΝΑΟΣ ΘΕΟΣ," *HSCP* 41 (1930): 61–62, = Nock, *Essays* 1:250. Cf. Habicht, *Gottmenschentum,* 165.

[28] M. Smith, "On the History of the 'Divine Man,' " in *Paganisme, judaisme, christianisme: Mélanges offerts à M. Simon* (Paris, 1978), 340, 343–44.

[29] S. R. F. Price, "Between Man and God: Sacrifice in the Roman Imperial Cult," *JRS* 70 (1980): 43.

[30] Callimachus, Hymn 4.165–66.

34. Arsinoë II and Ptolemy Philadelphus as Queen and Pharaoh of Egypt. Tanis, 270–246 B.C. British Museum, London. From *The Cambridge Ancient History*, 2d ed. (Cambridge: Cambridge University Press, 1984), vol. 7, pt. 1, pp. 13–15, pl. 13.

sycophancy, to both of which politically sensitive Greek administrators and beneficiaries of royal patronage would be wise to pay lip service), to dismiss it as such would probably be unsound. To call Philadelphus a god, given the broad range of nuances which characterized the significance of this term, was totally acceptable; *theos* merely implied recognition of a degree of authority in response to a ruler's mighty display of power.

What was the source of royal potency? Recently the traditional view that the ancient Egyptians considered their reigning pharaoh to be a deity in his own right has been challenged. Hans Goedicke maintains that it was not the king himself but rather the office of kingship that was divine.[31] Pursuant to numerous passages in Egyptian literature which emphasize the human nature of the Egyptian king, Georges Posener has argued that although the king was identified with certain deities—by means of representation in the form of a god or by exhibiting a feature or features unique to a specific divinity—the king himself was not divine.[32] It stands to reason, then, that the living Ptolemaic rulers of Egypt may have been similarly viewed: Ptolemy sat on the throne of Horus but it was the throne, not Ptolemy, that actually was divine.[33]

In his hymn to Zeus, Callimachus writes: "From Zeus come kings, for nothing is more divine than what issues from Zeus."[34] Similarly, at Edfu, Kom Ombo, and Philae, Ptolemaic kings were depicted crowned by the goddesses of Upper and Lower Egypt, Nekhbet and Buto; here, too, officially generated media portrayed the Ptolemies as divinely sanctioned, although in their own right they were not divine.[35] Kings were

---

[31] H. Goedicke, *Die Stellung des Königs im Alten Reich, Äg. Abhandl.* no. 2 (Wiesbaden, 1960).

[32] G. Posener, *De la divinité du pharaon* (Paris, 1960). See also W. Barta, *Untersuchungen zur Göttlichkeit des regierenden Königs, MÄS* no. 32 (Munich, 1975), 131–37.

[33] *Pace* Turner, "Ptolemaic Egypt," 132. On the distinction between the person and function of a king, see D. P. Silverman, "Divinities and Deities in Ancient Egypt," in B. E. Shafer, ed., *Religion in Ancient Egypt: Gods, Myth and Personal Practice* (Ithaca, N. Y., 1991), 58–87; H. Hauben, "Aspects du culte des souverains à l'époque des Lagides," in L. Criscuolo and G. Geraci, eds., *Egitto e storia antica dall'Ellenismo all'età araba*, Atti del colloquio internazionale, Bologna, 31 agosto – 2 settembre 1987 (Bologna, 1989), 465. See also Nock, "ΣΥΝΝΑΟΣ ΘΕΟΣ," 10 = *Essays* 1:209.

[34] Hymn 1.78–79.

[35] P-M VI: at Edfu: 136 (106–7) Ptolemy IV Philopator, 141 (152–53) *idem*, 164 (316–23) Ptolemy V Epiphanes, also 157 (291–94) a Ptolemy; at Kom Ombo: 188–89 (71–73) Ptolemy VII Neos Philopator, 184 (46) Ptolemy XIII; at Philae: 229 (228–34) *idem*. Compare the coronation scenes at Karnak: P-M II² 115 (364) Thutmose III, and 230 (20–21) Herihor. See also E. Hornung, *Conceptions of God in Ancient Egypt: The One and the Many* (Ithaca, 1982), 140–42, who argues that it was the accession ceremony, when the king assumed the insignia and trappings of the divine office, which had divine significance; and H. Bonnet, *Reallexikon der ägyptischen Religionsgeschichte* (Berlin, 1952), 395–400. See also E. Vassilika, *Ptolemaic Philae*, Analecta Orientalia Lovaniensia no. 34 (Louvain, 1989).

conceived as the representatives of traditional deities, especially Horus and Zeus, but not as their equals. This was the cutting edge of Demosthenes' and Diogenes' remarks.

The Socratic (Xenophon's *Cyropaedia*, Plato's *Republic* and *Laws*) and Aristotelian endorsements of the Good King's natural right to rule were no doubt well known to Greek intellectuals; but it was the Hellenistic philosophical schools that would elevate kingship from the natural to the divine plane—that is, kingship as a reflection of the divine—and catalog the Good King's many virtues.[36] Whether the position, voiced in the *Letter of Aristeas*, that the Ptolemaic monarch was human, ruling by the grace of God, owes more to the Jewish identity of the author or to his Greek education is, perhaps, a jejune question.[37] Various treatises of kingship were in general circulation, as confirmed by an anecdote preserved by Stobaeus: Demetrius of Phaleron is reported to have advised Ptolemy Soter to take an interest in books περὶ βασιλείας καὶ ἡγεμονίας on the grounds that "what friends do not dare to say to kings they write in books."[38]

No doubt the portrayals of Ptolemaic kings and queens in the attitude of traditional Egyptian deities represent an attempt to conciliate old pharaonic traditions with the new regime. At Karnak, Edfu, and Philae, for example, the Ptolemies parade the same iconography as, are assimilated and identified with, and even receive life from, the traditional gods of Egypt.[39] The identification of the Ptolemies with Greek divinities and proclamations of their divine ancestry ought to be similarly understood.[40] These were advertisements of the divine origins of royal power.

[36] E. R. Goodenough, "The Political Philosophy of Hellenistic Kingship," *YCS* 1 (1928): 55–102, echoed by C. Préaux, "Graeco-Roman Egypt," in J. R. Harris, ed., *The Legacy of Egypt*, 2d ed. (Oxford, 1971), 327–28. Cf. W. Schubart, "Das hellenistische Königsideal nach Inschriften und Papyri," *Arch. Pap.* 12 (1937): 1–26.

[37] *Aristeas to Philocrates*, ed. M. Hadas (New York, 1951), 226–27, 233, 242, 245. A similar claim, expressed by Diodorus at 1.90.2–3, probably derives from Hecataeus of Abdera's *Aegyptiaca*. For arguments that the writer of this letter assumed a thoroughly Greek persona, see V. Tcherikover, "The Ideology of the Letter of Aristeas," *HTR* 51 (1958): 63.

[38] Plut. *Mor. (Apothegm.)* 189D; Stob. 4.7.27.

[39] At Karnak: P-M II³ 199 (12c) Ptolemy III Euergetes I; at Edfu: P-M VI 144 (189) Ptolemy IV Philopator, 138 (125) Ptolemy VI Philometor, 140 (139) *idem*, 133 (95) Ptolemy X Alexander I; at Philae: P-M VI 238 (286–87) Ptolemy II Philadelphus, 239 (293 and 298) *idem*. Compare pharaonic scenes at Karnak: P-M II³ 62 Sesostris I, 89 (240–44) Thutmose III, 31 (81–82) Ramesses III, and 36 (129) Osorkon I. For discussions of the giving of life, consult Bonnet, *Reallexikon*, 418–20, and Lloyd, "Late Period," 293. See also Otto, *Priester und Tempel* 2:261–81; F. E. Adcock, "Greek and Macedonian Kingship," in *Proceedings of the British Academy* no. 39 (1953), 170; E. Otto, *Gott und Mensch nach den ägyptischen Tempelinschriften der griechisch-römischen Zeit* (Heidelberg, 1964), 63–83; Vassilika, *Ptolemaic Philae, passim*.

[40] On the identification of Ptolemaic kings with Greek deities, see J. Tondriau, "Rois lagides comparés ou identifiés à des divinités," *Chron. d'Ég.* 23 (1948): 127–46. See also A.

The second aspect of the ideology of Ptolemaic kingship addressed by Professor Samuel is military leadership, especially the defense of Egypt from foreign enemies. These military exploits, recounted in the historical accounts of Polybius and Diodorus Siculus, were also celebrated by Theocritus in his seventeenth idyll.[41] On monumental architecture throughout Egypt, Ptolemaic kings may be observed grasping captured enemies by their hair with one hand, while the other is raised in a smiting position.[42] This scene is virtually identical to the numerous pharaonic ones.[43]

Another aspect of the ideology of Ptolemaic kingship addressed by Professor Samuel was *philanthropia*. *Philanthropia* might be exhibited in such diverse ways as the promotion of peace, the bestowal of liberal benefits on priests and temples,[44] grants of asylum or amnesty,[45] relief from famine,[46] tax exemption,[47] and protection against abuses[48]—the last of which neatly ties in with his thesis. Numerous royal *prostagmata* (ordinances) issued in response to petitions requesting favors or the correction of abuses attest to the concern of the Ptolemies for *philanthropia*.[49]

F. E. Adcock cynically claimed that Hellenistic kings traditionally represented themselves as benevolent toward their subjects because this was part and parcel of playing the game of proper royal etiquette,[50] while

---

D. Nock, "Ruler-Worship and Syncretism," review of Otto and Bengston, *Zur Geschichte des Niederganges des Ptolemäer-reiches, AJP* 63 (1942): 218–19 = Nock, *Essays* 2:553; and Nock, "ΣΥΝΝΑΟΣ ΘΕΟΣ," 3–21 = Nock, *Essays* 1:204–18.

[41] Lines 86–94. In general, see E. Bevan, *The House of Ptolemy* (1927), reprinted as *A History of Egypt under the Ptolemaic Dynasty* (1927, repr. Chicago, 1968), and H. Heinen, "The Syrian-Egyptian Wars and the New Kingdoms of Asia Minor," *CAH*[2] VII.1, 412–45.

[42] At Karnak: P-M II[3] 226 (3) Ptolemy III Euergetes I; at Edfu: P-M VI 158 (297–300) Ptolemy X Alexander I, 121 (1–2) Ptolemy XIII; at Kom Ombo: P-M VI 188–89 (71–73) Ptolemy VII Neos Philopator, 200 (1) Ptolemy XIII; at Philae: P-M VI 214 (75–76) *idem.*

[43] At Karnak: P-M II[3] 170 (499) Thutmose III, 176 (522) Amenophis II, 55 (168) Sety I, 38 (141) Ramesses II, and 131 (488) Merneptah; at Medinet Habu: P-M II[3] 483 (12–13) Ramesses III; at Abu Simbel: P-M VII 101–2 (37–38) Ramesses II. Pharaonic parallels date at least as far back as the first dynasty: P-M V 193–94 Narmer palette. In general, see E. S. Hall, *The Pharaoh Smites His Enemies: A Comparative Study, MÄS* no. 44 (Munich, 1986). See also A. Spalinger, "The Concept of Monarchy during the Saite Epoch: An Essay of Synthesis," *Orientalia* 47 (1978): 12–36.

[44] *OGIS* 90 (Rosetta, 196 B.C.); cf. Theocr. *Id.* 17.106ff.

[45] *C. Ord. Ptol.* 53 (118 B.C.).

[46] *OGIS* 56 (Canopus, 238 B.C.).

[47] *OGIS* 90.12–13.

[48] *P. Rain.* inv. 24, ed. H. Liebesny, *Aegyptus* 16 (1936): 257–91 = *SB* V 8008 (mid-III B.C. Ptolemy Philadelphus); see also W. L. Westermann, "The Ptolemies and the Welfare of their Subjects," *AHR* 43 (1938): 282–83, and M. T. Lenger, "La Notion de 'bienfait' (philanthropon) royal et les ordonnances des rois lagides," in *Studi in onore di V. Arangio-Ruiz*, M. Lauria et al., eds. (Naples, 1953) 1:486.

[49] Lenger, "Notion de 'bienfait,' " 483–99; cf. *P. Enteux., passim.*

[50] Adcock, "Greek and Macedonian Kingship," 169.

William Linn Westermann questioned whether Ptolemaic legislation, insofar as it is known to us, demonstrated any real concern for the welfare of *Egyptian* subjects.[51] Claire Préaux noted that *philanthropia* ordinarily occurs in societies in which there is an immense disproportion between the wealth and power of the few and the poverty of the masses.[52] More to the point, however, is Marie-Thérèse Lenger's observation that the basis of Ptolemaic *philanthropia* rested primarily on the concept of the king.[53] For Egyptians no less than for Greeks, Ptolemy was the protector of oppressed subjects; there is considerable evidence of Pharaonic precedent for this as well, most notably the Egyptian pharaoh's duty to ensure *ma'at*.[54] Consider the instructions of a Ninth or Tenth Dynasty pharaoh to his son, Merikare: "Do justice, then you endure on earth; calm the weeper, do not oppress the widow, do not expel a man from his father's property, do not reduce the nobles in their possessions. Beware of punishing wrongfully; do not kill, it does not serve you."[55] I am not so rash as to suggest that *philanthropia* was a distinctly Egyptian as opposed to a Hellenistic concept, but rather that, at least insofar as the Ptolemies may have been concerned, there was already an established tradition for the pursuit of this ideal by the Egyptian king. Once established in Egypt, the Ptolemies appear to have dipped liberally into the springs of Greek philosophy—especially as supplied by the fourth-century Socratics, by Aristotle, and by Pythagoreans and Stoics—for rationalizations of their position as kings and of their *philanthropia*. Identical themes are echoed in Idyll 17, Theocritus' praising of his royal patron, Ptolemy II Philadelphus,[56] and in numerous papyri and inscriptions. Of course, the significant question (one that considerations of time prevent my addressing here) is the extent to which the Ptolemies actually lived up to the ideology of kingship they promoted—the fundamental distinction between *Idealbild* and *Realbild*.

As a social historian, I confess that I cannot imagine cultural exchange between the Greek and Egyptian inhabitants of Ptolemaic Egypt as having been one-sided. Nevertheless, the *communis opinio* among historians of Greek and Roman Egypt has traditionally been that Hellenic culture flourished in so alien an environment as Egypt as the result of a deliberate

---

[51] Westermann, "Ptolemies," 276. His conclusions are indeed sobering.

[52] C. Préaux, "La Bienfaisance dans les archives de Zénon," *Chron. d'Ég.* 19 (1944): 281–90.

[53] Lenger, "Notion de 'bienfait,'" 486.

[54] Bonnet, *Reallexikon*, 430–34; Hornung, *Conceptions of God*, 213–16.

[55] M. Lichtheim, ed., *Ancient Egyptian Literature: A Book of Readings*, vol. 1, *The Old and Middle Kingdoms* (Berkeley, 1973), 100.

[56] Theocr. *Id.* 17.106–14; Goodenough, "Political Philosophy," *passim*; and Schubart, "Hellenistiche Königsideal," 10–16.

policy aimed at promoting Hellenization. As examples, I need only point to the Alexandrian libraries and Museum. It is, moreover, argued that since the Ptolemies regularly appointed and promoted Greeks to senior administrative positions, ambitious Egyptians would assimilate themselves with all possible speed to Hellenic culture if they hoped to advance their careers. Nevertheless, in a land such as Egypt, where *terra sacra* enjoyed such venerable antiquity, and where Hellenistic Greeks, no less than Egyptians, subscribed to the efficacy of the old Egyptian cults, it is, I would argue, hard to sustain the conclusion that Egyptian religion did not exert an influence on the Greek colonists.[57]

Throughout the pharaonic period, Egyptian religion and administrative tradition concerned themselves intimately with the ideology of Egyptian rulers. They appear to have contributed no less significantly to the ideology of Ptolemaic kingship. The Ptolemaic monuments at Karnak, Edfu, Kom Ombo, and Philae, situated in plain view of all subjects, Egyptians and Greeks alike, celebrated an ideology of kingship that deliberately emulated pharaonic prototypes. These monuments do not advertise an Egyptian ideology of kingship as distinct from a Greek one, but rather demonstrate a coalescence of the two.[58] To balance Professor Samuel's emphasis on the Hellenic component, I have stressed the Egyptian.

It would be unreasonable to assume that the Ptolemies were uninterested in *Aegyptiaca*. Consider the traditions that imply Ptolemaic patronage of the Egyptian priest, Manetho, whose treatises on Egyptian history and religion were frequently cited by subsequent classical authors.[59] Whose benefit, if not that of the Ptolemies, did Hecataeus of Abdera's reconciliation of Egyptian antiquities with Greek political philosophy serve?[60] Indeed, as early as the sixth century B.C., Athenians and Ionian Greeks had been exposed to Egyptian traditions by virtue of their commercial activities at Naukratis and further inland, while fully a century before Alexander cast his spear into Asia or the Macedonians set foot on Egyptian soil, Herodotus so marveled at Egyptian traditions that the entire second book of his *Histories* was devoted to a discussion of them.

---

[57] See, for example, "The Refreshing Water of Osiris," forthcoming in *JARCE* 29 (1992).

[58] On Ptolemaic emulation of pharaonic precedents, see D. B. Redford, *Pharaonic King-Lists, Annals and Day Books: A Contribution to the Study of the Egyptian Sense of History*, SSEA Publication no. 4 (Mississauga, 1986), 204–5. See also L. Koenen, "Die Adaptationen ägyptischer Königsideologie am Ptolemäerhof," in E. Van't Dack et al., eds., *Egypt and the Hellenistic World*, Proceedings of the International Colloquium, Leuven, 24–26 May 1982 (Leuven, 1983), 143–52.

[59] Plut. *Isis* (361F–362B) Syncell., *Corp. script. hist. byz.*, 72. Both fragments have been conveniently incorporated in the Loeb Classical Library edition of Manetho, ed. W. G. Waddell and F. E. Robbins (London and Cambridge, 1940), frag. 80 and appendix I.

[60] *FGrH* III 264. Welles, 40–44, went so far as to dub this a "command performance."

The accounts of Diodorus Siculus and Strabo demonstrate that *Aegyptiaca* continued to fascinate Greek intellectuals into the Roman period. And is it not the remarkable intellectual curiosity of the ancient Greeks that posterity has lauded as the essence of Hellenism?

DISCUSSION

E. N. Borza: Is Professor Samuel suggesting that we have, to use Professor Hammond's term, a "coexistence" between a Ptolemaic version of traditional Macedonian monarchy and the traditional Egyptian bureaucracy? And could he also comment on the ethnic composition of the Egyptian bureaucracy? Assuming him to be correct, what is the economic engine that keeps this whole thing on track? He suggested that we cannot posit a kind of Ptolemaic trickle-down; perhaps we'll need a bubble-up theory or something like that. (Laughter.) But something has to maintain the whole structure despite the changes at the top. Professor Delia pointed out what I think may be lacking in his paper, and that is a reference to existing Pharaonic or even Egyptian-Persian institutions that kept things going. Another possibility is that forces external to Egypt helped shape the Ptolemaic economy. I have the impression that there was a more integrated economy in the eastern Mediterranean world following its conquest by Alexander. There is not time to pursue this, but I think it had something to do with the disruption of Persian authority in the East and new relationships among the Greeks, opening up new grain routes. To what extent would either Professor Samuel or Professor Delia concede that this new economy could have created a kind of marketplace that the Ptolemies had not planned for, but for which they eventually provided an organization in Egypt as a response? And that this new marketplace was perceived by Egyptians on all levels of society, and was related to the engine that kept the economy going, despite the imposition of a Macedonian kingship?

A. E. Samuel: The engine in its most fundamental form was of course the productivity of Egypt and the sale of grain. That's where the money came from. That's where the king was able to produce goods that produced coinage and revenue. The real problem at the core of your question is that we assume, from our own imperialistic experiences, that Ptolemy I, or Alexander, looked at this country with its Egyptian-speaking population and a minority of Greek merchants concentrated in a few places, and asked: How do we run this operation most productively? Since we have virtually no evidence for the first generation and a half, the period in which the adjustments and the decisions must have been made, we tend to seize on the solution which seems easiest, that they took existing pharaonic institutions and used them as much as they could—this being what *we* would have done, because we're as lazy as anybody else. But in fact we just don't know if that's what happened. It is also true that the situation itself does limit the number of options for running an economy based on the shipping of grain down to the king and then its sale abroad. What I was trying to suggest was that it doesn't make very much difference at the central level of operation how one does or doesn't use the existing engine so long as the output is what one wants. All of us here have become conscious of the great separations between Hellenism and non-Hellenic institutions wherever they encountered each other—there certainly is such a separation in Egypt—so even though the Egyptians may have outnumbered the Macedonians and Greeks in Egypt, and however many of the institutions were left intact, and no matter how prosperous, successful, and vital native tradition remained, there seems to have been very little crossover. If that is true, then we have to look at the way the king and his higher officials envisaged the operation out there, in terms of how they would see it as Macedonians and Greeks. And although they may have been forced to use Egyptian patterns, I suggest that they wouldn't *see* them as peculiarly Egyptian patterns. They would make such little adjustments in the language with which they would approach things as would make them into Macedonian or Greek patterns.

D. Delia: In reference to the economic engine, I'd like to interject that it's difficult these days since the building of the Aswan dam to understand the incredible fertility of Egypt. What really kept this whole thing going was the Nile. The crises occurred when the Ptolemaic administrators, pursuing self-interest, became too greedy.

E. N. Borza: What about the changes that resulted in the building of a larger export economy?

A. E. Samuel: I don't know. I think because of the traditional focus we have on Greek history in Greece down to Alexander, and then Greek history outside of Greece after Alexander, we overlook the very intimate relationship between Egypt and the Egyptian economy and the mainland of Greece and the Aegean from the fifth century on. I think they were much closer than tends to be reflected in our commentary. I think that what happened after Alexander was merely building upon and extending patterns that already existed. And the development of the territorial kingdoms may in fact have *impeded* to some extent the development of the eastern Mediterranean economy, which might have been easier for

Egypt to exploit before there was an Antigonus and a Demetrius and an Antipater. But I don't know if there is enough evidence to say.

E. Gruen: I like the idea that the Ptolemies did not have a carefully thought-out design or a rational plan. But let me press that idea a little bit. If I understand you correctly, part of the reason for what we take to be a very intricate administration was to attract Greeks from the homeland to come to Egypt and/or to find things for them to do once they were there, to give them niches, and to give them status. This is an appealing idea. But two questions: First, is that not itself something of a conscious plan, something of a rational purpose? And second, if it's true, why didn't the Seleucids or the Attalids do it?

A. E. Samuel: You touch on something I had to omit for reasons of time. Take the cleruchs, for example. The practice of cleruchy has been interpreted as a neat example of conscious policy: we have to pay these soldiers, how will we pay them, we give them plots of land. This is, I think, a construct to some extent on the basis of what we think we understand about medieval Europe. And the term "feudalism" came in—and went out—for Ptolemaic Egypt, to describe what I'm talking about. Modern scholars seeing things like the Revenue Laws were just stunned by so much marvelously elaborate bureaucracy. Because it seemed so minutely detailed it was taken to be rationally organized. The material was read that way. It is only after we have read the source material over and over again that we recognize that it is really very disorganized. There is a lot of regulation, but it is not organized regulation, so that documents like the Revenue Laws are no longer seen as royal legislation, but mostly as local compendia for informational purposes. If the establishment of Greeks on the land is to be seen as we traditionally saw it, as a means of paying the troops, and we have a rational organization, then yes, we have to see some rational planning. But let us suppose, as I hypothesize, that the reason these people were given land was to get them out there—that is, to disperse Greeks through the countryside so that the government would have Greek-speaking people familiar with the local areas. In other words, the plots of land were not given to pay the soldiers; there was enough income from grain to do that. The real problem was different: there was no one in Tebtunis, let us say, who spoke the language of the rulers. One solution to that was to get the Greeks to settle in the country. Now if it's rational planning to say, I want as many Greeks as possible to settle out there so that I have a Greek-speaking population to govern, it's rational planning at a very minimalist level. But that's what I'm suggesting: that the reason for the distribution of the Greeks through Egypt was simply to distribute Greeks through Egypt, and not much more. This would adequately explain why the Seleucids didn't do the same thing. It also would explain something that has not really been asked: why didn't the Seleucids use the cleruchic system? The economic base in Egypt required people to be throughout the *chora*. It really wasn't practical to create a lot of new quasi-Greek or quasi-Macedonian cities.

D. Delia: I think that the assumption that there was an overriding rationality for three centuries or more is an enormous one to make. What Professor Samuel is suggesting, rather, is that what we have is a series of individually rational responses to particular situations: the whole thing doesn't add up to one answer.

A. A. Long: I think Professor Delia made the point that Greeks would find it very difficult to treat Ptolemy as a god. But may not the reverse be true? I'm not sure what her expression was, but certainly we don't want to talk about "belief in" Ptolemy as a god. A Greek believed in a god just to the extent that he took the god to have some power over his life. The Stoics, for all their rationalistic theology—and at the highest level one might want to see Stoicism as moving toward a kind of monotheism—were actually radically polytheist as well. They allowed that there could be mortal gods. Even the cosmos, the physical world, which the Stoics regarded as a deity, perishes. How this relates to Hellenistic experience I don't know. But my other point is that perhaps in some way the experience of Hellenistic kings, at least from the point of view of how they affected people, could actually regenerate belief in gods. Because traditionally gods behave in this way: you hope that they will honor your prayers and not blast you away, but experience shows how erratic they are. Of course human gods are erratic too, but you have more direct access to them. You get my general point.

D. Delia: I don't think there's a contradiction here. The point I was trying to make was that there is a distinction between the king as a god, and the divinity of his office. I find it hard to believe that both Greeks and Egyptians considered, for example, Ptolemy VIII Euergetes II, who was embroiled in civil wars with members of his family on the very soil of Egypt, to be *the* god or a god. I think they may have considered the office of kingship divine, but not necessarily the person himself. The fact that he was mortal wasn't really something I was considering.

S. M. Burstein: What has been missing in this discussion so far, although Professor Delia tried to introduce it, is the question of the Egyptians. The impression created by Professor Samuel's paper is that greedy Greeks cruelly exploited Egyptians, but that is too simple. Omitted is a group of people whom scholars tend to ignore, the komarchs and *komatographeis* who were the indispensable intermediaries between the Ptolemaic government and the bulk of the Egyptian population. Colonial situations such as those in Ptolemaic Egypt provide opportunities for such men to accumulate greater wealth and influence than would be the case under native regimes, because in the final analysis it is only through their agency that governmental business gets done. Isn't it true, therefore, that much of the exploitation documented in the sources occurred because the Ptolemaic system created opportunities for "corruption" not only for Greeks but also for lower-level Egyptian officials, such as Menches of Kerkeosiris? After all, since by and large Greeks didn't learn Egyptian, such officials were irreplaceable.

A. E. Samuel: I'd like to respond to Professor Long's question first. There's a famous exchange between Peter Fraser and Brad Welles, in which Fraser remarked, "We know that Ptolemy I created Sarapis," to which Welles replied, in effect, "Of this statement the first half is false and the second impossible." Welles's point was that nobody creates a god. I believe that in fact these kings *were* seen as gods. Now what that meant was limited to what they could do for you. But I do believe that the average Greek in Egypt, by the middle of the third century if not before, had figured out that the Ptolemies could do something in some divine way, and were therefore to be treated as *theoi.*

This influences my response to Professor Burstein's question. If the occupation is not purely occupation by a superior force, but embodies some element of divinity—as must surely have been felt in the presence of Alexander—and if it is believed that there is a divine element in what has happened, then to some extent this affects the collaboration issue. The other aspect of the question Professor Burstein raised, that of Menches and the Egyptians, is that we don't know what Egyptians did to protest exploitation if they didn't speak Greek. There was no point in sending a complaint to Alexandria in demotic. What we really have is a barrier between the oppressed Egyptians and the official structure, created by their inability to write in Greek. Any complaints which exist are either the product of an Egyptian who used a scribe to put a protest in Greek, or of Egyptians who were at least partly Hellenized. I think that it was inevitable that Egyptians who spoke both Greek and Egyptian would be the people who occupied the so-called interface level of the bureaucracy. And it's equally inevitable that they would make a buck out of it. What I'm suggesting is that it isn't just these characters who used the bureaucracy to enrich themselves in this situation, but also the people within the Greek structure. At the same time none of this was *corruption.*

That's what I'm insisting on. The word "corruption" is the wrong term for it. This was just the way things were.

D. Delia: Yet it's clear that in the Ptolemaic ordinances exploitation was considered abusive. Maybe it's a matter of degree. A little bit of profiteering was OK, but if it was excessive, voices of protest were raised and ultimately the king had to do something about it.

S. Burstein: In this connection I think two points are worth noting. First, there is no evidence that any Greek writer ever knew that the Egyptian king was supposed to be a god. Indeed, the opposite is explicitly stated to be the case by Hecataeus of Abdera (*ap.* DS 1.95.5) and implicitly by Herodotus (2.142). Second, there is a full-blown third-century-B.C. Greek justification of divine kingship, namely Euhemerism. Ptolemaic divine kingship, therefore, fits well into a third-century-B.C. Greek context.

P. Green: The first thing that struck me was the extraordinary parallel with what goes on in the Soviet Union—the gap between central planning and what happens at the other end. I don't think there is any inconsistency between people *trying* to plan centrally, and this having absolutely no effect on actual output at the local level. This may well have been what was happening in Ptolemaic Egypt. There is plenty of evidence for organization and commands from the top. How far these orders were obeyed, and who actually drafted them, is not at all certain. The king will have put his initials on something that was probably drafted by a bureaucrat. Several things are suggestive. One of them is the closed financial economy of Egypt, very apparent from the different coin weights. This has something to do with the fact that Egypt imported practically all of her silver. She exported grain and papyrus. She didn't like this business of external trade, but it was absolutely necessary. On another point: the king, we are told, was expected to be military. Why? One thing that nobody has mentioned so far is the Coele Syria frontier, which was pushed north and south for hundreds of years by Seleucids and Ptolemies because the Bekaa valley, Lebanon, and north Syria were just as economically and strategically crucial then as they are now. The early Ptolemies took a tremendous interest in the eastern Mediterranean and the Aegean because they wanted control of the trade, not just for symbolic military conquest. I think Professor Samuel was right to argue that the shift in administrative emphasis was due to the weakness of people like Ptolemy IV and V. But doesn't that imply much stronger control on the part of the earlier Ptolemies, that they *did* know what they were doing, and controlled things to a significant extent? One of the things that Theocritus brings out in Idyll 17 is the number of lands that

Ptolemy has reduced. He didn't do this just for fun. And what about the corps of interpreters? That existed right from the beginning, and clearly was something well worth being in on. There are useful parallels here with the British Raj in India. And the collaborators are terribly important. The only people who collaborate actively are those who want to claw their way up in the existing system with a chance of real success. Christian Habicht has argued that even in the best of times, after two or more generations, they only formed about 2½ percent of the total population, but it's a very important percentage. I think we have to modify this view of a total lack of control from above. The fact that they weren't very good at it doesn't mean that they didn't try to do it and want to do it. In some respects, too, there *was* control: over the currency, for example. And what about those directives that in an emergency grain be shipped only to Alexandria? It may have been whistling in the wind. But there is a sense of control from Alexandria which I think you underemphasize.

A. E. Samuel: I think there's a difference between planning and direction. I see the evidence for direction. That is an attempt to get the maximum out of the grain crop, for example. What I don't see is detailed attempts at planning, to say, "Let us have so much grown here, and so much grown there, and so much this year and so much next year, and we will set our regulations up so that we get a better and more even result from the crop"—that's planning and that's what I deny. Secondly, in reference to the weakness of the leadership in the second century: what I'm suggesting is that in the third century the king had people like Apollonius, courtiers whom he knew personally and through whom he could get things done, such as taking care of foreign dignitaries and showing them around. This is different from a possible situation where the king would follow a chain of command from Alexandria down to the Fayum, using officials whom he might or might not have known. What I see in the second century is the absence of bilateral relationships between the king and his courtiers at the time of the regencies, and that's why you get the increase in the strength of the bureaucracy. So long as the king had a coterie of people that he could deal with there was some attempt to keep the bureaucracy under control.

C. M. Wells (Trinity University, San Antonio):   One observation: I think the absence of a clearly articulated distinction between the public and the private wouldn't surprise, for instance, a Roman provincial governor of the late Republic, who used his household to administer his province.

"The Base Mechanic Arts"?
Some Thoughts on the Contribution of Science (Pure and Applied) to the Culture of the Hellenistic Age

K. D. White

My first task must be to remove some misapprehensions and dispose of some widely held but erroneous notions about ancient science and technology. For example, we are frequently told that the Greeks had no word for science, as we understand that term. But they did have a word, *historia,* and even if we do not think much of Herodotus' pioneering "inquiries," it would be a bold man today who would deny the title of "scientific inquiry" to Theophrastus' *Inquiry into Plants (Peri phyton historia),* a work which laid the foundations of the science of botany. As for technology, it is surely time we stopped equating the term with mechanical inventions, or labeling applied scientists such as Philo of Byzantium with the obsolete term "mechanicians." The *Oxford Classical Dictionary,* even in its second edition, has no entry for technology, or for Ktesibios, while the hundred professors of the Museum are described, s.v. "Museum," as "research scholars." I think we must try to steer a middle course, somewhere between Finley's view of the ancient Greeks as "desperately foreign"[1] and the misguided notion that they were really "fellows of another college."[2]

Next, we have to dispose of some of the presuppositions encountered by those who embark on research in this area. They include the "Farrington heresy," which argues that everything in philosophy and science was

---

[1] M. I. Finley, *Aspects of Antiquity,* 2d ed. (New York, 1977), "Introduction: Desperately Foreign," uses the phrase as the title of a provocative attack on traditional views of the Greeks.

[2] The saying is attributed to various Oxford classicists of earlier generations.

going along swimmingly, following the pioneering enterprises of the Ionian *physikoi*, until Plato came along and spoilt it all with his insistence that (1) the prime aim of philosophy was not the investigation of nature and the cosmos but the acquisition of virtue, and (2) that epistemology must be based on the theory of Forms.³ Farrington's thesis, for which there was little evidential backing, exercised considerable influence over an earlier generation; the discrediting of some of his ideas has led to the neglect of the more positive aspects of his work, especially his views on the relationship of the Museum at Alexandria to the Lyceum and on the work of Strato of Lampsacus and Philo of Byzantium in relation to the use of experiment in science and technology, respectively.⁴ Particularly relevant to our discussion are Farrington's analyses of Strato's work on motion and on the compression of air.⁵ It is worth noting here that many of the devices invented by the *mechanikoi* of the Hellenistic Age were powered by compressed air, such as Ktesibios' water organ (see figure 35)—a point still ignored by most of those who write about the power resources of the ancient world.⁶

Our second presupposition is very deep-seated and has been made more difficult to dislodge since the late Sir Moses Finley lent the weight of his authority to it: the view that the economies of the classical world were undeveloped, their power resources very limited, and their technology primitive, with virtually no inventions and little in the way of innovation or development.⁷ In my *Greek and Roman Technology* (1984) I tried to review the evidence on several aspects of this central question regarding the range and importance of these technical developments, an area in which Hellenistic innovations were, in my opinion, of prime importance. Indeed, more than a decade ago the first holder of a Chair of Ancient Philosophy and Science at Cambridge, Geoffrey Lloyd, at the end of a chapter on applied mechanics and technology in this period, noted the ingenuity with which the writers on mechanics thought up new applications of a limited number of simple mechanical principles, the interest they displayed in the theoretical aspects of mechanics, and their recogni-

---

³ Benjamin Farrington, *Greek Science*, 2 vols. (Harmondsworth 1944, 1949), reissued in a single volume by the same publisher in 1961.

⁴ Farrington, *Greek Science*, 169ff.

⁵ Cf. Hero Alex. *Pneum.* introd. and 1.16.16ff.

⁶ That Strato provided a theoretical basis for the compressibility and elasticity of air as a source of power is conceded by J. G. Landels, *Ancient Engineering* (London, 1978), 128. It was the inventive genius of Ktesibios that put its properties to practical use in the pneumatic catapult (which got no further than the drawing board and was abandoned by Philo's time), and the water organ, (*hydraulis*), which not only worked but became the prototype for the development of a highly successful musical instrument.

⁷ The minimalist model, first presented by M. I. Finley in *The Ancient Economy* (London, 1983), still has its strong supporters; see, e.g., Peter Garnsey and Richard Saller's brilliant survey *The Roman Empire, Economy, Society and Culture* (London, 1987), 43–63.

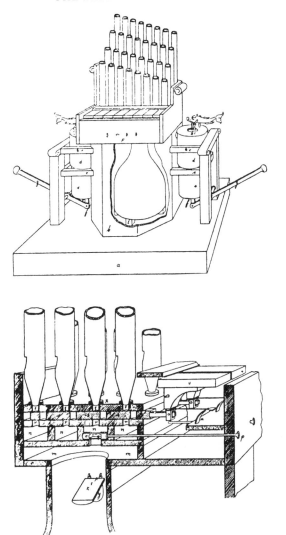

35. Reconstruction of Ktesibios' water organ. From K. D. White, *Greek and Roman Technology* (London: Thames and Hudson, 1984), p. 173, pl. 177. Reprinted by permission.

tion of the possibilities of applying mechanics to practical purposes, as well as to those of entertainment and miracle working.[8]

A few years later my former colleague at Reading, John Landels, produced in his book *Ancient Engineering* a lucid series of expositions, aided by diagrams, to demonstrate how many of the technical devices actually

[8] G. E. R. Lloyd, *Greek Science after Aristotle* (London, 1973), 105–6.

worked. In spite of this, G. E. M. de Ste Croix two years later described
the Greek world as "very undeveloped technologically, and therefore
infinitely less productive than the modern one"[9]—a statement that might
have carried more weight with the removal of the adverb "infinitely." In
support of this bold assertion he refers to the absence of so simple a
device as the wheelbarrow—though this also failed to get invented
throughout the Middle Ages, a period which is alleged to have witnessed
a series of great technical advances,[10] including the stern-post rudder
for ships, a device in no way superior to the steering oars of the classical
world.[11] In fact, as I hope to demonstrate, the Hellenistic Age saw a
variety of technical inventions and developments, as well as significant
advances in theory and methodology, including, for example, the introduction of experiment to test a theory. Rather than engage in such sterile
wranglings as those I have described, I propose to examine what evidence
we have about scientists and engineers, their operations, and their role
in the society of Hellenistic Alexandria.

Our sources of information consist of (1) the surviving written works
of practicing scientists, both pure and applied, and (2) any technical
devices which may be reasonably attributed to named inventors, such as
Archimedes' screw and the Ktesibian machine. As far as written sources
are concerned, our main difficulties arise from loss of the actual writings;
thus, whereas the pioneering works of Theophrastus, which laid the
foundations of the science of botany, survive in considerable quantity,
those of Strato of Lampsacus, Theophrastus' successor as head of the
Lyceum (c. 285–268), survive only in fragments cited by later authorities,
from which his ideas—which covered a wide variety of subjects, including zoology, pathology, psychology, and technology—have to be pieced
together. As for the technical inventions and innovations, it is, in many
cases, difficult to establish either dates or attributions. Thus the water-
lifting device known to the Greeks as the *cochlea*, or snail, may very well
have been invented by Archimedes, though the attribution cannot be
proved; and the double-action force pump known to antiquity as "the
Ktesibian device" may well have been invented by that talented engineer,
Ktesibios. This twin-cylinder pump was employed for a wide variety of
practical purposes, ranging from pumping out the bilges of merchant
ships to fire fighting;[12] an eight-cylinder version was still used by the
London fire brigade, and perhaps by its New York counterpart, well into

[9] *The Class Struggle in Ancient Greece* (London, 1980), 38.

[10] Lynn White, Jr., *Mediaeval Technology and Social Change* (Berkeley, 1962).

[11] See L. Casson, *Ships and Seamanship in the Ancient World* (Princeton, 1971), 224–28.

[12] Hero of Alexandria, writing an account of the device in the first century A.D., refers
to it as the "siphon used in conflagrations" (*Pneumatika* I.20); but Lloyd, *Greek Science after
Aristotle*, 101, unaccountably doubts whether it was ever used to put out a fire.

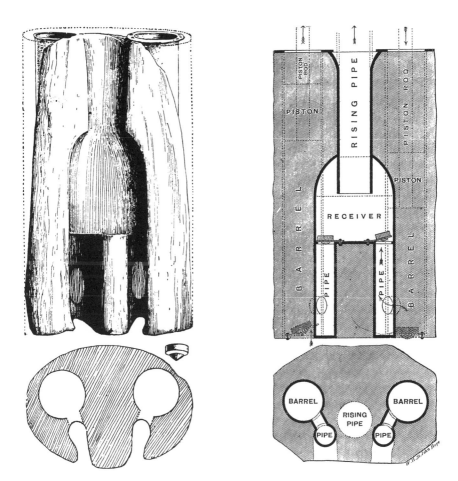

36. Ktesibian water pump from Silchester, England. From K. D. White, *Greek and Roman Technology* (London: Thames and Hudson), p. 16, pls. 4–5. Reprinted by permission.

the nineteenth century. Surviving specimens of the device—one of the more than twenty that have been located is illustrated in figure 36—have been collected, described, and classified for the first time, as recently as 1981, by an undergraduate student of University College, London.[13]

Regarding the important question of contemporary attitudes toward

[13] T. W. Battersby; "Roman Force Pumps; A Preliminary Survey," (B. A. diss., University of London, 1981). Battersby drew the important distinction between the small-bore pumps, with a delivered output equivalent to that of a garden hose, and the much more powerful type which could provide the head of water required for fire fighting and bilge pumping.

the Hellenistic world, and toward the forces that were thought to operate within it, the following passages, which may reasonably be attributed to Strato, are highly significant. The first occurs in Cicero's *De Natura Deorum* (1.13.35): "Strato the physicist was of the opinion that all divine power resides in nature, which is a power without shape or capacity to feel, containing in itself all the causes of coming-to-be, of growth, and of decay." The opinion expressed here springs from a worldview totally opposed to the prevailing Aristotelian view. Final causes in nature are out; nor is there any place in Strato's world for divine providence. Further, when he turned from theory to the investigation of physical phenomena, it seems clear that Strato endeavored to solve his problems by means of experimentation. The orthodox view on this question appears in a review of Farrington's *Greek Science*. Dismissing the author's claim that Strato both understood the need for experimentation and practiced it, the reviewer writes: "Experimentation as a systematic theory was unknown to antiquity, arriving only with the Renaissance."[14] There are, in fact, two passages by Strato which contain descriptions of a range of devices operated by compressed air, and which are crucial to the question. How far did Greek scientists carry out experiments designed to test hypotheses?

The first passage comes from Strato's treatise *On Motion*, as quoted by Simplicius in his commentary on Aristotle's *Physics* (916.10ff.), where the topic under discussion is the phenomenon of acceleration in falling objects. Simplicius noted that writers on the subject offer different explanations, but that few advance any *proof* of the fact that falling bodies, as they approach their destination, move faster. Strato, however, does just this. As Geoffrey Lloyd makes clear,[15] the importance of our text lies not in *what* the writer is trying to prove, but in the *way* he sets out to attempt the proof. He first uses a simple observation, of rainwater falling off the roof of a building; he then goes on to explain what would happen if a given weight of water were dropped from different heights. We cannot in this case prove actual experiment, but in our next passage (Hero Alex. *Pneum.* 1.16.16ff.) we certainly can. Here the topic is one that had been much debated—that of the existence and the nature of the void (*to kenon*) or vacuum. Hero describes the apparatus used; it is designed to show by experiment that (1) there are scattered vacua in the air, and (2) that air can be evacuated from a sealed globe-shaped container.

We come now to the second of our Hellenistic scientists, Philo of Byzantium, who worked in Alexandria around 200 B.C. Philo is one of several writers on technical subjects who are known to have had practical

---

[14] *JRS* 31 (1941): 149, quoted by Farrington, *Greek Science*, 177.
[15] *Greek Science after Aristotle*, 16.

experience in one branch of applied science or another, as well as being connected with the Museum or research institute established by Ptolemy Philadelphus; Philo's work was concerned with artillery, comprising mechanical arrow-firing catapults and stone-throwing ballistas. The stages of technical innovation and development in this field are well documented by a series of important finds, which include an artillery repair shop at Ampurias in Spain.[16] However, the most important fact revealed by recent research is the indication of *repeated experiment* as a means of establishing a method and a formula to be incorporated in the specification for the construction of different types of missile launchers.[17] Surely we have a clear indication that engineers in Philo's time were well aware of the need for systematic testing in order to isolate the relevant variables and determine their relationship. Philo in this passage evidently rejects the crude trial-and-error approach, along with a priori dogmatism, in favor of controlled experiment.

While Philo's name is associated with a variety of writings on scientific subjects, that of Ktesibios is linked with an equally wide range of inventions, most of which are based on the application of the principles of hydraulics. Little is known of the life of this outstanding technologist; but his lowly birth (his father was a barber) did not prevent him from enjoying royal patronage. His inventions included—in addition to the twin-cylinder water pump—a water clock, a pipe organ powered by an ingenious combination of water and compressed air,[18] and an improved catapult, operated by bronze springs instead of twisted animal sinew. He is also credited with a considerable number of inventions designed for entertainment, the so-called automata. These included a singing cornucopia, incorporated into the funeral monument erected by Ptolemy Philadelphus in honor of his wife and sister Arsinoë; and a cam-operated statue of the mysterious deity that figured prominently in the famous Grand Procession, where it carried out a continuous performance, enter-

---

[16] For details of Philo's important innovation in ballistics, the repeater mechanism for rapid-firing catapults, see Landels, *Ancient Engineering*, 183ff.; cf. also K. D. White, *Greek and Roman Technology* (London, 1984), 178, and references there cited, for this practical item of automation. The Ampurias finds included "a very primitive" (but doubtless efficient) "Vernier system" for the fine tuning of the torsion-spring catapult (Landels, *Ancient Engineering*, 115).

[17] Philo *On Artillery Construction* 3.50.20ff.

[18] The organ (*hydraulis*) was a composite invention involving a number of technical devices, making Ktesibios' organ the prototype for later developments. For a detailed account of the components and the operation, see Landels, *Ancient Engineering*, 26–27. These included a small windmill working a piston to supply the air; one of numerous instances of a basic invention not exploited for many centuries; the earliest windmill—a potentially vast power resource for the large-scale milling of grain—dates only from the ninth century A.D.

taining the festival crowd by standing up and sitting down.[19] The excitement produced by this very simple application of a rack-and-pinion gear may well be due to the fact that toothed gear wheels were a recent invention, which almost certainly meant that their possibilities were still being explored (there is a passage in the *Problemata* in which the author finds the reverse motion created by two intersecting cogwheels intriguing).

It is an easy step from the most famous inventor of his day (and presumably a very well-known figure in Alexandrian society) to the Museum with which he was associated. An impressive bibliography can be readily built up on this topic, but the material available about its working conditions and its environment is very limited. The House of the Muses was evidently a research organization, supported, like the Library, by a royal endowment. Traditional accounts of these cultural developments,[20] based as they are on the very limited accounts that have come down to us, assume that the Library, which rapidly acquired a worldwide reputation, was separate from the Museum; but it is more likely that both were parts of what might be called a research institute, which provided facilities for workers in a wide variety of disciplines belonging to what we would now call the humanities and the sciences. The House of the Muses housed and maintained an undetermined number of professors.[21] They were accommodated in a communal establishment, which might properly be described as collegiate since they enjoyed a common table along with the environmental benefits of a garden and the shady colonnaded walks that linked the different centers of activity. In addition to the Library, these also included a theater, which provided the accommodation needed for lectures.

As for research, tradition has tended to overemphasize the importance of the work performed in the Library, which laid the foundations of textual criticism, at the expense of the investigations associated with those various branches of pure and applied science for which the Museum became famous. A more balanced judgment informs the following comment by a recent historian of Hellenistic Egypt: "There is virtually no

[19] For details of the procession, and suggestions on the technical arrangements for operating the movement of the statue of Nysa, see the excellent commentary by Ellen Rice, *The Grand Procession of Ptolemy Philadelphus* (Oxford, 1983), esp. 62–67.

[20] See P. M. Fraser, *Ptolemaic Alexandria* (Oxford, 1972) 1:312–35, 2:467ff.

[21] Strabo 17.1.8, C.793–94 mentions the Museum among the prominent features of Alexandria. He describes it vaguely as forming part of the royal quarter, and he mentions the covered walk (*peripatos*), the assembly room (*exedra*, the term commonly used of the lecture rooms provided in the gymnasia), and a big hall (*oikos megas*), used as a common dining room or refectory (*syssition*) for the participating scholars (*philologoi andres*). The amenities also included a garden, complete with exotic plants and animals—a necessary provision for botanists and zoologists.

area of intellectual activity to which [the Alexandrian scholars and scientists] did not make a major contribution and in several spheres [Alexandria's] role was paramount."[22] Contrary to the commonly held opinion that under Rome the Museum and Library suffered a rapid decline into total obscurity, we have evidence that both were still operating many centuries later, even if not as vigorously as in their heyday; for Ammianus tells us that when he paid a visit to Alexandria (? c. A.D. 363) he found the arts and sciences still being pursued;[23] they included music, geology, astronomy, and, perhaps not surprisingly, astrology. Medicine was in the most flourishing condition of all the sciences there, enjoying such a high reputation that the only qualification an intending practitioner needed to produce was a statement that he had received his training in Alexandria. The most important scientific advances seem to have been made in pure mathematics, mechanics, physics, geography, and medicine. Considering the nature of the contributions made in modern research institutions, it is not surprising to learn that at Alexandria systematics and taxonomy were to the fore in many subjects, with Euclid's *Elements* as the most obvious example; nor that research in both pure and applied science was being pursued under the same roof, and in a number of outstanding cases, such as that of Archimedes of Syracuse, by the same person. This eminent scientist lived and worked in Alexandria, and while based there was thought to have invented the water-raising device that bears his name.

Snobbery and place seeking are common to a wide variety of societies; widespread too is the notion, enshrined in the word *banausos* and its derivatives, that those who work with their hands—applied scientists and engineers no less than those who earn their bread in the lowly confines of the workshop—are inferior to theorists. Attitudes vary widely toward different occupations: metallurgy has always been surrounded with an aura of mystery, and its products, like the Shield of Achilles, regarded as somehow miraculous—*thauma idesthai* in Homer's phrase. But what about the status of those who practiced both pure and applied science?[24] The passage usually cited in support of the "banausic theory" (Plut. *Marc.* 17) must surely be viewed in its historical context: Plutarch was no engineer but a pious country gentleman, and indeed somewhat addicted to Platonism. He is doubtless correct in suggesting that Archimedes valued his mathematical works above everything else. But how can we accept the statement that Archimedes—the inventor of the device which became so

[22] A. K. Bowman, *Egypt after the Pharaohs, 332 B.C.–A.D. 642* (London, 1986), 223–24.
[23] Ammianus 22.16.17–18, cf. 15.1
[24] On the relationship between science and technology, see White, *Greek and Roman Technology*, 12ff.

common in the complex irrigation systems of the Nile Delta that the papyri usually refer to it simply as *mechane*, "the machine,"—positively disliked "every art that serves the needs of everyday life?"

This is perhaps an appropriate signal to bring the present discussion to a halt, though not, I trust, to an end. I have missed out whole areas of investigation—notably medicine and astronomy—but I hope I have succeeded in establishing the need for unbiased enquiry into the science and technology of the Hellenistic Age, the activities of the scientists and engineers who lived and worked in the period, and their place in the society in which they flourished.

RESPONSE: JOHN SCARBOROUGH

Since its publication in 1970, I have been delighted to recommend Kenneth White's *Roman Farming*, the best account in any modern language of that most basic of ancient—and modern—human activities, agriculture. White's book remains a pioneering tome on the topic, reminding us of why the Romans would enshrine their curiously anachronistic farming virtues as a continuous theme in their literature, ranging from Cato the Elder's blatant denarius-grubbing advice manual on farming through some oddly reminiscent data on wine-stomps, bees and honey, and cattle diseases in the Byzantine *Geoponica* of the tenth century.[1] White represents the rarest of breeds in the field of history of science, technology, and medicine: a hands-on man, one who has delighted in the dirt and mud (let alone the questions of soils and their mineral variants) which always form the essence of farming. In his writing about ancient farming and technology he asks, again and again, the basic question, What is it? And in his deliciously technical manuals on Roman agricultural implements,[2] he shows just what plows and pruning hooks, axes and hoes *were*,

---

[1] The handiest Latin text and English translation of Cato is in the Loeb Classical Library volume Cato and Varro, *De re rustica*, ed. William Davis Hooper, rev. Harrison Boyd Ash (Cambridge, Mass., 1934). Before White's *Roman Farming* (London, 1970) there was little commentary on the specifics of Cato's agricultural lore; one of the better translations with brief commentaries was Ernest Brehaut, trans., *Cato the Censor on Farming* (New York, 1933). Even less is available on the *Geoponica*; the standard Greek text (with some discussion of Syriac parallels) is H. Beckh, ed., *Geoponica sive Cassiani Bassi scholastici De re rustica eclogae* (Leipzig, 1895). Remaining quite valuable is Wilhelm Gemoll, *Untersuchungen über die Quellen, der Verfasser und die Abfassungszeit der Geoponica* (Berlin, 1883).

[2] *Agricultural Implements of the Roman World* (Cambridge, 1967), and *Farm Equipment of the Roman World* (Cambridge, 1975).

besides furnishing technological data on how such presumably lowly objects were made, by whom, and where.[3]

Extending his scope, but employing the same essential questions, White produced the fundamental *Greek and Roman Technology*,[4] a book which indeed supersedes almost every work on the subject which preceded it,[5] yet specialist scholars appear not to have discovered how this volume also represents a major advance in the study of classical technology and science as a whole. Perhaps Kenneth White makes some scholars a bit uncomfortable with his clarity, with his insistence on reading the ancient texts on technologies for what they actually say, not what we expect or hope they might say in light of modern fads, whether Marxist, deconstructionist, or whatever. Crusty farmer and traveler that he is, White can easily sniff at the fancies of Farrington,[6] chastise moderns who would falsify ancient technologies in their attempts to formulate sweeping explanations of insoluble historical problems,[7] and generally chuckle at some of the inanities of writers who display their booklearning but not their command of how cogs and plowshares might actually work, or how the practice of medicine is always more than lofty theory and ideal conditions. White's maxim is "go and look." Simple. Direct. Difficult, but ultimately rewarding.

It seems to me that White has defined (perhaps unwittingly, but with unerring instincts) exactly why technology remains the province of nonhumanists, who are supposedly—or so we are repeatedly informed—the less-than-learned folk of our day: the engineers, the technocrats of various descriptions. Are they really so ignorant? Many, indeed, cannot write plain English; but similar qualities of proud fuzziness are common among the nonscientists, many of whom writhe happily in the slippery grip of in-house specialist jargon. Perhaps White is implicitly challenging these ordinary assumptions (that humanists can think and nonhumanists

---

[3] Sian Rees, *Ancient Agricultural Implements* (Aylesbury, England, 1981), is also a good introduction to the topic. White's *Bibliography of Roman Agriculture* (Reading, 1970), is a splendid, multilingual guide to the specialized literature, subdivided into listings on the texts, land surveying, legislation, crop husbandry, animal husbandry, arboriculture, forestry, prices, food and diet, and a number of other related categories (918 items).

[4] London, 1984.

[5] Including the frequently cited R. J. Forbes, *Studies in Ancient Technology*, 2d rev. ed., 9 vols. (Leiden, 1964–72), which is studded with errors, especially with respect to primary sources.

[6] Benjamin Farrington, *Greek Science*, rev. ed. (Baltimore, 1961).

[7] E.g., the fall of the Roman Empire attributed to lead poisoning, by Jerome O. Nriagu, *Lead and Lead Poisoning in Antiquity* (New York, 1983). A critique of such arguments is provided in John Scarborough, "The Myth of Lead Poisoning among the Romans," *Journal of the History of Medicine and Allied Sciences*, 39 (1984): 469–75.

cannot) when he considers just what technology in antiquity—and by extension in modern times—might actually have been. We are told that technology (broadly conceived) is applied science, so that whereas physics and pharmacokinetics in the laboratory are not technology, atomic energy and bottles of aspirin are. Or are they? Does theory precede application? White answers, "Sometimes," thus indicating why he engenders discomfort among simplistic seekers of systematics.

Technologies in the Hellenistic world were as varied in their own way as are ours, and one learns that if experiment is taken as a criterion for science and technology, then ancient science as a whole will rarely measure up to modern standards. Note that Kenneth White confronts this misapplication of historical analogy, even while he makes careful and precise observations on how the ancients *did* conceive of experiment; not only did Greek and Hellenistic scientists look for repeated instances in nature to suggest analogues in technology (as in the case of dripping rain applied to ballistics), but one has clear evidence that experiment was well known to Greek and Hellenistic science, even while antiquity allowed for variables such as modern science denies in advance. Continually implied in White's published scholarship and in his present paper is a simple if often ignored fact demonstrating the absolute difference between Greco-Roman and modern science. "Experiment" to us almost always means controlled experiment (laboratories, again); but to an Erasistratus, this would have been cheating, no matter what modern microbiologists might say about the essential techniques embodied in Koch's postulates.[8] It is thus arguable that ancient, as opposed to modern, "experiments" assumed natural variables; this also suggests why modern laboratory experiments on animal and human physiology turn out results which cannot predict exactly what will happen in the real world.[9] The reason, quite simply, is because controlled conditions are almost never the same as those that apply in the world at large—even in carefully monitored surgical theaters, such as those in which organ transplants take place.

---

[8] Named after Heinrich Hermann Robert Koch (1843–1910), whose *Untersuchungen über die Aetiologie der Wundinfectionskrankheiten* (Leipzig, 1878), trans. W. W. Cheyne as *Investigations into the Etiology of Traumatic Infective Diseases* (London, 1880), asserted that proof of the parasitic nature of traumatic infective diseases would be obtained when (1) microorganisms are observed in all cases of the disease; (2) the presence of those microorganisms is shown to be in such numbers and distribution as to explain all the symptoms of the disease; and (3) a well-defined microorganism can be established for the disease. A summary of Koch's career and achievements is Claude E. Dolman, "Koch," *Dictionary of Scientific Biography* (New York, 1973) 7:420–35.

[9] See, e.g., J. M. Padfield, "Making Drugs into Medicines," in D. M. Burley and T. B. Binns, eds., *Pharmaceutical Medicine* (London, 1985), 45–46.

Yet this unlimited variability never has prevented ancients or moderns from "going and looking": results in real science—ancient or modern—are frequently unpredictable, a fact quite invisible to chemistry students who might not progress beyond the cookbookery of freshman chemistry or the presumed invariabilities of the Krebs Cycle which explains human metabolisms.

Hands-on historians of science, technology, and medicine always seem to savor the evidence of the texts, so I am assuming Professor White will appreciate the introduction into this response of an experiment in Hellenistic times, an experiment fairly widely known by specialists in Hellenistic medical studies, but one which generally is misunderstood. The experiment is detailed in the *Anonymus Londinensis*,[10] parts of which probably incorporate the lost *Iatrika* of Meno,[11] a student of Aristotle who compiled opinions (*doxai*) of various medical thinkers and philosophies. In the version we have are various opinions of famous physicians and philosopher-physicians with the latest name dating to about 100 B.C., which suggests that we have an augmented and edited text of Meno plus more *doxai* added later for this private copy.[12] Here indeed is Hippocrates, a figure who has received too much attention from students of Hellenistic medicine,[13] as well as several other luminaries of medicine in the Hellenistic era, including one of the brilliant experimenters at the Alexandrian Museum, Erasistratus:

[10] Herman Diels, ed., *Anonymi Londinensis ex Aristotelis iatricis Menoniis et aliis medicis eclogae*, Supplementum Aristotelicum, vol. 3, pt. 1 (Berlin, 1893), remains the standard text. W. H. S. Jones, ed. and trans., *The Medical Writings of Anonymus Londinensis* (Cambridge, 1947; rptd. Amsterdam, 1968), while very useful, fails to specify dubious readings in the papyrus, and the translations sometimes suffer from these questionable interpretations of an often fragmentary text.

[11] Meno's *Iatrike synagoge* is attested in Galen's *Commentary of Hippocrates' Nature of Man* 1.2; J. Mewaldt, ed., *Galeni In Hippocratis De natura hominis*, Corpus Medicorum Graecorum V 9,1 (Leipzig, 1914), 15–16 = C. G. Kühn, ed., *Claudii Galeni Opera omnia* (Leipzig, 1828) 15:25–26. Jones, ed., *Anonymus*, 6, collects six further "testimonies" to a Meno who wrote on medical topics, but none indicates the contents of the full *Iatrika* as related by Galen.

[12] So Jones, ed., *Anonymus*, 4.

[13] *Anonymus* XIV–XX. As Jones, ed., *Anonymus*, 17–20, points out, the "Hippocrates" recorded here in the papyrus text is very disappointing for those modern scholars hoping to have found evidence of the brilliance of the so-called Father of Medicine. In fact, the text of *Anonymus* effectively disproved long-standing arguments which asserted "genuine works" by Hippocrates. See G. E. R. Lloyd, "The Hippocratic Question," *CQ*, n.s. 25 (1975): 171–92, in which one reads that questions of authorship (by Hippocrates or anyone else) are generally insoluble. As we have them, texts in what is called the Hippocratic corpus were probably pulled together sometime in the Hellenistic era, most likely in Alexandria: P. M. Fraser, *Ptolemaic Alexandria* (Oxford, 1972) 1:364–67, with references collected in vol. 2.

Erasistratus too tried to prove the proposition [i.e., that continuous, invisible emanations or evaporations of the finer elements within the body occur from the entire body without any external cause[14]]. If one were to take some suitable animal (a bird, for example), and were to set it down in a cauldron for some period of time without giving it food, and then were to weigh it along with the excreta that visibly have been passed, one will find that it is far less in weight because obviously a considerable emanation has taken place, perceptible only to reason.[15]

Professor White has rightly emphasized the connections between the notions of a vacuum as taught by Strato[16] and the concepts assumed by Erasistratus in "explaining" blood in the arteries observed when one of these large vessels has been severed (synastomoses thus must exist between arteries and veins).[17] If Alexandrian technologists could devise machines which employed compressed air and the principles of an artificially produced vacuum, then certainly the same principles could easily be applied to investigations of what we call physiology. But exactly what were Strato, Ktesibios, Philo—and Herophilus and Erasistratus—actually using as basic premises? Or more pertinently, what questions and/or assumptions guided inquiry (*historia*) in the most basic sense of that term?

One may begin, as does Professor White, with Theophrastus' masterpiece, the *Inquiry into Plants*, known usually by its Latinized title, *Historia plantarum*. Probably set down about 300 B.C., Theophrastus' *Inquiry* uses Aristotle's concepts of a morphological structure in nature to classify plants according to shape, providing the best botanical morphology and taxonomy until Carl Linnaeus' *Species plantarum* of 1753.[18] In nine books,[19] Theophrastus' inquiries incorporated all sorts of information,

---

[14] The origin of this notion of emanations may have been Strato, or more probably Aegimius. Heinrich von Staden, "Experiment and Experience in Hellenistic Medicine," *Bulletin of the Institute of Classical Studies* [London], 22 (1975): 179 n. 10.

[15] *Anonymus* 44–51. The translation is by von Staden, "Experiment and Experience," 180.

[16] Suggested, in particular, by frags. 54–67 in Fritz Wehrli, ed., *Die Schule des Aristoteles*, vol. 5, *Straton von Lampsakos*, 2d ed. (Basel, 1969), 20–25. Not all scholars agree with White's thinking; e.g., Heinrich von Staden, *Herophilus: The Art of Medicine in Early Alexandria* (Cambridge, 1989), 304 n. 229.

[17] See the incisive commentary in David J. Furley and J. S. Wilkie, eds. and trans., *Galen On Respiration and the Arteries* (Princeton, 1984), 31–37.

[18] Reprinted with introduction and appendices by W. T. Stearn and J. L. Heller, as *Carl Linnaeus: Species plantarum*, facsimile of the first edition, 1753, 2 vols. (London, 1957–59). Linnaeus' innovations in botanical nomenclature were strikingly original, as argued by John L. Heller, "The Early History of Binomial Nomenclature," *Huntia* 1 (1964): 33–70.

[19] Book 9 of the *Historia plantarum* often is termed "spurious" in the earlier literature, but the best witnesses among the manuscripts show that this ninth book is, indeed, part of Theophrastus' work. Benedict Einarson, "The Manuscripts of Theophrastus' *Historia plantarum*," *CP* 71 (1976): 67–76, esp. 68–69 n.

ranging from the experiences of professional *rhizotomoi* and semiprofessional *pharmakopolai* to his own observations (known to farmers, naturally) of growing seasons, fruits, flowers, properties of plant products (including those called *pharmaka*),[20] and—most importantly for consideration here—how plants fit into the world of nature (*physis*) as a whole. Questions of "life" as movement and change receive Theophrastus' brilliant modifications as he shows that such movement and change is obviously very slow by comparison to Aristotle's notion of *kinesis*,[21] but that plants form an essential part of a philosophical view of nature, more completely demonstrated by Theophrastus in his *Causes of Plants* (again known most commonly by its Latinized title, *De causis plantarum*).[22] In the *Inquiry into Plants* one finds botanical classifications, specific identities, and informational data as Theophrastus was able to gather them; in *Causes*, one receives an account of common and distinct characteristics of plants. Theophrastus' two works on botany function for plants as had Aristotle's six works for animals (his *Inquiry into Animals* gathered information and offered a classification of animals; *Parts of Animals, Generation of Animals, Motion of Animals, On the Soul*, and the shorter tracts called *Parva naturalia* all investigated common or distinctive characteristics). Assumptions in Theophrastus' works on botany are those of a Peripatetic world view, structured and related by form and function, and were quite scientific enough to remain the best books on botany until the European Enlightenment.

Much of Theophrastus' information on plants is from the world of "base" and "mechanical" learning, to use the phraseology of Professor White. Such data—like those of experts on ballistics or the facts recorded by inventors of gadgets, toys, and even the famous water raiser called the Archimedean screw[23]—emerge from the usually unwritten levels of a practical technology, not necessarily guarded as trade secrets (although many would be *technai*, along with the skills of medicine and surgery), but

[20] John Scarborough, "Theophrastus on Herbals and Herbal Remedies," *Journal of the History of Biology* 11 (1978): 353–85.

[21] In the enormous literature on this topic, one welcomes the succinct clarity of G. E. R. Lloyd, *Aristotle* (Cambridge, 1968), 46–49, 63–66, 115–116, and several other sections as listed under "change" in the index.

[22] Books 1 and 2 of *De causis plantarum* are available in a freshly edited and translated text by Benedict Einarson and George K. K. Link, *Theophrastus: De causis plantarum*, vol. 1 (Cambridge, Mass., 1976), with a brilliant introduction to the tract by Einarson. For the remainder of the work (bks. 3–6) one must still consult F. Wimmer, ed. and trans. [Latin], *Theophrasti Eresii Opera* (Paris, Didot, 1866; rptd. Frankfurt, Minerva, 1964), 218–319.

[23] K. D. White, *Greek and Roman Technology* (London, 1984), 23, 32. The origins of this device, supposedly invented by Archimedes, are murky. A. P. Usher, *A History of Mechanical Inventions*, rev. ed. (Cambridge, Mass., 1954), 129; *contra*, Thorkild Schioler, *Roman and Islamic Water-Lifting Wheels* (Odense, Denmark, 1973), 168.

known and passed down from generation to generation. Theophrastus' *rhizotomoi* of book 9 of the *Inquiry into Plants* are as skilled as the assumed *metallikoi* of his undeservedly understudied tract *On Stones*[24]—here are miners, to be sure, but also gem gatherers; and the tract addresses the basic questions of how things dug up from the earth took form initially (Theophrastus, following Plato and Aristotle, seems to believe that what we call "metals" came from water, and "earths," that is "mined earths," came from earth). I am quite fond of Theophrastus' short work *On Odors*,[25] which is very likely a surviving part of the lost book 7 of *Causes of Plants*; in *Odors* the technology of mixing perfumes and medicinal oils indicates skills which fuse with the skills related to olive oil.[26] Shelf life was certainly important; but, more essentially, Theophrastus wrestles with questions of smell and taste as sense perceptions which would enable Greek consumers to tell, rather precisely, good stuff from bad stuff. Philosophy's questions about higher sensations are applied to mold understanding of why some oils are better as media for certain ointments; and the common technologies of cheese making can be used to classify good cheeses by their rennets,[27] a technology derived from venerated farm lore. And when one reads about an effective fire extinguisher made from egg whites and vinegar,[28] one cannot escape the impression that Theophrastus' sources of information (in this case for the brief work *On Fire*) included practical experiments by military technologists. Theophrastus is indeed a scientist by whatever definition, but his premises are of his age, not those of botanical taxonomists, engineers, and physicists of the twentieth century.

    Professor White makes the essential point—not strongly enough in my view—that the research at Ptolemaic Alexandria was less a matter of technology than of scholarship, assisted by a library which supposedly contained all of the best works of Greek learning, from Homer to Hippocrates. Yet this library needs to be understood for what it was: a collection of literature from which resident savants could and did make scholarly commentary. To put it another way, scholars in Hellenistic Alexandria were devoted mainly to philology; perhaps this explains why the weird and often internally contradictory collection we know as

[24] D. E. Eichholz, ed. and trans., *Theophrastus: De lapidibus* (Oxford, 1965).

[25] Included in Arthur Hort, ed. and trans., *Theophrastus: Enquiry into Plants and Minor Work*, (London, 1916), 2:327–89.

[26] E.g., *Odors* 8–12.

[27] John Scarborough, "Nicander's Toxicology, I: Snakes" *Pharmacy in History* 19 (1977): 13 nn. 131–32.

[28] Theophrastus *On Fire* 59; Victor Coutant, ed. and trans., *Theophrastus: De igne* (Assen, 1971), 39.

the Hippocratic corpus should ever have been called "Hippocratic" at all.[29] Libraries mean librarians, and librarians mean catalogues,[30] and it became customary after about 250 B.C. to compile *pinakes* of subjects almost as a literary form, so that oddments such as Phlegon's *Marvellous Events*,[31] while purportedly deriving their learned *pinax* form from pseudo-Aristotelian matter under titles such as "Marvellous Things Heard,"[32] soon became listings of curiosa for their own sake.[33] Science? Of a kind, if classification in its most rigid definition is assumed.

Strato and Ktesibios may have theorized, and their followers devised, machines, perhaps to demonstrate how false in the so-called real world were Aristotelian concepts of motions (i.e., in simple physics); but one needs occasionally to be reminded that Greco-Roman science sought solutions to problems far different from those that moderns take for granted. The Greeks and their Roman successors certainly practiced science; but in no wise did they ever think in terms of atoms, subatomic particles, and molecules—terms characteristic of physics and chemistry only since Rutherford and Einstein, and especially since Crick and Watson's double helix of 1953. Nor did the ancients assume exact measurement to be absolutely essential, as do modern biochemistry and pharmacology. In fact, not only were the questions of Greco-Roman science generally founded on an interplay between philosophical premises (whatever the brand of philosophy) and technological tradition, but sometimes the older traditions of empirical (or experiential) data were employed to "explain" what the philosophers taught. Small wonder that John Riddle thinks of Dioscorides' *Materia medica* as a millennia-old sum-

---

[29] Fraser, *Ptolemaic Alexandria* 1:364, 783, with refs. in vol. 2.

[30] L. D. Reynolds and N. G. Wilson, *Scribes and Scholars*, 2d ed. (Oxford, 1974), 6–9. Rudolf Pfeiffer, *History of Classical Scholarship: From the Beginnings to the End of the Hellenistic Age* (Oxford, 1968), 123–51 (chap. 3: "Callimachus and the Generation of His Pupils").

[31] Probably written in the reign of Hadrian (A.D. 117–38). The remnants of Phlegon of Tralles' rather mediocre writings, along with *Marvellous Events*, include another quasi catalogue titled *Long Lives* (Περι μακροβιων), apparently copied from censors' lists of those who had lived more than one hundred years. *Long Lives* is little more than a list of names, but the tailpiece of this slight tract incorporates about seventy lines copied from the Sibylline books. Otto Keller, ed., *Rerum naturalium scriptores graeci minores*, vol. 1, *Paradoxographi: Antigonus, Apollonius, Phlegon, Anonymus Vaticanus* (Leipzig, 1877), 57–93.

[32] Included in W. S. Hett, ed. and trans., *Aristotle: Minor Works* (Cambridge, Mass., 1936), 238–325.

[33] E.g., multilingual listings of plant names or various names for drugs as contained in the works of Pamphilus (fl. c. A.D. 100), who also compiled animal stories which formed a major portion of the material later borrowed by Aelian and perhaps Timotheus of Gaza. Max Wellmann, "Pamphilos," *Hermes* 51 (1916): 1–64, and "Timotheos von Gaza," *Hermes* 62 (1927): 179–204. Pamphilus apparently reveled in list making, since we know of fish catalogues, crab names, fruits from trees, and several other similar lists. Carl Wendel, "Pamphilos" (25), *RE*, vol. 18, pt. 3 (1942), cols. 336–49.

mation of precise pharmacology;[34] and when one considers Lynn Thorndike's not yet widely accepted thesis of magic (and yes, throw in astrology
and alchemy, too) as the origin of modern science,[35] one is immediately
struck by the contrast with the questions—and their assumed answers—in ancient science as a whole.

Particularly satisfying was the earlier Greek notion of elements (finally
reduced to four), their qualities (also four), and—for humans, animals,
and plants—the semicanonical four humors first lucidly argued by the
author of the Hippocratic *Nature of Man*.[36] This tripartite theoretical
perception of the living biological universe was good enough to explain
almost everything until 1787, when, in a famous demonstration, Lavoi-
sier proved that water was *not* an element. The Greco-Roman theoretical
description using elements, qualities, and humors had incredible lasting
power. Quantities in such a system were almost irrelevant if an ideal
balance (viz. a *krasis* for the doctor's four humors) was more or less
presumed; so that when simple mechanical devices like Herophilus' pulse
counter (a portable clepsydra) appeared,[37] the measurement of pulse
rates simply was used as part of a preconceived diagnosis. Greek medicine had classified numerous fevers, so that when Praxagoras (a genera-

[34] John M. Riddle, *Dioscorides on Pharmacy and Medicine* (Austin, 1985).

[35] Lynn Thorndike, *A History of Magic and Experimental Science*, 8 vols. (New York,
1923–1958): the intentional joining of "magic" with "experimental science" in the title
indicates Thorndike's thesis, which is heavily supported throughout by the primary texts,
quite frequently drawn from manuscripts ignored by historians of science. And even
though well-edited texts are available for Greco-Roman astrology in its varied forms (e.g.,
Vettius Valens, Manilius, Ptolemy's *Tetrabiblos*, Firmicus Maternus, and several others),
modern scholarship which studies these writings in their own terms and historical contexts
is woefully lacking; thus A. Bouché-Leclercq, *L'Astrologie grecque* (Paris, 1899; rptd. Brussels, 1963), remains one of the better works on the topic. On Greco-Roman alchemy, the
old yet very serviceable Edmund O. von Lippmann, *Entstehung und Ausbreitung der Alchemie*
(Berlin, 1919), contains a wealth of careful judgments based on primary texts. Of course,
"magic" existed in swirling and continuously evolving forms, often intertwining with the
so-called rational arts, and modern scholars have occasionally broached the whiggish barriers to produce some excellent studies; see esp. G. E. R. Lloyd, *Magic, Reason and Experience:
Studies in the Origins and Development of Greek Science* (Cambridge, 1979); Garth Fowden,
The Egyptian Hermes (Cambridge, 1986); E. R. Dodds's classic, *The Greeks and the Irrational*
(Berkeley, 1951); and Ingrid Merkel and Allen G. Debus, eds., *Hermeticism and the Renaissance* (Washington, 1988), in which appear the following essays on antiquity: Moshe Idel,
"Hermeticism and Judaism" (59–77), William C. Grese, "Magic in Hellenistic Hermeticism"
(45–58), and John Scarborough, "Hermetic and Related Texts in Classical Antiquity"
(19–44).

[36] See the synopsis of these and similar matters in John Scarborough, "The Galenic
Question," *Sudhoffs Archiv* 65 (1981): 1–31.

[37] James Longrigg, "Anatomy in Alexandria in the Third Century B.C.," *British Journal
of the History of Science* 21 (1988): 455–88, esp. 470, with quotation from Marcellinus *Pulses*.
Great technical sophistication, however, seems clear: von Staden, *Herophilus*, 282–84.

tion before Herophilus) discovered how pulse rates were related to disease and how pulsation characterized arteries, the "new device" merely refined assumed diagnostics. Naming specific pulses engaged Herophilus' fertile mind, blessed as it was with facility in analogy and exactly appropriate associations: his *myrmekizon*, "crawling like an ant," or *dorkadizon*, "leaping like a gazelle,"[38] among other invented terms to describe abnormal pulses, were colorful and vivid, but they were simply another aspect of fevers already described. The evidence of a "gazelle pulse" simply refined *which* fever was in question.[39] Machines and medicine were seldom in partnership in Greco-Roman medicine, though there are exceptions: the racks and pulleys which painfully reset some fractures and dislocations,[40] and the technologically remarkable specula, surgical scalpels, dissection hooks, and needles (both fake and real), widely known in museum collections.[41] Even in military matters technologists improved slowly upon earlier designs of ballistic machines; pneumatic principles were recorded by Vitruvius and later Roman writers, but the infrequent use of such principles suggests a conservative attitude on the part of

[38] Galen *Synopsis of His Books on Pulses* 8, *Opera omnia*, ed. Kühn 9:453 = von Staden, *Herophilus*, 352–53 (text no. 180); and Galen *Distinction among Pulses* 1.28, *Opera omnia*, ed. Kühn 8:556 = von Staden, *Herophilus*, 344 (text no. 169): "ant" and "gazelle" pulses.

[39] Suggested by Marcellinus *Pulses* 11 = von Staden, *Herophilus*, 353–54 (text no. 182).

[40] Such machinery will occasionally puzzle modern scholars, given the corruption of later Greek texts—especially Oribasius (c. A.D. 320–c. 400), from whose works come many descriptions of the mechanical aids for resetting fractures and dislocations, including the *tripaston* (triple pulley) attributed to Archimedes. Cf. "Oreibasios" in A. G. Drachmann, *The Mechanical Technology of Greek and Roman Antiquity* (Copenhagen and Madison, 1963), 171–85, where the texts are translated and machinery diagrammed. Some Hellenistic physicians apparently specialized in this aspect of treatment with machinery: Markwart Michler, "Perigenes," *RE*, Supplement, vol. 11 (1968), cols. 1054–55, and *Die alexandrinischen Chirurgen* (Wiesbaden, 1968), 147–52. A brief overview of earlier practices with the so-called Hippocratic bench is in Guido Majno, *The Healing Hand* (Cambridge, Mass., 1975), 162–66.

[41] The best summary of the technologies employed for producing ancient medical instruments is by Gwynneth Longfield-Jones, "Surgical Instruments," in J. F. Healy, *Mining and Metallurgy in the Greek and Roman World* (London, 1978), 246–50. A number of medical tools are illustrated in John Scarborough, *Roman Medicine* (London, 1969; rptd. 1976), esp. pls. 33, 38–44; Ralph Jackson, *Doctors and Diseases in the Roman Empire* (London, 1988), pls. 23, 32; and Majno, *Healing Hand*, 355–70 ("The Celsian Surgeon and His Tools"). Many specimens in museums, however, have proven to be fakes, so that more recent literature normally will be quite careful with archaeological attributions; e.g., the fine summary by Lawrence J. Bliquez, "The Tools of Asclepius: The Surgical Gear of the Greeks and Romans," *Veterinary Surgery* 11 (1982): 150–57, and Bliquez's superb catalogue with comments, *Roman Surgical Instruments and Minor Objects in the University of Mississippi* (Göteborg, 1988). Especially valuable in reassessing our knowledge of ancient surgical instruments has been the work of Ernst Künzl, especially "Medizinische Instrumente der Römerzeit aus Trier und Umgebung im Landesmuseum Trier," *Trier Zeitschrift* 47 (1984): 153–237, and *Medizinische Instrumente aus Sepulkralfunden der römischen Kaiserzeit* (Bonn, 1983).

military authorities—quite similar in this to authorities in medicine. Innovation, then and now, in both fields, is almost always defined as dangerous.

And yet we see Strato, Ktesibios, and Philo pushing, as it were, at the
boundaries of their technologies. Why not improve the capacity of
springs by changing from hair to bronze? The crossbow would emerge
many centuries later from a miniaturization of this idea. Why not exploit
the artificial production of a partial vacuum (something not found in
nature)? Or more to the point of Alexandrian science as a whole, why
not test the hypothesis of Aristotle's "intelligent heart" by looking to see
just what the head contains (to test the opposite notion descended from
Plato), just what the heart really does, and how it actually appears *in* the
human body? Would structure suggest function? Aristotle thought so,
much as he argued for the oddly formed *entoma* which jointedly wiggled,
wobbled, and buzzed everywhere.[42] So also we see that the burning question for anatomists and physicians in Hellenistic Alexandria was one
formulated in the matrix of philosophy: Does the head rule, or does the
heart?

Once again, that Tiber frontier looms in our analysis. Almost everything we know about Alexandrian medicine and physiology (excepting
Nicander, with whom I will close my brief remarks—and he is not Alexandrian anyway) comes through the filter of Roman writers: Celsus in
the reign of Tiberius;[43] Rufus of Ephesus, Aretaeus of Cappadocia, and
some bits in Soranus of Ephesus in the early second century;[44] the diar-
rhea-of-the-pen Galen of Pergamon (A.D. 129–after 210);[45] and Caelius

[42] See the excellent analysis of ancient entomology by Ian C. Beavis, *Insects and Other
Invertebrates in Classical Antiquity* (Exeter, 1988), which supersedes all earlier work on the
topic.

[43] W. G. Spencer, ed. and trans., *Celsus: De medicina*, 3 vols. (Cambridge, Mass.,
1935–38).

[44] Rufus: C. Daremberg and C. E. Ruelle, eds. and trans., *Oeuvres de Rufus d'Éphèse*
(Paris, 1879; rptd. Amsterdam, 1963). Aretaeus: C. Hude, ed., *Aretaeus*, Corpus medicorum
graecorum vol. 2 2d ed., (Berlin, 1958). Soranus: J. Ilberg, ed., *Sorani gynaeciorum libri
IV: De signis fracturarum; De fasciis; Vita Hippocratis secundum Soranum*, Corpus medicorum
graecorum vol. 4 (Leipzig, 1927); Owsei Temkin, trans., *Soranus' Gynecology* (Baltimore,
1956), translated from Ilberg's Greek text.

[45] For these revised dates and their textual foundations, see Vivian Nutton, "Galen and
Medical Autobiography" (1972), "The Chronology of Galen's Early Career" (1973), and
"Galen in the Eyes of his Contemporaries" (1984), all conveniently reprinted in Vivian
Nutton, *From Democedes to Harvey: Studies in the History of Medicine*, Variorum Reprints, nos.
1–3 (London, 1988). For a listing of most of Galen's huge body of works, see Helmut
Leitner, *Bibliography to the Ancient Medical Authors* (Bern, 1973), 18–40. For a discussion of
Galen's influence, as well as some notations on texts and translations published since 1970,
see John Scarborough, "Galen Redivivus," *Journal of the History of Medicine and Allied Sciences*
43 (1988): 313–21.

Aurelianus of probably about A.D. 400.[46] These are our major texts and authors for information about Hellenistic Alexandrian medicine, anatomy, physiology, pharmacology, and some small specifics on surgery. Celsus and Caelius Aurelianus are in Latin, the rest in a high-flown and artificial Greek, sometimes openly imitative of the "best" medical writer, Hippocrates.[47] Galen especially is part of that dreary revival of the fourth-century-B.C. Greek called, charitably, in its second-century-A.D. Roman counterpart, the Second Sophistic.[48] Yet the Romans did pick out the basic methods, assumptions, and results of the work performed by Herophilus (about 280 B.C.) and Erasistratus (about 260 B.C.): they both dissected human cadavers;[49] and they both made anatomical discoveries which formed the basis of what was known of internal anatomy until late medieval times. Maybe what they found was sufficient. Cerebrum, cerebellum, medulla oblongata, *neura* going all over the body: Herophilus. The brain ruled. Or did it? What *were* these "white sandalthongs?" And why were two of them crossed (*chiasma*) before they entered the eyes? Were tendons and nerves the same? What of the internal structure of the human female? Uterus and other parts? Were they truly analogous to male structures? Were the older theories right regarding conception? Seeds and soil? Hot seeds making baby boys? Did dissection answer the old questions? In a way. The brain *was* complicated, the cerebrum of man was fuller of ridges and creases (convolutions) than comparable cerebra in sheep, goats, and such. Higher intelligence explained now by more diffuse convolutions? Perhaps. And blood? One found blood in dissection only in the veins: Erasistratus.

It was not until Galen's simple double-ligation demonstration,

---

[46] I. E. Drabkin, ed. and trans., *Caelius Aurelianus: On Acute Diseases and On Chronic Diseases* (Chicago, 1950).

[47] Aretaeus of Cappadocia, especially, composed his writing in Ionic Greek, the dialect of the Hippocratic works. Hude, ed., *Aretaeus*, x–xxv. See also Karl Deichgräber, *Aretaeus von Kappadozien als medizinischer Schriftsteller* (Berlin, 1971). Kudlien's attempt to redate Aretaeus into the mid–first century—the reign of Nero (A.D. 54–68)—has not found wide acceptance among students of Roman medicine: Fridolf Kudlien, *Untersuchungen zu Aretaios von Kappadokien* (Wiesbaden, 1963).

[48] G. W. Bowersock, "The Prestige of Galen," in *Greek Sophists in the Roman Empire* (Oxford, 1969), 59–75. Along with fourth-century-B.C. Attic orators (Demosthenes, Aeschines, etc.) taken as models of style was the philosopher Plato, whose limpid clarity evoked admiring imitation among second-century-A.D. Roman literati—including Galen. See Phillip De Lacy, "Galen's Platonism," *AJP* 93 (1972): 27–39, and "Plato and the Intellectual Life of the Second Century A.D.," in G. W. Bowersock, ed., *Approaches to the Second Sophistic* (University Park, Pa., 1974), 4–10.

[49] John Scarborough, "Celsus on Human Vivisection at Ptolemaic Alexandria," *Clio Medica* 11 (1976): 25–38. See also Wesley D. Smith, "From Hippocrates to Galen," in *The Hippocratic Tradition* (Ithaca, N.Y., 1979), 177–246, and "Notes on Ancient Medical Historiography," *Bulletin of the History of Medicine* 63 (1989): 96–98.

recorded in his *Blood in the Arteries*,[50] that one *knew* blood was in the arteries of a living human being. And even earlier, strict thinkers could easily criticize results obtained from animal dissections as not applying to man, even by analogy. Yet Galen's genius as a comparative anatomist recognized similar genius in Aristotle's work—so Galen stuck by his guns, and analogy was the watchword in anatomy until the Renaissance. In some senses, human dissection did not tell very much about human existence (except for better descriptions of the actual parts and of their relationships one to another) not already intuited previously. Pulse lore was sophisticated before the Museum was established, and since quantitative notions were not particularly valued it did not occur to either Erasistratus or Galen that a closed circulation might explain the functions and forms of both heart and vessels. So analogy remained, and was satisfying, for almost two millennia.

Finally, I will illustrate the "base mechanic arts" thesis by considering Nicander of Colophon (fl. c. 130 B.C.), whose poems, *Theriaca* and *Alexipharmaca*, have survived almost intact.[51] Farm lore on spiders, scorpions, insects, toads, poisons, and antidotes, all put into poetic hexameters. Homeric hexameters. Nicander, of course, was compelled to coin words to ensure correct scansion, with the result that these two poems were a miserable hodgepodge of half-recognizable and sometimes freshly invented words which caused even the ancient scholiasts to scratch their skull.[52] But two factors stand out regarding these poems, which became standard textbooks on toxicology: first, one could memorize them easily, since Nicander's poetic techniques for coining epithets mimicked Homer rather precisely; second, one could take pride in recognizing all those Homeric allusions (now reduced to fine-spun and esoteric learning and newly minted words), since a really well-educated person of the day would know Homer by heart. Farmers would be aware that a "large, black grape" (*rhox*) described the black widow spider to a tee, so Nicander (or his source, an obscure Apollodorus of c. 250 B.C.[53]) inserted the term for vivid contrast while detailing gruesome symptoms.[54] And what did farmers and rural folk do for snake bite? What one would expect: treated themselves, with time-tested remedies, also recorded by Dioscorides two hundred years later. Most victims of snake bite—even of cobra envenom-

---

[50] Galen *Blood in the Arteries* 6.5 = *Galen*, ed. Furley and Wilkie, 168–71.

[51] A. S. F. Gow and A. F. Scholfield, eds. and trans., *Nicander: The Poems and Poetical Fragments* (Cambridge, 1953).

[52] Annunciata Crugnola, ed., *Scholia in Nicandri Theriaka* (Milan, 1971). Marius Geymonat, ed., *Scholia in Nicandri Alexipharmaca* (Milan, 1974).

[53] John Scarborough, "Nicander's Toxicology, II: Spiders, Scorpions, Insects and Myriapods," *Pharmacy in History* 21 (1979): 7–8 nn. 51–73. Beavis, *Insects*, 47.

[54] Scarborough, "Nicander's Toxicology, II," 7. Nicander *Theriaca* 719–24.

ation—survived.[55] Worse were the poisonous concoctions of aconite, potions made from blister beetles, and the scorpion stings which still carry off many children and elderly people in North Africa. So much for Cleopatra's asp; there were easier ways to go, as any farm boy could have told her.[56]

DISCUSSION

E. N. Borza: Clearly the Greeks were interested in theory and speculation. This is evidenced, as Professor White pointed out, by the work of the Alexandrians. Someone once observed that, had the theory that was developed by Alexandrian science been translated into machinery, Julius Caesar could have conquered Gaul on a railway system. But that didn't happen. To what extent did the theory and speculation among Greek scientists, especially the Alexandrians, have practical applications and affect the real world?

K. D. White: If we turn to hydraulics, surely the record is quite impressive. The Archimedean screw is a very efficient piece of machinery. It did the job that was needed, in Egypt, where you needed to lift considerable quantities of water on a very shallow gradient. With a man-powered treadmill you got adequate power to do all the irrigation you needed. Basically, a society gets the technology that it requires. The inventive capacity for the steam engine certainly was there, but was the motivation there that would be required to produce the kind of big technical advances you're thinking about? In addition to the Archimedean screw they had the water wheel used as a mill. Vitruvius describes this, and we have the entries on milling in the edict of Diocletian of A.D. 301, which mention the water mill. We now have enough evidence from actual remains to show that the story that the water mill wasn't exploited until the Middle Ages is complete nonsense. No less than three water mills have been identified on Hadrian's wall.

J. Scarborough: I think the question as you pose it contains modern technological assumptions. I would answer with a question. These theories that you imply are nonpractical—why would they last for so long? Think of the fact that your great-great-great-great-grandfather would

---

[55] Scarborough, "Nicander's Toxicology, I," 17–18 nn. 147–53.

[56] The famous tale of Cleopatra's suicide has puzzled scholars since the Renaissance. Saul Jarcho, "The Correspondence of Morgagni and Lancisi on the Death of Cleopatra," *Bulletin of the History of Medicine* 43 (1969): 299–325. One of the better summaries of texts and problems is Francesco Sbordone, "La morte di Cleopatra nei medici greci," *Rivista Indo-Greco-Italica* 14 (1930): 3–22.

still be talking about a physical and medical universe made up of humors. What gave such notions their staying power?

S. M. Burstein: What about the *saqia*? This is an animal-driven water wheel in which the animal's circular motion is translated by a series of cogwheels into the motion of a rotating vertical wheel to which jugs are attached. Archaeology suggests that this device was invented and spread during the Ptolemaic period. This certainly sounds like an example of the practical application of the sort of cogwheel speculation that was going on at this time. Moreover, it is hard to understand its spread except as the result of a deliberate effort. Or am I wrong on this?

K. D. White: No, you're absolutely correct. In addition, I think we should note the difficulties involved in identifying the metal and wooden parts of all sorts of machines. There very well may have been machines in use which we simply can't know anything about.

P. Levi: What technology is nowadays expected to accomplish is the concentration or the transference of energy. And we know from the raising of obelisks that the practical mathematics were quite highly developed. It's quite clever to raise a monolithic column or an obelisk. But I take it that what went wrong with the Hellenistic rulers' exploration of different techniques is that they had too much man power—they had too many slaves. To have slaves is, apart from being wicked, inefficient, because you may use a million men where one machine could have done the job.

K. D. White: In antiquity they got along well enough with man power, and when necessary with animal power. The column drums for the Parthenon were conveyed in wagons with as many as thirty-eight oxen pulling them. Are you suggesting that they could have invented a source of power more efficient than thirty-eight oxen pulling the wagon to move stone, if they hadn't had slaves?

P. Levi: Well, I'm not quite clear how many fields thirty-eight oxen would have grazed, but it makes quite a lot of fields for the oxen working in the quarries. And so there is some inefficiency. What I claim is that the motive was lacking for innovation.

K. D. White: You're only using the oxen for a very limited time in certain seasons of the year. The rest of the time they're down on the farm working and eating their heads off.

P. Woodruff: I want to ask Professor White about the thesis that ancient scientists knew nothing of controlling experiments. His example of Philo of Byzantium showed that they could incorporate controls: for experimenting with artillery they varied only the bore of their catapult, keeping everything else the same, and saw what happened to the trajectory.

K. D. White: On the strength of that example you could say that controlled experiment was understood.

M. Gagarin: Philo's experiment, because it was a mechanical experiment, required a certain precision of measurement. The goal was to make a catapult that would follow a certain trajectory. You had to have a certain amount of control built into the experiment. But in other cases they didn't have that degree of precision in measurement, and they didn't need the control, because the purpose of the experiment was different. I think Philo's experiment does not show that they had any *concept* of controlled experiment, but rather that for certain purposes they needed and used controls. In the case of the exhalations of the bird you didn't need to control the experiment if all you were proving was the theoretical point that exhalations take place. Precision is irrelevant, since all you were trying to prove is that there *were* exhalations. I would suggest that the longevity of some of the physiological theories is precisely because you don't have the possibility for measurement and control and the sort of certainty and testing in experiments in that area that you do in the mechanical areas. So in the mechanical sciences this need for precision would necessarily lead to greater efficiency of machines, whereas—how do you prove or disprove the theory of the four humors?

J. Scarborough: For the ancient mind the idea of an experiment to prove the existence or nonexistence of the four humors was irrelevant. People always ask, "Why didn't the Greeks discover the circulation of the blood?" as if they were looking for it. Well, they weren't. Why not? They had the idea after a while that blood functioned much as the philosophers had argued that things function: as a part of how the body worked in life. *You* might object that that doesn't answer anything; but it did for them. Even Leonardo studied anatomy much as Galen and Vesalius studied it. You look and you see and you explain. How do you explain? You have preconceived ideas and theories. You test them and see if they fit. The answer is always yes, they do. It comes down to the fact that the way you ask the question is almost as important as the answer you're looking for—which is postulated by the question you're asking. The problem is to formulate the question in a way that would be understood by the ancient mind. That's hard because of our scientific background.

P. Green: I think Peter Levi was right to bring in the social aspect of this question, which runs all the way through. A central problem is that regarding alternative sources of energy. Why were they not used or exploited? I think Professor White slightly skirted the issue of the water wheel chronologically, because in fact it did turn up much later than one might expect, and precisely when man power, if not animal power, was running rather short. Professor White mentioned Hadrian's wall and Diocletian; these are late. Now why was there no steam engine when all the components were present? Professor Levi raised the problem of the availability of slaves. I think that is only the beginning of it. If you look away from technology for a moment, what you find throughout antiquity is a paranoid terror of revolution. It's no accident that the Greek and Latin terms for making a revolution are *neoterizein* and *res novare*—that is, just doing something new. In quite a few treaties and drafts for constitutions there are provisions that allies must go to the assistance of any allied state suffering from a revolution. It's not so much that slaves were available, which indeed they were. No, the ruling classes were scared, as the Puritans said, of Satan finding work for idle hands to do. One of the great things about not developing a source of energy that did not depend on muscle power was the fear of what the muscles might get up to if they weren't kept fully employed. The sort of inventions that were taken up and used practically were the things that needed muscle power to start with, including the Archimedean screw. On the other hand, consider that marvelous box gear of Hero's: it was never used. That would have been a real conversion of power. What got paid for? The Lagids tended to patronize toys, fraudulent temple tricks in large quantities, and military experiments. Dissection was only tolerated when there was an enlightened Ptolemy who was prepared to back it. After that it went out again.

K. D. White: There is a famous passage in Suetonius' life of Vespasian in which a technician appears before the emperor to advocate some kind of new device, we're not quite sure what. But the answer of the emperor to an aide is, give him a reward and send him away, and please leave me here to feed my little people. *Sine me pascere plebeculam meam.* I think this is in line with what you're saying. Apart from the slaves, *pace* Professor Levi, there were lots of underemployed free citizens, and *plebeculam meam* surely refers to them. The lack of employment was not confined to slaves; it included underemployed free citizens.

S. M. Burstein: The common wisdom that cheap slave labor inhibited the development of technology in antiquity should probably be reconsidered for two reasons. First, slaves are expensive, not cheap. Second, as the history of the antebellum American South indicates, the use of slave labor is not incompatible with the development of labor-saving technology, provided—and it is an important proviso—that the technology increases the productivity and value of the slaves.

A. A. Long: I think one has to look at the so-called failure of technology to develop also in relation to the theoretical sciences. Here I'm partly agreeing with John Scarborough on the absurdity of the notion that you would try to prove the existence of the four humors. Why prove them? It's self-evident that they're there! In the case of astronomy: Greek astronomy is an astonishing achievement. But of course it was based, except for the brief moment of Hipparchus, on assumptions that we see as totally false. There just wasn't a sufficient reason to invent, for example, the telescope when you had an astronomical theory which, with extraordinary mathematics, could fit the appearances. You *can* save the appearances with Ptolemaic astronomy. Copernicus could have hunches that things were wrong, but it was only when Galileo showed that the moons of Jupiter were actually going around Jupiter that you had any basic evidence for questioning that kind of astronomy. So economic conditions are only one factor; but we also need to look at the state of the theoretical sciences to see why technological devices were not invented when we might think that there was a reason for them.

P. Green: But would this apply to the parallel science of medicine? There you have a similar blockage. There were no thermometers, very little dissection, no instruments that allow you to do more than you can with the naked eye. The whole theory is based on what you can judge with the naked eye and with the sense of touch.

A. A. Long: That's because, I would say, you think you have a totally comprehensive theory which will account for the appearances. The application of the elements to the notion of the humors, plus what you think you know about anatomy, seems to be sufficient.

Hellenism and Persecution:
Antiochus IV and the Jews

Erich S. Gruen

The reign of Antiochus IV brought momentous upheaval to the land of the Jews. Judaea had, for nearly a century and a half, enjoyed a relatively untroubled existence under the suzerainty first of the Ptolemies, then of the Seleucids. But turmoil struck in the 170s B.C., followed by civil strife and then a hideous persecution. Antiochus IV Epiphanes (figure 37), it appears, endeavored to extirpate Judaism altogether from the Holy Land. That endeavor, stunning and memorable, stands in dramatic contrast to all that had gone before. Early Greek attitudes toward the Jews, insofar as they can be discerned, were more often favorable than unfavorable. The Jews, in turn, became increasingly familiar with and adaptive to Hellenism.[1] Seleucid rule in Palestine had been respectful and protective of Jewish institutions.[2] Antiochus' reversal of form thereby becomes the more striking—and the more baffling.

The issue has ramifications well beyond the circumstances and events of the persecution. The Jews, to be sure, played only a small part on the grand stage of the Hellenistic world—or even in the vast realm nominally under the hegemony of the Seleucid kings. An imbalance of information, it can be claimed, brings undue notice to the Jewish nation, obscuring the fact that in the sphere of high politics and amidst the titanic clashes

---

[1] Texts on early Greek views of the Jews are conveniently collected by M. Stern, *Greek and Latin Authors on Jews and Judaism*, 2d ed. (Jerusalem, 1974), 1–96. On Hellenic influence in Palestine, see, most significantly, M. Hengel, *Judaism and Hellenism* (London, 1974).

[2] See, especially, the declarations of Antiochus III; Jos. *Ant.* 12.138–46. For his successor Seleucus IV, note II Macc. 3.2–3.

37. Antiochus IV Epiphanes. Gold stater, minted at ? Antioch. British Museum, London.

of the Hellenistic monarchies the Jews were hardly more important than the denizens of Pontus or Cyrene. True enough—up to a point. Yet no apologies need be made for reopening the subject. It carries significance on a broad front and for substantial reasons: not only because of the long-range religious and cultural influence of Judaism for which this persecution—and the reaction it provoked, the Maccabean re-volt—proved to be a pivotal moment in history, but also because the episode presents our best-documented example of the tensions between Hellenism and native traditions in the Near East, and the strains inherent in imperial rule over disparate societies in the Hellenistic Age. The drive to resolve this intractable puzzle remains potent, and justifiably so: why did Antiochus IV break sharply with the long-standing policy of both the Ptolemies and the Seleucids in Palestine and engage in a brutal repression with such fateful consequences for Jewish history and for Hellenism in the East?

It will be prudent first to review the salient facts. Not all, of course, can be detailed, and many are controversial as to precise chronology and meaning. But an outline of the principal events leading to and surround-ing the persecution is vital.

The Seleucids gained supremacy in Palestine through the victories of Antiochus III in the Fifth Syrian War at the beginning of the second century B.C.[3] The king entrenched his success by showing favor to the

---

[3] For sources and discussion of the Fifth Syrian War, see M. Holleaux, *Études d'épigraphie et d'histoire grecques* (Paris, 1968) 3:317–35; F. W. Walbank, *A Historical Commentary on Poly-*

Jews for their assistance against his Ptolemaic rivals. He expressed gratitude through a number of measures that bestowed privileges and promised tangible assistance. These included aid in rebuilding the war-bat-
tered city of Jerusalem, repair of the damaged temple, the restoration
of exiles, subsidies for sacrificial expenses, various exemptions from and
reductions of taxes, an endorsement of traditional Jewish religious prescriptions, and an express declaration that the Jews were to govern themselves under their own ancestral laws and institutions.[4] Those benefactions set the tone for three decades of cordial collaboration between the
Seleucid regime and the Jewish nation. Greek *poleis* flourished in Palestine (see figure 38), and Jewish intellectuals felt the influence of Hellenic
culture.[5] Appointment of the high priest, it appears, was subject to the
approval of the Seleucid monarch.[6] But that office remained in the hands
of the Oniads, the family that previously controlled it; and its occupant
in the early third century, Simon the Just, both cooperated with Antiochus III in implementing the restoration of Temple and city and received high praise in the contemporary work of Ben Sira, a prominent
advocate of traditionalist Jewish values.[7] Mutual advantage in the relations between Jewish leaders and the Seleucid overlord persisted in the
years of Onias III, successor to Simon the Just, and Seleucus IV, heir to
Antiochus III. Jerusalem, so the author of II Maccabees reports, enjoyed
complete peace and exemplary administration of the laws through the
piety of Onias and the generous subsidies of Seleucus.[8]

The serenity did not last. Trouble began late in Seleucus' reign, stem-
ming from individual ambitions and family rivalries within the Jewish
state. A quarrel erupted between the High Priest Onias III and a certain
Simon, financial overseer of the Temple. The latter, so the hostile account in II Maccabees implies, sought to extend his responsibilities to
regulation of the market, thereby prompting appeal to the king's representatives and a suggestion that the funds contained in the Temple treas-

---

bius (Oxford, 1967), 2:523–25, 546–47; and most recently, D. Gera, "Ptolemy, Son of Thras-
eas, and the Fifth Syrian War," *Anc. Soc.* 18 (1987): 63–73.

   [4] Jos. *Ant.* 12.138–46. On the authenticity of these decrees, see E. Bickerman, "La Charte
séleucide de Jérusalem," *REJ* 100 (1935): 4–35; cf. the discussion of V. Tcherikover, *Hellenistic Civilization and the Jews* (New York, 1959), 82–89. And see now T. Fischer, *Seleukiden
und Makkabäer* (Bochum, 1980), 1–10.

   [5] Tcherikover, *Hellenistic Civilization and the Jews*, 90–116; Hengel, *Judaism and Hellenism*,
58–106. One should not, of course, undervalue the continuities of Jewish traditions, as
rightly noted by F. Millar, "The Background to the Maccabean Revolution," *JJS* 29 (1978):
1–21.

   [6] Cf. Jos. *Ant.* 12.237.

   [7] See Tcherikover, *Hellenistic Civilization and the Jews*, 80–81; Fischer, *Seleukiden und
Makkabäer*, 6–8.

   [8] II Macc. 3.1–3.

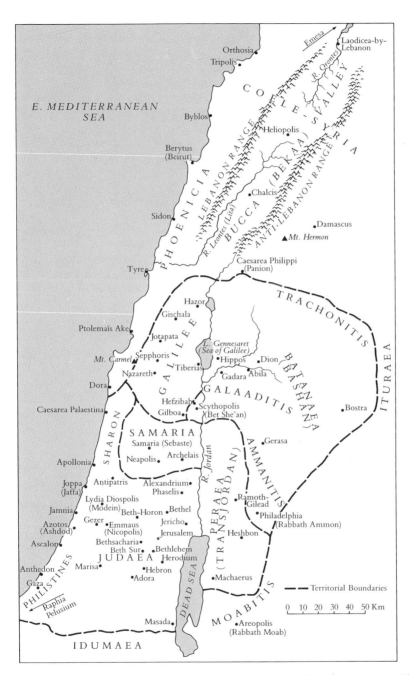

38. Map of Palestine and Phoenicia. From Peter Green, *Alexander to Actium: The Historical Evolution of the Hellenistic Age* (Berkeley: University of California Press, 1990), p. 498.

ury be made available to the Seleucid regime.[9] The climax of the clash
is told in the wonderful tale of Heliodorus, the royal minister who endeavored to confiscate the Temple funds. Heliodorus, impervious to human
pleas, was turned back at the Temple gates by the arrival of a magnificent
horse which kicked him and two gloriously handsome young men who
beat him to a pulp—causing the wretched minister to be carted off in a
litter acknowledging the sovereignty of the Jewish god.[10] The story, of
course, is apocryphal. But there is no reason to question the underlying
facts and circumstances: a split in the Jewish leadership, appeals to the
arbitration of Seleucus, and the attractiveness of Jewish finances for the
Seleucid monarch who still had the burden of a heavy indemnity owed
to Rome. But he evidently stopped short of confiscation—doubtless a
matter of policy, not the result of intervention by two angelic youths and
the hooves of a golden horse.

Civil strife, however, intensified. Simon escalated his attacks upon
Onias III, and one of the High Priest's supporters was murdered, thus
causing him to seek the intervention of Seleucus. The timing proved
unfortunate for Onias. His trip to Antioch came at or very near the time
that Seleucus himself was assassinated in 175, the throne passing now to
his brother Antiochus IV, newly arrived in Syria after nearly fifteen years
as a hostage in Rome. Worse still for Onias, his removal to Antioch left
him vulnerable at home. His own brother Jason seized the occasion to
aim for the High Priesthood. The new ruler in Antioch concurred. Jason
shrewdly offered cash, a bribe as represented by II Maccabees, in fact a
promise to increase revenues through higher taxes. That proposition
would appeal to Antiochus, who needed funds to bolster his image and
to finance his ambitious plans.[11]

The Jewish leader, who had already changed his given name from
Jesus to Jason, had a further proposition that Antiochus would find
attractive. What he now suggested was a dramatic advance in the Hellenization of Jerusalem. He offered yet more cash for the authority to institute a gymnasium and an ephebate and to register the "Antiochenes" in
Jerusalem.[12] What is meant by that last phrase is much disputed and

---

[9] II Macc. 3.4–7.

[10] II Macc. 3.8–30. Analysis of the story in E. Bickerman, *Studies in Greek and Christian History* (Leiden, 1980) 2:159–91; J. Goldstein, *II Maccabees* (New York, 1983), 198–215.

[11] II Macc. 4.1–8; an inaccurate version in Jos. *Ant.* 12.237. On Antiochus IV's accession, see O. Mørkholm, *Antiochus IV of Syria* (Copenhagen, 1966), 38–50; Walbank, *Historical Commentary*, 3:284–85. To take the monetary transaction as an outright bribe is to adopt the bias of the author of II Maccabees; cf. Goldstein, *II Maccabees*, 227.

[12] II Macc. 4.9: πρὸς δὲ τούτοις ὑπισχνεῖτο καὶ ἕτερα διαγράφειν πεντήκοντα πρὸς τοῖς ἑκατόν, ἐὰν ἐπιχορηγηθῇ διὰ τῆς ἐξουσίας αὐτοῦ γυμνάσιον καὶ ἐφηβίαν αὐτῷ συστήσα-σθαι καὶ τοὺς ἐν Ἱεροσολύμοις Ἀντιοχεῖς ἀναγράψαι; cf. I Macc. 1.14; Jos *Ant.* 12.240–41.

need not be resolved here. Scholars have interpreted it either as the installation of a Greek *politeuma* of Hellenized Jews within the city of Jerusalem or as the wholesale conversion of Jerusalem into a Greek *polis*, a new "Antioch-at-Jerusalem."[13] It is hard to imagine just what would be meant by the latter. Certainly Jerusalem did not adopt a full panoply of Greek political institutions, nor did she abandon her traditional structure of governance. The "Antioch-at-Jerusalem" comprised, at most, a select body of individuals keen on the promotion of Hellenism. The discernible consequences lie in the sphere of culture rather than politics. The gymnasium soon materialized, attracting the elite of Jerusalem's youth and even enticing many in the priestly class who became patrons of the *palaestra*. For the author of II Maccabees that constituted the apogee of Hellenism in Jerusalem.[14]

The euphoria did not last. Jason held sway as High Priest for little more than three years. He had entertained Antiochus lavishly at Jerusalem, producing even a torchlight parade in his honor to show Jewish support for the king's prospective conflict with Egypt. He displayed continuous dedication to the furtherance of Hellenism, even dispatching an embassy to Tyre with cash to finance sacrifices to Heracles at the quinquennial games attended by the king. And in 172 or 171 he sent another mission to provide funds urgently requested by Antiochus, presumably for purposes of mobilization against the Ptolemies. The High Priest had acted with exemplary loyalty and cooperation.[15] It was not enough. Internal rivalries in Judaean ruling circles resurfaced. Menelaus, the envoy sent by Jason with revenues for the king, lusted after supreme power himself. He took a leaf from Jason's book, promised Antiochus more money than his superior had provided, and won the king's consent for his own appointment as High Priest.[16] The new appointee was outside the family of the Oniads which had held a monopoly on the office, thus marking a sharp break with Jewish tradition. Antiochus, however, was on the brink of a major and expensive campaign. The intricacies of Jewish political rivalries did not much concern him. Augmented revenues were decisive.

---

[13] For the *politeuma*, see E. Bickerman, *Der Gott der Makkabäer* (Berlin, 1937), 59–65. For the *polis*, see Tcherikover, *Hellenistic Civilization and the Jews*, 161–69; Hengel, *Judaism and Hellenism*, 277; E. Schürer, *The History of the Jewish People in the Age of Jesus Christ*, rev. ed. by G. Vermes and F. Millar (Edinburgh, 1973), 1:148. K. Bringmann, *Hellenistische Reform und Religionsverfolgung in Judäa* (Göttingen, 1983), 84–92, argues vigorously for the *polis* but recognizes that only a select number of Jerusalemites would be enrolled as members by Jason and that the continuation of Jewish institutions would produce a hybrid form. A moderate view in E. Will and C. Orrieux, *Ioudaismos-Hellenismos* (Nancy, 1986), 117–19.

[14] II Macc. 4.11–15; cf. I Macc. 1.14–15; Jos. *Ant.* 12.241.

[15] II Macc. 4.18–23.

[16] II Macc. 4.23–24. A garbled version in Jos. *Ant.* 12.237–38.

Menelaus' tenure as High Priest intensified turmoil and civil upheaval.
The new High Priest, we are told, acted in an arbitrary and tyrannical
fashion, even expropriating gold plate from the Temple treasury—a
credible report in view of the income he had contracted to raise for
the crown. Jason was forcibly exiled from Judaea and sought refuge in
Transjordan. Menelaus, brother of that Simon who had harassed the
earlier High Priest Onias III, now finished his brother's job, arranging
for Onias' assassination. He accomplished the deed, so II Maccabees
reports, through the connivance of Andronicus, one of the king's chief
ministers. Reaction from the populace was sharp and unusually aggressive: not only indignation at the murder of Onias but a growing resentment at the heavy exactions imposed by Menelaus. Popular feelings burst
to the surface. They issued first in a petition to the king to punish Onias'
assassin, and later in a lynching of Menelaus' brother Lysimachus. The
latter had plundered the treasury, probably to pay arrears owed to Antiochus. Pressure extended even to the Jewish Council of Elders, which
began proceedings against Menelaus and brought charges before Antiochus. The king intervened twice in this tumultuous series of events: to
order the execution of Andronicus, accused assassin of Onias, and to
acquit Menelaus of the charges leveled against him. Antiochus would
have preferred a more stable situation in Judaea, but his attention was
concentrated upon Egypt. Menelaus, at least, was beholden to the crown
and more likely to remain loyal than any alternative leaders. The result
was to leave Menelaus in power but also, no doubt, to harden Jewish
resentment against the Seleucid throne.[17]

Antiochus had gathered resources and recruits for an assault on
Egypt. The king conducted two major campaigns, the first in 170/69, the
second in 168, with the intent of bringing the Ptolemaic realm under his
suzerainty. The initial thrust earned considerable success, a smashing
victory over Egyptian forces, capture of territory, and the enthronement
of a young Ptolemy who would be a client of Antiochus Epiphanes. The
blatant power play, however, encountered stiff resistance in Alexandria.
Antiochus returned to Syria in late 169, perhaps to build additional resources and fire power. He readied another invasion for spring 168,
which resulted in notable advances for the Syrian cause. Egyptian opposi-

---

[17] II Macc. 4.25–50. Whether Andronicus was, in fact, the murderer of Onias III has
often been doubted. He is probably the same Andronicus executed by Antiochus in 170
for the slaying of the king's young nephew; DS 30.7.2. This does not itself diminish the
likelihood of Andronicus' responsibility for Onias' death. But it does supply a more plausible motive for his own execution. Antiochus was more concerned with affairs of his court
than with rivalries in Judaea. Cf. Tcherikover, *Hellenistic Civilization and the Jews*, 469 n. 40;
Mørkholm, *Antiochus IV*, 45, 141; Schürer, *History of the Jewish People*, 150 n. 31; Hengel,
Judaism and Hellenism 2:185–86 n. 142; Goldstein, *II Maccabees*, 238.

tion crumbled, Antiochus seized the ancient city of Memphis, became Lord of Upper Egypt, and set his sights on Alexandria itself. It was a high-water mark for Seleucid authority in the region. But not for long. The colossus from the west had just concluded a decisive victory over Macedon at the battle of Pydna. News of that victory released the Roman mission headed by C. Popillius Laenas and charged with terminating the Sixth Syrian War. Popillius arrived in Alexandria at the opportune moment. Antiochus' forces had just reached the outskirts of the city at the suburb of Eleusis. In one of the most celebrated episodes of antiquity, the Roman envoy confronted Antiochus Epiphanes and delivered the *senatus consultum* that demanded an end to hostilities. The king hesitated and requested a recess for consultation with his staff. Popillius Laenas, in a stunning display of arrogance, took a stick, drew a circle in the sand around Antiochus, and asked for a reply before he stepped out of it. This time, it was clear, the Roman meant business. Antiochus meekly evacuated his troops from Egypt and his fleet from Cyprus. The "Day of Eleusis," as it came to be known, cast a dark cloud over Seleucid aspirations and the reputation of Antiochus Epiphanes.[18]

What impact did these dramatic events have upon the history of Palestine and the nation of the Jews? A contemporary Jewish source provides the most direct testimony, in the form of prophecy—which its author knew to have been fulfilled. The Book of Daniel reports Antiochus' endeavors in the Sixth Syrian War, his devious dealings with the Ptolemaic royal house, and the two campaigns against Egypt, each followed by an assault upon Judaea.[19] Those statements can be fleshed out by information in I and II Maccabees and in Josephus. The specifics of chronology remain very much in dispute, but the general outlines are relatively clear.[20]

---

[18] On the events and chronology of the Sixth Syrian War, see sources and discussion by W. Otto, "Zur Geschichte der Zeit des 6 Ptolemäers," *ABAW* 11 (1934): 40–81; E. Bickerman, "Sur la chronologie de la sixième guerre de Syrie," *Chron. d'Ég.* 27 (1952): 396–403; Mørkholm, *Antiochus IV*, 64–101; Walbank, *Historical Commentary* 3:352–63. A briefer review, with further bibliography, in E. S. Gruen, *The Hellenistic World and the Coming of Rome* (Berkeley, 1984), 650–60.

[19] Dan. 11.24–31. See L. F. Hartman and A. A. DiLella, *The Book of Daniel* (New York, 1978), 296–99.

[20] A fundamental uncertainty arises over the question of whether dates in I Maccabees, given according to the Seleucid era, follow the Macedonian or the Babylonian calendar. The first year of the former runs from c. October 312 to October 311, the latter from c. April 311 to April 310. The author of I Maccabees may indeed have employed both systems, thus compounding the confusion; cf. Bickerman, *Gott der Makkabäer*, 155–68; Mørkholm, *Antiochus IV*, 160–61; J. Goldstein, *I Maccabees* (New York, 1976), 21–25, 540–43. Bringmann's recent argument, *Hellenistische Reform und Religionsverfolgung*, 15–28, that the author consistently used the Macedonian system, is attractive but unpersuasive.

The mixed successes of the first Egyptian campaign brought Antiochus back home in late 169. The need to shore up his finances seemed especially critical. The Temple at Jerusalem proved to be an inviting target. Since the High Priest Menelaus had himself requisitioned some of its wealth for the Seleucid cause, Antiochus did not scruple to march troops into the holy city, enter the Temple, and cart off priceless treasures to Syria, thus causing widespread lament and embitterment.[21]

The enriched resources enabled the king to undertake his second invasion of Egypt in spring 168. But his absence then gave occasion for renewed civil conflict in Judaea, this time at a yet higher level of violence. A report reached Palestine that Antiochus had been slain in battle, thus inspiring dissidents to grasp at opportunity. Jason returned from exile, crossing the Jordan with a thousand men, and attacked Jerusalem. The regime of Menelaus had doubtless suffered opprobrium and unpopularity because of the High Priest's compliance with Antiochus' looting of the treasury. Menelaus, so Josephus remarks, had the backing of Judaea's premier commercial magnates, the family of the Tobiads, whereas the bulk of the populace stood by Jason. But Jason squandered his advantage. He took control of the city, forcing Menelaus and his supporters to seek refuge in the citadel, but wreaked vengeance for his setbacks by conducting murderous purges of his fellow citizens. The slaughter generated a sharp reaction that drove Jason back to Transjordan and sent his fortunes into a tailspin. He concluded his career as a wretched outcast in Sparta, where he perished unburied and unmourned. Menelaus resumed control of his war-torn nation.[22]

[21] I Macc. 1.20–28; Dan. 11.28; cf. Jos. *Ant.* 12.249, *C. Ap.* 2.83–84. The author of I Maccabees sets the event in the year 143, which would translate to October 170 – October 169 by the Macedonian system or April 169 – April 168 by the Seleucid system. Either one would suit a return after the campaign of 169. Schürer, *History of the Jewish People*, 152–53 n. 37, combines this testimony with that of II Macc. 5.11–21. But the latter is explicitly dated after Antiochus' second departure for Egypt; II Macc. 5.1: τὴν δευτέραν ἄφοδον. . . εἰς Αἴγυπτον. It will not do to interpret this as "the second phase of the campaign," Schürer, *History of the Jewish People*, 128–29, nor to see it as Jason of Cyrene's effort to validate the prophecies of Daniel, Goldstein; *I Maccabees*, 45–51, *II Maccabees*, 246–47. This is not, of course, to deny that some elements in II Maccabees do, in fact, refer to the Temple robbery of 169; notably II Macc. 5.15–16, 21. Cf. J. Dancy, *A Commentary on I Maccabees* (Oxford, 1954), 67–71. On the chronological problems, see the summary in Will and Orrieux, *Ioudaismos-Hellenismos*, 138–41.

[22] II Macc. 5.5–10; Jos. *Ant.* 12.239. Tcherikover, *Hellenistic Civilization and the Jews*, 186–92, argues that Jason's coup was foiled by a rising of the Jewish populace rather than by resistance from Menelaus and his supporters, an attractive hypothesis but unattested and unverifiable. The entire episode is often transferred to 169 on grounds of II Maccabees' reference to the plundering of the Temple in subsequent verses; II Macc. 5.15–16, 21; Schürer, *History of the Jewish People*, 153. And the coup has even been seen as supplying the motive for Antiochus' return from Egypt in 169; Goldstein, *II Maccabees*, 249–53. But the contamination of II Macc. 5 with some data that belong to 169 is insufficient to remove

The "Day of Eleusis" fell upon Antiochus Epiphanes in the summer of 168. The king had to beat a retreat from Egypt; he had heard, also, of the upheaval and violence that wracked Palestine in his absence. Antiochus, so the Jewish sources assert, returned to Jerusalem in a fury, ordering his soldiers to conduct a massacre in the city, the outcome of which, according to II Maccabees, was the death of 40,000 Jews and a like number sold into slavery. His authority was to be established unambiguously and ruthlessly. Before withdrawing to Syria, the king installed officials, presumably with garrisons, to keep the Jews under heel: Philip in Jerusalem and Andronicus at Mount Gerizim in Samaria. They would also provide a bulwark for the regime of Menelaus.[23]

Those measures were only the beginning. Antiochus prepared even more drastic moves toward the subjection of Judaea. Some time in 167 he dispatched Apollonius, commander of mercenaries from Mysia, with a force of 22,000 men, to terrorize the populace of Jerusalem.[24] His orders, according to II Maccabees, were to massacre all adult males and sell women and children into slavery. Such instructions, of course, cannot possibly have been carried out, since Jews continued to inhabit the city. But rumors of wholesale terror may well have been encouraged, thereby to cow the populace into submission. Apollonius stayed his hand for a time, lulling the Jerusalemites into false confidence, then launched an attack on the Sabbath when unsuspecting crowds had gathered on his invitation to review a military parade. Numerous innocent citizens were slain, the city ransacked, and parts of it set on fire.[25] The temporary

the tale of Jason's coup, explicitly placed in Antiochus' second campaign, to that year. Josephus, *Ant.* 12.240, indicates that Menelaus and the Tobiads went to Antiochus for assistance against Jason, an item accepted as fact by Hengel, *Judaism and Hellenism*, 281. But Josephus is here plainly confused, for he has Menelaus petition the Seleucid king for a gymnasium and other Hellenic institutions, a policy actually initiated by Jason seven years earlier; II Macc. 4.7–17.

[23] Dan. 11.29–30; II Macc. 5.11–14, 22–23. The intervening lines probably refer to the expropriation of Temple treasures in 169, but it is not impossible that Antiochus extracted yet more cash from that source. II Macc. 5.11 associates Antiochus' rage at Judaea with receipt of word that the land was in rebellion. Whether this refers to Jason's coup or to the whole sequence of events concluding with his ouster cannot be determined.

[24] I Macc. 1.29 fixes the time as two years after Antiochus' seizure of the Temple treasury, i.e., 143 of the Seleucid era, probably by Macedonian reckoning from April 167 to April 166. There is no sound reason to place the event in 168, as does Bickerman, *Gott der Makkabäer*, 161–68; Tcherikover, *Hellenistic Civilization and the Jews*, 188–89. See Goldstein, *II Maccabees*, 263–64. For Apollonius' title, see II Macc. 5.24. The text of I Macc. 1.29 has him as a chief financial official, but this may be due to a mistranslation of the original Hebrew; F.-M. Abel, *Les Livres des Maccabées* (Paris, 1949), 15; Goldstein, *I Maccabees*, 211–12.

[25] I Macc. 1.29–42; II Macc. 5.24–26; cf. Jos. *Ant.* 12.248. The thesis of Tcherikover, *Hellenistic Civilization and the Jews*, 188–89, that a Jewish revolt preceded and prompted Apollonius' appointment, has no textual support.

39. The Citadel, Jerusalem. Photo: Ronald Sheridan.

terror was then succeeded by a more permanent presence. Seleucid forces occupied a citadel, the Akra (site uncertain) and installed there a military colony, an "abode of aliens" according to I Maccabees, a place for "a sinful race and lawless men." In all likelihood, the garrison expanded with the addition of renegade Jews, the "Antiochenes" enrolled by Jason as citizens of the *polis* or *politeuma* a few years earlier; and foreign settlers, the "people of a foreign god" as designated by the author of Daniel.[26] The Akra would serve as a rampart of Seleucid strength in

[26] I Macc. 1.33–40; Dan. 11.39; Jos. *Ant.* 12.252. On the site of the citadel, much disputed, see Schürer, *History of the Jewish People*, 154–55 n. 39; Goldstein, *I Maccabees*, 214–19; Will and Orrieux, *Ioudaismos-Hellenismos*, 168–69 n. 58. Goldstein, *I Maccabees*, 123–24, argues that Antiochus' idea stemmed from the example of Roman military colonies. But the Greek institution of a cleruchy or a *katoikia* supplied a more direct and more appropriate model; see I Macc. 1.38: κατοικία ἀλλοτρίων; cf. Tcherikover, *Hellenistic Civilization and the Jews*, 188–89. The actual ethnic composition of the *katoikia* remains uncertain; cf. Bringmann, *Hellenistische Reform und Religionsverfolgung*, 128; Goldstein, *II Maccabees*, 106–12; extensive bibliography in Fischer, *Seleukiden und Makkabäer*, 32–33.

Jerusalem for the next quarter of a century. Dissident Jews took the only recourse remaining to them: flight, escape to the desert and mountains, and preparations for guerilla resistance.[27] Antiochus IV Epiphanes now readied his most extreme measures. Installation of the physical presence of Seleucid force would be followed by direct interference in the spiritual realm. All previous policy by his predecessors was cast to the winds. To the shock and consternation of the Jews, Antiochus seemed determined to stamp out their religion itself. The king implemented this extraordinary scheme through a series of drastic decrees in the latter part of 167.[28] If the author of I Maccabees is to be believed, Antiochus laid the basis for his moves with a broad edict, issued throughout his realm, which commanded conformity in law and religion. Its authenticity, certainly in the form given, is questionable. But it may well represent a general call for allegiance in the Seleucid kingdom.[29] In any case, Antiochus directed subsequent measures quite specifically at Jewish practices, in damaging and disastrous fashion. He forbade burnt offerings, sacrifices, and libations in the Temple; he ordered the erection of altars, shrines, and images, the sacrifice of pigs and other impure animals, the elimination of circumcision, the burning of the Torah, and a range of activities that would require violation of Jewish practices and profanation of religious life. The dictates applied not just to Jerusalem but to the towns of Judaea generally, and evidently also to Samaria. Disobedience brought the death penalty.[30]

Nor did the king confine himself to proclamations. He saw to their implementation. His agents entered the Temple, defiled it with illicit intercourse, piled unclean offerings upon the altar, and compelled Jews to eat pagan sacrificial victims and to parade with wreaths of ivy at Dionysiac festivals. The Temple itself was now rededicated to Zeus Olympios and the sanctuary at Mount Gerizim to Zeus Xenios.[31] The fateful day

---

[27] I Macc. 1.38; II Macc. 5.27.

[28] I Macc. 1.54 places the climactic deed on the 15th of Kislev in 145, i.e., December 167. Bringmann's endeavor, *Hellenistische Reform und Religionsverfolgung*, 29–40, to set all the preceding events, from Jason's coup through the "abomination of desolation" in 168 is unconvincing. He fails to account for the statement in I Macc. 1.29 that Apollonius' appointment came two years after Antiochus' plundering of the Temple in 169.

[29] I Macc. 1.41–43. Cf. Hengel, *Judaism and Hellenism*, 284–87. For Goldstein, *I Maccabees*, 119–21, Antiochus promulgated the edict at the beginning of his reign, without explicit attention to the Jews as such. Dancy, *Commentary*, 76 dismisses it too summarily as "fantastic."

[30] I Macc. 1.44–51, 56; Jos. *Ant.* 12.251, 253–54. Antiochus' agent in delivering the message is described as γέροντα Ἀθηναῖον in II Macc. 6.1. Whether this means "the old Athenian," "Geron the Athenian," "the old Athenaeus," or "an elder of Athens" need not be decided. On the Samaritans, see Jos. *Ant.* 12.257–60; elsewhere, II Macc. 6.8.

[31] II Macc. 6.2–9.

of the "abomination of desolation," probably the introduction of a pagan altar into the Temple at Jerusalem, was the fifteenth day of Kislev, December of 167. Ten days later came the first sacrifice of a pig on that altar, an act of unspeakable desecration for the people of Judaea.[32] There was valiant resistance among many of the citizenry. But the soldiers of Antiochus ruthlessly punished dissent, torturing and executing those who preferred martyrdom to capitulation.[33] The measures of the king were devastating and calamitous. They represented a total reversal of Seleucid policy—and a watershed for Jewish history. It is hardly surprising that scholars through the ages have offered a wide variety of explanations for this astounding turn of events—or that the puzzle remains unresolved. A review of the proposed solutions will be salutary; to be followed by a new attempt.

A favorite answer prevailed through most of the earlier scholarship, and still claims adherents: that Antiochus saw himself as a crusader for Hellenism, and attempted to impose conformity on his realm. On this view, Jewish recalcitrance became a sore point and an embarassing aberration; the king resorted to compulsion to enforce compliance.[34]

The thesis receives support in certain key texts. First and foremost, the decree of Antiochus, cited above, declaring to his entire kingdom that all were to become one people and each would abandon his own customs.[35] That explanation is buttressed by two subsequent passages in II Maccabees. The order to enforce Antiochus' extremist measures against the Jews in 167 includes a sanction for executing those who did not choose to convert to Greek practices.[36] Also, a later letter by Antiochus V, reversing his father's policy, describes it as seeking a transformation of Jews to the ways of Greece.[37] Josephus adds a letter of Epiphanes, responding to a petition from the Samaritans, which acquits them of charges leveled against the Jews, since they elected to live in accordance with Hellenic customs.[38] From the perspective of two and a

[32] I Macc. 1.54, 1.59; Dan. 11.31; Jos. *Ant.* 12.253; *BJ* 1.34; DS 34/5.1. It is not absolutely clear to what the "abomination of desolation" refers; Will and Orieux, *Ioudaismos-Hellenismos*, 147–51.

[33] I Macc. 1.57, 60–64; II Macc. 6.10–11; Jos. *Ant.* 12.255–56.

[34] See, e.g., E. Bevan, *The House of Seleucus* (London, 1902) 2:162–74; Schürer, *History of the Jewish People* 1:147–48; *SEHHW*, 2d ed. 2:703–5; H. Bengtson, *Griechische Geschichte* (Munich, 1960), 482.

[35] I Macc. 1.41: καὶ ἔγραψεν ὁ βασιλεὺς πάσῃ τῇ βασιλείᾳ αὐτοῦ εἶναι πάντας εἰς λαὸν ἕνα καὶ ἐγκαταλιπεῖν ἕκαστον τὰ νόμιμα αὐτοῦ.

[36] II Macc. 6.9: τοὺς δὲ μὴ προαιρουμένους μεταβαίνειν ἐπὶ τὰ Ἑλληνικὰ κατασφάζειν.

[37] II Macc. 11.24: τοὺς Ἰουδαίους μὴ συνευδοκοῦντας τῇ τοῦ πατρὸς ἐπὶ τὰ Ἑλληνικὰ μεταθέσει.

[38] Jos. *Ant.* 12.263: ὅτι μηδὲν τοῖς τῶν Ἰουδαίων ἐγκλήμασι προσήκουσιν, ἀλλὰ τοῖς Ἑλληνικοῖς ἔθεσιν αἱροῦνται χρώμενοι ζῆν.

half centuries later, Tacitus offered a similar interpretation: Antiochus strove to stamp out the Jewish superstition and to introduce the institutions of the Greeks.[39] How plausible is that motive? Antiochus IV certainly projected himself as a great benefactor of the Greeks. His generosity is well attested and widespread. Benefactions extended to Athens, Delphi, Delos, Argos, Achaea, Arcadia, Boeotia, Rhodes, Byzantium, Chalcedon, and Cyzicus. He earned his reputation as foremost among Hellenistic kings for patronage of Greek cities and cults.[40] Antiochus' assiduous efforts in this regard, of course, carried practical value, lending substantial prestige to the king in the international world of the second century. But dedications in shrines and subsidies for public events or institutions at various ancient Greek sites by no means betoken a drive to spread Hellenism to the Near East. The equation is facile and misguided.

The royal edict recorded in I Maccabees that required all nations to forsake their own traditions and become one people carries little credibility, at least in that form. Still less credible is the author's immediately subsequent statement that nations everywhere complied with the directive. The available evidence shows the contrary to be true. Eastern cities and territories under the suzerainty of the Seleucid kingdom continued to mint coinage with local symbols and types; the great temples at Uruk and Babylon betray no trace of Hellenization; and the priests and officialdom of the ancient sites retained native titles and responsibilities.[41]

The king, so some have argued, promoted his own worship as an incarnation of Zeus Olympios and visualized imposition of a syncretistic cult that could unify the peoples of his dominion.[42] However, that notion also finds little support in the ancient testimony. Antiochus did pay special attention to Olympian Zeus, and he employed the title of *Theos Epiphanes* for his own epithet; but there are no grounds to infer that the monarch identified himself with Zeus Olympios, let alone that he strove to employ ruler cult as a means of consolidation in his realm. The worship of that deity in Seleucid lands preceded Antiochus IV, and the king

---

[39] Tac. *Hist.* 5.8: rex Antiochus demere superstitionem et mores Graecorum dare adnisus.

[40] Polyb. 26.1.10, 29.24.13; Livy, 41.20.5. See, especially, Mørkholm, *Antiochus IV,* 51–63; cf. Walbank, *Historical Commentary* 3:287–88; E. S. Gruen, *Hellenistic World,* 189–90.

[41] Bickerman, *Gott der Makkabäer,* 90–92; Dancy, *Commentary,* 75–76. See now the collection of material and discussion by S. Sherwin-White, A. Kuhrt, and R. J. van der Spek, in A. Kuhrt and S. Sherwin-White, *Hellenism in the Near East* (Berkeley, 1987), 1–31, 48–52, 57–74.

[42] Cf. Dan. 11.37–38; Bevan, *House of Seleucus* 2:154–55; W. W. Tarn, *The Greeks in Bactria and India,* 3d ed. (Chicago, 1984), 190–91; *SEHHW* 2:704; Dancy, *Commentary,* 47.

showed favor to a variety of gods and cults.[43] The fact that the worship
inaugurated in the Temple at Jerusalem in 167 was that of Zeus Olympios does not imply unity and uniformity. For at the same time Antiochus
ordered the sanctuary at Mount Gerizim to be dedicated to Zeus Xenios.[44] In any event, the establishment of the new cult came late in the
series of events, at the time of Antiochus' most savage repression; it does
not exemplify a long-standing policy of Hellenization to which the Jews
objected. Nor had the king determined to eradicate Judaism as an aberration. His measures applied only to Judaea and Samaria. Nothing suggests
an extension to the Jews of the Diaspora.[45] We can then safely and happily discard the notion of Antiochus Epiphanes as crusader for Hellenism, driven by the resolve to have Greek civilization penetrate throughout the Near East, or to unify his holdings through a cultural and
religious homogeneity that was upset by recalcitrant Jews. Ideological
fervor did not characterize the schemes of Antiochus IV.

A more plausible approach prefers pragmatism to ideology. The king,
on this analysis, concerned himself more with concrete advantages than
with lofty goals. The question of money arises repeatedly in the story, a
motivating force and a determining factor. A crushing indemnity had
been assessed against Syria by Rome in 188, thus putting severe strain
on her resources and limits on her aspirations. Income from Judaea
represented a critical source of revenue. That fact manifests itself in the
reign of Seleucus IV, when the Jewish minister Simon offered to release
cash from the Temple for the king, and when Heliodorus considered
forced entry into the sanctuary for the same purpose. Antiochus' ambitious ventures, it could be argued, helped give rise to conflict within
Judaea, as rival leaders bid for his favor through offers of increased

---

[43] See the evidence and discussion in O. Mørkholm, *Studies in the Coinage of Antiochus IV of Syria* (Copenhagen, 1963), 7–75; Mørkholm, *Antiochus IV*, 130–33; Hengel, *Judaism and Hellenism*, 284–86; J. G. Bunge, "'Theos Epiphanes' in den ersten fünf Regierungsjahren des Antiochos IV Epiphanes," *Historia* 23 (1974): 57–85, 24 (1975): 164–88.

[44] II Macc. 6.2. Cf. Goldstein, *II Maccabees*, 272–73. According to Dan. 11.37–38, the deity was not even reckoned among the ancestral gods of the Seleucid house; hence perhaps a blend with the Syrian god—and hardly a means to foster Hellenism. On the nature of the god and his cult, much discussed, see the incisive analysis of Bickerman, *Gott der Makkabäer*, 92–116; scholarly literature collected by Fischer, *Seleukiden und Makkabäer*, 35–38. Bickerman's view of the cult as syncretistic and assimilationist is criticized by Millar, "Back-
ground," 12–13, and Will and Orrieux, *Ioudaismos-Hellenismos*, 149–51.

[45] I Macc. 1.51; Jos. *Ant.* 12.257–63. A possible exception lies in II Macc. 6.8, referring to extension of the persecution to Jews in the "neighboring Greek cities," at the instigation of the "citizens of Ptolemais"—or perhaps "of Ptolemy." On either reckoning, this applies to local circumstances within or in the vicinity of Judaea. It in no way implies extension to the Diaspora. Cf. Abel, *Livres des Maccabées*, 363–64; Hengel, *Judaism and Hellenism*, 287.

tribute and immediate cash subsidy. The king backed first Jason, then Menelaus, for the tangible returns that would support his aggressive expansionism. Hostility within Judaea to Menelaus and his party only bound Antiochus more closely to them. Expropriation of funds from the Temple, with Menelaus' direct assistance, gave the Seleucid monarch the boost needed for his renewed invasion of Egypt. The backlash against Menelaus, however, caused consternation. Jason's attempted coup threatened not only Menelaus but the pro-Seleucid elements in Palestine generally. Antiochus, after his forced evacuation of Egypt, had no choice but to shore up the regime of Menelaus with every means available; hence the citadel, the garrison, and the intimidation of the populace. But Menelaus needed more to retain his hold on power: a thorough cowing of the opposition. This would strengthen the hand of Menelaus' follow-ers by giving them control of the cult and protect Antiochus' interests by keeping his partisans in central authority. So Menelaus persuaded his patron to crush dissidents through religious oppression. The motives that drove Antiochus were practical and political: cash for his military adventures and security for his position in Palestine. Such, in brief, is the gist of the pragmatic thesis, recently and forcefully argued.[46]

The case clearly has merit—up to a point. Additional cash was always welcome. Higher tribute payments would fuel Seleucid schemes of ag-grandizement. And Antiochus' seizure of Temple funds in 169 surely had the Egyptian venture in view. But financial considerations do not tell the whole story, and it would be hazardous to place too much weight upon them. The indemnity imposed by Rome had evidently not crippled Seleucid resources. Antiochus, as we have already noted, was liberal in his benefactions; much of the Greek world profited from his gifts, dona-tions, and subsidies.[47] Further, one must recall what is often forgotten: Antiochus had paid off the last installment on the indemnity in 173—four years before his assault on Jerusalem.[48] Financial demands from Rome were no longer at issue, and the kingdom was solvent.

The political motivation is as fragile as the economic. Conjecture has it that Antiochus committed himself to Menelaus as the principal bastion of strength for Seleucid interests in Palestine and that the offensive against Jewish traditions aimed to smash Menelaus' rivals and to keep him in power.[49] A single statement in Josephus alone can be cited. And it applies to the year 163, after the death of Antiochus Epiphanes, in the

---

[46] See Bringmann, *Hellenistische Reform und Religionsverfolgung*, 111–40; more briefly in "Die Verfolgung der jüdischen Religion durch Antiochos IV: Ein Konflikt zwischen Judentum und Hellenismus," *Antike und Abendland* 26 (1980): 176–90.

[47] See above.

[48] Livy 42.6.6–7.

[49] Bringmann, *Hellenistische Reform und Religionsverfolgung*, 126–35.

midst of the Maccabean rebellion. Lysias, chief minister to the new boy-
ruler Antiochus V, advised the king to authorize the slaying of Menelaus,
who, he claimed, had persuaded Epiphanes to force Jewish abandonment of their ancestral faith and was thereby the source of troubles for
the Seleucid realm.[50] That text cannot, in fact, bear the weight set upon
it. Lysias had his own reasons for seeking the eliminaton of Menelaus,
and the young monarch was in no position to check the accuracy of his
allegations. One may doubt, in fact, that Lysias even charged Menelaus
with having instigated the religious persecution. Josephus plainly drew
his data from a parallel passage in II Maccabees. Lysias there also prods
the wrath of Antiochus V against Menelaus, denouncing him as responsible for all the troubles in the kingdom. But nothing is said in that passage
about Menelaus prompting religious repression; this was an inference
added by Josephus.[51] Nor is it likely that Menelaus, a Jew from the
upper echelons of society, and one well aware of the proclivities of his
countrymen, would foster a policy calculated to spark explosive upheaval—an upheaval that threatened to sweep him away with the debris.
Persecution of the faithful hardly seems a prudent means to secure Menelaus' hold on power. Quite the contrary. Pragmatic politics cannot
explain the decision.

A very different theory has Antiochus look not to Greeks or to Jews,
but to Romans. Therein lay his inspiration. The Seleucid had resided for
more than a dozen years in Rome, technically as a hostage for the good
behavior of his father and his brother, in practice treated as an honored
guest.[52] Those years allowed for observation and instruction. The later
actions of the king in his own homeland have been traced to events and
institutions experienced in Rome. The establishment of a *polis* or an
enclave of "Antiochenes" in Jerusalem in 175 had, it can be argued,
certain analogies with Roman extension of citizenship to Italian communities or segments of Italian communities. Antiochus conceived the idea,
with Roman practice in mind, to grant privileges to "Antiochenes" in
various cities who would serve as centers of loyalty to the Seleucid regime.
The later introduction of a garrison, the Akra, in 167 had as its goal
protection and enhancement of the "Antiochenes" in Jerusalem, while
adding new soldier-settlers who would also obtain citizen privileges. And
the outlawing of the Jewish religion, with the accompanying measures
of persecution and ferocious repression, also has a Roman analogy: the

---

[50] Jos. *Ant.* 12.384: τοῦτον γὰρ ἄρξαι τῶν κακῶν, πείσαντ' αὐτοῦ τὸν πατέρα τοὺς Ἰουδαίους ἀναγκάσαι τὴν πάτριον θρησκείαν καταλιπεῖν.

[51] II Macc. 13.4: Λυσίου ὑποδείξαντος τοῦτον αἴτιον εἶναι πάντων τῶν κακῶν.

[52] The year of his arrival in Rome is not certain—189 or 188; Mørkholm, *Antiochus IV*,
22–23. On his honored status at Rome, see Livy 42.6.9; Asconius 13 Clark.

fierce measures taken by the government against the Bacchanalian cult in 186—one of the years in which the Seleucid prince resided in Rome. The senate and magistrates demolished places of worship, punished the sect's adherents, and severely curtailed its activities. Antiochus, like his former mentors, could claim to be suppressing degenerate rites and restoring a purer, pristine religion.[53]

The idea is ingenious and alluring, but also fanciful and farfetched. Nothing in the evidence suggests that the stay in Rome had so profound an impact on Antiochus' actions and policies. It is difficult to imagine that the young hostage would have gained so intimate an acquaintance with the principles of Roman colonial policy—or indeed that he had access to the decision-making process that implemented it.[54] The conjecture that Antiochus created the "Antiochenes in Jerusalem" as a form of Roman citizen colony, founders on the fact that the initiative for the move came not from Antiochus but from Jason, the Jewish would-be High Priest—a man who had never had experience of Rome.[55] As for the presumed parallel between suppression of the Bacchants and the assault on Judaism, differences loom much larger than similarities. Most significantly, the Romans professed to be cracking down on an alien creed, foreign to national traditions, whereas Antiochus imposed an alien creed while seeking to eradicate a national tradition. No testimony alludes to the desire or even the claim to revive ancestral practice in a purer form. And if experience of the Bacchic affair had an influence on Antiochus' policy, it is most peculiar that among the grievous burdens imposed on the Jews was the obligation to don ivy wreaths and join the procession at the festival of Dionysus![56] The Roman hypothesis can be confidently abandoned.

Ancient testimony on the king includes numerous incidents of eccentricity and oddity. The monarch who could lavish gifts upon communities in most grandiose fashion also disported himself in most unlikely ways. Observers wondered about his sanity. And jokesters played with his epithet, changing *Epiphanes* to *Epimanes* ("madman"). Antiochus regularly violated court etiquette and took pleasure in roaming the streets, ex-

---

[53] So Goldstein, *I Maccabees*, 104–60; somewhat modified, with the basic thesis intact, in *II Maccabees*, 104–12.

[54] Goldstein's proposals that Antiochus enjoyed the patronage and friendship of various highly placed Roman political families, *I Maccabees*, 105–7, are pure speculation.

[55] Goldstein attempts to get around this objection by placing Antiochus' general decree inviting conformity at the beginning of the reign and seeing Jason's move as a response to that invitation; *I Maccabees*, 120–21. This simply multiplies the conjectures and, in any case, undermines the putative link to the Roman experience. Did Antiochus suddenly recall that experience only when Jason proposed to register "Antiochenes"?

[56] II Macc. 6.7.

changing shoptalk with artisans and craftsmen, conversing and carousing with commoners and riffraff. He showed up unannounced at parties, sometimes to take personal charge of the entertainment, bringing his own instrument and musicians, while astonished guests headed for the exits. He could be equally amusing on public occasions. The Roman experience may not have inspired persecution, but it did inspire mimicry. Antiochus delighted in shocking onlookers by removing royal attire, donning the white toga of a Roman candidate, and circulating among the public to solicit votes as if running for the aedileship or the tribunate. And he would carry the charade to its conclusion, performing like a Roman magistrate, presiding over lawsuits, and delivering judgments in mock solemnity. The king was endlessly inventive in surprising his countrymen. He snubbed friends but stopped strangers in the street and plied them with gifts. He embarrassed the highborn with childish toys, but would transform an unsuspecting commoner into an instant millionaire. His visits to the public baths gave occasion for revelry and practical jokes, which included the pouring of priceless ointment that had Antiochus and his fellow bathers slipping and sliding in hilarious frolic.[57]

Should one then abandon rational explanations for the assault on Judaism? Perhaps it was just another example of aberrant behavior by a monarch who gloried in the unorthodox and the bizarre? That would be an easy solution, but not a very satisfactory one. The political, diplomatic, and military successes that stand to Antiochus' credit belie the representation of him as a demented crackpot.[58] Moreover, the ruthless and thorough measures taken to stamp out Judaism possess a character altogether different from the quirky, idiosyncratic, playful, and topsy-turvy behavior designed to shock and amuse. An answer to the puzzle must be sought elsewhere.

An influential scholarly thesis affixes blame not on Antiochus, but on the Jews—or rather a segment of the Jews. Initiative for the reform movement came from the Jewish leadership itself and reflected internal conflict within its ranks. This was no Seleucid scheme. Jason brought the idea of a gymnasium and ephebate to Antiochus. As delineated by the author of I Maccabees, it represented the efforts of lawless Jews to ingratiate themselves with the peoples surrounding them, for their separation

---

[57] Polyb. 26.1 offers the most reliable catalogue of Antiochus' eccentricities. See further Livy 41.20.1–4; DS 29.32, 31.16. Mørkholm, *Antiochus IV*, 181–86, questions Polybius' authority here, without compelling reason. The mimicry of the Romans has been taken seriously by some scholars; e.g., Bunge, "'Theos Epiphanes'," 67; Walbank, *Historical Commentary*, 3:286.

[58] See the treatment by Mørkholm, *Antiochus IV*, passim; in brief, Gruen, *Hellenistic World*, 647–63.

had been the source of much suffering.[59] This set the Hellenizing trend in motion and also produced a rift between the Hellenizers and the traditionalists in Jewish society. Antiochus was the beneficiary rather than the instigator. Conversion of Jerusalem into a Greek *polis* or *politeuma* delivered a heavy blow to Jewish conservatives, effectively undermined ancestral practices, and stimulated other Jews to curry Seleucid favor by moving still further away from tradition. Hence Menelaus obtained power as a more "radical Hellenizer," generating a split with the faction of Jason. The extremist actions alienated much of public opinion in Judaea, making Menelaus ever more dependent upon Antiochus for his authority. Menelaus' urging, therefore, brought about the Seleucid garrison in Jerusalem, the intimidating terrorism of Apollonius, and even the sweeping prohibition of Jewish religious practices. The apostates pressed for abolition of Mosaic law and all ancestral ordinances ranging from dietary restrictions to circumcision. The insistence on full-scale assimilation would entail either forced conversion or elimination of their opponents. The "abomination of desolation" climaxed a concerted campaign to dissolve Judaism in its conventional form and replace it with a syncretistic worship suffused with Greek ideas and adapted to the Hellenistic world. The contest throughout represented a fundamental struggle between Judaism and Hellenism.[60]

The matter is, however, not so straightforward. Divisions among the leadership certainly plagued the course of Jewish history in this period. But did they open a genuine cleavage between Judaism and Hellenism? Did the escalation of tensions reflect an increasing push toward Hellenization that energized the support and encouragement of Antiochus? Did the initiative for change consistently come from Jewish reformers or apostates who were responsible not only for the injection and augmentation of Hellenism but for the persecution of Jews who clung to the old ways? Those issues merit serious review.

One might expect to find the confrontation of Judaism and Hellenism as a central and repeated theme in the contemporary or near-contemporary Jewish literature. In fact, it is almost altogether absent. The work of Ben Sira, composed in the early second century, reiterates traditional

---

[59] I Macc. 1.11.

[60] The classic statement of this position is to be found in Bickerman, *Gott der Makkabäer*, 117–36, reinforced and expanded by Hengel, *Judaism and Hellenism*, 277–309. Other scholars, who do not fully subscribe to this view, nevertheless concur in seeing Hellenization as responsible for the division among the leadership and in interpreting the contest as one between Hellenism and Judaism; e.g., Tcherikover, *Hellenistic Civilization and the Jews*, 152–74, 193–203; C. Habicht, "Hellenismus und Judentum in der Zeit des Judas Makkabäus," *Jhrb. Heid. Akad.* (1974), 97–104. A general discussion of the issue in Will and Orrieux, *Ioudaismos-Hellenismos*, 124–26, 149–51.

precepts and denounces those who yield to the temptations of wealth, who fall away from righteousness, who oppress the poor, who abandon fear of the Lord or the teachings of the Law. But he nowhere contrasts Jews and Greeks, and gives no hint that a struggle for the conscience of his fellow countrymen was being waged by Hellenizers and conservatives.[61] Nor does the Book of Daniel provide comfort for the theory. Written at the very time of the Maccabean revolt, the work's apocalyptic visions set the experience of the Jews squarely in the context of battles among the great Hellenistic powers: divine intervention and a last judgment will deliver the Jews from the foreign oppressor. This is not a cultural contest for the soul of Judaism.[62] Similarly, I Maccabees, although composed well after recovery of the Temple and the entrenchment of the Hasmonaean dynasty, does not express the discord as one between Judaism and Hellenism. The absence of this polarity becomes more striking.

The phrases do appear in II Maccabees, our fullest source on the relevant events. The author describes Jason's innovations as bringing his fellow Jews to a "Greek way of life." And the implementation of his reforms constitute the high point of "Hellenism."[63] The order to enforce the new cult in 167 authorized the king's agents to execute those who refused to convert to "Greek ways."[64] And, as earlier noted, Antiochus V's letter referred to Jews who resisted change to "Greek practices."[65] A few passages also designate "Judaism" as the principle upheld by rebellion against the Seleucids.[66] But the author nowhere juxtaposes the two phrases as opposites. The fact deserves emphasis. Were Judaism and Hellenism incompatible?

Jason introduced a gymnasium and the ephebate to Jerusalem, and he arranged for the registration of persons as "Antiochenes" in the city.[67]

---

[61] The quotations and summaries provided by Hengel, *Judaism and Hellenism*, 131–53, refute his own efforts to see Ben Sira as an opponent of "Hellenistic liberalism." None of the material makes any direct or indirect statement to that effect. A similar inference by A. Momigliano, *Alien Wisdom* (Cambridge, 1975), 95: "His book . . . quietly reaffirmed Jewish traditional faith against the temptations of Hellenism." See now the proper skepticism of Goldstein, in E. P. Sanders, *Jewish and Christian Self-Definition* (Philadelphia, 1981) 2:72–73. Ben Sira's prayer for deliverance from foreign rule, 36.9–17, is, of course, a different matter.

[62] Dan. 11.2–12.3. See Momigliano, *Alien Wisdom*, 109–12. The reference in 9.27 to Antiochus making alliance with many hardly implies a "Hellenizing party."

[63] II Macc. 4.10: πρὸς τὸν Ἑλληνικὸν χαρακτῆρα τοὺς ὁμοφύλους μετέστησε. 4.13: ἦν δ' οὕτως ἀκμή τις Ἑλληνισμοῦ.

[64] II Macc. 6.9: μεταβαίνειν ἐπὶ τὰ Ἑλληνικά.

[65] II Macc. 11.24: τοὺς Ἰουδαίους μὴ συνευδοκοῦντας τῇ τοῦ πατρὸς ἐπὶ τὰ Ἑλληνικὰ μεταθέσει.

[66] II Macc. 2.21, 8.1, 14.38.

[67] II Macc. 4.9.

None of these measures involved elimination or alteration of religious rites. Nothing in the Hebrew Scriptures forbids gymnasia, military training for youths, or enrollment as citizens of a *polis* or *politeuma*. Although the author of II Maccabees brands the innovations as unlawful, he also provides material for his own refutation: the priests themselves welcomed the gymnasium and were eager to participate in exercises in the palaestra. They evidently did not consider it inconsistent with their sacerdotal functions.[68] Even Jason's closest allies would not cross the line from Hellenistic reform to religious compromise. The envoys he sent to Tyre with cash for sacrifice to Heracles at the quinquennial games declined to contribute to the pagan festival.[69] They shrank from idol worship and kept to the Law. The measures of Jason's High Priesthood stopped short of interference with traditional religion. The motive for those measures is accurately described in I Maccabees: a desire to foster good relations with neighboring peoples, isolation from whom had been the source of much evil.[70] The cultivation of Greek ways need not undermine the practice of Judaism.

Factional quarrels within the Jewish establishment brought turmoil and division. But where is the evidence that factions divided on the issue of Hellenism? Menelaus, it is commonly assumed, outbid Jason for Seleucid favor by out-Hellenizing the Hellenizer. The assumption lacks all foundation. Personal rivalry and political ambition alone can be inferred from the texts. Jewish sources brand Menelaus with venality, corruption, ruthlessness, treachery, murder, even sacrilege for expropriating Temple funds—but not with Hellenism.[71] Menelaus may indeed have had little sympathy with the Greek institutions sponsored by his rival Jason. Antiochus found him serviceable as a conduit for cash and an enforcer of loyalty in Judaea. The king did not require Hellenic credentials from his Jewish supporters.

The actions taken by Antiochus against the Jews belong in an entirely

---

[68] II Macc. 4.14. It is often asserted that Hellenizing Jews had so far departed from tradition as to compete in the nude and even to undergo some form of reverse circumcision in order to conform to Greek practice. The silence of II Maccabees on this point is potent testimony against it. The most that the author can say is that they wore a Greek-style hat; II Macc. 4.12. So, rightly, Goldstein, in Sanders, *Jewish and Christian Self-Definition* 2:77–78. The reference in I Macc. 1.15 and Jos. *Ant.* 12.241 to the concealment of circumcision may perhaps apply to behavior after the repressive measures of 167—which included a ban on circumcision.

[69] II Macc. 4.18–20.

[70] I Macc. 1.11; cf. Bringmann, *Hellenistische Reform und Religionsverfolgung*, 189; Will and Orrieux, *Ioudaismos-Hellenismos*, 116–19.

[71] II Macc. 4.23–50. The fact is noted by Goldstein, *I Maccabees*, 159, and Millar, *JJS* 29 (1978): 10–11. Josephus' reference to Menelaus as petitioning Antiochus for a gymnasium is an obvious confusion with Jason; *Ant.* 12.240–41.

separate category. He seized moneys from the Temple after his first
Egyptian campaign, with the collaboration of Menelaus. And after the
second campaign, he implemented those extreme measures, ranging
from the massacre of citizens to the prohibition of religion, that put all
previous behavior in the shade. What reason is there to believe that the
party of Menelaus put him up to it? Once the putative link between
Menelaus and Hellenism is severed, the main prop for the conventional
theory falls. That Menelaus exerted any influence over Antiochus may
be seriously questioned. One item only suggests it: Lysias' later allegation
to young Antiochus V that Menelaus bore responsibility for all the
realm's troubles, an allegation intended to justify his elimination.[72] The
statement lacks both specifics and objectivity. Lysias had an ax to grind
and no facts to provide.[73] It is unlikely in the extreme that Menelaus
prodded the Seleucid ruler to eradicate Judaism and terrorize its adherents. The one relevant piece of testimony points in the opposite direction.
Three years after the outbreak of the Maccabean revolt, Menelaus
helped to arrange an amnesty for the disaffected rebels and to restore
to Jews the privilege of adhering to their dietary laws. The man responsible for the repression of Judaism would hardly have been used as inter-
mediary for reconciliation.[74]

Blame for the persecution can be lifted from the shoulders of the
Jews themselves. They aggravated their own difficulties with internal
divisiveness, but the divisions did not break down neatly into Hellenizers
and traditionalists. Personal and familial quarrels played a role, as did
private ambitions and possibly political sympathies.[75] But the idea of a
stark confrontation between Judaism and Hellenism should be dis-
carded—and with it, the thesis that ardent Hellenizers prodded the king
of Syria into persecuting their coreligionists, banning their creed, and
inflicting an alien cult upon the temple. II Maccabees, in fact, reckons
the Hellenizers as among the victims of the king.[76] Apart from Lysias'
partisan and tainted allegation, our evidence is unanimous: it is Anti-

---

[72] II Macc. 13.4.

[73] Josephus' statement, *Ant.* 12.384, is derivative and unreliable. See above.

[74] The fact is recorded in a letter by Antiochus IV in 164 to the Jewish council and
people: II Macc. 1.27–33. The proper sequence of letters in that collection is disputed; see
the discussion in C. Habicht, "Royal Documents in Maccabees II," *HSCP* 80 (1976): 1–18.
Goldstein, *II Maccabees*, 418–20, drew the proper conclusions with regard to Menelaus. So
also Bringmann, "Verfolgung," 182.

[75] Josephus, *Ant.* 12.239–40, reports that the Tobiads backed Menelaus, while a majority
of Jews supported Jason. Elsewhere, Josephus suggests that conflict in Judaea divided
partly along pro-Seleucid and pro-Ptolemaic lines; *BJ* 1.31–32. That passage, however, is
a hodgepodge of confusion. Bringmann, "Verfolgung," 185, assigns it more weight than
it deserves.

[76] II Macc. 4.15–16.

ochus Epiphanes who must take responsibility for the savage onslaught against Judaism.[77]

Where then to turn for an answer? Until the final, ferocious act of the drama, the king had played a relatively passive or evenhanded role. Jason instigated the Hellenistic reform, Antiochus merely endorsing and benefiting from it. He benefited further when Menelaus contracted to raise the tribute and thereby won the Seleucid's backing as High Priest. Antiochus intervened when requested in immediately subsequent years, acquitting Menelaus at his trial, but condemning his own minister Andronicus. He did not pursue an activist policy in Palestine. Even the sequestering of funds from the Temple in 169 may have come at the suggestion of Menelaus, who had exploited that source once before, and now accompanied the king in stripping most of what remained. In any case, the objective was war on Egypt, not punishment of Jews. Antiochus had hitherto taken only a secondary interest in Palestinian affairs. But the measures implemented after the second Egyptian campaign created a wholly new situation. They cannot be explained in terms of Hellenization, intra-Jewish rivalries, or even pragmatic advantages. Stationing of a garrison, mass executions, terrorism, prohibition of the faith, and sweeping persecution shifted matters onto an altogether different plane. They did not evolve smoothly or logically out of what came before. Something happened in 168 to convert Antiochus Epiphanes into a rampaging monster.

II Maccabees offers an ostensible explanation. Jason raised an insurrection in that year, while Antiochus was campaigning in Egypt. The attempted coup against Menelaus ignited a civil war in Judaea. When news reached the king, so reports the text, he reckoned it as rebellion, flew into a fury, and made Jerusalem a prize of war. There followed the succession of terrorist measures that culminated in the "abomination of desolation."[78] The rage of Antiochus is plausible enough, but cannot suffice as explanation. Rebellion in his rear might inspire retaliation and subjugation; but it hardly accounts for the brutally thorough and detailed prescriptions which, if adhered to, would be tantamount to the abolition of Judaism. Those measures ran the risk of alienating even the king's staunchest supporters in Judaea. Investigation reaches an impasse. One

---

[77] Dan. 11.30 states only that Antiochus stayed his hand with regard to those Jews who abandoned the holy covenant—not that he was acting on their advice and instigation. That the king took the initiative is clear from Dan. 11.32.

[78] II Macc. 5.11: προσπεσόντων δὲ τῷ βασιλεῖ περὶ τῶν γεγονότων διέλαβεν ἀποστατεῖν τὴν Ἰουδαίαν. Cf. Abel, Livres des Maccabées, 352–53. In the view of Tcherikover, Hellenistic Civilization and the Jews, 186–203, Antiochus' anger directed itself not against Jason and his followers, whose coup had already failed, but against a popular rising that had expelled Jason, intimidated Menelaus, and seized control of the situation.

eminent scholar announced despair, and declared an understanding of
Antiochus' deeds to be beyond reach.[79]
    The despair may be premature. One contemporary source addresses
the question directly, and must be attended to. The author of the Book
of Daniel asserts that "the king of the north" in his second invasion of
the south will suffer a different outcome from the first. The ships of the
Kittim will come against him, causing the king's withdrawal. He will then
loose his wrath upon the Holy Covenant, taking care only for those who
forsake that covenant. His armed forces will defile the sanctuary and the
pious, and he will impose the "abomination of desolation."[80] Interpretation of the text is not controversial. Daniel plainly refers to Antiochus
Epiphanes' second campaign against Egypt, its abortive conclusion when
Rome intervened, the ignominious retreat, and then the oppressive and
devastating measures inflicted upon the Jews.[81]
    The explanation has both psychological and political plausibility. Anti-
ochus was compelled to abandon his Egyptian adventure at Popillius
Laenas' brusque command and infamous swagger stick.[82] Not only did
the withdrawal terminate Antiochus' long-cherished dream of extending
suzerainty over the Ptolemaic realm; it also came under humiliating circumstances that threatened to shatter the king's reputation throughout
the lands of the Near East.[83] The rage of Antiochus IV is readily intelligi-
ble. It could not, of course, be vented against Rome.[84] But the upheaval
in Judaea came at a convenient time and offered a suitable target. The
introduction of a garrison and the intimidation of the populace by state
terrorism had a larger design than simply to punish the Jews. It would
announce Antiochus Epiphanes' resumption of control to the diverse
peoples and nations nominally under the Seleucid regime. The "Day of

---

[79] Millar, "Background," 16–17: "There seems no way of reaching an understanding of
how Antiochus came to take a step so profoundly at variance with the normal assumptions
of government in his time."

[80] Dan. 11.29–31. On the date of the work, see Hartman and DiLella, *Book of Daniel*,
9–18; Schürer, *History of the Jewish People*, vol. 3, pt. 1, 245–50.

[81] The Septuagint even translates the Hebrew *kittim* as "Romans." See further Hartman
and DeLella, *Book of Daniel*, 270–71.

[82] For Popillius' intervention, see Polyb. 29.27.1–10; Livy 45.12.3–8; DS 31.2; App. *Syr.*
66; Just. 34.3.1–4; Cic. *Phil.* 8.23; Vell. Pat. 1.10.1; Val. Max. 6.4.3; Porphyr. *FGrH* 260
F50; Plin. *NH* 34.24; Plut. *Mor.* 202F. See also, for Egyptian evidence, J. D. Ray, *The Archive
of Hor* (London, 1976), 127–28.

[83] Not that Rome herself intended to humiliate Antiochus. Popillius' intervention ended
in amicable fashion; Polyb. 29.27.6; DS 31.2.2; Livy 45.12.6; see E. S. Gruen, "Rome and
the Seleucids in the Aftermath of Pydna," *Chiron* 6 (1976): 76–77. But the perception of
a forced withdrawal could do serious damage to Seleucid prestige and authority.

[84] Indeed Antiochus soon dispatched a mission to Rome to offer congratulations for
Pydna and thus regained Roman favor; Livy 45.13.2–3, 45.13.6.

Eleusis" was to be buried under a barrage. Antiochus would answer any potential questions about his withdrawal from Egypt by taking the offensive in Palestine.[85]

The initial measures, however, did not suffice for the king's purpose. He determined to stamp out Judaism. The reasons can hardly have been religious or ideological. Nor can an outburst of anger explain the sweeping actions that took place a year later. Judaea would serve as a conspicuous showcase for Seleucid power. The antiquity of the Jewish faith and the tenacity with which its adherents clung to it were well known to Greeks and natives alike in the Near East. Whether they voiced approval or disapproval, they acknowledged the strength and endurance of Jewish traditions.[86] Eradication of the creed and forcible conversion of the faithful would send a message throughout the ancestral kingdom of the Seleucids—the message that Antiochus had accomplished what no ruler before him had hoped to achieve: the abandonment of Jewish belief at Seleucid command. Antiochus Epiphanes would put the "Day of Eleusis" behind him for good.

The concern for image and reputation can be illustrated further. In the immediately subsequent year Antiochus staged a dazzling demonstration at Daphne, a suburb of Antioch. Invitations were issued to towns all over the Greek world, in order to ensure a diverse and widespread audience. The king put on a splendid show: a grand parade of armed forces including both nationals under his control and mercenaries in his pay. Infantry, cavalry, chariots, and elephants marched in procession. More than 50,000 men displayed armor, weaponry, and handsome accoutrements. The nonmilitary aspects of the parade were equally impressive: 800 ephebes with gold crowns, 1,000 cattle for sacrifice, numerous images of gods, lesser divinities, and heroes, 200 women sprinkling perfume from gilded jugs upon the crowd of onlookers, and vast quantities of silver and gold plate—much of it from Egypt—carted by the attendants of the king. As is obvious, Antiochus presented a pageant to exhibit the power and wealth of his kingdom, a signal to the Hellenic world of east and west that he had withdrawn from Egypt only to collect resources of awesome extent for even greater ventures. Projection and propaganda dominated.[87] The spectacle was very much in character. It fitted Antiochus' repeated practice of dedicating objects and bestowing gifts upon

---

[85] Cf. also Josephus *Ant.* 12.246, who relates the return from Egypt, through fear of the Romans, directly to the assault on Jerusalem: ὑποστρέψας γὰρ ἀπὸ τῆς Αἰγύπτου διὰ τὸ παρὰ ʻΡωμαίων δέος ὁ βασιλεὺς ʼΑντίοχος ἐπὶ τὴν ʻΙεροσυλυμιτῶν πόλιν ἐξεστράτευσε.

[86] See the texts collected by Stern, *Greek and Latin Authors*, 20–130.

[87] Polyb. 30.25–26; DS 31.16. See Mørkholm, *Antiochus IV*, 97–100; J. G. Bunge, "Die Feiern Antiochos' IV. Epiphanes in Daphne im Herbst 166 v. Chr.," *Chiron* 6 (1976): 53–71; Walbank, *Historical Commentary* 3:448–53.

shrines and cities of Hellas to advertise his means. The calculated eleva-
tion of his stature evidently worked. A Greek inscription from the Near
East hails him as "savior of Asia," and Diodorus identifies him as the
strongest of all kings in his day.[88] Antiochus exploited the image in the
closing years of his life to overawe his subjects, consolidate his realm, and
engage in further aggrandizement.[89]

Persecution of the Jews belongs in this category. The complicated tale
had many facets. Inner turmoil began with clashing ambitions among
the Jewish leadership, contests for power entangled by the introduction
of Hellenic institutions and aggravated by financial obligations to the
Seleucids. Those elements can explain the civil strife, the fierce divisions,
and the compromise of traditions that characterized relations between
the warring factions and the king. But the savagery and repression of 167
require a different explanation. Here responsibility rests with Antiochus
Epiphanes. The persecution did not grow out of factional quarrels, ideological divisions, or financial needs. It served the ends of the king as a
display of might, a sign that he had suffered no setback, indeed had
emerged with greater strength. The international image of the ruler and
his dominion were at stake. Antiochus victimized the Jews in a Seleucid
power play.

But the power play, in the end, backfired. Antiochus acknowledged
his error too late. The persecution galvanized Jewish resistance, issuing
in the Maccabean revolt that ultimately liberated the victims and gave
independence to the nation.

RESPONSE: M. GWYN MORGAN

Professor Gruen has provided us with an ingenious and a fascinating
interpretation of what has long been considered an insoluble problem in
Hellenistic and Jewish history. By raising new questions not only about
Antiochus Epiphanes' intentions and policies, but also about the context
in which they should be set, Professor Gruen has, I think, helped to
clarify the issues involved and the lines any scholarly explanation must
follow. But raising new questions, as we all know to our cost, is not always
synonymous with producing new answers. It would take us too far from
our immediate topic to discuss whether the "Day of Eleusis" was, or was
thought by Antiochus himself to be, the unmitigated disaster for the

---

[88] The Near Eastern inscription: *OGIS* 253; improved text by M. Zambelli, "L'ascesa in
trono di Antioco IV Epifane di Siria," *Riv. Filol.* 88 (1960): 374–80; cf. Bunge "Feiern,"
58–64; S. Sherwin-White, "A Greek Ostracon from Babylon of the Early Third Century
B.C.," *ZPE* 47 (1982): 65–66. On Antiochus' power, DS 31.17a.

[89] DS 31.17a; App. *Syr.* 45, 66; Porphyr. *FGrH* 260 F56 (subjugation of Armenia); I
Macc. 3.31, 3.37; II Macc. 9.1–2; Jos. *Ant.* 12.293–97; cf. Polyb. 31.9.1 (campaign in Persis).

Seleucid which it is almost invariably said to have been. For even if, as I believe, it was not such a setback,[1] it may still be argued that this signifies little. All that matters, so it may be maintained, is whether the Jews thought it a royal humiliation.

To this narrower question too the evidence as a whole will permit only an answer in the negative. The passage from the Book of Daniel, on which Professor Gruen has placed so much weight, cannot really support the linkage he seeks between the "Day of Eleusis" and the king's conduct in Judaea. The ships of the Kittim will come against Antiochus, so we are told, causing him to withdraw from Egypt. Then he will loose his wrath against the Holy Covenant. Like so much else in the Book of Daniel, the first statement is chronological, not causal.[2] Once we recognize this, the prophecy falls back into line with the accounts of the other Jewish sources, which certainly report that Antiochus was angry with the Jews for what they were doing, but in no way link either party's behavior with events outside Judaea.[3] This leaves only Édouard Will's theory that the rumor of Antiochus' death which set in motion Jason's seizure of Jerusalem was itself a garbled version of the incident at Eleusis.[4] For that, however, the chronology is surely too tight. Antiochus himself left Egypt only a few days after Eleusis and needed but a few more to reach Jerusalem. In this same brief span of time Jason had to hear (or manufacture and spread) the rumor of the king's demise, gather together his small private army, emerge from Transjordan, and, seizing control of Jerusalem, "set the gate on fire and shed innocent blood."[5] The rumor must have surfaced earlier, generated by Antiochus' being out of contact with his own subjects because lost in the wilds of Egypt, as indeed he was between late March 168, when he began his second campaign, and the start of July, when he put in an appearance outside Alexandria.[6] Even then the Jews had reasons aplenty to wish for the king's death: during the winter of 169/8, between his two expeditions into Egypt, Antiochus

---

[1] My original response was preoccupied, excessively, with this aspect of the situation: see "The Perils of Schematism: Polybius, Antiochus Epiphanes and the 'Day of Eleusis,' " *Historia* 39 (1990): 37–76. Despite all the revision which has taken place since, my thesis remains the same.

[2] See the characterization of this work by E. J. Bickerman, *The God of the Maccabees* (Leiden, 1979), 14ff. The original German edition, unfortunately, was not available to me.

[3] See II Macc. 5.11; Jos. *Ant.* 12.246–47 (somewhat confused).

[4] E. Will, *Histoire politique du monde hellénistique, 323–30 av. J.-C.*, 2d ed. (Nancy, 1982) 2:337.

[5] II Macc. 1.8; cf. O. Mørkholm, *Antiochus IV of Syria* (Copenhagen, 1966), 143.

[6] Antiochus set out for Egypt *primo vere* (Livy 45.11.9), and appeared outside Alexandria shortly after Pydna, having descended from Memphis *modicis itineribus* (Livy 45.12.2).

had helped himself liberally to the treasures in the Temple at Jerusalem and walked off with 1,800 talents.[7] To all this it may legitimately be objected that the Jewish sources can themselves be discounted, since they invariably take a parochial view of events, disregarding important happenings in the larger world outside Judaea. But if we grant the supposition that the "Day of Eleusis" had the kind of effect Professor Gruen has posited, we are still faced with the fact that a persecution launched late in 167 was at best a work of supererogation. Once Antiochus appeared in Judaea in July or August 168, he lost no time in proving that he was, and meant to remain, master in his own house by sacking Jerusalem and razing its walls.[8] This was an assertion or reassertion of Seleucid authority which only the blind could ignore. Not that the Jews were cowed, of course, and prophecies about the Kittim could well have flourished in this climate. But such sentiments were essentially whistling in the dark; and that the king could—and so far as we know, did—ignore.

This in turn raises an altogether weightier consideration, the extent of the king's interest in Jewish affairs at any stage. All the evidence we have shows clearly that anything which interested Antiochus personally he took in hand personally, be it a major enterprise like a campaign into Egypt or a minor matter like wrecking somebody else's party.[9] The only case I have been able to find where his interest was not matched by personal involvement was the seizure of Cyprus at the start of 168, and in that he could not participate because he was planning to lead his army overland on his second expedition into Egypt and could not be in two places at once.[10] Now the truly remarkable aspect of Antiochus' dealings with the Jews after the sack of Jerusalem in 168 is that he personally had nothing more to do with them. Every subsequent move, from the promulgation of the edict which began the persecution to the counterinsurgency measures its enforcement necessitated, was left to subordinates. On this ground alone, it is hard to avoid the conclusion that the entire episode, large though it may bulk in Jewish history, was of minor import to the king.[11]

This, moreover, seems to have been the view the Jews themselves took of the situation, inasmuch as their sources insist that Antiochus' only interest in this business, as in most of his other dealings with them, was

[7] II Macc. 5.21; cf. I Macc. 1.20; Jos. Ant. 12.247, C. Ap. 2.83–84.

[8] I Macc. 1.31.

[9] Cf. Polyb. 26.1; DS 29.32; Livy 41.20.

[10] Livy 45.11.9.

[11] Cf. E. Bevan, The House of Seleucus (London, 1902) 2:162; A. Bouché-Leclercq, Histoire des Séleucides (Paris, 1913) 1:291; W. W. Tarn, The Greeks in Bactria and India, 2d ed. (Cambridge, 1951), 193.

money.[12] This too could be discounted, no doubt, as a deliberate slur, meant to belittle the king by having him cause massive suffering for the most petty and paltry of reasons. But its essential accuracy is surely confirmed by the way in which the Samaritans evaded the persecution: begging the king not to confuse them with Jews or blame them for Jewish crimes, they pointed out that if they were left to their own devices, they could increase the royal revenues—an argument Antiochus bought happily.[13] Admittedly, this seems to fit ill both with what we might surmise the king's financial situation to have been at the time, and with his molesting Jews to get money while getting money by not molesting Samaritans; but these difficulties are apparent rather than real.

To take first Antiochus' financial situation, we know that he spent money like water throughout his reign and, whenever possible, replenished his treasury by robbing temples. This much is generally agreed. The question is whether he had money enough to function in his customary lavish manner during 168 and 167, and we cannot simply assume that the kingdom was solvent. During his first campaign in Egypt in 169, he had carefully refrained from looting,[14] meanwhile incurring the costs not only of this expedition but also of *douceurs*, 150 talents of goodwill, distributed around the Mediterranean at the end of the year.[15] So there can be little doubt that the 1,800 talents taken from the Temple in Jerusalem during the winter of 169/8 was swallowed up by these debts and, still more, by his preparations for a second campaign, launched in spring 168. From that second expedition, it is true, he returned laden down with booty, but much of that booty—as Polybius tells us explicitly—he paraded at his great festival at Daphne in 166.[16] In other words, it was either booty still in 166 or it was booty reserved to finance that festival. It could not be turned into cash in the interim without loss of prestige, and what the king needed in the interim was ready cash, such as the Samaritans promised him.

Which brings us to the more important question of how Antiochus hoped to improve his cash flow by persecuting the Jews. Professor Gruen

---

[12] Cf. Jos. *Ant.* 12.248–50. Other similar references: II Macc. 4.1–9 (cf. Jos. *Ant.* 12.237); Jos. C. *Ap.* 2.83–84; I Macc. 3.27ff.

[13] Jos. *Ant.* 12.261–64.

[14] Porphry. *FGrH* 260 F49a.

[15] Polyb. 28.22.

[16] Polyb. 30.26.9. Polybius also says (30.25.1) that the stimulus for the festival was provided by the magnificent games which L. Aemilius Paullus held at Amphipolis to celebrate his victory at Pydna, in early 167; but it would be unwise to see this as the entire explanation (cf. J. G. Bunge, "Die Feiern Antiochos' IV. Epiphanes in Daphne im Herbst 166 v. Chr." *Chiron* 6 [1976]: 53ff.), and Antiochus almost certainly had in mind some sort of parade from the moment he left Egypt in 168.

has stressed, and rightly so, that there is very little evidence for friction between Greeks and Jews prior to Antiochus' reign. This is not to say that all was sweetness and light. In religion and culture the two peoples were far enough apart to create a situation not unlike that which manifested itself when the British and the Chinese came into contact in the nineteenth century: each found the other incomprehensible *and* inscrutable.[17] So far as Antiochus himself is concerned, it is easy enough to assume that, as a Greek long absent from his homeland because of an enforced stay in Rome, he was particularly insensitive to Jewish beliefs and practices. However, we have no real evidence that his father or his brother before him had understood them any better. Antiochus III had favored the Jews primarily because they supported him against the Ptolemies.[18] And whatever Seleucus IV had thought he was doing, his minister Heliodorus had tried in 175 to carry off treasures from the Temple in Jerusalem and had done so—as Professor Gruen concedes—at the bidding of one faction in an internal struggle within the Jewish community. On the Greek side, therefore, I am far from convinced that we can talk of a change in policy, when the dominant trait in Seleucid policy is neglect in peaceful times and intervention when conditions are, or are thought to be, disturbed.

As for the Jews themselves, there were, to be sure, priests in Jerusalem eager to ape Hellenistic custom, but that tells us little about the views of the priesthood as a whole, less about the feelings of the common people in the city, and nothing at all about the attitudes of the Jews out in the countryside—and it was in the countryside, as Bevan remarked long ago, that the strongest opposition was offered to Antiochus' edict.[19] Not that it follows from this that the factional struggles within the Jewish community were fueled exclusively, or even largely, by differing views on the values of Hellenization—though one can see why some might doubt its worth. The important consideration is that these struggles had been going on, for any number of reasons, since the last years of Seleucus IV, and that the standard means of gaining the upper hand, already elaborated, was to outbid one's rivals at the Seleucid court by promising the monarch larger sums of money. It was in Antiochus' best interests, in other words, to allow the Jews to be molested. He received his money up front, and he probably had no idea (those responsible taking every care not to tell him) how far the persecution would be carried, or what repercussions it might have.[20]

[17] Byron Farwell, *Queen Victoria's Little Wars* (New York and London, 1985), 13.

[18] Jos. *Ant.* 12.133–53; cf. Bouché-Leclercq, *Histoire*, 1:237.

[19] Bevan, *House of Seleucus* 2:174, 176.

[20] The Jewish sources say that at first there was little opposition to the edict; Daniel 9.27; I Macc. 1.43, 52, 2.16, 18, 23, 44, 6.21, 10.14. This could be true (though the champions

This leaves one last point to make, apropos the timing of the persecution. One of the most serious difficulties in Professor Gruen's thesis, it seems to me, and a consideration which has attracted far less attention than it merits, lies in the eighteen-month gap between the "Day of Eleusis" and the launching of the persecution in December 167. One could perhaps argue that it took time for the impact of Eleusis to sink in, time for the Jews to become restive, and time for Antiochus to respond—but there is no evidence to support any of this. Or one might maintain that the king, having decided to mount a comprehensive attack on the Jews and Judaism, sat down with his councillors and took the time to work out in detail exactly what measures were best calculated to outrage Jewish sensibilities—but Professor Gruen himself has proved that the king planned no attack on Judaism as such. Once we grant the possibility that one faction within the Jewish community sponsored the edict as a way of crushing its opposition, the matter of its timing is most simply and economically explained as a piece of sharp practice. It would have taken such people no time at all to work out what measures should and what measures should not be included in the edict. What counted was getting Antiochus to approve the document, and that could best be done when the king was totally absorbed by another project, oblivious to the risks involved in such an edict and concerned only with the funding of his latest extravaganza. In December 167 Antiochus was already wrapped up in his preparations for the festival at Daphne.[21]

None of this is meant to excuse Antiochus' behavior. Whatever the facts of the case, he must bear the ultimate responsibility for the persecution. On the other hand, there is no more reason to drag the Romans into this melancholy episode than there is to lay every last ounce of blame on the king. As Tarn observed many years ago, "whatever he did to the Jews, they have had an ample revenge."[22]

DISCUSSION

S. M. Burstein: To say that Antiochus tried to stamp out the Jewish religion is not, I think, quite right, since he did not attempt to eliminate the worship of Yahweh. This is clear from the fact that the Samaritans were exempted on the basis of their opportune "discovery" that they were Sidonians, not Jews. Rather he tried to crush Torah-based religious practice in Judaea. In other words the conflict between the Judaizers and

---

of the edict can hardly have expected this much success), or it may have been intended to flatter the Maccabees, or it may rather reflect differing attitudes between town and country.

[21] Cf. Polyb. 30.25.1, 12.

[22] Tarn, *Greeks*, 183.

Hellenizers was essentially over practice, not belief. In this connection, although Antiochus' anger and his proclivity to loot temples may have been factors in his actions, he had to have had Jewish collaborators. For two reasons the best candidates for this role certainly were the Antiochenes in Jerusalem, who presumably were citizens of a Greek entity, an Antioch, that could not have had the Torah as its basic law. First: because only a minority of the Jewish residents of Jerusalem became Antiochenes, the Hellenizers must have thrown in their lot with Antiochus. Second, and more important: Antiochus' pogrom, which interestingly extended into the countryside, reflects a knowledge of Jewish practice that, so far as we know, could not have been found in the Greek ethnographic tradition concerning the Jews.

E. S. Gruen: To take your second point first. The so-called Hellenizers who remained in the Akra did so after the Akra had been established and after the crackdown by Antiochus. This does not establish prior collaboration with Antiochus. The meaning of Antiochenes in Jerusalem remains obscure. I do not myself believe that all of Jerusalem was turned into a Greek *polis*. The phrase may apply to those who wanted to display their assimilation to the outside world, to show themselves as international figures, not simply Jews. Now of course the Antiochenes in Jerusalem were not all Jews. Certainly some—maybe most of them—were Greeks, or Syrians. But opting for citizenship in this *politeuma*, if that's what it was, need not mean abandoning Judaism.

D. Delia: The idea of a fifth column is exciting, but it sounds like an anticipation of what went on in the great Jewish revolt of the first century A.D. Josephus has a lot to say about that—or, I should say, he doesn't have quite enough to say about it, because he represents only part of the fifth column. Another point is that already for over a hundred years the Torah had existed in Greek, in the form of the Septuagint. And so it wasn't necessary for Jews to explain Jewish culture to Greek-speaking monarchs.

E. S. Gruen: Yes, that is true. But to what degree the Septuagint was known outside Alexandria, outside the Diaspora, or in Palestine itself, is more questionable. It seems not impossible that at least those Jews who made a point of exhibiting their Hellenization would have contact with Hellenized Jews in the diaspora, and that Antiochus himself or his advisers would be well aware of Jewish practice.

A. E. Samuel: I wonder if we really have the straight story at all. Professor Gruen acknowledged at the beginning that our sources are pro-Hasmonean. When we read Josephus we read someone who is embarrassed about the whole affair. And yet from Josephus we would recognize that the Jews really were a pain in the neck, and had been a pain in the neck to the Roman administration for some time before the revolt. When we read the letter of Claudius, we see that the Jews had been practically demolished in one of the worst and most horrific pogroms—much worse than the one Antiochus had launched. And Claudius is stern about that. He doesn't approve, and he thinks the Alexandrians should stop mistreating the Jews. "But if the Jews keep up what they're doing they'll see what a gracious ruler will do to them!" Somehow I see the events in 167 as fitting into the kind of political and ethnic atmosphere that is reflected by the events of the first century A.D. and the reactions of somebody like Claudius as expressed in the letter.

E. S. Gruen: But the fact is that Josephus is not so hard on the Jews in this particular episode. What he does provide is an interpretation that is not in either I or II Maccabees: that this struggle was, in part, one between Seleucid-leaning Jews and Ptolemaic-leaning Jews.

A. E. Samuel: I guess my main point is that we may be unaware of the extent of Jewish unrest in the period before the oppression, and that if we are unaware of events that could be by design on the part of our sources.

E. S. Gruen: When Caligula began his pogrom, a long history of Jewish difficulties lay in the background. There had been no comparably long history of Jewish troubles with the Seleucids. The argument that Antiochus sought to suppress rebellious Jews overlooks the fact that the only rebellion had been an internal uprising by Jason against Menelaus. And, more importantly, Menelaus had won. Jason had already been driven back across the Jordan, and Menelaus was back in control when Antiochus entered. And the king blasted the so-called Hellenizers. A very interesting passage in II Maccabees reports that the Hellenizers were themselves victimized by Antiochus. So he had not come to champion the Hellenizers against the rebels. He intended to persecute them all, and this despite the fact that there had not been a long history of unrest.

M. G. Morgan: I'm not as convinced as you are that there hadn't been that much trouble before 167. You said at one point that the early Greek references to the Jews are more often favorable than unfavorable. This is not the same as saying that they're *always* favorable. Something's wrong. Similarly when you talk about Ben Sira you make the point that if Hellenism were a major issue he would have mentioned it. But the point about

Ben Sira, it seems to me, is that he's much more concerned to point out
what the Jews are falling away from than what they are falling into. So
Hellenism would not get mentioned. However, I think that even if there
had been friction before Antiochus hit his stride, it cannot have been
important. Any serious strife between Ptolemaic and Seleucid Jews would
have had Antiochus in there personally. He only went through Judaea
three times. There's the visit in the 170s; he carts off the temple treasures
after the first Egyptian expedition; and he sacks the place after the second. That's it. He never goes back again. I think for him the major
concern was "Let's have the money!"

E. S. Gruen: Well, I wouldn't want to suggest that Antiochus ever
thought he had enough money, nor that money was unimportant. What
I *am* suggesting is that desire for money cannot explain the pogrom.
When Antiochus did want money from the Jews he got it. He got it from
Jason, he got it from Menelaus, and he took it himself in 169. The idea
that the only way he could get money from the Jews was to eradicate
Judaism seems to me extraordinary.

M. G. Morgan: I'm not saying that Antiochus couldn't get money from
the Jews, what I'm saying is that it took more time than it needed to take.
And I think that you can argue that as a general rule he did not get as
much as he wanted.

P. Green: I think we've got to look a little more closely at Antiochus'
motives and at what was happening in Judaea. Antiochus wanted money
on this particular occasion because what he was desperate to do was
to emulate his father. Antiochus III had carried out this great eastern
anabasis, which in fact was largely a masterpiece of public relations and
ad hoc diplomacy rather than actual conquest. His son, too, saw salvation
in the east. Now, if you are going to make an anabasis to the east, you
need money, but even more you need peace behind you. You do not
need rebellions and explosive trouble. This brings me to the Jews. I agree
with Professor Morgan that there had already been more trouble than
Professor Gruen is disposed to admit, and I think we also have to look
forward, to evaluate the whole recurrent pattern, the kind of trouble the
Jews produced from the Maccabean revolt through Masada. The point
is, it's *ideological* trouble. That's what distinguishes the guerrilla resistance
in the *chora*—the trick known as *anachoresis*, vanishing into the countryside, raiding in the Vietnam style. The Maccabees were absolutely brilliant at this, and as we know, it's a technique that can cause endless
trouble. I think we should probably give Antiochus some credit on his
own terms for grasping, instantly, just what was different about the Jew-

ish resistance: that is, that their political guerrilla movement was intimately tied up with the ideology of their religion. What he didn't realize
is that you couldn't get rid of this by violence. He tried it. But before he
died he called the whole thing off. He sent a rescript back from the east
saying, in effect, abandon the policy of religious repression, give them
back their rights. It was a clear admission on his part that repression
simply didn't work. In other words, unlike so many Seleucids he was
ready to concede that he had made a mistake. We have to give him credit
for two things: for seeing what the trouble was and where it lay; and,
when violence didn't work, for changing his mind. But I think the pogrom was an attempt to wipe out the ideological element in what indeed
proved, subsequently, to be to a most appallingly troublesome and stubborn resistance movement.

E. S. Gruen: Your characterization of Jewish resistance and troublemak-
ing holds from the Maccabees through Masada. But that resistance began
after the pogrom. The notion that the pogrom was a reaction to a Jewish
rebellion *may* be right, but it lacks any support in the texts. That is why
Tcherikover, who knew that there was no evidence in the texts, but who
believed fervently that there *was* a Jewish rebellion before the Romans
entered, invented one.

P. Green: There is one enormous piece of evidence, which has been
mentioned again and again, and that is simply the raiding and despolia-
tion of the Temple. If that wouldn't unite them, heaven knows what
would.

E. S. Gruen: That is why I want to take up your second point: you are
absolutely right that according to Jewish testimony Antiochus repented
of his crackdown before his death. The testimony has been questioned,
but let us assume its truth for the sake of argument. Antiochus realized
that he had made a mistake. If so, he made that mistake precisely because
there had not been previous Jewish resistance. He had miscalculated.
When it was brought home to Antiochus that his policy had failed, he
cut his losses. But that is because of the experience that followed the
pogrom; it does not *explain* the pogrom.

P. Green: But what your explanation doesn't explain is precisely why
he attacked at this point. There had to have been *something* to cause his
action. Otherwise it would have been like any revolt anywhere else which
didn't involve this element.

M. G. Morgan: Now, Antiochus is steaming in 168; I still don't see the idea that he then gets the planners to go work out the details, and only comes out with his persecution a full year later.

E. S. Gruen: It was certainly not my thesis that he was steaming and raging and that fury explains the decision. That is a thesis that some others have argued. They have assembled all of Antiochus' quirky eccentricities and concluded, "Eleusis, that was the final straw, he went round the bend." No. He knew what he was doing. He did have a definite policy in mind, that is, to demonstrate to the Near East that Eleusis was not a defeat. He was very concerned that it not damage his prestige. He was worried about his image in the lands that were scattered, fragmented, and only very loosely held, though nominally under the control of the Seleucid realm. This was one way of demonstrating that he was still master of his own house. And not only that. Why did he select the Jews here? They represented a people whose tenacity not only in their beliefs but also in their independence and autonomy was well known throughout the Near East. If Antiochus could show that he had brought even the Jews under heel, he could salvage and even enhance his reputation. But, as we all know, it didn't work. In retrospect, the failure seems foredoomed, and hence mad. But only in retrospect.

A. E. Samuel: I wonder if we shouldn't see it also in the perspective of its timing? Consider the parallel case of the sack of Thebes. Here was a chance for Antiochus to give his soldiers some money and excitement—and at the same time a chance to really show off, to demonstrate that any opposition would result in violent repression: "Don't nobody move!" as the Western gunman says.

CONTRIBUTORS

E. N. Borza	Professor of History, Pennsylvania State University.
S. M. Burstein	Professor of History, California State University, Los Angeles.
Diana Delia	Associate Professor of History, Texas A and M University.
Peter Green	Dougherty Centennial Professor of Classics, University of Texas at Austin.
Erich S. Gruen	Gladys Rehard Wood Professor of History and Classics, University of California, Berkeley.
David M. Halperin	Associate Professor of Literature, Department of Humanities, MIT.
N. G. L. Hammond	Professor Emeritus of Greek, University of Bristol.
Frank Holt	Associate Professor of History, University of Houston.
Peter Levi	Fellow of St. Catherine's College and former Professor of Poetry, University of Oxford.
A. A. Long	Professor of Classics, University of California, Berkeley.
M. Gwyn Morgan	Professor of Classics and History, University of Texas at Austin.
J. J. Pollitt	Dean of the Graduate School and Professor of Classical Archaeology and History of Art, Yale University.
Martin Robertson	Lincoln Professor Emeritus of Classical Archaeology and Art, Oxford University.
A. E. Samuel	Professor of Greek and Roman History, University of Toronto.
John Scarborough	Professor of Classics and History of Pharmacy and Medicine, University of Wisconsin, Madison.

K. D. White   Professor Emeritus in Ancient History,
                      University of Reading.

Paul Woodruff   M. H. Thompson Centennial Professor of
                      Philosophy, University of Texas at Austin.

Index

291

to, 245, 247; frontiers of, 6, 65, 103, 230; hostages at, 254–55, 268; indemnity on Syria, 240, 252, 253; Italian citizens of, 254; and kingdom of Meroë, 65, 66; medical writing at, 230–32; military colonies of, 248n26; and Nubia, 65, 66; patronage of art at, 97, 101, 106–7, 108, 109; portraiture of, 101; preoccupation with sex, 4; provincial government of, 210; Ptolemy VIII at, 177; relationship with Greek East, 6; resistance to principate of, 157; and Stoic philosophy, 153, 157; study of Plato at, 159; suppression of Bacchanalian cult, 255; technology of, 220; tutelage of Egyptian monarchy, 191; war with Macedonia, 15, 22, 245. *See also* "Day of Eleusis"
Rosetta stone, 188–89
Rostovtzeff, M. I., 6, 193; on capitalism, 173, 174nn11–12; on Greek economic system, 3, 173, 174nn11–12; on the Ptolemaic state, 194
Roxane, 17
Rufus of Ephesus, 230
Rutherford, E. R. (nuclear physicist), 227

Sabrakamani, King, 40n4
Sacroidyllic paintings, 107. *See also* Art; Paintings
Ste Croix, G. E. M. de, 214
Samaria, rule of Antiochus IV over, 249, 250, 252, 267, 269
Samos, Ptolemy Philopator's rule over, 183n30
Samothrace, 81, 91
Sarapis (deity), 54, 196, 208; cult of, 182; images of, 73, 91
Sardis, 21
Satraps, 10, 13; portraits of, 72
Science: applied, 217, 219, 222; banausic theory of, 9, 219; experimentation in, 216, 217, 222–24, 235; Farrington heresy of, 211–12, 221; Greco-Roman, 227; mechanical theories, 212; of metallurgy, 219; at Museum of Alexandria, 6, 219. *See also* Alexandria, Museum of; Mechanics; Medicine; Technology
Scopas (general), 188
Scopasian heads (Tegea), 86

Sculpture. See *Doryphoros*, Old fisherman; Old market woman; Portraiture; Procne; Statuary; Terme boxer; Terme Hellenistic ruler
Sebiumeker (Meroitic deity), 48
Second Sophistic, 231
Seleucid dynasty, 206, 207; ancestral gods of, 252n44; portraits of, 78
Seleucid empire, 9; allegiance to, 249; campaigns against Ptolemaic Egypt, 209, 244–46; conflicts within, 183n30; control over Ephesus, 184n30; effect of Indian culture on, 60; in India, 56, 58–59, 65; rule of Palestine, 238–42, 271
Seleucus I Nicator, 15, 76; accession of, 28n13; Chandragupta's gifts to, 60n16; colonies in Mauryan empire, 61; Indian campaigns of, 56; murder of, 17
Seleucus IV Philopator, 238n2, 240, 252, 268; assassination of, 242
Self-mastery, 155, 164; Socratic idea of, 142–46. See also *Enkrateia*
Seneca, Lucius Annaeus, 157
Septuagint, 262n81, 270. *See also* "Letter of Aristeas"
Serapis. *See* Sarapis
Sesostris I, 200n39
Sety I, 201n43
Sextus Empiricus, 157, 159n1
Shabaka, 48
Sheep, pasturing of, 114
Shield of Achilles, 131, 219
Sibylline books, 227n31
Sicily, in Theocritus, 116–18
Sicyonian paintings, 108. *See also* Art; Paintings
Sidonians, under Antiochus IV, 269
Silanion (sculptor), 72
Simon (overseer of Temple of Jerusalem), 240, 242, 244, 252
Simonides (elegiac poet), 129
Simonides the Younger, 38
Simon the Just (Jewish High Priest), 240
Siphnian treasury friezes, 85
Sippas, recruitment of soldiers by, 19
Skepticism, 140, 141
Slavery: in Aristotle, 140; as impediment to technology, 234, 236–37; portraiture of, 135; in Theocritus, 120–21

Designer: Ina Clausen
Compositor: Maryland Composition
Text: 10/12 Baskerville
Display: Baskerville
Printer: Malloy Lithographing, Inc.
Binder: Malloy Lithographing, Inc.